ESSAYS IN CONSTRUCTIVE THEOLOGY

A Process Perspective

ESSAYS IN CONSTRUCTIVE THEOLOGY

A Process Perspective

Bernard Eugene Meland

Edited by
Perry LeFevre

Exploration Press, Chicago

Copyright © 1988 by Exploration Press of the
Chicago Theological Seminary

Printed in the United States of America

Exploration Press
Chicago Theological Seminary
5757 University Avenue
Chicago, Illinois   60637

ISBN: Cloth: 0-913552-38-0
      Paper: 0-913552-39-9

Library of Congress Catalog Card Number: 87-82148

Contents

Editor's Note

Bernard Meland has long been one of the creative voices of the Chicago school of theology. Across the years he has published widely both in books and in journals. Much of this material is out of print or otherwise inaccessible. It seemed important to the Editors of Exploration Press to bring together a representative selection of Meland's essays for the contemporary theological community as we have previously done in the case of Paul Tillich, Daniel Day Williams, and James Luther Adams. In Meland's case we have been able to ask him to choose the material he would wish to include in this volume. We had hoped that Meland might be able to write a retrospective introduction to the work, but it has seemed to him desirable to let a short 1967 essay on the mytho-poetic dimension of faith within modern culture serve as orientation to his thought.

We have, as in the other volumes mentioned, reproduced Meland's papers photographically for economy's sake. We have used Meland's personal copies of the printed articles. A few of these included hand-written corrections. We have let these author's corrections stand.

In a paper analyzing Meland's contributions, Daniel Day Williams once wrote: "To read his works is to live through the reflection of a sensitive mind the struggles of American liberalism to come to terms with the realities of contemporary history and to find poise and guidance within the Christian tradition when it is creatively appropriated." A new generation of readers may well come to appreciate Meland's sensitive approach to the tasks of constructive theology.

Perry LeFevre

How Is Culture A Source for Theology?

Bernard E. Meland

On first hearing the question put this way I recoiled from recognizing in it any suggestion of my own theology; for at best it seemed a wrong-headed way of expressing whatever truth might be implicit in it. Yet the fact remains that it was my theology in part that evoked the question. And this must mean that what I say and what I do in theology conveys the impression or the judgment that there is some substantive relation between theology and culture. I am not sure that, by adding one more paper to what I have already written, I will be able to make my position any clearer with regard to this issue. However, seeing this issue in the context of my method as a whole, and thus in relation to other aspects of my thought, should help toward bringing forth an answer to the question.

In any case, I take it that the Council's purpose in asking me to present this paper is more tactical than theological. It is, no doubt, to present to our distinguished friends and colleagues, Williams and Spiegler, a specific target at which to aim. I can just hear the members of the Divinity Student Council reasoning among themselves and saying, "Meland is diffuse enough even when he is precise. Let us then narrow the range of this diffusion." So be it! I shall try to provide you with such a target; but I warn you, the target may turn out to be a flying saucer.

I

My theological method presupposes that all human existence takes place within a particularized orbit of meaning. An orbit of meaning is determined by the cultural history of a specific people. Interchange with alien and rival orbits occur from time to time; hence syncretization and secularization are intermittently present. Yet, historically speaking, primordial drives within a culture achieve sufficient focus in the form of sensibilities, modes of awareness, and reflection to generate both a characteristic mind-set and a persistent thrust of the psyche. One has only to look around, or to move around, among the various well-defined culture-groups of East and West to get some intimations of these contrasts in historical development. The human response, therefore, is hedged about by two kinds of limitations: 1) the limitation of finitude or creatureliness which applies to all men; and 2) the limitation of cultural orbit of meaning which prepares the human mind and psyche within a given area of human association to receive and to react to occurrences in specific and characteristic ways.

The tendency of every people is to employ the terms of their orbit of meaning universally; i.e., to speak for every man. The effect of this tendency has been to impel each cultural faith to conceive of itself and its perspective as being singularly significant, if not absolute, and thus to resist alien forms of religious witness. A first step as a prolegomenon to theological method is thus to attain self-understanding as a participant in a cultural faith, and to acknowledge as well as to accept the limitations of its historical witness. A second step, however, is to take adequate measure of the relative situation in which each cultural witness stands: namely, to recognize that, while the life of every man is seen to be ambiguous by reason of his creaturely and cultural limitations, it is at the same time borne forth by, and in its daily moment of existence is impelled to bear witness to, an ultimate depth of reality. To my knowledge, Radical Empiricism was the first metaphysical interpretation of human existence in the West to lift up the simultaneous presence of an ultimate dimension of reality and the humanly imposed immediacies *within the stream of experience*. Almost a generation before Existentialism and Phenomenology had become household words in the theological and philosophical vocabulary, Radical Empiricists were reacting against the abstractness of Hegelian idealism, insisting upon taking human existence seriously both in its concrete immediacies and in the depth of its participation in this ultimate dimension of reality.

The basic imagery of my thought, following from this orientation of Radical Empiricism (which I have since come to speak of as Empirical Realism) presents existence in this twofold manner, as embracing simultaneously dimensions of immediacy and ultimacy. On its subjective side, I see existence as a stream of experience; in its objective aspect, as a Creative Passage. I use the term "Creative Passage" as an ultimate reference in the way traditional metaphysics employed the term "Being" or "ground of Being." Back in the nineteen thirties I found it useful to point up this radical empirical note of existence as a stream by setting the notion of "Becoming" over against "Being" and thus spoke of my thought as a philosophy of becoming. I still hold to this essential contrast in the main, though I have come to see that, on the one hand, there is no becoming that is without something that is persisting, giving to every moment of becoming its identity; and, on the other hand, that, except as one absolutizes the notion of becoming in the modernistic sense of indefinite and uninterrupted progress, one must acknowledge that there are periodic plateaus and even critical instances of regression and defeat within this stream of experience. Thus I came to see that to speak of existence as being simply an event of becoming seemed sanguine, or at least unrealistic. Yet the stress upon the notion of becoming, I would hold, is justified, certainly as a process among other processes; or even by way of pointing to a prevailing tendency among those complex occurrences of incessant "coming into being and perishing" which make up our daily existence. As a way of settling upon a more neutral term, therefore, taking account of both being and becoming and of their interplay, thus acknowledging persistence and creative change, I have come to think of the Creative Passage as being the most basic characterization of existence as it applies to all life, to all people, to all cultures.

Furthermore, I have come to see the reality of God as being of a piece with the Creative Passage. For reasons which may become clear, I have recoiled from trying to envisage or to define God in any complete, metaphysical or ontological sense, preferring instead to confine attention to such empirical notions as *the creative act of God* and *the redemptive work of God in history*. Much of the meaning we appear to find in life, we bring to it, as Kant observed, through our own forms of sensibility and understanding. But as James and Bergson were later to remark, countering the stance of Kant and Hume in one basic respect, the nexus of relationships that forms our existence is not projected, it is given. We do not create these relationships; we experience them. Huston Smith, speaking in Rockefeller Chapel a few Sundays ago, put this point incisively, saying, "Man's basic matrix is not man-made. It is given with existence." And from this matrix comes resources of Grace that can carry us beyong the meanings of our own making, and alert us to goodness that is not of our own willing or defining. This goodness in existence which we do not create, but which creates and saves us, is the datum to which I mean to attend. It is literally a work of judgment and grace, a primordial and provident goodness, the efficacy of which may be discerned in every event of creativity, sensitivity, and negotiability. Thus I am led empircially to speak of God as the Ultimate Efficacy within relationships.

One may wish to go beyond this empirical line of inquiry to enlarge upon or to give further intelligibility to the claims that are made for it. I have always held that such a metaphysical vision can be justified to the degree that it has some empiricial basis, i.e., if its primal perceptions can be said to have a basis in experience or in history. A metaphysics that is purely a work of the imagination, however valid it may be internally as an exercise in logic, has seemed to me to be a floating vision having only the value of wishful thinking or of a reverie as an aesthetic creation. But where a sense of ultimate persuasion arises in experience, or out of events in history, as a serious estimate of the character of events that are daily encountered, one's judgments can be said to be empirically anchored in the realities of existence. Such apprehensions may be taken seriously as interpreting experience to some degree, however vaguely or ambiguously they may have been gleaned. One may thereupon seek further intelligibility by extending the vision of the mind, cautiously moving out from these basic apprehensions imaginatively and speculatively; but always with a restraint consonant with empirical demands and with the limitations of our human powers of inquiry. On this basis I have ventured to enlarge upon this empirical persuasion by projecting it into a metaphysical vision, albeit a modest one. It is understandable, perhaps, that I should have availed myself of the stimulating imagination of Alfred North Whitehead in this undertaking since he took it upon himself, as he said, to complete the task begun in Radical Empiricism by William James and Henri Bergson. But my response to Whitehead with regard to this crucial empirical datum has been qualified by preferences of my own. For example, Whitehead, in considering where one might begin in one's metaphysical explication of the creative act of God, pondered the primal alternatives which Western history offered, namely the Hebraic and the Platonic myths. Whitehead decided that the Hebraic myth of creation was too primitive for modern metaphysical speculation and thus chose to build upon the Platonic myth. I have chosen otherwise, not on philosophical grounds, but on grounds indicated by hints from cultural anthropology. The Hebraic myth, I would hold, is not only more basic to Western forms of thought and sensibility than the Greek myths, but it has been more pervasive in its influence in shaping the human psyche of the West as well as its religious institutions. The Platonic myth has been influential at the level of philosophical reflection, but in other areas of cultural expression its influence has been marginal and intermittent. It is true that Christian theologians have assimilated Platonic imagery in certain areas of their thought, but in dealing with what might be called the basic theological formula, the *imago dei*, by which the Christian understanding of man and of his relation to God have been explicated, they have resorted to imagery that roots in the metaphor of the Covenant and in the biblical story of creation.

In any case, you may find it helpful to know that *Faith and Culture* and *The Realities of Faith*, as well as the earlier efforts of mine in *Seeds of Redemption* and *The Reawakening of Christian Faith*, represent a concern to bring emergent and organismic insights to bear upon our religious history as this cultural and religious history takes its rise out of the Judaic-Christian myth or primal beginnings. It would be accurate to say that my efforts parallel Whitehead's metaphysical vision and, at certain crucial points, partake of it; but they do not stem directly from it, as you can see from the qualifications I have just cited.

Within the Creative Passage there occurs the passage of history, not as a single stream, but as diverse cultural currents, each of which has its own dynamic structure, integrating through memory, precedent, custom and much more, the sequence of events and actualities that have constituted its living stream. The dynamic passage of events within each culture has given form to a *Structure of Experience* which can be said to be the enduring structural residue of the cultural history within its particular orbit of meaning, as seen from within the perspective of every present moment of that history. The Structure of Experience is thus the present immediacy within the total and inclusive Creative Passage. The distinction between these terms is somewhat comparable to the distinction implied in the contrast between "Essence" and "Existence," though the context here is the culture, rather than individual man.

Within each Structure of Experience there is to be found a persisting, elemental myth, giving shape to its cultural *mythos*, expressive of the hard-earned, endurable modes of response, subliminal for the most part, which have formed within that orbit of meaning. A third step, then, is to come to an adequate understanding of this phenomenon of myth in the culture, and of the *mythos* that continues to shape its orbit of meaning. Myth is the elemental response of a people to what is ever present as an ultimate demand and measure upon human existence. It reaches to the level of the creaturely stance which a people will assume in speaking of their existence. It affects and shapes not only language, the mode of thinking and speaking, but sensibilities of thought, psychical orientation, and thus psychical expectations. In our more sophisticated and technical theological speech, this cultural *elan* is often expressed in universal terms as the response of the individual: e.g., *sensus numinous*, "sense of destiny," "idea of the holy," "ultimate concern," etc. In using such terms one may intend to transcend the cultural myth, or he may simply mean to point to a quality of response implied in all myths which can be legitimately assimilated by modern man and correlated with his use of reason. As a way of evoking general acceptance of this elemental response within the modern ethos, these terms serve a purpose; but they do not do justice to what is culturally expressive of this *elan*. In fact, in employing such terms, modern theologies have tended to emulate the Enlightenment in individualizing, and then universalizing, the religious response. The concreteness of the response within its cultural history is thereby dissolved; and thus the efficacy of the response as a persisting psychical orientation of thought and experience within that cultural history is readily overlooked, if not ignored. It is in recognition of this fact that I have argued for retaining a concern with the mytho-poetic mode of thought and awareness in modern cultures, and with the kind of elemental outreach which it conveys. This, in my judgment, is consonant with retaining the psychical depth of the cultural response. And I urge this as an accompaniment of, rather than as an alternative to, efforts to rationalize experience.

However transitory specific myths may be, or the mythologies that arise as explications of what has been discerned in myth, the shaping of the human psyche, its sensibiliies, modes of apprehension and reflection, are more enduring. Thus the outgrowing of specifically formulated myths and mythologies does not imply necessarily a relinquishment of the *mythos*, which is the deep-lying orbit of meaning giving structure and direction both at the level of the human psyche and within the realm of imaginative and cognitive experience. Insofar as a people remain elemental in some respect, which is simply to be responsive to primordial and ultimate demands in existence, they participate in this deep-lying *mythos* of the culture. But even in becoming sophisticated, enabling one to disavow or to ignore this elemental response, modern men will not wholly relinquish the *mythos*, for their disavowals, and possibly their alternative secular affirmations, will partake of, or be defined against, and thus to some extent be defined in terms of, what has once been elementally embraced. The reasons for this persistence of the mythical forms of sensibility and cognition are subtle and devious; for they have to do with the shaping of the human psyche at a subliminal level, both individually and collectively. Simply dealing with the problem at the level of conscious meaning will not reach to formative influences of *lived* experiences, or of history as it has been lived.

The Judaic-Christian *mythos*, I contend, underlies and is formative of the sensibilities and psychic outlook of our Western culture. The Christian expression of this *mythos* bears witness to a specific occurrence in our history in which the saving work of God became manifest as a New Creation; that is, the creative work of God assumed a new and decisive degree of concreteness. This, I am inclined to believe, was made possible by the emergence of a sensitivity and qualitative response within the human structure, enabling God to assume a new degree of concreteness in human history. Nothing ontologically new occurred in this New Creation; that is, nothing new ontologically occurred in God's character. But something quite new as a social energy was released into history, giving rise not only to new expectations, new hopes and possibilities within existence, but to new understanding of the movement of goodness and grace within relationships that form and hold us in existence. A vivid sense of the energies of grace and judgment being ever-present as a resource beyond our own energies and efforts came into human lives, opening their lives to the depth of their creative ground or matrix wherein relationships were made redemptive and recreative.

It is this New Creation as a redemptive goodness in the relationships of history to which the Christian *mythos* bears witness, either explicitly or implicitly; and in this sense, it is the deepest vein of our structure and experience.

Now there are various forms of participation in the *mythos* within any culture. And here I come to a distinctive emphasis in my own theological method.

II

Looking at the more recent history of our Western experience, we may identify at least three fairly distinct forms of participation in the *mythos* of our culture: 1) the cultus, 2) individual experience, and 3) the wider, so-called secular domain of experience within the culture. For purposes of brevity, I shall speak of the latter form simply as culture. These three forms of participation overlap, even intermesh; yet one can detect boundaries between them at certain points. The fact that there have been issues between individual Christians and the faith of the church, for example, or between the church and society, not to speak of tensions between individuals and society on grounds of conscience or belief, is evidence of the distinction of which I speak.

Since the terms "culture," "cult" or "cultus," and "individual experience" are important to my presentation, let me try to make clear what I mean by them. Culture, as I use the term, connotes the total complex of human growth that has occurred within any clearly defined orbit of human association, expressing its prevailing sentiments, style, and way of life. This is a shorthand way of saying what I have written in *The Realities of Faith*, where I defined culture as being

> the human flowering of existing structures and facilities, becoming manifest as an ordered way of life in the imaginative activities and creations of a people, their arts and crafts, their architecture, their furniture and furnishings, their costumes and designs, their literature, their public and private ceremonies, both religious and political. It is in their formative ideas, giving direction to their educational efforts and customs, as well

as to their religious notions and practices, their social graces and manners; in their habits of eating and body care; in their modes of livelihood and the social organization that follows from them.[1]

Culture, then, is any society seen in terms of its total human expression, wherein the accumulative qualities of *lived history and experience* are made vivid and distinctive. To be sure, spatial demarcations in the history of peoples are by no means fixed or enduring; yet there has been sufficient durability of large and small blocks of human society throughout the world's history to enable one to say that there have existed "clearly defined orbits of human association" in which distinctive and pervading qualities of experience have developed. Mobile and unstable as these demarcations have been, they suffice for speaking in a general way of varying human cultures, distinctive clusters of human growth evincing a particular structure of experience. Thus, in speaking of man or men, of people or the human community, we deal in abstractions until we conceive of these men or communities within historical orbits of association that have yielded distinctive cultures.

The cult, or the cultus, is generally defined as a particular system of worship, including its body of belief, its organization, as well as its ceremonial. Often the cult exists as a culture within culture. That is to say, the cult becomes so effective in redefining an orbit of spatial existence for its devotees within the culture as to exclude much that is expressive of human growth outside its restrictive orbit, thereby rendering it nonexistent for its own defined purposes. Yet this exclusion is never totally effective; for even under the tightest controls, certain minimum lines of communication between cult and culture are made necessary, even if they have to be underground and clandestine.

The history of our Western experience presents considerable variety in the relations between cult and culture, ranging from the secretive encounters of the catacombs to the quasi-secularized religious societies of recent liberal vintage. To whatever extent religious organizations and culture may have coalesced, however, each of them has nevertheless continued to be in some sense a particular focus of religious witness and practice.

Now in Western society there has emerged a third distinctive focus of the religious witness, namely the individual, or the individual experience. In the earliest stages of Near-Eastern and Western experience, individuality was virtually nonexistent. Personality, insofar as the term existed, was understood to mean corporate personality, expressing the mentality or spirit of a people through individual representatives. Even throughout early Christian history this sense of conformity to the corporate image persisted, both within religious and political societies. Individuality appears to have been an outcome of the rise of the city states in Greece and Rome and the consequent dissipation of corporate control or even or corporate ties. Nonconformity in religious and political spheres was by no means an innovation peculiar to that period of our history, but nonconformity as an expression of individual experience, rivaling both cult and culture, was.

In subsequent years, say from the eleventh century on, this particular form of religious witness, rising from and resting upon the authenticity of individual experience, was to become increasingly formidable in challenging, and at times radically altering, the religious witness of both cult and culture.

Now I mean to argue that the Christian witness, rather than being contained, as it were, within the community of believers commonly identified with the formal organization of the church, has been exercised, with varying degrees of definitiveness, throughout Western history, acquiring a distinctive focus, with varying degrees of intensity, in these three areas or vortices of experience.

This way of looking at the witness of faith presupposes, as I have said, the concreteness of God's working at the level of the Creative Passage in each moment of historical time and a symbolical (or cognitive) participation in the *mythos* arising from the witness of the living Christ. In some instances, the former may be vividly known as concrete experience, with little or no knowledge or its symbolic reference. In other instances, the symbolic level of its meaning may be readily acknowledged and verbalized without experiencing a vivid sense of the empirical realities of Spirit as these are concretely encountered. I am trying to be attentive to both levels, to the empirical as well as to the symbolical. I am concerned to say that responding to the revelatory event in Jesus Christ is not just a matter of perpetuating the recollection and psychical shaping of an historical event through memory and tradition, but of experiencing a work of judgment and grace concretely in the depth of present events and relationships. Participation in the *mythos* provides the first, and gives illumination to these occurrences and encounters, actual response to the efficacy of judgment and grace, as these come to us in events and relationships, provides the second, giving concreteness and reality to what is borne forth as a witness of faith.

Now, perhaps, with this explanation, it will become clear why, in formulating a theological method, I choose to speak of correlating three vortices of the Christian witness. One who takes the cultural history of the West seriously as being integral to Christian history, and who envisages both of them as occurring within the Creative Passage, will be encouraged to see theological method as a comprehensive dialectic between its primal source in the biblical witness to the New Creation and present participation in the efficacy of Spirit, along with the contemporary forms of witness to this depth in our historical experience and existence. This method may seem somewhat reminiscent of Schleiermacher's appeal to the religious consciousness. It is, however, more inclusive in what it considers to be relevant to the witness of faith. And further, the method I employ is more organismic, more contextual in its understanding of the dynamics of faith, regarding it, not just as a teleology within consciousness, but as a dynamic nexus of formative relations within the culture itself. Again, the pattern and movement of the method I have outlined may seem to have affinities with that of dialectical theology; but on examination, or perhaps on the face of it, it will prove to be more complex than the dialectic between kerygma and proclamation. The latter is a church dogmatics, and presupposes a single strand of witness issuing from the preaching of the Word in the churches. My own method presents a theological texture with diversified yet interwoven strands of witness, with the faith of the church forming the central strand of the vertebrae.

Even as I emphasize the importance of culture as one vortex of Christian witness, I recoil from speaking of it as a *source* for theology lest this way of expressing it should seem to say more than I intend. It is a source of data for theology in the sense that the religious consciousness was such a source in Schleiermacher's theology. Yet the data of theology, whether gleaned from culture, the church, or individual experience, points us to deeper realities which speak through these data. Thus I am concerned to say that each of these vortices points beyond itself to the living Christ as a continuing work of the New Creation, revealing the Infinite Structure of grace and judgment in each generation of history. Together they point as well back to the primal witness in Scripture wherein the Christ-event as a defining datum is available to Christian faith. However one views this luminous center, one cannot ignore its controlling force in theological construction. It is the fulcrum which gives leverage to every other doctrine. Everything relevant to Christian theological inquiry, formally speaking, fans out from that focal event. If the phrase "source for theology" is applicable to any datum, it would seem to apply to this revelatory event. Having said this, however, it is pertinent to observe that, materially, this formal center, the Christ-event, may not be the starting point for every Christian, or for every theologian. That which prompts one to be theologically reflective or inquiring may be some specific occurrence in one's experience, some situation of impasse or crisis, of release or heightening. Such reflection may arise from some poignant reports of the human story in modern literature or the arts; it may begin with the tragic cleavage between human groups within society at large, with the struggle for unity and identity within contemporary church life. Such reflection may follow from solitary moments of anxiety that tear men and women apart in their loneliness and sense of meaninglessness. All such instances present vortices of human experience in which the realities of existence come vividly and critically into play; where, in a word, ultimacy and immediacy traffic together. These instances suggest, too, how volatile experience itself really is; how ever-present the energies of judgment and grace are, how concretely real the life of the Spirit actually is, and why it cannot be contained within institutional forms of man's own making. It is this underlying conviction about the freedom of the Spirit as it arises out of the Creative Passage, and as it emanates from the New Creation that was discerned in Jesus Christ, that impels me to look beyond ecclesiastical forms for these acts of witnessing, even as I try to give full attention to the proclamations of the Kerygma within the community of the church. Yet, in speaking of the freedom of the Spirit, I would not wish to be understood as saying that these energies of grace and judgment appear and do their work without benefit of structure or human form. On the contrary, they occur within the relationships, and not just certain *sanctified* relationships, relationships set apart in this community or that. "The Spirit bloweth where it listeth." And in this sense the entire culture in which the Word is proclaimed, wherein the primal *mythos* is conveyed, shared, and participated in, is made resonant with varying degrees of relevance in the focal event of the Christian story.

III

Now that I have made the point that the source for theology, substantively speaking, is the dimension of ultimacy within history and within present immediacies, and that this Ultimate Efficacy of Spirit is received within our structured experience, I can be free to point up the way in which culture plays a role in shaping our encounter with its realities, and in giving verbal or symbolic response to such encounters.

In the first place there is simply the matter of language itself, forms of speech, characteristic modes of thought, facilities for inquiry and the imagery of thought that is employed in any given period of history in carrying the verbal and intellectual business of theology. This was a major emphasis of the early Chicago School under Shailer Mathews, who argued that the social mind of every age was formative both of the problems that arose, precipitating theological discussions, and of the analogies and social patterns by which solutions to problems were sought and found. I have added my weight to this effort, pointing out in addition that the imagery of thought in any period of history within a culture tends simultaneously to offer new opportunities, not only for seeing into problems and issues, but for seeing realities afresh, even for repossessing what has been lost to previous generations by reason of restrictions which its imagery of thought imposed; and to enclose the new generation within the frames of meaning that are particularly appealing and illumining to it. I have pressed this point sufficiently, perhaps, in my later writings, so I shall not burden you with it further. What I should like to do instead is to argue that the culture makes a concrete contribution to theological understanding and thus, in a way, to tantalize you with the suggestion that the culture may be more substantive as a source for theology than I have acknowledged.

I shall begin by pointing out what has been lost to theological understanding because of the tendency to conceive of the witness of faith too narrowly and exclusively. The formal accounting of Christian theological history, say between the fourth and seventeenth centuries, has adhered rather rigidly to the doctrinal history of the cultus. Our theological history, therefore, in large measure is the story of the Christian consensus. It records the line of Christian thinking emanating from the victory of the majority or the party in power in church councils over competing views and viewpoints, with some marginal reference to minority groups or individuals who provided some opposition to this Christian consensus. As a history of dogma, i.e., as a history of Christian belief that became controlling and mandatory, this accounting is fairly reliable. As a history of the Christian witness, however, it is highly selective, consciously biased, and apologetically inadequate. Except for isolated instances of this Christian witness beyond the firm line of conformity within the church, much of the non-conformist expression of the Christian witness has probably been permanently lost. Thus we have come to know the Christian story and the Christian witness within this vast ancient and medieval period largely through the authoritative, doctrinal deliverances of the established church. One large exception to this statement can be made; and this exception points up one important bit of evidence for the thesis for which I have implicitly pled in my writings on Christian theology, namely that the culture provides an important supplement to the church's formal witness to the faith. The exception is that intermittent shafts of reflected light from the environing culture filter through these cultic discussions sufficiently to give hint of divergent views and voices. For an accounting of this cultural witness we have been largely indebted to church historians. Incidentally, I should like to say that one of the important reasons for having rich offerings in church history, in addition to historical theology, is that church historians are more likely to do justice to this witness of faith within the culture beyond that of the formal cultus than historians of theology. Church historians are the true secularists of theological seminaries. They mingle with literary and political historians, with architects, dramatists, and art collectors. They even visit bawdy houses, dives, and beer cellars, looking for artifacts that will fill in their story. I have evidence of this if anyone is interested.

The church historian, when he has been imaginative, resourceful, and enterprising, has provided us with our best accounts of this witness of faith issuing from the culture; though often he has done so with a sense of guilt insomuch as he conceived himself to be a *church* historian, and as such, so he thought, should confine himself to more recognizable church activity and functions. But I would argue otherwise. What has been expressive through the culture, say within the medieval period, and captured in church history, is not just a pale reflection of that found in the formal cultus, nor a spillover from it; rather it is the gospel story re-enacted and communicated with the subtlety and sensitivity of the creative talent within art forms: in the medieval miracle plays, in the cantos of a *Divine Comedy*, in wood carvings, in painting, or even in the floor plan of a cathedral. It is this story amplified or exemplified in the disciplined speech of philosophers, publicists, statesmen or poets. It is this story critically confronted and countered, yet with an integrity of mind and heart that lends fiber to its presentation. Christianity so conveyed may or may not speak through the churches. Often it has not. Furthermore, artists and scholars are a crafty lot. At times they speak out of the independence of genius, however much they may be sponsored or seemingly controlled by conformist thinking. The hidden nuance or emphasis, if it must be hidden, can be a carrier of new overtones of meaning and intention. Orthodoxies have been satirized, taunted, and eventually undermined by the subtle innovations of a creative talent. What is present in any period of history as a force bent on creativity within disciplined and imaginative minds, or the skill of craftsmen, can loom as a tidal wave of renascence and reform, with power to overthrow the established church and to break asunder its consensus of belief and practice. Bear in mind that, before the dams of conformity began to break in the fourteenth to the sixteenth centuries, much that was brewing as intimations of renascence and reform was issuing from this cultural witness of faith.

But I should not want to convey the impression that these sensitive and creative voices of the culture had value only as a dissonant and disruptive force, countering the dogmatic consensus. On the contrary, one should take account of the fact that such voices arose within the church, and in large measure concurred with the historic consensus to which orthodoxy was committed. Yet, in being zealous participants in the culture of the period as well, they were able to bring to this established line of dogma fresh insight and nuances of thought that saved the orthodox confessions from becoming inflexible stereotypes. They were able to do this principally because, as participants in some restive or creative area of the culture, they had assimilated into their thinking and feeling some of the creative ferment of the period that was either pertinent to the idiom in which the witness could be significantly conveyed, or expressive of the truth of the faith within an idiom that was relevant to the period. Significant figures both in Roman Catholic and Protestant history can be cited to illustrate this point. Some of them were known as renaissance men; others as reformers; but whether reformers or renaissance men, they were ambiguously involved both in the church and in the culture.

Once the historic cleavage came in Christendom, setting culture and cultus apart from each other more vividly, say in the seventeenth century, their interrelation became a more self-conscious, more strained, and possibly more tenuous, yet no less inescapable. By this I mean that, even after the seventeenth century, cult and culture in the West were held within a common orbit of meaning by reason of the historical interweaving of the common strands of experience. What issued from this organic complex was a contextual outcome of historical occasions that could not readily be set aside by conscious decision or by indecision. Nevertheless, we must acknowledge that the modern period of Western culture has presented a different and more perplexing picture with regard to the cultural witness of faith. The very fact that the church's authority over culture, and over the arts and sciences of society, had broken left cultural activities and the various disciplines of learning to pursue a more forthright and thus a more vigorous course along independent lines of inquiry and interest. In time this was to have the effect of causing the formal church to retrench in its public activity, and of causing those activities within culture outside the church to loom as a more formidable and cohesive organization of life, set over against the churches. It became possible, under these circumstances, to conceive of the church as being the sole embodiment of what persisted as the Christian witness, and to view the culture as a secular force in the face of which Christianity and the church were at bay.

The growth of lay Christianity within the free churches in the seventeenth century and following was to alleviate this situation temporarily as demarcations between church and culture among them became less pronounced; but it was to become apparent that, even under these circumstances, the issue between the two could not be ignored or set aside. However, with the free churches having accepted the "right of private judgment" in matters of faith and belief as a guiding principle in the conduct of church affairs, this issue tended to take the form of setting the religious conscience of individuals over against the tyranny of power exercised by political sovereignty. Later, within the American experience, the reverse of this situation was to occur as it became necessary to restrict the expression of partisan voices in the churches with regard to the affairs of the state.

Yet the most serious threat to the Christian witness within the modern period was to come from another source: namely, in the emergence within Western culture of sciences, philosophies, and other creative disciplines, along with social institutions, that were to rival, and then challenge, the church and its ethos. With the appearance of this more explicit form of secular knowledge and activity within Western culture, the sense of its continuity with the Christian *mythos* has become difficult to sustain. Roman Catholic scholars and churchmen have forthrightly declared the modern period of the West to be a post-Christian era in culture. And the implication of their characterization has been that only in the authoritative institution of the Roman Catholic Church is the witness of faith to be found and acknowledged. The orthodox line among Protestants has simulated this ecclesiastical judgment; thus theology in this context has meant specifically *church theology*. The Free Church tradition in Protestantism, and later Liberal Protestantism, has, in general, veered from this orthodox line only in insisting upon an appeal to the right of private judgment, which in Liberalism became an appeal to religious experience or to a judgment of fact. Out of this Free-church and Liberal heritage has come a form of theologizing which has often eschewed the formal traditions of church doctrine, combining in its stead a selected body of Scripture with present-day claims based upon individual experience and judgment. Among non-liberal Protestants of the Free churches, the culture has tended to be more and more excluded from their concerns, leading finally to a dissociation of theology and culture as explicit and as decisive as in orthodox traditions. These non-liberal Protestant free churches have adopted a policy of "Christ against culture" which has implied even more disavowal of any cultural influence in theology than in orthodoxy.

Liberal Protestantism has taken a different stand on this issue. Along with its concern to give credence to the witness of individual experience, liberal Protestantism has sought to avail itself of the guidance and control of the cultural disciplines in the interest not only of achieving relevance in its interpretation of Christian faith but of bringing integrity and intelligibility to its formulations within the modern idiom.

Now my efforts must be seen in relation to these several established procedures. I have argued that theology cannot adequately convey the witness of Christian faith by conceiving of its task within the bounds of the institutional church. I have argued further that it cannot do so by undertaking to express it simply in terms of individual experience or judgment, as clarified and tested by contemporary cultural disciplines. What I seek to add to these, even within the modern period, is the data which comes from the witness of the culture within which both church and individual have achieved their historical experience.

Now you will readily see that to argue that the culture in our modern Western experience is or can be the bearer of the Judaic-Christian witness, despite all that has happened in Western history, takes a bit of doing. Neither orthodox nor liberal theologians are ready to concur with such an argument; which means that neither the approach to Christian history within traditional categories nor the understanding of the Christian experience within historical liberal categories can provide the structural basis for enlarging the scope of the Christian witness to include culture as its third vortex. In this respect, I find myself moving into a post-liberal methodology.

My method, I am inclinded to believe, rests precariously upon the assumption that our culture cannot extricate itself from the Judaic-Christian *mythos*, any more than any existent event can relinquish its past as it lives on in the shaping of its present structure and dynamics; or, to speak of human events, as one lives on in the present shaping of one's individuated psyche and structure of experience. One can modify and discipline the emotions attending these past valuations, one can summon them, insofar as they are articulate within one's conscious experience, to confront the demands of new occurrences and new knowledge. Thus, in part, this primordial shaping can be altered; but, in part, it cannot be altered. To the extent that its shaping goes deeper than man's conscious awareness, it tends to elude the conscious efforts modern men may employ to advance their sophistication, with indifference to elemental demands. And in this I mean to take issue with modernism as such, as we have come to know it in the West.

But I seek to rest my case not simply upon the persistence of this elemental shaping of our structure of experience, but on the soundness of what is implied in this elemental dimension of existence, however much its historical working out in Western culture may have proven offensive to sophisticated and disciplined minds of the modern period. By the elemental dimension of existence I mean simply living with an awareness of the fact of birth and death, confronting man's existence, its range of opportunity for human fulfillment, not only within these acknowledged limits defined by birth and death, but with creaturely feelings appropriate to them. Simply living within these limits on a sophisticated level, shunting off emotions, anxieties and inquiries evoked by an appropriate elemental depth of our nature, is the usual commonplace pose of sophisticated modernity. It is a pose that was given intellectual credence a generation ago by the psuedo-scientific dictum, "all beginnings and endings are lost in mystery," thus seeming to release the modern, informed mind to be attentive only to this span of existence between beginnings and endings, as if no mystery or ultimacy attended these years in between. While this cleared the board for a more simplified and controllable form of intellectual inquiry, it condemned it to shallowness, however refined and precise its disciplines might become. Elementalism, I would hold, is simply a capacity to acknowledge humbly and humanly this fact of existential limitations, defined and symbolized by the events of birth and death, and to experience creaturely feelings appropriate to such limitation and dependence.

Now there can follow all grades of response to this inescapable fact, expressing such feelings in many different modes. But, however expressed, as long as the elemental dimension of existence is alive and assertive in modern experience, it will be continuous with what is primordial as a mythical response.

Thus, while I understand what can be implied historically in speaking of modern culture as being post-Judaic-Christian, namely, that disavowals and estrangments exist between secularized segments of our society and the practicing cultus of Jews and Christians, I do not acknowledge that this modern culture, by its disavowals and alienations, has extricated itself rom the primordial *mythos* of the culture that has shaped the dynamics of the human psyche and its ethos within its orbit of meaning. Its very secularization, in its peculiar way, bears a kind of witness to the faith it disavows.

Thus, while I understand what can be implied historically in speaking of modern culture as being post-Judaic-Christian, namely, that disavowals and estrangments exist between secularized segments of our society and the practicing cultus of Jews and Christians, I do not acknowledge that this modern culture, by its disavowals and alienations, has extricated itself from the primordial *mythos* of the culture that has shaped the dynamics of the human psyche and its ethos within its orbit of meaning. Its very secularization, in its peculiar way, bears a kind of witness to the faith it disavows.

If one argues that this is indeed a pale and hollow form of witness, more negative in its implications than the assertion that our doubts are of a piece with our faith, I would reply that it is in fact quite otherwise. And it may be this very fact that lends force to the various proposals that are being made these days advocating a "religionless Christianity." (Cf. *Honest to God* by John A. T. Robinson). Undoubtedly the effort to achieve a new Christian worldliness, or to "secularize the gospel" is motivated in a variety of ways: in some instances it appears to be prompted by a dubious concern to attain intellectual and cultural respectability for religion, reminiscent of the modernistic zeal of the twenties; in other instances it appears to be favored because it promises to be an astute way of carrying on the apologetic task in the modern world among "its cultured despisers." For the most part, however, this new mood among us seems to be embraced simply out of weariness with formal Christianity, a kind of modern-day recurrence of the lay Christianity that has periodically burst forth throughout Christian history as a revolt from within, bent on "cleansing the inward parts." It is quite possible, however, that these present-day efforts to bring the Christian witness incognito into secularized centers of the culture will yield some unexpected results. Committed Christians may discover amidst these so-called secularists resources of judgment as well as of grace that will radically transform and possibly deepen their own understanding of the Christian gospel. Anxiety, alienation, and despair, when humanly confronted as stark realities, can have a dimension of meaning, and possibly an impact, that eludes their liturgical or theological rendering. Experiencing gross indifference to human sensibilities, the raw exercise of power, and contempt for human sentiments of every kind can alert one to the hardness of heart in humanity as few sermons and scriptural homilies can convey. And, conversely, under other circumstances, encountering the human goodness of people outside the churches, sensing the quality of their discernment, judgment, and discipline of spirit, despite their seemingly secularized ways of living and thinking, may put to shame the churches' stereotyped estimates of human nature.

What I am insinuating by these oblique remarks is that there are resources within the culture that lend a sense of reality to this gospel of grace and judgment to which the Church bears witness, but to which, the church as *church*, and Christians as *Christians*, may be but vaguely atuned. To apprehend the realities of faith as energies of grace and judgment concretely at work in culture, in human relationships, in the crises and triumphs of human enterprise, is no small or insignificant theological achievement. And a theology that is quickened to discern this dimension of the Christian witness has access to the very realities that speak forth through the Scriptures when they say, "Behold, and see!"

Faith, we may then discover anew as church people, is not a memory merely, recalled in creed and litany, not just the story of our lives re-enacted in pageantry and ritual, not a will to believe despite all evidence to the contrary. Faith partakes of all these acts of reminiscence and decision, we will affirm; but we will discover that it is this and more. And this *more* of faith, we will find, issues from the realization that what we read about in Scripture, celebrate in sacrament, and proclaim through the Word, is a truth of immediate experience, a truth that transpires within every epochal occasion to visit upon every nexus of relationships, its offering of grace and judgment. Our faith, we may be startled to find, is not just a faith in the Scriptural memory of the Christ-event, not just a symbolic transfer from an ancient to a modern idiom, but faith in the reality of a New Creation that meets us in every event of betrayal or blessedness, in every experience of sin and forgiveness, in every encounter with defeat and despair, and in the joys of the resurrected life that follows again and again upon this experience of judgment and grace as we mingle with our fellows, of whatever confession, or of no confession, and as we stumble into or out of the stark tragedy-laden events of these harrowing experiences of present-day history.

I have done my best in these pages to declare a truth about the Christian faith that will not let me go, and which motivates my every word in formulating a Christian theology. That truth is that the realities of this faith are living, vital energies in the immediacies of experience. As such they are no respecters of persons or situations, or forms or institutions; though they exist and transpire through forms and institutions. But the forms we provide will not contain them—neither intellectual, aesthetic, moral, or institutional forms. I have said elsewhere that "the Christian gospel leaps beyond the sanctuary into common places, like a fire that is no respecter of structures, particularly of those that would enclose or contain its flames." So, too, with these energies of grace and judgment of which the Gospel speaks. This does not imply, I would argue, that the forms, institutions, and structures which we create in order to express, convey or clarify this life of the Spirit are of no avail. They are of the utmost importance when we are dealing with the problem of our own understanding of these realities, or with our own efforts at disciplining our capacities to receive and to respond to them. Every conscientious concern to achieve intelligibility in apprehending the Christian faith speaks out of an integrity of mind that carries its own justification. Every caution to preserve a sense of dignity and restraint in our approach to what is holy attests to the depth of our witness of faith, and to a humility that is proportionate to it. Every intimation of sensitivity in act or expression in bearing witness to our faith gives evidence of the disciplining to which we have submitted in restraining egoistic passions and feelings, thus summoning them to a more discerning level of wonder in worship. In each of these ways, let us confess, we do go astray, making idols of our human forms of sensibilities, our categories, our codes of conduct; yet through each of them we open ourselves to the chastening effects of a human grace that is akin to the sensitivity that is in God. We do not become divine by becoming more human; but neither do we attain spirituality by denying our humanity! Yet, when we pursue these human capacities and sensitivities under the judgment of grace, which is a good not our own, they can become the disciplined instruments of devotion and inquiry despite the fact that, as human forms, they present a possible threat as barriers to what is real and good beyond our human measure.

I must add a footnote to these concluding remarks. I am confident that some of you will feel that I have exaggerated the role of culture in theology, even falsifying its relation to the church. You may wish to criticize what I have presented, saying, "But don't you recognize that Christians themselves are people of the culture? The culture is in the churches, even as the churches are within culture. The distinctions you make here are arbitrary and misleading."

I am glad you asked that question. In reply I must say: to be sure, Christians are people of the culture, and to that extent the culture is in the churches, even as the churches are within culture. In our modern society the lines of cleavage or demarcation are not sharply drawn. Nevertheless, they exist because there are distinctions between the people of culture who are within the church, and the people of culture who are without it. In this respect, Christians, who are also people of the culture, do not fully embrace or express the culture in all its dimensions of human goodness and evil. Let me put the matter bluntly and boldly: I mean to express a conviction that neither the glory of the human spirit, nor its degradation in major key, appears within the community of the committed. You can qualify that in whatever way you wish. It does require qualification in order to be reasonably accurate. But face the extreme assertion of this conviction first: there is something about Church Christianity that depresses the creativities of men, that foreshortens their imaginative and critical powers and impels them to suspect concern with qualitative attainment, thus lulling them into or even summoning them to a preference for mediocrity. We should now qualify the assertion by saying that neither the glory of the human spirit, nor its degradation in major key, appears *readily* within the churches. By this I mean to acknowledge that there are to be found within the churches those for whom these human creativities mean much, and who in themselves express this qualitative outreach of the human spirit. But they are lone voices, crying in a wilderness. It is true that they who speak in this way are lone voices crying in the wilderness of modern culture as well; but the fact remains that when they appear, they appear as a more formidable expression of this dimension of our humanity. And thus, simply on the pragmatic basis of turning to where they are, I tend to urge that theology, in order to be attentive to the meaning of man in terms of his human creativities, and the glory that is visited upon his structure of existence by reason of them, needs to have access to the resources of the cultural witness.

In a similar way, I would agree that Church Christianity has little access to the depths of human degradation; thus, while Christian preachers and theologians speak freely of human sin and moral evil, their encounter with it tends to be circumscribed. Often it tends to be more formal than material. Don't misunderstand me. I am fully aware that church people, themselves, are sinners. Whether we are speaking in Niebuhr's terms of the sin of pride and arrogance that issues from men's so-called "higher natures," or the shabby instances of clandestine sexuality in church circles that periodically breaks into the open in scandal sheets, there is no lack of human degradation among people of the churches. What is less available to the religious consciousness that is confined to its circles, however, is a concrete awareness of such human evil in its massive, persistent, and organized expression, such as appears in the work-a-day world of the culture, where evil, as a surd of insensitivity, perverseness, and violence appears in demonic form. Our awareness of this dimension of the human spirit and its structured existence as theologians tends to be remote, meager, and second-hand. Thus our knowledge of man is partial, truncated, symbolic. If we venture to reach beyond our contained Christian outlook, we speak abstractly or obliquely about these surmised depths of human evil without really knowing the context in which they occur, without noting the ambiguities that attend such human evil in the *lived experience* of men.

All I mean to say here is that the church theologian who presumes to speak out of a witness of faith concerning the human situation that has been insulated from that situation as it actually occurs in the teeming life of culture must admit to being deprived of material resources for his discipline. His theological critique, like his sermons and homilies, must, in the nature of the case, be "sicklied o'er with the pale cast of thought" peculiar to one who remains remote from the realities of which he speaks.

Now I am giving the impression, no doubt, that I mean to argue for immersing the theologian in the hubbub and hovels of culture, when actually I mean no such thing. Many theologians who have become awakened to this cultural dimension of the Christian witness, and to the resources it brings to the theological task, will readily follow this course, and find identification in their own experiences with the problems to which they address themselves. I concur in this provided one recognizes the limits to which one can go in pursuing this course profitably as a disciplined inquirer. But being receptive to the resources of culture in pursuing one's theological task is more a state of mind than a state of life, implying an readiness to receive the life of culture freely into one's own life as one's own history and experience, and to think and participate in its as being of a piece with its depths of reality. It then becomes a way of conceiving the revelation of God in Christ, as well as of understanding the plight and possibilities of men's souls. One for whom the Gospel and culture must be segregated moves within a theology of containment, wherein the demarcations between spiritual and secular, the sacred and the profane, are sharp and unyielding. And in that containment neither the full meaning of the Gospel, nor the full meaning of the culture, nor for that matter the full meaning of man as man, can be known or understood.

The life of God, as it appears within the structures of history, is a vast movement of grace and judgment, touching the whole of people's life. There are distinctions and specializations of practice and performance within this historical pageant of creativity and redemption, giving rise to different vortices of witness, bodying forth our human response to this life in God. But no one of these vortices, no one of these specialized functions, can exhaust, or fully contain, what is given in this good not our own, as it issues forth from our life in God.

The Breaking of Forms in the Interest of Importance 2

Bernard E. Meland

The affinities between the cultural unrest of the nineteen sixties and that of the nineteen twenties, the era in which my generation grew up intellectually and culturally, are striking to the point of being disturbing. In view of this fact, one can understand and even sympathize with the tendency among many of my contemporaries to make glib comparisons between them. Yet, one would do well to guard against being taken in by them, for, despite obvious similarities, the two eras of cultural revolution are not really comparable. The issues of today differ, not only in kind, but in range and complexity; as does the temper and mood of thought, not to mention the intensity of feeling that is expressed in action. The nineteen-twenty revolt of youth in this country followed upon disillusioning developments resulting from World War One and the inability of the League of Nations to cope with its political consequences. That mood of disillusionment cut more deeply into the personal idealism of European youth and their communities than in our own country. In fact, except for some darker veins in the American literature of the period, the American mind, even among the younger generation, remained impervious to a sense of despair. Theologically the sun was still in the heavens. Evolutionary idealism and the pragmatic theory of knowledge were intact. Even Reinhold Niebuhr in those years, then a young minister in Detroit, Michigan, clung to the hopes of a personal idealism despite the growing cynicism that threatened his mood and mode of expression, as his first book, *Does Civilization Need Religion?* (1926) gives evidence. Henry Nelson Wieman's first book, *Religious Experience and Scientific Method*, published in the same year, expressed a sharper attack upon appeals to personal idealism, intent upon disclosing the ambiguities of human intentions; yet his stance at that time showed no awareness of or even concern for the social dimensions of his own realistic attack. Not until the mid-thirties and later was he to address himself to such issues.

The locus of unrest among my own generation in those years, as I recall, centered in an appraisal of the cultural outlook as such. What was loudly denounced among college and university students and among prophetic

commentators of the time, was the discrepancy between America's pretensions to ideal ends or purposes and the disclosure of crass practices belying
that public image. The ferment of our thinking as college students associated with religious activities on campus in this context centered in our
misgivings about religious organizations, especially the churches, and the
discrepancies we detected between their institutional practices and what we
understood to be the spirit of Christian living. The phrase "organized Christianity" had for us the same pejorative connotation that the word "establishment" has for the present generation of college and university students.
We in our restive concerns were for releasing Christian incentive from the
confining and distorting perspective of the "organized church." In our efforts to understand Christian motivation and its prophetic zeal as a cultural
force, we were, of course, concurring with what had already been pursued
at a pace among liberal and modernist churchmen. And, no doubt, we partook of the same limiting, cultural imperialism that attended that era of
Social Christianity. For, in retrospect, one can see, as Robert Handy has
pointed out in his recent appraisal of the social gospel, that "the social
gospel," whether of the Rauschenbusch or the Shailer Mathews variety,
partook of the "Manifest Destiny" thesis which had motivated Western expansion. Christianity and Democracy had come to mean pretty much the
same thing. And *making the world safe for democracy* took on a missionary
zeal that visibly advanced the export of our sensibilities, hopes, and aspirations, along with our moral biases and political designs, intent upon extending *the American way of life* to all mankind. Undoubtedly what shapes our
American foreign policy today, as it has done since the nineteen-twenties
and earlier, is this commitment to our "Manifest Destiny," vastly ac-
celerated by our confrontations with World Communism.

1. The Broadened Base of our Humanity

By contrast with that earlier period of social revolution, the revolt of
mind in the present-day is more extensive and complex than the revolt of
youth in the twenties; so much so, in fact, that they partake of different
worlds of experience. For one thing, and perhaps the most obvious one, the
"Manifest Destiny" principle, justifying Western expansion, has become
suspect, if not routed. Thus the present cultural revolt is epochal in dimension in that it does in fact mark the end of an era. We used that phrase, "the
end of an era" in the twenties and early thirties, but it had provincial meaning compared to the present scope of change and dissolution.

What stands between that earlier period of cultural and theological innovation and the present one is a radical break in our conception of humanity; hence in our way of expressing what might be called our humanizing *intentionality*. Much is involved in the transitions effecting this changed image of man; but, in my judgment, no series of events has been more decisive in altering man's conception of himself and his culture the world around, and of transforming man, himself, into a new, eruptive, and dynamic power within modern cultures, than the many declarations of independence among subjected people, beginning with India's proclamation in 1947 and continuing year by year, reaching a climactic point in our own history in 1964 with the passage of the Civil Rights Act. If one can appraise this sequence of events objectively, one cannot fail to see that it is epochal to a degree not matched by any single, social innovation in the lifetime of modern man. Quite apart from the specific cultural revolutions that followed from these events, or that led up to them; or, perhaps more accurately, were coherent with them, yet transcending their specific implications, is the stark inexorable fact that *the baseline of our humanity has been broadened.* More people are now legally established as human beings in our time than has been true in all of human history. One has to stand back and take in this stark, innovating fact, with all that it implies, before one can sense what is really upon us as a given of our present-day cultural experience, both as a burden in what this implies for social change, and as a promise of what it could imply in human fulfillment. A sizable number of the pre-thirty-year-olds have taken it with remarkable perceptiveness, shock, and excitement. This is why they express such disbelief concerning our social institutions and their commonly accepted mores, loosely designated with pejorative overtones as "the Establishment."

This broadened base of our humanity intrudes a new and possibly disturbing dimension of what it means to be human. There is, for one thing, an elemental quality that comes alive in the new humanity that puts to rout many of the cherished sensibilities that have given form and style to our cultural behavior and history in thr West since the time of the Renaissance, much of which was reactiviated in the Liberal era with its own modifications. These inheritied cultural sensibilities and style, particularly during the Liberal era, elevated human personality in terms of its individual attainments as being the accepted good. Personality was made the criterion of what is *good*, and for some, of what is *God*. Educational theory, aiming toward evoking and nurturing this ideal personality, was to correlate with this humanizing ambition, subtle influences from both science and industry in which notions about the survival of the fittest were readily translated into judgments about who might be fit to survive and who might not. Nurturing the ideal of personality thus succumbed to the more vigorous and ruthless objective of equipping capable individuals with the capacity and personal appeal to make their way in the competitive drive toward private and public enterprise and social acceptance. The elemental thrust of the new mode of humanity that is erupting all about us distrusts this individualized conception of humanity as being tailor-made to conform to a social establishment of free-enterprise, with its class distinctions that accord with financial, professional, and social success and esteem. At the same time they see this mode of economy, and the culture that is consonant with it, as being indifferent to the humanizing qualities of experience which give recognition and support to individual identity in the midst of an accelerating mass culture. There is a difference, by the way, between this current concern with individual identity and the earlier preoccupation with personality that was later to succumb to the lures of an aggressive individualism. The concern with identity implies recognition and appreciation of the worth of the individual human being in the context of communal relations; as contrasted with the stress upon singling out and elevating individuality on the basis of initiative, audacity, and attainment. In a word, it is the humanity of all individuals, their identity as persons, rather than individual enterprise or achievement as such that is to the fore in this present mode.

This revolt, however, is not simply a turning back upon a former lifestyle. It is a spirited reaction and resistance as well to what is increasingly being recognized as a massive mechanization of the processes of life within the modern community, made evident by the ever expanding use of technological devices by industry, government, and its enlarging war machine. Among some of the younger generation, the revolt is also a very personal and partisan impatience with their own upbringing under a permissive and affluent laissez-faire liberalism; among others, for whom affluence was never a problem, the revolt partakes of deep-seated, historical resentment and hurt, which is the psychic toll of lived experiences endured and now cast off. When the variant forms of discontent among the former are merged with the vast movement of the disinherited, recently given franchise, a wholly new quality of mind and spirit inadvertently intrudes to make the mixture of revolt a heavy brew, indeed. The present upheaval among modern youth thus presents a medley of of disillusionments and protests. No single characterization will suffice to identify or to describe its *elan* or its *intentionality*. Such unanimity as intermittently occurs stems from an avowed resistance to the established order of things, however conceived. Within that common disenchantment a vast variety of motives, desires and intentions are astir.

II. The Issue of Past and Present

Given this decisive sense of having come into a new age of delayed opportunity and promise, as against one that may well pass into oblivion, this recalcitrant generation responds readily to any appeal or urging to forget the past as a resource of the educational experience of the present. In this mood, higher education in all of its customary and disciplined modes of inquiry impresses many of them as being, either irrelevant to their enthusiasms, or suppressive of them in the interest of perpetuating an established mode of life which still persists in defiance of this vivid, contemporary fact that the baseline of humanity, legally and culturally, has broadened.

The placing of higher education under the judgment, if not the directive, of this radically contemporary fact of revolt and cultural change tends to foreshorten the range of inquiry as it sharpens its focus. This, it seems to me, is what intrudes the telling, educational issues. This change of perspective is then readily translated into a stance demanding confrontation between getting knowledge and understanding that is sharply oriented toward social and political action, on the one hand; and, on the other, of pursuing the long-range mode of historical and analytical inquiry, bent on viewing the present scene within the larger context of cultural history. Considering the aimless and omnibus manner in which historical and philosophical understanding of our cultural and religious background is often conveyed, the impatience among these younger contemporaries with what is offered as education within the present crisis is understandable. This, however, is a problem of long-standing. It is by no means peculiar to the current upheaval. If students think it is, that would be one argument for their reading history to see how much tradition lies back of their recalcitrant and non-conformist state of mind.

Along with this impatience with what is regarded as "education as usual," goes the conviction that what is being offered as education in the conventional mode partakes of the very ethos that antedates the current crisis, and thus is inescapably suppressive of the creative ferment that provides motivation and lure to the present generation.

Now the stance I find necessary to assume as an educator toward this critical impasse in higher education is one that presumes to be neither acquiescent nor defensive. Acquiescence to this new mode of modernity represents, in my judgment, a gullible acceptance of the plea for relevance, on the one hand; and on the other, an uncritical acceptance of the way the issue is posed in the current protest between past and present. Concern for relevance, I agree, is indispensable in shaping any present-day curriculum or mode of study; but such a concern can be highly misleading as it is commonly exercised. Given optimum meaning, relevance can mean bringing learning into a sharpened focus so as to give intelligence a vocation within the immediacies of experience. In actual application, however, relevance tends to mean being attentive to, or completely absorbed in what is currently in fashion in thought, or what is causing a great stir. This can be impoverishing of thought and inquiry, and can render its counsel of short duration. Relevance in its optimum sense implies, not curtailing inquiry to keep it focused upon current interests, but a selective use of both historical and contemporary resources at hand so as to bring maximum and pointed illumination to bear upon issues pressing for consideration. Relevance in this sense need not mean the elimination of historical and reflective dimensions of inquiry, but a selective handling of the data so as to point it up with an economy of clarification toward such issues. No student, simply because he is in heat over contemporary issues, should be permitted to side-step or evade disciplined inquiry of an historical or analytical nature. Yet, it should be possible within the kind of curriculum that is formulated, as preparation for participating in the contemporary world, to find ways of bringing such historical and analytical inquiry to bear directly upon contemporary concerns, instead of causing the student to assume that such inquiry is simply delay-action, or even a detour around the critical points at issue.

Coming to know just how the past forms a dimension of the present may be the most helpful way to achieve a stance of relevance. The perceptual act that impels us into action within the immediacies of our experience somehow has a way of silhouetting this that is immediately felt and attended to as if it were singularly ourselves, our world, the world in which we are now involved. But, as Merleau-Ponty was to discover, no act of perception, however sharply focused or presently informed, is solely an act of immediacy. It carries in its heightened awareness an intentionality that subtly insinuates past experience and valuations into every present act. And it strikes against, or in concert with, forces, situations, human valuations which, like every conscious experience, intrudes into this immediacy the present thrust of a past inheritance. No immediate act is simply a reiteration of past experience; yet it bodies forth within the innovations, the rebellious protests, the glimpses of discovery prompted by present occasions, a whole complex of occurrences which now present themselves out of a past inheritance as a present shaping, qualifying and impelling present experience.

Alfred North Whitehead was to bring to process thinking a similar correlation of past and present in his reconception of causal efficacy in relation to the creative act. By contrast, the dynamics of Modernism, which preceded both process thought and phenomenology, had little in its idiom of thought to illumine this subtle interplay of past and present. This was the structural limitation of theological modernism, causing it to give a primacy to the present which its own methodology belied. Much of our present thinking in education, whatever the discipline, which seeks to meet the demands of those who are in protest, seem to reflect a similar structural limitation, though for different reasons. The Modernist's adherence to an idealistic mode of evolutionism committed him to ongoingness as an assured and inevitably ascending movement of life. In his commitment to ongoingness, past history could be illuminating only in retrospect. The past as presently experienced was not really a live or meaningful notion to him. What has come into our present mode of critical thinking, in large measure due to Whitehead's revised notion of *causal efficacy*, along with the phenomenologists' notion of *intentionality*, is a vivid sense of past experience selectively and competitively entering into each moment of our immediacy as a genuine dimension of its innovation and creativity. This reconception of the past selectively envisioned as lived experience casts new light upon historical meaning; and possibly upon the way we may fruitfully attend to history.

This realization has led me to see the crisis of education in one of its important aspects as turning upon an adequate assessment of the role of our understanding of past experience within our immediacies.

III. Form and Frustrations of Form

Closely allied with this issue of past and present is that of form and the disruptions of form, as these enter into the shaping of historical experience. In this era of social revolution, form, like the word "establishment," has become synonymous with what is suppressive of the new life struggling to be born. Hence the disruption of form is looked upon as the initial step toward releasing the creative possibilities of the new. That this is a provincial and commonplace way of conceiving of the creative opportunities of the present age can be demonstrated by a perusal of events during any historic revolution. It is not enough, however, simply to insist that they who are in revolt be apprised of their provincial assessment of form and structure, as these appear in established institutions and mores. For what is being provincially expressed as a revolt against form and structure may, within its limited purview, be a legitimate resistance to what form and structure invariably tend to become in relation to the dynamic thrust of lived experience. Hence, this provincial witness against present forms and structures, within the limits of its awareness, bespeaks an appropriate judgment upon all form and structure within the immediate history that would presume to suppress or to frustrate, not only innovating occasions of human expressiveness, but human identity and expressiveness itself.

Form, as Whitehead has pointed out, is always a tentative stage of consolidating creative effort, and of giving it social or individualized expression; but where life is in growth, it is always in process of breaking forms in the interest of importance. Importance here has the meaning of a creative reordering of experience and effort in response to presently discerned insight and disciplined effort, looking beyond the immediate toward further goals that could be more defensible and significant.

Creativity, when it is more than sheer ongoingness, and partakes of a qualitative advance in experience, occurs within individual persons, as it emerges in corporate form, simultaneously as a vision of possibility, and as a restive incentive toward reform. The latter, in a way, always exaggerates the potency of the current threat as well as the promise of any corporate expression of such creative advance; for its spokesmen are generally those who are fully committed, and possibly most integrated with that vision in their own experience, acts, and decisions. On the other hand, the overt social expression of such creative advance actually understates its full possibility and threat as well. It does so precisely because of latent powers of realization and commitment implicit in those many participating individuals who, at any time, may come into full realization of what they had but tacitly and tentatively affirmed. Creativity within any epoch, and one might add, within any community, thus proceeds at various levels of innovation and intention. To suppose that it can readily be made unilateral, or brought into one concerted mode of creative advance as a unified and consistent movement of social reform is to ignore the stubborn fact of structure and form that is implicit in every instance of innovation. For existence itself, at whatever level of attainment, presupposes structured experience. This imposes limitations of vision as well as possible attainment, even as one strives to reach beyond one's present level of actualization, or beyond the level of cultural attainment that defines the community. The pluralism of actualization within any community or culture means that creativity transpires within a variety of contexts; hence, creative advance is not to be identified solely with any one singular thrust toward innovation, or new growth, but is to be seen as occurring simultaneously at many levels, within many contrasting configurations of effort and intention. In every instance, the breaking free of forms that have become closures upon the creative outreach, rather than the structural means of bodying forth its intentionality, is to be seen as being of apiece with creativity itself as it transpires

within any individual experience. The breaking of forms as a total communal act raises other problems. The conflict that generally ensues as a consequence of such planned and pointed iconoclasm may not be described
simply in terms of the creative and the uncreative; for the existing forms do
not sustain life evenly or equally; and conversely, existing forms or structures do not, categorically, pose a threat to qualitative attainment under all
circumstances.

Thus, the very focusing of the opposition in social revolt in terms of
fighting "the establishment" tends to be misleading. It then seems to provide
the warrant for destroying all form and structure indiscriminately. It also
tends to formulate and to focus the thrust of innovation in negative terms as
being preeminently an act of dissolution, and to dissipate energy in effecting
such dissolution; whereas commitment is not to the death of the old so
much as it is to the birth of the new. And this implies a shift in the expen-
diture of energy in the interest of importance. Importance, in this context,
takes on the meaning of one's vision of destiny, impelling one to assume the
burden of opportunity laid upon everyone who chooses life, rather than
death. I realize that many who are presently in revolt assume that there is
no possibility of the new until the old has been demolished. It is this thesis
which, in part, I am challenging as being a romantic assessment of dynamic
change, and a failure to apprehend and to assess potentialities of structure
within the so-called "establishment" which, instead of being suppressive of
change, stand ready to body it forth as a new occasion of creativity.

In order to see more clearly what the constructive dimension of "the
frustrations of established order" can mean we need to give further attention to this word "Importance" in its generic meaning. Whitehead has
elevated the notion of Importance above all others, setting it in contrast to
"matter of fact," which is the notion of mere existence. Matter-of-fact, he
says, is "tinged with the notion of compulsive determinism . . . It is the
recognition of the goingness of nature in which we, and all things of all
types are immersed. It has its origin in the thought of ourselves as process
immersed in process beyond ourselves."[1]

The recognition of the *goingness of nature* readily leads to the assumption
of sheer ongoingness as being the inevitable persistence of what is presently
occuring. The sense of "Importance" is always the leap of the mind and
spirit beyond what is presently occuring, a leap beyond, either in the mood
of impatience with what is, or in expectation of what could be. Importance,
says Whitehead, is derived from "the immanence of infinitude in the finite."
In the spirit of Whitehead's analysis, I would add, that importance is the
restive and impatient, even rebellious, yearning within any period of time
and within any single human experience, in the interest of realizing and ex-

pressing this larger vision of human identity and possibility within these immediacies that seem otherwise to persist in habitual, almost mechanical responsiveness to the matter-of-factness of existence itself.

Since sheer ongoingness carries within its own monotony of operations the tendency to express and to support life within the species or level of subsistence that has become accommodated, or been accommodated to its ongoingness, there will always be a large number of casualties who are unaccommodated, and for whom ongoingness is in itself a dread to be endured, hopefully with the possibility of an ultimate release; or for whom ongoingness becomes an evil to resist, and hopefully to change in the interest of a more bearable and fruitful existence. Such eruptions of protest against sheer ongoingness which, as experienced, is menacing to existence, may or may not partake of the larger vision of importance; although, as a witness to what is presently deficient in experience, it tends to be consonant with it. Neither does it necessarily stem from any ultimate consideration or concern, having religious or philosophical motivation. More often than not it will be conceived more provincially, or even locally, in terms of intrenched power and the unrelenting power within established communities. Thus "ongoingness" takes on the meaning of life-as-it-is in this place and time, and "matter-of-fact," the connotation of the system of social operations that supports and makes life-as-it-is. Importance, too, in this context, carries restricted meaning as a will to break through the impasse of intrenched power by striking at the powers themselves. Confrontation under this vision of existence thus tends to become a power struggle in which unaccommodated levels of the human community pit their uncertain strength against securely intrenched structures of power within the stable community. Given this hard-core encounter between intrenched power and the thrust of communal groups presently empowered by a sense of purpose directedly toward destroying the present power structure, what is implicitily significant as an expression of Importance is often obscured, or misread as being sheer rebelliousness and disorder which can be routed or stemmed only by restoring order. It is necessary to recognize, therefore, that while the hard-core confrontation with existing institutions of repression and matter-of-fact stability appears to be the significant thrust toward innovation, countering the present misuses of structure and power, it tends, in resisting this matter-of-fact premise, only to emulate its example, pressing one set of facts expressive of "existence mere" against a more formidable set of facts concerned only with "existence mere."

In the background of every such confrontation are the vast number of instances of dissent and dissociation from the matter-of-fact hypothesis: young people, for example, who are concerned in their own private or restricted ways with the lure of importance, vaguely conceived, which reaches beyond this matter-of-fact existence, if only as a subjective revolt against what matter-of-factness tends to become. This, too, becomes a dubious resource, either as an ally of consciously rebelling, unaccommodated segments of humanity, or as a witness to importance in its larger connotation. Nevertheless, such unassertive dissent is not to be dismissed as being of no consequence because of its unfocused, subjective stance; for it remains a mode of expressiveness that is potentially supportive of both.

Rebellion within our culture today is desperately serious business. It is not to be regarded as an outburst of rebelliousness for its own sake nor a temporary mood of despair or disdain that will pass, given time. Neither is it to be supinely discredited as being the social and psychological consequence of an age of permissiveness and misdirected affluence. It is in the full sense of the word a traumatic uprising against what the American experience has become. It voices impatience with matter-of-factness in all of its unyielding forms: with the mind-set of the military establishment and its civilian adherents; with mounting mechanization through technological and industrial advances; with rigid adherence to a morality of law and order; with ther unrelenting bias toward masculinity that dominates American society, with all that that connotes in exercising muscular vanity and aggressiveness and disdain for sensitive, appreciative, and imaginative ends. The current outcry against the pollution of our environment, the rising concern with ecology, the resistance to acts of war, the neglect of human needs among impoverished peoples, the yearning for tenderness and care in human relationships, all these are expressive of the outreach of the human spirit toward importance among many of our contemporaries. Despite the seeming disproportion of bombast and disruptiveness in the protests among the generation now in revolt against established forms and sensibilities, the protests are prophetic. They express deep yearning for *importance* as against the trivia, the deadening inertia, and the brutalizing aggression of the matter-of-factness in our institutionalized existence. The incredible impasse between those who see what is happening as a creative surge toward newness of life, and those who resist what is happening as being simply disruptive and destructive of a cherished mode of life, makes invalids of us all, whatever our motivations may be.

What is needed in any cultural situation, and desperately so in our own at the present time, is a sharpened focusing upon this that transcends, yet, within limits, is inclusive of both the tepid and the violent forms of reaction against *matter-of-factness* in living, when the latter has become deficient of vision or even contemptuous of it. This that transcends, but which could mightily motivate such resistance of the human spirit is, I am proposing, the commitment to *Importance* as a beacon of promise beyond the present morass of hostility and frustration. Perhaps this is but a secular way of expressing what all idealizationsa of the human spirit have ventured; or, for that matter, what all religious and moral valuations of man's existence in some way have affirmed. The fact that this kind of commitment can be stated in secular terms has its advantage, given the temper of our times. But I would insist that Importance is more than just a secular way of saying what religion and morality and various idealizations of life have declared. In Whitehead's words, "Importance is a generic notion which has been obscured by the overwhelming prominence of a few of . . . its innumerable species." Whitehead continues:

> The terms 'morality,' 'logic,' religion, 'art,' have each of them been claimed as exhausting the whole meaning of importance. Each of them denotes a subordinate species. But the genus stretches beyond any finite group of species. There are perspectives of the universe to which morality is irrelevant, to which logic is irrelevant, to which religion is irrelevant, to which art is irrelevant. By this false limitation the activity expressing the ultimate aim infused into the process of nature has been trivialized into the guardianship of mores, of rules of thought, or of mystic sentiment, or of aesthetic enjoyment. No one of these specializations exhausts the final unity of purpose in the world. The generic aim of process is the attainment of importance, *in that species and to that extent which in that instant is possible.*[2]

The final sentence gives the clue as to how the ultimate vision of Importance is made effectual in the immediacies of experience. The attainment of importance in any historical period is proportional to the circumstances and to the subjective aims expressed in any given situation—"in that species and to that extent which in that instant is possible." Within every situation in which the matter-of-fact aspect of sheer ongoingness poses a threat to the elemental will-to-live creatively and expressively, the forms which hold life and which body it forth in that structured existence come under the threat of rejection, and under the judgment of that infinite measure of Importance. Forms, unless they are the bearers of life, deteriorate into becoming the suppressors of it; in which case they become the debris that follows upon life's dissolution. The concern I am intent upon pointing up here, is that this beacon of promise beyond our hostilities and frustrations which designates Importance is more than a vision, merely. It is inherent as energy within the human spirit and in human communities. This energy is expressed in minimal ways as a will-to-live forward expectantly. In more significant form it is expressed in various grades of decision to live creatively toward whatever attainment is envisageable and manageable—*in that species, and to that extent which in that instant is possible.* Such decisions will take definitive form in the pursuit of imaginative ends, in a concern for addressing human need, in experiencing the joy and wonder of human relationships, in creating experiences of beauty as well as in responding to them. When these several individual projections of the human spirit assume communal or corporate form, they take on great dimension as a social force, though, in becoming so coordinated, they may suffer some recession in imaginative power and expectation. Nevertheless in communal or coordinated form, they become a resource for encouraging further individual expectations and commitments. As a social force, they become a challenge to all existing social structures, not simply as a threat to the inertia of their Matter-of-factness, but as a summons to transcend the ennui and frustration which their inertia engenders, and to resist their repressiveness.

I have been discussing the matter of Importance as a generic term within the idiom of process thought; but it is discernible in many other ways. For, being a generic notion, it comes readily into view whether the concern is with intentionality, as in phenomenology, or with the lure of an ultimate good, as in many forms of idealism. The way Whitehead has posed the issue between Importance and Matter-of-factness, however, even as he relates them, gets at the problem within a context in which the issue is erupting all about us. And for that reason, his formulation of it ontologically speaks directly to our situation as educators. We should not be content, however, with vague talk about ultimacy as an ontological notion, but press with all the imagination and perceptiveness at our command to bring its illumination to the troubled concerns of this vital immediacy.

The key of discerning the direction which education must take in the present situation would thus seem to be suggested by this secular way of stating the vision of human identity and destiny as a summons to reach beyond the inhumanities of our matter-of-fact existence to attain some measure of our humanity in more significant form. The educational task, then, would be to identify and to clarify these intimations of Importance as they appear in the immediacies of conflict and change. This is no easy task, and mistakes will be made in the effort; but it is the crucial effort to distinguish between "the children of light and the children of darkness"; and it will set the whole program of change and innovation in a deeper and more defensible context than is customarily contemplated. Similarly, it will give to the educational process itself, bent on participating in the vital events of our current history, authenticity and purpose. Instead of following such will-o'-the-wisps as "being relevant," "timely," "modern," "insistent," "or where the action is," educators would purpose in their hearts to address the issues of life in their ultimately significant demand, as they present themselves to us within these immediacies, within the disciplines in which we work, informed and illumined by other disciplines which may be available to us as scholars and teachers.

Areas of new experience and understanding serve as apertures in what presently envelopes our conscious experience, through which we are enabled to see the possibilities of creaturehood afresh and with new zest in this historic moment of living. In responding to such occasions, we act as men awakened to our historic opportunity of creaturehood. This is relevance of the highest order. To fail to act hopefully and expectantly in response to such occasions is to relinquish our humanity as creatures, as human beings; and thus to respond simply as inert entities within the passage of time.

TRADITION AND NEW FRONTIERS 3

By BERNARD E. MELAND

WE are witnessing in theology and in the literature of our day an unprecedented appeal to traditions of the past as solutions for our present predicament. We are told by Catholic writers, such as Maritain, Dawson, Bruni, and Sheen, that our hope is in recovering the spirit and method of St. Thomas Aquinas; and by Protestant theologians—Emil Brunner, for example—that our starting-point must be "the Reformation Confession of faith." As a man of letters T. S. Eliot counsels us against following *After Strange Gods,* and John Crowe Ransom (in *God Without Thunder*) adds, "With whatever religious institution a modern man may be connected, let him try to turn it back toward orthodoxy." This turn of the tide in present-day Christian thought, carrying us back to familiar shore lands of the past, raises anew the question of the relation of our forward striving to the assured traditions and standards of our past heritage. To one who has felt the lure of the open sea and whose thinking has been caught up in the outward tide, this urgent concern to return to tradition can make little or no appeal. Yet even he recognizes at times that his frontier faith is continuous with an age-old enterprise of human thinking and formulation. Wisdom argues their correlation; but how shall he relate his forward venture to that ancient heritage without abandoning the call of the sea? And how can one pursue the emerging values of these growing frontiers and remain enamored of tradition? I shall undertake to examine this issue, not by considering the arguments of the several proponents of tradition as over against their contemporary opposites; but by inquiring into the basic matter which tends to divide all traditionalists, of whatever sect or school, from the experimentalists and the forward-venturing men of their times.

I

Our bias is to overstress the significance of the past because in its accepted standards, we find the criterion for judging the values of the present. The great majority of men and women, when they are reflective at all about life, turn to the past for their source of stimulus and guarantee of value. Even when they are unreflective about it, they view the present as a rebel offspring from a parental past and bend every effort to keep the fugitive in the tradition of his heritage. There is a degree of wisdom in this acquiescent regard for tradition. Wherever value has emerged with undisputed clarity, it wears the garments of the past. No critic of discerning taste disputes the excellence of the Parthenon, or the literary eminence of Virgil, Dante, or Milton. No interpreter of the arts disputes the view that the classical achievements in stone or the painting of the Italian Renaissance will live. Men of genteel taste may prefer Botticelli to Michaelangelo; but the certainty that each possesses enduring worth is assured. Doubtless there is something in our mentality that conditions us for this bias in favor of the old and the accepted. We become accustomed to these recognized forms and they, in turn, impose a standard, more or less arbitrary, which compels emerging creative works to conform to type. The same tendency manifests itself in literature, in philosophy, and in political, economic, and religious doctrine. Incurably and to an unhealthy degree, we are susceptible to the claims of the past and of things ancient.

Nevertheless, this persistence of the past's standards is empirically justified. Men have lived with these things and have found them unfailingly good. They have communicated meaning and satisfaction of such proportion and quality that men's understanding and hunger have been inevitably orientated to them. Furthermore, time has lifted these ancient things out of the temporal stream and given them that objective meaning and value which repeated approval bestows. Consequently, whether it is a ritual, a Chippendale chair, or a wall hanging, if it bears the distinction of approval through the centuries, it is rightfully a unique work of art with verified value, so far as judgment of this sort is able to define value.

Recognizing all this, I should not wish to appear to be minimizing the significance of tradition, or of the accepted goods of the past. On the other hand, there is always the possibility that reverence for the past and its heritage may obstruct the whole course of the life process; may, in fact, become so resistant to its vital streams as to frustrate its creative thrusts. The traditionalist, with all his refined discernment and his concern for the recovery of reality in the present, may be the least sensitive to existence of value when it becomes operative in current life. To be aware of value, one needs to be alert to the growing frontiers as well as to the achievements of the past.

II

Orienting human living to the frontiers of existence, however, requires more than a sensible view of the past in relation to the present. It demands an entirely different perspective with which to envisage value. One way of defining the difference is to say that it requires commitment to a biologically, rather than a mathematically, motivated philosophy. Or, one might say, it requires awareness of *value in process,* as over against value in finished and static form. I am not altogether satisfied with this statement of it, for in a very real sense the concept *being* carries a quality of meaning and value which *process* can never attain so long as it is in flux. The quality of the human spirit which issues from the total being of a life long lived, compared with the emerging qualities of the person in growth as observed at various stages, gives something of this difference. Yet this total being is always the organic unity created by life in process. To that extent, *being* depends upon growth for the quality of existence peculiar to its character. (This would not hold true of realities considered outside of the historical process, but I am considering here historical realities in relation to the past, present, and future dimensions.)

If this course of reasoning is sound, it follows that realities within the historical stream, whatever their form, continue to embrace value so long as they front a future in which actual value may pass into active relation with possible forms that give rise, in turn, to yet-unrealized conditions of value. Even the works of established art, while they would retain the objective merit which they possess as creations in their own right, would diminish in their total scope of value were they to become mere monuments of time, divorced from the continuing stream of conscious appreciation and appraisal. This is not to say that their important values are subjective; but rather to point out that created value in the stream of history has organic connections with emerging forms of value; and apart from that continuing creative life of existence and expression, its value shrinks to the significance of milestones and museums.

An organic view of history thus impels us toward the expectant future, toward the perilous open where the highways are not clearly marked, and where the meanings and the standards of value are not sharply defined. One needs a new psychological and mental pattern to be able to travel this road with a sense of rewarding experience. Too much reluctance to accept change and uncertainties will make it hazardous and painful. On the other hand, it does not follow that to pursue this path enjoyably, one must seek change and uncertainty and nothing else. Too much emphasis has been given to the modern man's interest in change and his relinquishment of certitudes, resulting in a distortion of his actual concern and outlook. The true modern has never been a devotee of the contemporary in the shallow sense. He has simply been attentive to the most luminous point of the moving reflections of history. Or to change the figure, he has been alive to the growing edge of the planetary culture, and has sought to aid its growth toward the new fulfillment, never assuming that this was the end. All the while he has been sensitive to definitely experienced and finished states of value; yet his chief devotion has been to the creative passage of events that carries life to still greater possibilities of value.

He who feels the lure of this perilous open does not cringe before the breakdown of cherished doctrines or creeds, or even codes of conduct. If he is thoughtful, he will not gleefully accept this chaos, nor treat it lightly. He will be sobered by its consequences, knowing that travail attends the time of change; yet he will recognize in these instances, and in their freedom from fixity, fresh opportunity to bring the creative possibilities of the present into richer realization. Likewise with his estimate of decaying cultures or forms of government: not committed to any existent good as a final end, he will not be frightened into feeling that the dissolution of one system means the death of all system and order. Underneath these established forms, there is process. No established form was ever anything but an approximation to what might have been, had conditions been more favorable for complete actualization. We tend to become accustomed to one mode of living and enjoy the certitude of predictions which this customary existence affords; but it is the grip of habit and the comfort of the rut, more than discernment of value, that impels one to this choice.

When vision has been lifted and sensitized to this greater devotion, to the possibility of actual good in this deep, persisting creative order underlying established forms, the passing of the existent structure is less an evil than an opportunity for the actualization of greater good. It is at this point, however differently they may express the rationale of it, that all current philosophies shaped by biological concepts come together, in contra-distinction to all rival theories orientated to a traditional heritage. The one sees the human venture in its highest expression as a cause committed to further a creative newness and its potentialities; the other views it as a cause to preserve and implement that tradition which the human spirit, in its finest flowering, has thus far achieved. The latter leads to an ardent crusade for enlightened orthodoxy; the other to the vigorous promotion of adventurous and experimental living.

One might say that this commitment to the perilous open has always been the philosophy distinctive of American life. Hartley Burr Alexander, in his essay, *The Faith That Is America* (Personalist, Spring 1938), has said, "Our gaze is intensely toward the future. Failure to perceive this radical difference in the orientation of life gives account of the inability of so many Europeans to grasp America's meaning. The men of Europe judge us by what they see, and they are doubtless justified if they see little that is not barbarian. But we judge ourselves by what we hope and mean to achieve, and perhaps, even if but half consciously, by that impulsive vitality."

The perilous open is the frontier of promise and also of possible failure. It is the far country fronting the open road of planetary growth. They who are themselves in growth and who can respond to the lure of earth-growth, will take to this path, continuing the human venture. But only they who have the faith that moves mountains travel this way.

III

We who cherish this American faith do well to recognize, however, that this forward thrust in our thinking tends to contemporize our thoughts to the exclusion of valid reference to the past. This has been particularly evident wherever our American faith has given expression to philosophic or religious beliefs. Orienting religious and philosophic thought to the growing frontiers is not accomplished simply by translating its fundamentals into terms consonant with contemporary life. For the world of life is more than the present with an immediate future. And the reorientation of religion implies more than literally translating dogmas. We need to avoid the short-range perspective that characterized Positivism and which seems to have attended most forms of Modernism. Despite the fact that Modernism brought historical perspective into its interpretations of religion, the past, as a spiritual dimension, rarely entered into its conception of the spiritual life or into its practice of worship. The reasons for this, I believe, are three-fold: Modernism, like Liberalism, was a reaction against authoritarianism in religion. Consequently, all recollections of the religion of the past, liturgically emphasized, seemed to carry over the temper of an authoritarian faith in a disturbing way. Furthermore, the historical study of religion, upon which Modernism developed, tended toward the view, characteristic of all social-historical thought influenced by Spencerian evolutionism, that the superior forms of any historical phenomena, were to be found in its later, rather than in its earlier, stages. Consequently, the mature values in religion were sought in recent or even present periods. Again, Modernism has been strongly inclined toward rational standards of value, leaving the appreciative approach to the historic past neglected. These three tendencies have given Modernism a bias toward contemporaneousness which has greatly limited its range and qualitative expression.

Some corrective has come to our perspective in recent years. The protest against authoritarianism in religion has assumed better balance. Consequently, much of the aversion to liturgical reference to the past has subsided. Readiness to recall the past, or to call upon the past, is not taken to be merely a reverting to the appeal to authority. Again, the assumption that the course of history presents a continuous and upward evolution, placing present forms at the peak of the process, has become unconvincing as a generalized observation. While certain obvious advances in civilization, due to developing theoretical knowledge in the sciences and the continual improvement in technological equipment, are clearly acknowledged, comparable or corresponding achievement in the spiritual culture of recent times is not so readily admitted. Upon closer observation, in fact, it becomes quite clear that spiritual integration has not been possible in recent periods to the degree achieved in earlier and far simpler civilizations. While it does not follow that historic spiritual cultures of the past can be profitably set up as the ideal or authority for the present, Neo-Thomism to the contrary notwithstanding, it nevertheless becomes apparent that certain cultural periods of former years loom as guiding stars still in the firmament of the ages. And the wealth of historic recollection and tradition, suggestive of these high moments of spiritual achievement, continues to be a stimulus of great significance to the modern age. Now, through the appreciative approach to this traditional heritage, religion may communicate its spiritual stimulus and value to contemporary life without seeming to impose its formulas and forms authoritatively. This, in fact, it must seek to do, else the spiritual life of the present suffers impoverishment.

IV

How to accomplish this appreciative rapport with the past in a way that will secure its spiritual stimulus without becoming limiting in spirit and vision, is a staggering problem. The immensity and difficulty of the problem, however, should not turn us aside from its undertaking. For no satisfactory adjustment between practicing religion and the modern outlook can be accomplished, in my opinion, until this basic problem of relating the present to its past heritage is dealt with adequately. The simplest solution is, to be sure, to take the course of Humanism and Modernism: clarify the objective by decisively parting company with the past, and project religious idealism as a forthright modern faith, trimmed to fit these times. I am persuaded that this is not a solution, but an escape from the most pressing aspect of the problem. I cannot concur with the judgment that to undertake to relate modern religion to the historic faith in any way is to play deceptively with symbols and meanings. This seems to me to be a forced integrity. Apologetics is not the impelling motive back of this concern for correlation. It goes deeper than a fear to be out of step with convention, or a will to believe *somehow or other*. The real motive is aesthetic in the fundamental sense. It is the concern for completeness, demanding that elements of appreciation as well as utility shape modern man's faith. To one for whom the aesthetic measure of life has significance, truth is more than the literal deduction or induction we call knowledge. Truth is the whispered wonderings of the wise, and the wistful wisdom of simple and good men. Truth is that aura of felt meaning rising out of hard-earned experiences in living, which becomes the continuing spiritual heritage from generation to generation. Truth is the illumination that lingers from age to age, through literature, the sacred epics, great art and the haunting music of the masters and common folk. Truth is the echo of other dawns, and the sobering lament of their shadowed nights, uttering the profound reminder: *Man passed this way before!*

This is the heritage of insight and vision that religion must continually hold before the passing present. But it must present it in such a way that it appears for what it is. For it is just as imperative to realize what truth is *not*. Truth is not a fact or a system of facts to be taken literally. Truth is not belief to be taken authoritatively. Truth is not infallible law to be imposed with coercion. Truth is the poetry of this human venture, conveying the spiritual heights and depths of the human spirit.

When truth is seen in this light, the full force and relevance of inherited truths becomes apparent. All the sacred lore, the pageantry of ritual, the songs and satires of ancient bards, the wisdom of philosophic men, impassioned songs out of solitude where men felt a Presence, the ardent cries for justice, the silent solemnity of the cathedral, the arts of brush and pen, these and other numerous testaments of the human spirit become authentic overtones of the present, resounding as the waves of the sea with the world's eternal memories. They who have listening thoughts may sound the depths of this echoing heritage. They who have eyes to see may behold its silent drama, vividly illumining the cavalcade of time.

V

So significant has this heritage of memory appeared to some that they have been tempted to regard it, in itself, the spiritual life of man. To cherish these recollections, to recall their meaning and to live up to their stimulus, was to feel the common experience lifted to the realm of the spirit. This temptation has led to spiritual desuetude. For the resources of the spirit are not in the past alone. Neither are they in the present alone; nor in the unborn future. The spiritual life of man is the synthesis of *memory, awareness,* and *imagination.* It is the selective integration of *persistent, existent,* and *possible* value, entering into every moment and event of experience. When men make memory the essence of the spirit, tradition hangs heavily upon the present, suppressing its authentic creativity. And when they make awareness this essence, the vistas of the farther range fade from view. If there is to be a singular expression of the spirit, imagination affords the most creative and extensive approach to life; yet, while it lends length and openness to life and impels it with creative zeal, it renders all significance and values of life implicit in *being* as nothing, in deference to the ruthless process of incessant *becoming*.

Relating these three aspects of every moment is not a simple achievement. It is, in fact, so difficult that men and institutions have usually abandoned the undertaking for the easier effort, following one to the exclusion of the others. Our present tensions, as in all periods of history, rise out of the antipathies between these contrasting views. There is no simple way of relating them. One cannot bring contrasting elements into a simple synthesis, or render them expressions of identity. Only by coordinating their contrasts, as in the symphony or in the painted canvas, can they be harmoniously resolved.

When this is translated for practical procedures, the problem of worship becomes clearly posed. For worship in its public expression, contrary to much opinion, is neither mere aesthetic recollection, communicating the past, nor mere motivation for present commitment and action. Worship is the sobering envisagement of life's profoundest realities as they impinge upon the present in the experience of living. Worship, when it is full-orbed, communicates, sensitizes, and impels. Through its experience, the winged truths of ancient men come into vision. Through its adventure, issues of the present world loom with proper importance. Through its stimulus, the will to live realistically, in devotion to the order of reality which is God, takes hold of and transforms men.

WHY MODERN CULTURES ARE
UPROOTING RELIGION 4

By BERNARD EUGENE MELAND

THE prevalence of "anti-Christian" and "anti-religious" movements in countries throughout the world where new cultural awakenings are in process is arresting. Since the establishment of the Chinese republic in 1911, both Christianity and Buddhism have been threatened by developments in revolutionary China; and there are prominent Chinese statesmen, like Hu Shih, present ambassador to the United States, in *The Chinese Renaissance*, who advocate the dissolution of Confucianism as well. While the elevation of Shinto to the status of an official national cult may seem like a revival of religious zeal in modern Japan, it is clearly a decisive step in the opposite direction, making the state the ultimate object of devotion, and placing the religions of Japan in a precarious and depreciated relation to the national life. Even in India, while many attempts have been made to reawaken national pride in the religious heritage of the Upanishads and the ancient Vedas, anti-religious tendencies have appeared. And in the Western Hemisphere, the reactions against organized religion in countries like Russia, Turkey, Germany and Spain are too well known to need comment. But to limit reaction to these areas would be to view the situation only superficially. For in modern cultures that are struggling to maintain democracy, the temper of secular disdain for established religion is evident.

Why this uprooting of religion in modern culture? Why in an age when faith is at a premium, are historic faiths being cast out? The answer has its political and economic aspects; but let no one who would know the truth of the matter stop with these obvious explanations. The issue goes deeper than political strategy. Because the tension has given way to open conflict in totalitarian nations, we have been led to think that this is a fight between religion and Fascist states. The real issue, however, is in the relation of historic religious faiths to modern cultures, whatever its language or form of government. The present conflict between religious faiths and modern cultures grows out of deep-seated historic differences between a cultural outlook concerned with emerging values in the present world process and a faith that looks away from the world of life.

I

What is the proper relation between historical religions and living cultures? In a recent discussion of "Tradition and New Frontiers" (CHRISTENDOM, Summer, 1940) I undertook to give an answer to this question. In brief, the conclusions were these: The present will always have need of rapport with the heritage of insight that comes through association with the past. For the truth that is tradition represents the enduring wisdom of the race, distilled from a vast and far-reaching social experience, as well as from more individual high ventures of sensitive, solitary spirits. To hold this inherited vision before us who walk in the present is the task of the religious cultus; and it does so through recollective mediums in worship, in sacred song, and in the reading of sacred scriptures. But to make *memory* the sole agent of the spiritual life is to reduce religion and the church to a cult of the past; and thus to set it at variance with the present flow of experience we call the living culture. Tradition then, as we have said, hangs heavily upon the present, suppressing its authentic creativity.

Religion becomes full-orbed when it succeeds in keeping the present faith sensitive to the inherited wisdom, yet compels it to confront the immediate and emerging issues of life with a responsible realism that relates the ancient heritage to the ongoing stream of culture. To turn from this living culture as a world alien to the spiritual tradition, is to sever the vital connection between the inherited faith and the ongoing life of the race. It is to make of religion an insulated tradition.

One will say that religion must stand apart from culture. There has been, in fact, a growing insistance in recent years that the role of religion in any society is to provide a criterion for evaluating the course of culture and to pronounce without fear or favor its judgment upon the ways of men. This insistence upon the prophetic function of religion is peculiarly pertinent today. But the claim that religion must provide an objective criterion of value should not be confused with the claim that religion must abandon all responsibility for culture and detach itself from culture. This is the vicious assumption that prevents clear thinking on the main issue involved. Religion must seek an objective criterion of value; but it must seek it in order to restore a center to the living culture.

What is frequently overlooked in this preoccupation with the prophetic interest is that religion also has an even deeper and constructive function within culture which is prior to the prophetic function, because it is more organic and integral. That deeper function is to make vivid and impelling the sovereign end toward which all social forces properly move. Religion, when it is healthy and robust, is both a unifying propulsion toward maximum value, providing cohesion and direction to the common life; and a prophetic vision, releasing an acidulous ferment which *cleanses the inward parts*. Unless these two seemingly contradictory aspects of its function are operative — its cohesive and cleansing force — religion becomes either vacuous or merely acrid, thus failing of any constructive end.

I am not persuaded that the only alternatives are uncompromising protest or cultural assimilation. There is a responsible propheticism which may strive to serve the ends of both God and man through a functional critique of culture that envisages possibilities of the fulfilment of supreme value, however partial, in the human culture — a culture at once unworthy, yet most worthy of social reclamation.

II

Christianity is in danger in these trying times of developing into an insulated tradition to the extent of becoming an alien within modern culture. It has already reached that status in Russia and in Germany. And in these cultures religion is being cast out. The fact that in both Russia and Germany present political leadership has reached the point of outraging the prevailing social conscience of the West, tends to exaggerate our sentiment in behalf of religious groups that are being persecuted by this political tyranny. This is a natural humanitarian response; but it is a sentimental reaction nevertheless. And it detours thinking from the social issues that are basic to the matter. Political tyranny in government is a symptom of an organic disease in culture that goes more deeply into the structural life of society. To say that it is an inevitable consequence of social dissolution may seem to justify it unduly; yet a realistic view of social crises seem. to say just that. Thus, to pose the issue as if it were a clash simply between arrogant usurpers of power and entrenched spiritual authority, overlooks events that have issued in tyranny and which have issued from unyielding elements in the social tradition. The point we are insisting upon is that in every contemporary culture, and this applies especially to the West, where religious tradition tends to insulate itself and its cultus from the dynamic configuration we call the living culture — a culture that moves experimentally toward new social ends, and which responds creatively to new discoveries, new inventions, new technological advances, and thus new human insights — religion develops as a malignant growth within the social organism which becomes increasingly unassimilative and predatory. And when the situation becomes critical, removal of the malignant growth seems inevitable. The predicament in which the Russian Orthodox Church found itself in 1922 (see Spinka, *The Church and the Russian Revolution*) during the early stages of the Soviet republic, when the Church was placed in the position of decisively opposing defensible proposals of reform which were obviously in the interest of the common life, is an illustration in point. Again, the response of the Orthodox Church to the critical situation that developed among the peasants during the famine in the Volga region in 1921, and the governmental reaction that followed, is an instance of this cleavage in modern times. Such crises makes evident the extent to which an insulated church will go in placing the needs of the culture secondary to the laws of the cultus.

III

The conflict between the Nazi state and German Protestantism again illumines the contemporary impasse between cultus and culture.

The situation of the Protestant Church in modern Germany presents a confused maze of conflicting ideologies and loyalties. Here we see the curious phenomenon of a cultus clinging to the principle of state support while at the same time repudiating the culture of the state and refusing all responsibility for it. Century old traditions lie back of this contradictory stand of German Protestantism. As Tillich observes in *The Religious Situation*, "The peril of Protestantism lay in the fact that it was a protest and that it did not achieve an adequate realization" (p. 154). That is the first factor underlying this contradiction. When true to its tradition, it "must protest against every religious or cultural realization which seeks to be intrinsically valid." This means that German Protestantism cannot properly assume any constructive interest in the cultural problems of the commonwealth upon which it depends for physical maintenance. And, if it is consistent with its traditions, it can project no ideal of culture. And because it has no formulated ideal of culture, it is led to insist upon a dualism between religious faith and any expression of culture, whether it be in the sphere of education, social philosophy, or government. This is precisely the emphasis that the neo-reformist theology of Karl Barth, which is the backbone of the Protestant reaction in Germany, has been led to take. Thus the relation of German Protestantism to the cultural regime in modern Germany amounts to a situation almost identical with that of the Orthodox Church and Soviet Russia, though for different reasons. But in both cases, the impasse between cultus and culture derives from elements in the religious tradition that insulate religion from the growing social experience. Now I am aware of the fact that this resistance to cultural change, even this capacity to resist cultural change, is precisely what gives German Protestantism its significance in the present crisis. It is also what explains its predicament. And it becomes a question of considerable importance how significant an ethic of martyrdom actually is, after all, where defiance of the cultural situation, without social responsibility for its ends or its problems, is the only concern dictating Christian action.

For the ascetic mind this question is unimportant; because for it human culture and its issues have no religious importance. But for the person who embraces the life of culture with responsibility as a participant, this withdrawal from the constructive tasks of society, into defiance of the culture and in defense of the cultus, can only mean the abandonment of the corporate spiritual task.

In defending the Confessional stand against totalitarianism, one should not overlook the psychological factor that has given large followings to the various folk faiths that have arisen in Germany since the last World War. Wholly apart from their crude and excessive claims for racial purity and the cultural superiority of the German folk, these faith movements express a fundamentally sound discontent with the prevailing supernatural theologies which alienate religious men and women from their sustaining culture; and on the other hand, they reveal a commendable concern for turning religious devotion into a creative social force. The totalitarian and racial doctrines of National Socialism render these efforts viciously restrictive; but one misrepresents matters when he infers from this turn of events that the cultural attempt to integrate religious responsibility in culture must lead to restrictions so evident in Nazi Germany.

We who are not in the midst of the conflict are in no position to pass judgment upon those who do battle to the death for a principle. But, seeing the consequences of a religion of protest, devoid of a positive ethic or philosophy of culture, one might at least ponder the question whether any end, other than martyrdom, can be served by such a faith.

IV

Where the religious outreach of a people stiffens into an arbitrary concern to preserve a tradition, the creative forces of the culture forge ahead with indifference to spiritual ends; or else fashion, as best they can, a working faith for the new venture. In either case, the established forms of religion became alienated from the growing culture. There is little left for them to do then but to wither and die, or to generate vitality through reactionism. Having lost their opportunity to provide motivation and direction to the new social efforts, they presume to stand in judgment of culture *in the name of a higher loyalty*. That they are justified in pointing culture to a loyalty beyond its boundaries, is not to be questioned. What is to be questioned is the assumption that religious institutions that have become insensitive to the creativity of the environing culture through their own ingrowing tendencies, possesses the criterion, or can point to the criterion, by which culture is to be judged. There is a difference between saying "Lord, Lord," and actually doing his will. There is a vast difference between denouncing the contemporary course of society and illumining that course with a vision of God.

For this reason one may not assume that because religious groups take a firm stand against the trend of the times, they are bringing the judgment of God to bear upon the situation. They may simply be blocking passion with passion, born of an irrational disdain.

This is not to say that religion is to become assimilated by cultural forces. I should agree with Reinhold Niebuhr when he says that "Religion can be healthy and vital only if a certain tension is maintained between it and the civilization in which it functions." (*Does Civilization Need Religion?*, p. 69.) I should also agree with his concluding assertion that "the moral effectiveness of religion depends upon its ability to detach itself from the historical relativities with which its ideals are inevitably compounded in the course of history." (*ibid.*, p. 222.) But neither tension nor detachment of this sort serves a religious purpose unless they proceed from a source of judgment that is intelligible enough to men to provide them with a criterion for their moral judgments concerning culture.

That is why to declare the judgment of God upon culture without recourse to the Divine Criterion, and without ears to hear with unmistakable clarity, the Voice of him who speaketh, is to enthrone impassioned zeal and to give it the authority of objective right.

It does not follow that to maintain a certain tension between religion and civilization or to achieve detachment from historical relativities, there must be commitment to the dualism of other-worldliness. It may require, rather, commitment to the dualism inherent in the natural life-process; or, we should say, to the order-giving growth within that process that transmutes the chaos of change into emerging value. Recourse to this objective criterion is not by the revelations of irrationality, but by the insights of sensitive and patient inquiry into the meaning of the Sovereign Value to which loyalty and commitment are to be given. No man will find this value through reason alone. Nor will he find it without reason.

V

The insulation of the cultus from the living culture in Russia and Germany had doubtless developed beyond that of any religious situation to be found in our own country. And the political turn of events in these two situations, as we have observed, make the impasse more critical. Yet we should not let these differences blind us to the fact that sectarian faiths wherever they exist tend toward this kind of insulation and thus are always potentially malignant growths. Their malignancy to any culture is in proportion to their hostility to the creative advance within that culture and to their power as a social force to arrest that growth. A society that is in growth can assimilate a surprising amount of this independent cellular structure before a lag occurs; or perchance growth is arrested. And in a democracy where there is separation between sectarian religion and the state, the assimilation can continue almost indefinitely. It is interesting to recall that in present-day totalitarian cultures, free religious cults have incurred comparatively little conflict with state authority. The conflicts have arisen where sectarian faiths have been socially and financially identified with the state. And the solution to church-state conflict proposed by the government representatives, both in Russia and in Germany, was discontinuance of state support of religion, placing all faiths on a voluntary basis.

This analysis would seem to argue that if sectarian faiths are to persist as independent cults within the culture, separation between cult and state is the most favorable safeguard against the kind of malignancy we have cited; and against possible conflict between cult and culture. Sectarian faiths, so existing, however, will always constitute a luxury of the commonwealth. They exist for the purpose of appeasing special religious temperamental preferences; but in so far as they manifest indifference to the cultural growth or, as in some instances, exert hostility to such growth, they must always remain a liability to the corporate life as a cultural whole. Their continuance therefore necessarily depends upon how long the commonwealth can carry the liability without serious impairment of its social cohesion and cultural advance.

VI

Religion in American culture, however, must aspire more and more to the achievement of its deeper function in providing a unifying propulsion toward the growth and actualization of value in our common life. When the churches begin to move forthrightly in this direction, they will discover that they are not alone in this high concern. For the deepening of the common life is not merely a priestly or prophetic interest; but a venture in which all persons and institutions, sensible to the higher life, can share. Thus religion, when it gets beyond the meager role of perpetuating a sectarian tradition to embrace this living faith, can become the first concern of all responsible people. It can become the most mighty of movements in our midst.

What is the content of this living faith which may become the concern of all responsible people? In summary form, it is the age-old vision of a commonwealth of spiritually-impelled men and women, made articulate, persuasive, and operative in American life. Let us not waste time in perfectionist thinking; or in repeating Utopian dreams. What we need more than finished plans or ideals, once the direction of our faith is envisaged, is the recognition of practical steps that will gradually transform the corporate processes of our common life into a functioning organic unity. When some measure of organic unity is achieved, the processes of the corporate life become the media by which men and groups may experience significant satisfactions and by which the citizenry may achieve continuous growth toward life's fulfilment. This is the substance of all high visions of the possible commonwealth from the eighth century Hebrew prophets and Plato down to our own day.

But it need not remain an ideal pattern; it can be made the description of social processes becoming operative at various stages and with varying degrees of completeness. Our concern here is to make clear that to the degree that the corporate life achieves this kind of functioning it begins to function as a religiously-motivated commonwealth — religious because its processes make possible the release of creativeness in individuals and in groups, and because these processes create conditions favorable to human growth. Whatever contributes to the fashioning of the social process toward this end, serves the religious transformation of our culture.

Such growth toward organic unity within our American culture will come about, not through the initiation of more movements, more causes, more platforms, nor through legislation; it will come through internal spiritual growth. It will come about as the result of a renaissance of those spiritual functions in the more intimate social groups such as the family, the village and town community, and similar centers of cultural cohesion. Too long we have dissipated these natural groups in the interest of pursuing a glamorous course of individual careers, with its stress upon "contacts" and "cultivation," requiring artificial group associations. A sounder culture of the spirit waits upon a recovery of life around the hearth and upon a restoration of civic life and civic resources within the community.

This is no idle dream about what ought to be. Developments toward such spiritual growth of the corporate life are already taking place. A single group of experiments will serve to make vivid the kind of religious functioning we are pointing to. I refer to the remarkable renaissance of community life among Michigan towns, resulting from long-time educational projects conducted by the University of Michigan. In the reclamation of these Michigan towns we have a striking illustration of the operation of a spiritual dynamic in society. These Michigan projects developed out of a concern to facilitate educational work among youth out of college. The dearth of community resources in the way of cultural aids made educational efforts futile. When attempts were made to improve this situation, serious obstacles were encountered. The community was buzzing with busy-ness, but much of it was self-defeating. Haphazard, sporadic, competitive and uncorrelated programs among the adults were providing considerable activity, but it all fell short of meeting any genuine local need. Worst of all, it was difficult for any organization or group to work toward any genuine end in the community because all such effort was frustrated or blocked by in-groups, sometimes by a single person who gripped the community like an octopus, and prevented anything being done that might take the power or prestige out of their hands. Through patient adult education, these obstacles were overcome. Community "bosses" who had found satisfaction in frustrating creative efforts in the towns were helped to find satisfaction in applying their talents and strategic positions to significant community advance. As a result community organizations were correlated and harnessed to functional needs. Step by step the various competing and conflicting forces within the community were transformed into co-operating agencies of larger and mutual ends, until a new sense of power for social achievement took hold of the community. For the first time its citizens began to feel democracy in action in a realistic and practical way. And we might add, in a religious way. (From a report on the Branch County experiment, by Howard Y. McClusky.)

Now if this spiritual renaissance of the corporate life of villages and towns can be taken as the *type* for the cultural creativity within the commonwealth, the possibilities for the religious functioning of the social process in American culture may begin to appear. Many groups and institutions in society have a responsibility in shaping this spiritual growth. Churches, theaters, civic associations, industries, schools, and many other agencies become potential participants. Preachers, educators, scientists, philosophers, poets, artists, engineers, workingmen, and industrialists, all become possible contributors to this emerging spiritual culture. What is important to recognize is that all cannot do the same job; nor work in the same way. Each has its own peculiar function and distinctive genius; and each its limitations; and these determine the kind of relation each may have to this corporate task. Let us recognize frankly that none of these institutions is fitted by its inheritance or by its present policy to contribute significantly to this cultural growth; for each is under the domination of an "art-for-art's-sake" and a "church-for-the-church's-sake" policy. Potentially, however, the contributions are enormous. There is hope in this fact: That they may begin growing in capacity and in purpose to participate in this most important of all cultural objectives.

The extent to which the churches can grow toward this end remains ambiguous. Persistence in a primary concern for the inherited tradition, in isolation from the creative social culture. obviously precludes significant participation in this larger task. There is every likelihood, however, that enlightened church groups, among all the denominations and cults, will discover ways of relating their respective traditions and cult-practices to this end. How they will do so must be answered by each of them. There is ample precedent for assuming that among the liberal churches and synagogues a growing group will be found who will feel this responsibility increasingly. And from them will come the church's chief contribution to this task.

This religion of renaissance within the common life is not alien to the Christian religion. The Christian tradition, in fact, becomes pregnant with stirring meaning when it is brought to bear upon this kind of spiritual awakening. All the thrilling utterances of the prophetic voices from Amos to the Christ come echoing down through the centuries:

> "Behold I will do a new thing; now it
> shall spring forth; shall ye not know it?
> I will even make a way in the wilderness,
> And rivers in the desert."

Only in the light of our present awakening we may see in this prophetic tradition something more than the gospel of an *everlasting Nay;* we may see beyond negation, in the vision of the good life, a reaffirming *Yea!* Like the welling up of new spirit that accompanied the folk movement of St. Francis' time, when religion left the cloister and became a quickening faith within the towns, this spirit of the ampler life may become a transformative working in our own life and day.

The times *are* ripe for "a superhuman flowering of mutual value and meaning" in American culture. When the churches identify themselves with this supreme task of the hour, the people will rise up and call their name *blessed*.

THE PERCEPTION OF GOODNESS 5

BERNARD E. MELAND*

THE attempt to justify the Christian view of the world and of human experience has generally turned upon the kind of appeal to evidence which has entailed argument and persuasion. The underlying assumption here has been that such justification must rest exclusively upon intellectual assent. Theology, in following this line of apologetics, has lifted the intellectual issue to a pre-eminence which seemed to suggest that the acquiring of religious truth is, ultimately, a theoretical problem. Impatience with this form of apologetics centering upon logic or doctrine has led religious thinkers to react against dependence upon reason in religion and to insist that *faith* or *experience,* rather than any theoretical concern, should take priority as being the heart of the matter. In this reaction, often such discipline as had been brought into religious thinking through the intellectual analysis of doctrine was lost, causing religious expression to assume some form of appeal to experience, to sentiment, or to practical zeal with indifference to, often with disdain for, the restraint and discrimination which the theoretical interest in religion had manifested.

The dissipation of discipline in religious feeling and experience has made for a serious loss of discrimination in religious judgment. Yet, it must be ac-

knowledged, on the other hand, that this discontent with the imbalance implied in the rational emphasis has certainly been warranted and could hardly stop short of such disavowal of discrimination whenever the drive of religious feeling or experience issued forth in elemental form. For the appeal to faith and experience had actuality on its side. Even the intellectual analysis of religion, when carried to its profoundest level, must conclude that the religious response arises out of an orientation of the human psyche in which the depths of experience press for a sense of meaning and direction. Doctrine and theoretical judgments of right and wrong have come as a consequence of mature reflection upon these primordial moments of religious awareness and perception.

Despite the propriety of the intellectualist's concern with an analytical discipline, and the soundness of the appeal to experience in religion, one must admit that both emphases have inadequately expressed the meaning and basis of the religious response. For neither of them has focused sufficiently upon the initial act of faith or of religious experience to realize that the religious relationship rests basically and ultimately upon a form of discernment which comes to each man or to each group as a report from experience when life is lived profoundly and vigorously with in natural events. The issues of life, in their simplest as well as in their most perplexing form, yield up evidence of God and of the goodness of

* Bernard E. Meland is professor of constructive theology in the Federated Theological Faculty of the University of Chicago and one of the editors of the *Journal of Religion.* He is author of *Seeds of Redemption, America's Spiritual Culture, The Reawakening of Christian Faith,* and other volumes.

existence. The religious response is initially a form of perceptiveness which opens up the fact of this quality within experience and which conveys the import of its meaning for all of life.

Now religious perception is, in my judgment, a peculiar kind of seeing. I do not mean that it is esoteric, different in every conceivable way from other forms of perception. I mean simply that it has its own specific data, its own preoccupation, its own qualitative effects, and its peculiar sequence of consequences. Religious perceptiveness is a way of looking upon the world, of apprehending and appreciating people, of discerning relations within experience which open up its depth and dimension of meaning. People vary in their capacity for such perceptiveness. Individuals vary in perceptiveness at different stages of their life-span. Conceivably the advancing of years should deepen the grasp of life's meaning; yet this does not always follow. For responsibility during the forties or fifties might crowd out the sensitive reports from the experiences of earlier years as household duties and vested interests restrict the line of vision. And the growing sense of insecurity and isolation among the aged might accentuate the claims of the ego to the extent of removing all sense of responsible relations with other people and with events. This does not argue that religious perceptiveness is most common and sharpened among the young, for they, too, have their problems of egocentricity and preoccupation as well as limited incentive to attend to ultimate concerns. If the childlike quality of wonder is essential to the religious response, the capacity to be humbled without reacting to emotions of inferiority is equally pertinent. And this involves the ele-

ment of distance in living which comes with maturity of experience. Religious perceptiveness, therefore, though not confined to any one age, appears with varying grades and depths of discernment.

Religious perception is a capacity which responds to nurture. For, like poetic perception or perceptiveness in the employment of any skill, it improves its act of discernment as the human consciousness, the bodily feelings, and the total response of the human psyche are brought into a persistent and absorbing concern with the datum or data which define its object and the character of events revealing the quality and intention of its object.

Yet, such nurture comes best as an indirect consequence of affection for the quality of events to which this datum has relevance and of participation in the events which issue in this quality of experience. In this way, nurture is a transformative process which happens to one as a result of one's seeking a higher end than one's own edification. The important concern in religious perception is, not the self-conscious quickening of one's perceptiveness, but the recognition of the quality of events which awakens or elicits religious affection and which fixes the human psyche upon the source and center of this qualitative character as an ultimate object of devotion.

I

The character of events which becomes peculiarly evident to religious perception is a qualitative occurrence in life to which the word "goodness" may be properly applied. "Goodness" is an exceedingly difficult term to clarify. Without some base from which to work, the word can be made quite meaningless. In the context of this discussion the word "goodness" will be understood to convey a quality of meaning which points the human emergent beyond its own ambiguous perfections to intentions or occurrences which move Godward. This quality is not dissociated from natural or human structures, for its operational route *is* these very structures which give actuality to meaning. One could speak of it in the way in which the emergent philosopher has spoken of any novel meaning which appears in a structure where a new complexity of relations gives intimation of new meaning in process of forming but which in its present state is but incipient in character. "It does not yet appear what it shall be." Enough appears, however, to indicate that a quality not wholly its own is emerging from the structure. Goodness would then be to the human structure what psychical activity would be to the physical existence in a structure of mechanism.

Goodness gets its character as meaning, then, from these intimations of a higher-than-human working within natural and human structures. God, being qualified by his goodness, as Whitehead has phrased it, exemplifies a certain character of relations to the world and to the human community. These relations express a concern for meaning and for conditions which are creative of this meaning. God's goodness may thus be viewed operationally as his participation in events which move toward qualitative attainment. This is what is implied in the creative act of God.

The reach toward clarification of this profound happening within the structures of the world is always met with some degree of frustration, for quite obviously the human mind in pressing for understanding of this qualitative

happening in events is struggling to envisage what exceeds its sight. Yet the human mind does catch intimations of its working in acts of beneficence or of judgment which arise in situations and in relations between human beings, often in conjunction with situations of extremity involving, for example, such responses as remorse, repentance, and forgiveness. These acts reveal a sensitivity at work in human beings which can radically transform both the individual and the situation in which the person's life is cast. Often a situation of conflict between people—it may be between parent and child—reaches such an impasse that the two life-streams seem to seal up against each other. They cannot effect a complete insulation from each other once they have been interpenetrative. Each bears the burden of the other's life in his own structure of experience. But a sufficient degree of hypnosis is effected in the mood of alienation, possibly through autosuggestion, to enable each of them to pass by on the other side so as to avoid any direct encounter between them. This condition of congealment may continue until one or the other is moved to a sense of the tragedy of the relationship. Such a momentary glimpse of the total meaning of a situation may be enough to enable one to break through the fortress of the ego which pride has reared, and with this one, swift, penetrating glance the citadel may crumble. For in such instances the redemptive act works swiftly, or it does not work at all. This instantaneous escape from the self-contained view is enough to start the deflation of the ego which may then begin in remorse and move toward repentance. And the repentant act elicits a response of forgiveness. The forgiven state, in a way, changes no single fact.

The lifetime of unintended injury may not be undone. Time being real, effectual, will not turn back; and it may not be in its power to heal. Yet forgiveness transforms the tragedy of time that has been lived into a situation which makes tragedy acceptable and accepted. The injury no longer rankles. Relations are no longer strained. The individuals are no longer estranged. The healing that cannot alter conditions in fact does alter the perspective in which the facts are borne. Thus the transformative power of the repentant heart releases both a healing and a creative force into the relations between the two people.

In situations which press men and women to a sense of their extremity, where the resources of self-help seem spent, these re-creative and healing events break in upon human relations, often spontaneously as if unanticipated, to transform a situation of despair into hope.

Again, intimations of goodness come in situations where abundance presses upon conscious experience. This, too, is a form of human extremity in that it becomes a joy too great to bear. The cup runs over. Joy is a welling-up out of gratitude for grace which abounds. The capacity for joy not only accompanies the capacity for appreciative awareness in that such awareness opens up the world of meaning to the receptive consciousness but also releases the bodily feelings from possessive demands which would otherwise intrude an acquisitive outreach. The peril of selfhood is thus, in effect, removed, or at least diminished, as the bounds of the self are extended.

The movement of the human psyche toward ends not its own in this appreciative way awakens a sense of identity with other life or with other events.

This, too, is perilous, as I shall point out in a moment; nevertheless, it is the route to that summit of experience where the vision of God and the vision of man converge. In this orientation of the psyche, love as an outward movement toward people and toward the Source of all goodness is made increasingly controlling in contrast to that condition of self-love which separates people from one another by its inward movement toward the many egocentric foci. In the one instance the relations which bind life together are acknowledged and made the resources of living; in the other, the relations, if acknowledged, are resisted and, where possible, severed. More often, however, where the look of the self is self-ward, the relations go unnoted, though by no means unencountered.

The movement of the psyche toward identity with other life is not, psychologically speaking, a relinquishment of the self. The center of sensory organization within the personality structure of the organism remains as an individuated channeling of meaning. Only the bodily feelings become transformed in their automatic responses by the appreciative consciousness which receives the good of the world as its good. The identifying marks of goodness move God-ward and other-men-ward instead of simply self-ward.

The emotion of joy is a response, then, acknowledging the fulness of life's meaning and a confession of one's incapacity to receive its fulness or to hold even a portion of it for any extended period of time. Hence, the cup runs over.

II

Joy as an emotion can be intelligible only to the consciousness which is capable of an outward movement toward an experience of identity; for the movement self-ward can yield no such sense of the fulness of life. The demand for self-satisfaction is insatiable. Self-seeking may subside for moments at a time, as hunger and passion and similar cravings may be assuaged. In this sense satisfaction can be so achieved. The rhythms of the body are formed by its rising and receding hungers. But a vast gulf stretches between sheer bodily satisfaction and the emotion of joy. They are in no sense comparable in dimension or in level of meaning.

Now a problem intrudes here which is often magnified into a stumbling block for those who would hold body and spirit together. What I have just said about the contrast between bodily satisfaction and joy will seem to border upon asceticism with implications of self-denial and especially denial of bodily satisfactions. I have no intention of asserting either of these denials to an ascetic degree. Certainly I would insist that any concentration upon bodily satisfaction such as is implied in sensuality, in whatever form, aggravates the demands of the self in a possessive sense. The line between bodily delight and sensuality is often a very thin one; nevertheless, there is a proper demarcation between participation in the bodily senses and indulgence which enslaves the spirit of man. Bodily delight, which, of course, includes many forms of self-satisfaction, can be consonant with the outward movement of the psyche in the sense that community or the interrelation of life, when it is a genuine correlation of interests, becomes an instance of *individuals in community*. Such community, in which the concrete goods are acknowledged and accounted for, is of a greater complexity of relationship with a higher degree of qualitative ten-

sion than the communal form in which individuality is canceled out or in which sensory capacities are obscured as in asceticism. Solitary asceticism and mass society have one basic trait in common: both have relinquished the creative tension between the living center of the sensory self, which fosters individuality in the bodily feelings, and the demands beyond the self. There is a truncation of spirit whenever this tension is destroyed or obscured.

There is a further reason why bodily delight may not be depreciated in deference to the emotion of joy. Any perception of goodness giving rise to such an emotion invariably manifests itself to the individual as a bodily feeling; and the persistence of its meaning as a re-creative force of the personality is made possible by its retention in the bodily feelings. There can be no sharp dichotomy, therefore, between the sensory self and some "higher" self, or between the self and the not-self, even though the distinction is made between a pattern of response within the individual which moves self-ward and one which extends the individual's concerns appreciatively beyond the self.

III

The outward movement of the human psyche leading to identity with the full range of life and meaning enlarges the scope of sensitivity, making one responsive to a greater range of appreciative awareness; but, in so doing, it also increases the range of pain and suffering. It is in this sense that joy and sorrow are concomitant experiences. The extension of the range of feeling is inevitable where identification with other centers of living or concern occurs. Thus the problem of evil mounts as a feeling event in proportion as the appreciative consciousness extends its reach.

It is at this point that the perception of goodness falters. For even in the individual consciousness which has won its way to an awareness of meaning beyond the restrictive bounds of the self, the vision of meaning in which both good and evil are encountered will invariably be more attentive to events of evil than to events of goodness. There are several reasons why this will occur. For one thing, evil, more often than not, releases bizarre and violent configurations of destruction and pain, as in the earthquake or the blinding storm, which are readily discernible; while goodness may come into one's path with the quietness of sun and of gentle rain. The import of evil, or, better, the urgency of judging and denouncing evil, impresses even the religiously sensitive person as a topic of greater significance than the designation of goodness. A subtle influence motivates the choice of emphasis here. Even the person concerned with religious meaning is susceptible to the appeal of power over goodness. And the denunciation of evil yields an illusion of power in the name of goodness. Thus, if one can champion goodness with a feeling of power through fighting against evil, he is apt to choose this course as being more suited to his reforming zeal, leaving to poets and mystics the more gentle and ambiguous art of perceiving the good. To be sure, a further motive often enters in. Metaphysically, some would hold, the goodness of God can be approached only through negation of evil. The good, it will be claimed, is not given in structured events. If it appears, it is ? a grace that is given on God's initiative. One will know when this decisive event occurs, one says, for God himself will make it known. This conception of goodness dissociates the goodness of God from the events of common goodness so sharply as to leave no alternative but to define the religious act as the perception of evil. The perception of goodness could have only idolatrous connotations.

Against both this indiscriminate identification of power and goodness and this extravagant abstraction of goodness I would argue for a religious discernment which attends to the qualitative events within the concrete structures of experience giving intimation of God's grace and goodness.

A greater degree of discrimination in religious discernment is demanded, however, as perception of evil and perception of goodness crowd into consciousness to counter one another or to create a disturbing tension which is not readily resolved. The tendency of the human mind to want to balance accounts between conflicting forces and to give intellectual allegiance to whatever figure survives below the line as debit or credit causes it to cancel out the creative tension between good and evil and thus to be oblivious to real differences. Lurking beneath this habit of mind is, again, the insidious inclination to capitulate to survival power, even to worship it. What prevails in the balance of forces is thus accounted right, whether it be good or evil.

The discrimination which religious perception tries to make here is one that dissociates the mind from inevitable allegiance to sheer, ambiguous power without dissociating power and goodness. This implies a purer vision of goodness or, rather, a perception of goodness which is committed to meaning and quality rather than to sheer force—which is a way of saying that goodness and whatever prevails are not accounted synonymous. Goodness, if it is a quality of meaning, remains good whether or not, in the balance of forces and tendencies, it prevails under any given circumstance. Purity of religious perception consists precisely in this capacity to perceive goodness in the complexity of events where evil abounds. It is not an act of ignoring evil, or of ignoring the power of evil, but an act of realistically holding in view, under vivid contrast, both good and evil as they operate in concrete events. The resolution of the conflict between good and evil is not wholly the work of man; nor is it wholly in his hands. This raises the troublesome question as to how far and in what sense men may fight the evil they apprehend and fight for the good which they cherish. One who makes an easy resolution of this problem will be overlooking the creative character of events as well as the ambiguity of men's valuations and affections. In a creative situation, good and evil intermingle, often to the human perspective in indistinguishable form. The ambiguity here arises from the tension between novel and persisting value and from the differences in the way men assess the claims of novelty and of persistent events. Creativeness demands an interrelating of these facets of meaning; but only the creative act itself can effect the transition through which interrelation occurs. The habits and fixations of men tend to line them up on one or the other side, impelling them either to a stubborn resistance toward novelty or to a championing of novelty for its own sake, thus countenancing ruthlessness toward all created goods.

These seemingly opposite characteristics among people, the one impelling people to cling steadfastly to what is given, the other pressing individuals toward innovation, have a common basis in the tendency to equate goodness with what one personally cherishes and in which one finds his own sense of security. Basically this is an egoistic drive which ignores the note of judgment upon one's self and leaves the reconstructive forces, which are objective to one's existence, uncalculated. Generally, the person for whom the past and its fixed meanings offer the greater degree of security will identify God with past values and set him at odds with creative change, while the individual whose sole security lies in the promise of the future will define God exclusively in terms of novelty or creative change as the breaker of patterns, the creator with a mailed fist. In both instances, God is made in the image of one's own valuations, which, in turn, have been defined by one's intimate sense of need and desire.

The resistance to creative change in large part arises from the conviction that change itself is but a manifestation of transitoriness and that changelessness is in itself the basic good. A metaphysics of long standing underlies this conviction—one in which *the good* can be mathematically delineated as an eternal structure. The commitment to novelty also arises from a basic conviction—the conviction that sheer process is a sovereign source of good. Thus, whatever issues from its occurrence is good or is better than the structure through which it has broken in its advance toward the novel event. Emergence in its profound meaning is never simply change; it is re-creation or reconception. It is a transformative occurrence in which the elements of an older structure are thrust into a new order of relations. The new is never the polar opposite of the old. Each stands in a formative relationship, the one qualified by the other. The old can never be the same, now that the new structure has actualized some portion of the possibilities which were implicit in its existence. The new, however different, moves out of a context which is always the receding past. It bears in its organic being the accumulative and transformed residue of whatever past has preceded its actuality.

Now the perception of good as over against evil in this creative passage of events becomes difficult in proportion as one is inflexible in either direction. Goodness then tends to be defined in relation to one or the other point of fixation. Yet the good is always in the act of qualitative attainment wherein emergence wrests from past structures the qualifying influence which can be assimilated into the new. Where value cannot be so assimilated, it forms as an accumulation of obstructive energy, registering defeat in every subsequent act. Having dissociated itself from the ongoing stream in which creative meaning is being fashioned, it has no part in the creative purpose itself. Its defeat thus becomes increasingly evident as its own dissolution of structure occurs, in its every act of resistance. On the other hand, where partisans of novel advance remain indifferent to this qualifying event, wherein the increment of persisting value is assimilated, their very thrust into novelty has the same dissipating effect. At best, such a thrust can boast but a seasonal triumph which must be readily dissolved as soon as its meager resource of energy and insight is spent.

IV

Religious discernment is always an act of awareness in the midst of crea-tive advance; yet it is not always preoccupied with the moment of change. It is a process of attending to persisting features of quality which rise from experience, attesting to the goodness of existence in the form of a fruition of creative change. This is one source of generalized notions such as mutuality, love, tenderness, forgiveness, beauty, order, truth, and peace. The concrete occurrence of these qualitative meanings is always a process, a happening having to do with relations and qualities of response arising from these relations. But it is their nature to have enduring effects in the sense of eliciting subsequent processes with affinities for these qualities and of giving direction to processes such that the goodness of existence which has become actual by reason of their occurrence persists, both as a qualifying effect upon all processes and as a matrix of meaning which generates new events in kind.

These generalized notions, therefore, are not just abstractions of the mind. They are, as it were, distillations of quality from concrete occurrences which, in becoming cumulative, give a sort of texture to experience within the relationships in which such events persistently occur. Thus they live on in events. In this form they are called overtones and depths of experience which add a dimension of feeling to the experiences of people who live within such a relationship. Anyone who has achieved some measure of this depth in experience in living with people or with some one person, or in relation to some place, will recognize immediately the persisting quality of goodnes- to which I am pointing.

These overtones elicit from the group life itself a consensus of meaning and valuation by which a society or a culture come to a common understanding of such general notions as truth, beauty love, order, and the like. Thus it may be said that, while the individual philosopher may arrive abstractly at a definitive conception of these terms through arduous analysis, the group as a whole, or people living within the common experience of the group, come to have a sense for these meanings and these values in concrete terms, *by acquaintance*, one may say, through the life they have lived together. This fact will help to explain why such general notions take on a cultural coloring. It is often assumed that these notions are nothing but predilections of the culture. This is a half-truth. They will always assume some cultural character when they are encountered in concrete form, for they are actual ingredients of some context of living experience. Abstractly they can be distilled from any culture or from many cultures. Concretely they exist as overtones of some actualized meanings or values within events which have been known and felt by actual people within a given pattern of living.

Once these overtones and depths of experience, to which we give the names beauty, love, order, community, etc., form within a given relationship, they have the force of actuality, even though they are not readily designable or measurable; for they generate the quality of meaning which enters into every experience within that relationship.

The presence of these overtones and depths of experience is what gives profound reassurance to the human psyche, at times amplifying and heightening the intellect's grasp of discernible meanings; at other times, serving as a ballast when the mind moves toward despair. When we have discerned the import of this feeling context, much of which envelops the structure of events with an imperceptible fulness, we will have penetrated to the empirical basis of faith.

The Structure of Christian Faith 6

BERNARD E. MELAND

Three years ago Professor Paul van Buren wrote an article that appeared in RELIGION IN LIFE under the title "The Dissolution of the Absolute." I was invited by the editors to respond to this article in a symposium that was scheduled for the summer issue of 1965. Van Buren's manuscript reached me in Bombay, India, shortly before I was to leave for the University of Poona, where I was to give the Barrows Lectures. In view of the awkwardness in timing I began puzzling in my mind as to how I might word a convincing letter to the editors withdrawing from the symposium. Mrs. Meland, though she was gravely ill at the time, sensed my distress. She calmly remarked, "I should think you would find it easier just to write the article instead of using all that energy to get out of the assignment." Her censorship was all I needed to prod me into action; so within a matter of hours I had the article in the mail on its way to the United States. Thus do our wives enter significantly into our creative scholarship.

Written in haste between snatches of reflection, as I stared out from the balcony of my apartment in Bombay overlooking a vast expanse of the Arabian Sea, what I said in that article had to be very much off the cuff. Under the circumstances there was no choice. What I shall say in this article presents some further thoughts on the subject, thoughts which have formed in my mind since that memorable year in the face of subsequent events which have been more devastating in their impact upon the life of faith than the dissolution of absolutes or any other conceptual crisis.

After enumerating various ways in which the world view and habit of thought represented by the notion of the Absolute have disappeared from the modern scene, Professor van Buren summarized his argument, saying,

> The dissolution of the Absolute, then, is a broad cultural shift which may be investigated and documented from a number of angles. It is a change that

has affected our thought and language in ways so fundamental that they are not always noticed. Few have taken as little account of this shift as have the theologically inclined, although it should be evident that religion and theology are as much or more touched by the dissolution of the Absolute as any area of human activity

Then, as if weighing the consequences of what he was asking, he continued:

> To ask theology and religion to accept the dissolution of the Absolute, to open their eyes to the world in which they live, is admittedly to ask much. It means that religion must not only become much more guarded in speaking of God (if not give this up altogether); it means also that more care be exercised in speaking of "unique revelation," "absolute commitment," and some single "ultimate concern." It is to ask of the life of faith that it be lived as a certain posture, involving commitments, but held in balance with many other commitments; a certain willingness to see things in a certain way without feeling obliged to say that this is the only way in which they can be seen. The question may be fairly asked whether theology and faith can survive this shift of focus; whether Christianity, for example, which has for so long proclaimed . . . a single and unique point of reference as the only valid one, with a single and unique revelation of this truth, can learn to live in a world from which the Absolute has been dissolved.

In my response to van Buren, I commended much that he had said in describing the modern situation, but disagreed with the implications he had drawn or inferred from that characterization. "With the stance of the Christian in the present age," I wrote,

> for which Professor van Buren pleads in his closing paragraph, I am heartily in accord. He has stated bluntly and forcefully that a Christianity that persists in claiming absoluteness for its faith to the point of discrediting all other perspectives and cultural witnesses does so at the cost of being itself discredited by the critical consensus of our age. . . . My difficulties with Dr. van Buren's paper are not with his stated conclusions, but with implications that are drawn or inferred as he marshals the resources of contemporary thought in support of his argument.

Now the issue here is twofold, but basically it is simply one of certainty as against uncertainty with regard to the outcome of existence. In fairness to Professor van Buren's discussion, this was not the issue he was raising directly. He was concerned more explicitly with the problem of varying perspectives upon ultimate truths, or upon the breadth of faith claiming to respond to a revelatory event in history which traditionally had been deemed absolute. The loss of such an absolute in theology was what was troubling him. This is the other wing of the issue. In this article I wish to address myself to what seems to me to underlie all such expressions of concern about the relativity of faith and the loss of absolutes.

Given the relativity of perspectives within a pluralistic culture, how much certainty can we have in matters of faith? And an accompanying question is, How much uncertainty can we live with?

Van Buren overstates the matter, I believe, when he says that earlier generations of Christians could affirm the ultimate end of faith as an absolute, and thus had no occasion to waver in their commitment to faith. I see far more evidence of insecurity in these earlier writings, and a great deal of evidence of doubt and disbelief. It is easy to be overimpressed by the assurances of the ancients, not realizing that, in an authoritarian era, it would be precisely these documents in positive thinking that would have survived, while the literature of despair and disillusionment might very well have been suppressed or destroyed. Even so, the strains of anxiety and uncertainty do persist in these ancient writings. And when one comes to Reformation literature, particularly the writings of Luther, the note of despair rises to pathological heights, and the words of assurance appear to have been said with a tremor, echoing the lines of the distraught father in the Gospel of Mark: "Lord, I believe, help thou my unbelief."

What van Buren means to bring into focus, of course, is the strange, new world of man's own making stemming from the Enlightenment period, and its progressive dissociation from any imagery of providential care offering an assured destiny. In analyzing the problem in this way, however, he overlooks the fact that the kind of certainty implied in the notion of the Absolute is really more akin to this post-Enlightenment period than to periods of Christianity antedating the seventeenth century. It would, in fact, not be amiss to argue that the Absolute was a creation of this modern, liberal period, supplanting the authority of the Church and Scripture. For the Absolute implies a rational certainty established by logical argument out of concern to find points of fixity and ultimate reference in a world of finitude and change. Isaac Newton was able to provide this imagery for his generation and for generations following in a natural philosophy based upon the concept of absolute space. Modern idealists in the lineage of Hegel were able to give completion and a sense of ultimacy to every fragmented span of existence in projecting their concept of absolute mind. In our own time Charles Hartshorne, having assimilated the notion of change as a controlling idea in his philosophy of becoming, nevertheless is impelled to re-establish a sense of absolute assurance concerning the ultimate goodness of God by meticulously developing his logic of perfection. So you see, while the Absolute has been in dissolution for many years in many areas of our culture, as van Buren has noted, its ghost or some apparition strangely like it keeps haunting these modern scenes. It would seem more to the point, perhaps, to argue that the Absolute dies hard; for the shadow of ultimate certainty, first initiated in the dogma of authority, to be followed by biblical literalism and an appeal to reason, has a strange hold upon the human mind. And conversely, the ability to sustain the venture of faith in the face of uncertainties calls for a childlike trust that is not readily come by in our sophisticated age.

On the other hand, in the face of this persisting concern with absolute certainty, there have been counter developments in the most disciplined areas of experience, in theology as well as in modern science, setting themselves against absolute notions—against Newton's notion of absolute space and against Hegel's absolute mind. But these instances of rejecting the Absolute represent not just a secularizing of life and thought, as van Buren seems to think; they express a more serious and sensitive probing of the realities that reach us in concrete experience. In a word, the Absolute has been shown up as being itself a phantom of our conceptual world, and as having little to do with the concrete realities of existence as they are lived. I would say that the Absolute has dissolved all about us not through neglect, as van Buren would have it, but through the most spirited and persistent efforts of sensitive minds of our age, both in religious and scientific studies, aiming not at robbing us of a sense of reality, but at recovering it after centuries of captivity in a wasteland of conceptual abstractions.

It can be argued, I think, that the Christian witness of faith, in its most elemental as well as in its most discerning expressions, has never assumed absolute certainty, or relied upon it. It assumed an attitude of *trust*. But this is not the same as absolute certainty. Whenever people of lesser sensibilities with regard to faith have undertaken to depict or to dramatize the Christian faith, they have usually made a mockery of it, parading Christians as impassioned zealots declaring with bombast and fervor the assurances of their beliefs. The movie versions of Christian history usually offend in this way. I am not denying that many Christians do embrace the faith in this way. And it is true that where institutions and the letter of Scripture are placed above the spirit, there develops a fanatical preoccupation with certainties. Not one jot or tittle of the law, ecclesiastical or biblical, is to be overlooked, for they add up in their entirety to a dogma or absolute certainty in faith.

Such a concern with certainty is neither profound nor sensitive in its response to the realities of faith. And ultimately it is dehumanizing of faith itself; for in its zeal for minutia and exactitude, it is unattuned to the travail of existence, to the cry of the human spirit, to the pain and anguish, joy or ecstasy of fallible man. It is common observation that an inflexible display of certainty invariably tends toward intolerance in one's witness, arrogance in exercising judgment upon others, and narrowness in one's sympathies or in one's understanding of the human situation.

It can be said too that the dissolution of absolutes has gone hand in hand with a growing realization of the nature of human existence as it is concretely envisaged, and with the growth in sympathies among men, regardless of race, creed, or color. The human reality, seen as a primordial demand upon our thought and beliefs, as being the sacred lamp of being and the bearer of the divine grace and judgment as it comes to us in our experience, has steadily shattered these preoccupations with inflexible dogmas of certainty that have no defense or standing, except in our moral pretensions and our intellectual pride. Faith, when it is really faith, assumes a more humble stance.

On the other hand, the quest for certainty as an intellectual purchase upon this unsettling flux of experience can be made more defensible in that it often arises, not out of the pride and pretensions of a particularistic witness of faith, but out of a disciplined concern to alter or cope with "the mind's allegiance to despair." Here a margin of intelligibility may suffice. And this can readily be correlated or integrated with one's venture in faith. Or such a form of inquiry may be prompted by an aesthetic sensibility of thought, preferring to have some order and precision in one's response to these realities of faith, rather than simply trust in one's open awareness. One will then move toward some reasoned resolution of the contraries and contradictions that plague one in his experience of faith. He may even undertake to formulate a total vision, candidly acknowledging it to be analogical, yet offering in effect a reasoned, logical structure of faith. Several efforts of this kind have appeared in recent years, of which the massive architecture of faith in Alfred North Whitehead's *Process and Reality* is an eminent example. More recently similar formulations in this tradition have appeared, notably Hartshorne's *The Logic of Perfection*, Daniel Day Williams' *The Spirit and the Forms of Love*, John Cobb's *A Christian Natural Theology*, and Schubert Ogden's latest book, *The Reality of God*. My former colleague and friend, Bernard Loomer, often announced his intention of writing a book on *The Logic of Christian Faith*. In all of this creative effort, there is the intention to wrest from the welter of empirical realities evoking the response of faith a reasoned view which can offer a firm and literal sense of certainty amidst the relativities of modern existence.

I share deeply in the mode of thought within which these men work, and have great admiration for the competence and integrity of their efforts as well as confidence in the spirit of their inquiry. Insofar, however, as these impressive efforts have been understood or interpreted as a concern to re-establish an absolute faith, even in modern terms within the checks and balances of an empirical method, I have argued against them. I have done so for various reasons, but chiefly because I have come to see that faith is a narrow way of negotiation within existence, not a broad way based on a generalized view of principles and propositions. And my reasoning here follows from what I have come to see to be the structure of faith itself.

In stating what I understand to be the nature of this structure, I think I give interpretation to a quiet but persistent view of the Christian witness that has been particularly powerful in meeting the crises of existence, and it may be what has made the Christian witness enduring even amidst the dissolution of high sounding and pretentious dogmas of the faith.

I would put it this way: The structure of Christian faith is symphonic rather than logical. There is a logic implicit within its minor themes, but the overall movement of its affirmations presents a dissonant situation in which contraries are simultaneously acknowledged and disavowed, in which resolution and peace are somehow attained, but not without the price of conflict, pain, and suffering, and not without a sense of taking into oneself, of bearing the burden, of that over which one has triumphed.

In short, the resolution of faith is not a logical argument into which everything reasonably fits, but an arduous and long-suffering venture in negotiation in which conflicting claims, reasonable in their own right, are somehow adjudicated, or brought into a livable correlation without achieving full conformity or uniformity of meaning and purpose.

And the outcome of the negotiations, be it conquest over sin or remorse, the transcending of grief, or a total summation of experience against the years of travail and fulfillment, is never one of total victory, and in that sense conclusive. Where the realities of experience are soberly assessed, it is always one of assurance, tempered with restraint and with lingering misgivings. Assurance is sufficient, however, to impel one to move toward a relinquishment of one's own pressing anxieties and distress, not with despairing, nor with a blandishment of naïve hope, but in trust. This I find to be the critical stance of the man of faith who cuts a path between naïve hope and despair.

Presumably there is an ultimate resolution of all conflict and striving in the final destiny of God. And the Christian philosopher, eager to anticipate this ultimate resolution, has sought to envision it as a structure of meaning and to designate the logic of its perfection. With the logical assurance of this ultimate destiny established (albeit a destiny in which all persons and events realize their fulfillment in the consciousness and life of God), the Christian philosopher finds the chaos and pain of our present striving, our conflict, bearable, and even justified. This kind of logical demonstration of the vision of faith is more a venture in understanding or anticipating the ultimate outcome of existence than a direct inquiry into the nature and resources of existence itself.

It is apparently felt by the one who undertakes this kind of rational quest that, except as this ultimate vision of God as a guarantee of the final good of existence *is* logically assured, the very effort to negotiate existence with any degree of hope or incentive is in jeopardy, and perhaps futile. Now it should be said that this concern with some demonstration of our final assurance is not as alien to the life of faith as theologians commonly assume. Put in the philosophic mode as a logically demonstrated perfection of good, it seems to the theologian to state the truth of the faith too explicitly as a realized goal. Protestant theologians especially have preferred to emphasize the precariousness of existence with its possibility of despair, and to move toward the assurance of salvation by way of Christology rather than through a logical demonstration of God's goodness. A word about this distinction in a moment.

What the theologian needs to recognize is that such logical demonstration is aimed at providing a reasonable basis for the faith he affirms, not a substitute for that faith. The aim of the philosopher, however, often does go astray, and thus what was initially ventured as a form of inquiry to mitigate "the mind's allegiance to despair," and thus to open the human spirit to the appeal of faith, does result in becoming the mind's answer to despair, and thus in fact a substitute for faith.

The theologian is justified, in my judgment, in resisting this kind of philosophical substitute for faith simply on the grounds that our visions of rationality, when projected toward final meanings, can only be in the form of a venture in understanding, abstractly considered. It says, in effect, this is how it could be, given certain presuppositions which we are presently committed to assuming. It thus becomes a bold, though usually a highly disciplined, projection of the lines of continuity, extending out from initial premises, controlled by forms and categories along with conceptual rules designed to guide its long-range reflection. Although such reflection means to be a commentary upon what has been historically and is presently occurring, given the ultimate vision of orderliness, it is really focused upon the ultimate outcome, insofar as it speaks of God and of our life in God. With this vision of what is ultimately real, it is assumed we will then be able to see life in its proper (that is, in its ultimately assured) perspective. Always this vision of God in his ultimate perfection and life viewed in relation to its ultimate end and purpose remains controlling and normative for judgment.

Christology, on the other hand, is not God in terms of logical perfection, but God in his concreteness, God reconciling the world unto himself, God taking upon himself the form and burden of actuality, God becoming man, enjoying the simple joys of a carpenter's family or the rugged pleasures in the fisherman's community, alternately partaking of the solitude of the open sea or the arduous climb of some steep ascent. But Christology envisages also God in the form of a man enduring commonplace bigotry and smugness of people in authority, or of people in common places possessed and dominated by the canons of their own self-righteousness. Thus Christology envisages deity not in its majesty and power as supreme ruler, but as suffering servant, taking up the cross of humanity that is borne by all men who suffer from the insensitivities of creaturely existence, both those of their own making and those of other men with whom their lot is cast.

Christology, precisely because it presents the God-man within perspectives amplifying the imperfections of existence, has posed an insoluble issue for certain philosophical architects of faith who could tolerate only a vision of God resting back ultimately and singularly upon the logic of perfection.

If there is any truth in the current declaration, "God is dead," it lies in the disavowal of that singular view of perfection in God insofar as it presents him as being immune to the joys and pains of existence and of the vision of God that lends a pale cast of unreality to this veil of tears by way of coming to a logical solution of contending contraries which would seem to give the lie to this kind of ultimate unity and peace.

I find the Christian gospel in its starkest and most realistic utterances coming to terms with these contending contraries that give character and substance to the events of existence. I find it affirming, on the one hand, that we are born into a community of love and forgiveness, as disclosed both in a primordial vision of creativity and in the ultimate vision of God's perfection, and this affirmation is its key assertion, from which other constructive assertions follow. But I find it asserting too that we are born into a world of insensitivity, terror, and cruelty, a world of narrow loyalties and strife, of bitterness, self-striving, pride, and competitiveness. In short, we are born into a situation of sickness and health, of growth and decay, of hope and despair.

Now the impatient resolution of these contraries, either in the direction of proving a final perfection or in the direction of declaring an ultimate despair, short-circuits theological inquiry, enabling it to sublimate the intricacies and inconsistencies of lived experience in the generalized vision of God, or to capitulate too readily to the slings and arrows of outrageous fortune on the assumption that this is the way life is. In the one instance, destiny is too obviously designated and assured; in the other instance, cruel fate displaces all sense of destiny.

If my remarks so far are not too oblique or elusive, you will see that I tend to cast my lot as theologian with interpreters of the Christian faith who see it as a narrow way rather than as a broad way of generalized knowledge. I see it as a disclosure accompanied by discernment that issues forth out of the responses we make in seriously confronting the demands and opportunities of each moment of living. And each moment of living is itself an act of living forward.

Seeing experience as an incessant act of living forward carries certain implications. Each turn of events is in part borne forward by the momentum of an initial rhythm of living which carries its own implicit trust in the current of action. So there is, on the one hand, a level of animal faith, as Santayana once put it, which generates an unreflective will to live and, on the other hand, a level of conscious decision wherein these acts of living are negotiated by each of us with the resources for decision and response at hand. Keeping this in mind, one can understand the emphasis given to the immediacy of grace and judgment as energies effecting or conditioning our acts or decisions.

The existentialist reading of experience strongly asserts the power, travail, and ecstasy of creatural existence, of the mysteries of the Kingdom and the concrete acts of decision and response, of the Jamesian *More* and the visible event in the stream of experience. But if an emphasis must be declared, it is clear that, while the abstract vision of God in his ultimacy is a kind of lodestar holding inquiry and the act of living forward in their courses, the disclosures of this ultimate vision as a fact of experience in the concrete pathos and promise of existence, as these loom in individual and communal instances, form the burden of inquiry. This is why grace and judgment, sin and forgiveness, despair over the magnitude of human evil, anxiety, or absurdity, and the redemptive life remain the perennial topics of inquiry in pointing to realities of the human situation for modern, secular man, as they were for archaic and medieval man.

Much has changed in the way modern men formulate these truths of faith. Nothing has changed, however, so far as I am able to see, in what ultimately and immediately confronts modern men as the stark truth of existence and the elemental needs they intrude in the face of any ultimate reckoning, or in the face of any immediate encounter with events of experience that evoke some kind of reckoning with what meets one, both in death and in life.

There remains for me to say a final word about how the words we form into an interpretation of Christian faith for the modern day actually speak to the conditions of men, wrestling with the realities of faith as living energies of the social experience. Whatever we may say about the relevance of Christian words and doctrines to the modern mind, the realities of spirit and the human spirit to which they bear witness are inescapably present in our human situation. This expresses a certain skepticism about the semantic task of conveying Christian meaning to modern men, but an implicit faith in the persistence of what was initially designated a new creation, opening the experiences of men and women, of whatever age, to the redemptive good offered through grace and judgment. This view identifies me as an elementalist (not to be confused with a fundamentalist), meaning that *we live more profoundly than we can think*, not only when we are unable or unwilling to think profoundly, but even when we address ourselves in the profoundest way possible to the issues of our existence.

Theology, important as it is in dealing with the problematics of faith, has limited value in clarifying or evoking the faith. It is instrumental, not substantive, in providing the resources we need for living and for confronting the inevitable and forever baffling event of dying. Where the exigencies of existence erupt to press upon one existential demands of profound moment or to disrupt the web of relations that has formed the meaningful content of one's existence, the words one has affirmed as a theology, or even as a credo, assume a strange and detached status, awaiting the confirmation or disputation in experience. It is not that the event alters the words one has affirmed; only in the crisis of loss and deprivation the reality of their meaning is now full upon one and demands something more than reaffirmation or consent to them when they are reasserted by another. I am able to report, as no doubt others of you can, that what confronts one in the dissolution of tender relationships that have given continual support, incentive, and direction to one's living, not to speak of the tender graces of companionship, is not readily assuaged, either by the philosophical vision or by theological judgments that presume to give form and substance to one's affirmation by faith. Theology is no cure-all for the ills and deprivations that beset us in human living or in human dying. These reasoned views do provide a backdrop to the events that transpire, and to that extent set the stage for reflection upon these events, and in time will offer resources by which reflection and inquiry can be helpfully nourished. But living and dying, and the human responses to these occurrences, are more complex than reflections about them, or than any intellectual query evoked by them. Here one sees that the truth of the faith as lived experience is mediated to such situations not through words that abstractly state our human situation or that reiterate the vision of our ultimate end. These, in a way, are cold, remote austerities that in that context somehow do violence to the tender feelings and emotions which more accurately convey the tragic sense of separation and loss. They must await their time when the structures of the mind can be received in ways consonant with the bodily feelings. The truth of the faith as lived experience is mediated in such critical situations of grief and deprivation through a vivid uprising within immediate relationships of the very community of love and forgiveness that forms the ultimate ground of man's existence. It is here that we learn what we mean to one another in the ultimate aspect of our existence. We are literally the bearers of grace and redemptive love to one another, and there is no concrete nature of God, no new creation except as it is made incarnate in these relationships that hold us in existence. Conversely, we are also the bearers of demonic evil, transmitting to our fellows whatever is expressed through us of the surd of insensitivity that resists and defiles the communal growth of love and forgiveness.

It is in this sense that I would speak of the energie of grace and judgment as being social energies—real, explicit instances of efficacy carrying forward the creativity, sensitivity, and negotiability within the Creative Passage, and of the surd of insensitivity being an accumulative psychical barrier to the redemptive good, or a counterforce of demonic magnitude striking at the very core of being and becoming itself.

Because theology deals with issues of such immediate and ultimate import, its problems can never be resolved, other than as tentative solutions to a complex of queries whose answers elude any final formulation. But the truth of the faith, I repeat, lies not in these formulations, or in any word or symbol as such, but in the realities of grace and judgment of which they speak, realities that sustain, alter, and ultimately redeem our human ways.

Faith and Critical Thought 7

BY

BERNARD E. MELAND

THE ACCUMULATIVE EFFECT of social disillusionment throughout recent years has had no small part in returning us to a theological mood which has always been familiar to Protestants—one in which the infirmities of man's will have been made stark against a backdrop upon which the goodness and greatness of God's will have loomed. Whenever this mood returns, something in the relationship between theology and philosophy snaps; for the mention of this contrast between man and God recalls an imagery which goes deep in Christian thought. Here the presuppositions of theology and philosophy appear to be basically at odds with each other; for in the one, faith is made prior to reason, while in the other, reason, if not prior to faith, is more determining of its results. Faith has implied a relationship of man's volitional nature to God so that man's total being is receptive to the influence of God's sovereign nature upon this thinking, willing self. Reason has had a twofold meaning in Christian thinking. When it has been assertive as an autonomous capacity in man it has generally invited the strictures of the theologian, even to the point of being dismissed altogether from aiding religious inquiry on the assumption that it is simply the intellectual exemplification of man's arrogant and rebellious will. Reason employed within the perspective of faith, however, has been another matter; for this represented the human mind become repentant and humble and thus receptive to the divine demands, yet ready to employ its human faculties to the utmost within the bounds of this humility.

There is a real problem here, one with which Christian theologians have continually struggled. What is the relation between discursive thought and the appreciative awareness implied in the act of faith? What is the correlation between meanings derived through attention, critical reflection based upon the appeal to a criterion, and meanings which emerge out of a full-orbed relation to undefined data in which critical powers, including the focus of attention, are relaxed, made susceptible to the intrusion of a wide range of data beyond the self; unhampered by the barriers of egoism or by egoistic assertiveness? Somehow the insistence upon faith as implying a higher order of meaning takes on a measure of significance when viewed in this context. The contrast between faith and reason becomes the contrast between knowledge bearing the limitations and restrictiveness of the aggressive, self-conscious ego—knowledge formed by the instruments and facilities of human assertiveness— and insight, understanding, or awareness imparted through an act of relinquishment: a waiting, a giving of the discerning self to the full impact of the event or utterance in which God's meaning is being imparted. This form of appreciative awareness, I feel sure, is a contemporary counterpart of the insight which the Reformers and earlier Christian thinkers sought to take hold of in their insistence upon the special order of meaning derived in the act of faith.

Now it is not enough to say that awareness is not knowledge; that to become knowledge, this sensitive awareness must be subjected to the criterion of critical judgment and evidence, and, accordingly, that awareness is but the raw stuff of knowledge which reason and observation provide. This shunts off the real import of this orientation which is thus prior to knowledge. It makes it instrumental to knowledge implying that it can have no importance for thought except as it is reduced to knowledge. Yet its importance lies precisely in the opposite direction. When it is reduced to knowledge, it becomes particularized in terms of the preferences, biases, restrictiveness of the criterion that suggests the nature of evidence. The intrinsic importance of this wider awareness which the word "faith" connotes

lies in the peculiar orientation of consciousness which turns it recep-
tively toward data or toward a datum which may be only partially
apprehendable. What is reduceable to knowledge may be of less significance than the fulness of meaning which resists particularization.

Faith, or the appreciative awareness unattended by critical intrusions, is the art of human response to this fact of fulsomeness in
the datum that is of ultimate concern to the creatural experience, and
to all existence. It is the thrust of the creature toward the source of
his creaturehood·in an effort to nullify as far as possible the limiting
effects of his own creatureliness. This he cannot do wholly; he can
only seek to do it by achieving such abandon as he is capable of doing.
when, mindful of the source of life, he takes leave of his creatural
self-interest.

I shall try to illustrate this contrast by citing two different approaches to understanding alien cultures. One procedure is to come
to a decision in one's own mind as to what constitutes a sound human
culture, suitable for the nurture of the human spirit—in other words
formulate a criterion of sound culture. A sound culture is:

(a) Democratic in its organization of life.

(b) Concerned for the well-being of its citizens, *i.e.*, attentive to standard of living, health, security.

(c) Adequately industrialized to facilitate the production and distribution of goods so that both democracy and
human well-being can be assured.

As a criterion of culture, this meets the basic requirements as
many would see the problem. Presumably one might follow the suggestion of the late Wendell Willkie and others and bring to the world
such a new standard of living, looking to the establishment of a sound
culture the world around. But a moment's thought will reveal how
American this criterion is. It is, in fact, envisaging the ideal possibilities of the world culture through the purview of the American
experience.

A second procedure would begin with the recognition that a

world culture is as yet unexplored and unknown country. We stand within our several fragmented cultures looking out upon one another in a new relationship—that of critical interdependence and of compulsory cooperation. Not only do we not know the possibilities of world living ahead, but we are only meagerly acquainted with one another as cultures. Our statistical knowledge will aid us in understanding certain physical facts bearing upon each of us individually and upon the conditions that connect us as one people. But the emerging world culture as a *qualitative meaning* involving associated values, appreciations, aspirations, the things that sustain man and that nurture the human spirit, that shape into a world community, these are as yet unformulated in any single culture—on a world pattern.

Physical well-being is a major motif of the American society; but it is secondary to the zest for life that arises from the simple human joys where life itself has become an art, where handicraft and the communal sharing of the creative gift are as indispensable as the assurance of bread.

The qualitative richness of this emerging life waits upon (a) receptiveness to values yet unanticipated or known, because they are beyond the scope of social experience in each culture; (b) readiness to receive the stimulus of this larger reality into one's own social experience and to be shaped by new meaning so derived; (c) willingness to let the conflict of cultural values have right of way without undue insistence upon any criterion of cultural good. This will mean the relinquishment of the cultural ego in the effort to be receptive to meaning and value beyond the range of one's own restricted social experience.

Now the life of faith in contrast to the restrictively reasoned life is comparable to this second procedure. And the rational effort, bound to the demands of a criterion, must always bear some resemblance to the first one. The importance of this attitude of faith or appreciative awareness to thinking lies in the humility that it gives to the act of thinking itself. And this is especially important in all religious thinking. By giving humility to the act of thinking, the process of thinking retains that orientation for which Christian thinkers have always pleaded, namely one in which sensitivity to God routs the arrogance of man's reason. Such an orientation will help to keep us clear as to the importance of what we call the designations of deity, or the empirical evidence. These are important to our thinking, but important because of the limitations inherent in our thinking, not because of the nature of evidence itself nor because of the superiority of empirical method over the practice of faith. These designations, in fact, are crutches that we employ because of our inability to walk entirely by faith.

It should be made clear, then, that devices of exact thought to counteract the failings of inexact thought breed their own form of deception, just as recourse to inexactness to counteract an oppressive accuracy degenerates into error and sordid sentiment.

Faith stands to reason as love transcends the law. But faith can be made to betray all truth in unreason just as love can be made sordid and sentimental without the restraint of observing law. I am simply trying to lift up the intent of Protestant thinking in its classical form to show that despite its failure to carry Christian thought forward in its revolt against scholastic rationalism, it seized upon an attitude of mind which is indispensable to the religious mind, and indispensable as well to the full effort to apprehend religious truth.

Now when one asks, "But what does this 'attitude of faith' or sensitive awareness accomplish that contributes either to the theological task or to the religious life?" The answer is apt to be inconclusive and the effort to justify its worth somewhat groping. Early Protestantism overcame this ambiguity by attributing to it a personal assurance of God's goodness and grace which, when apprehended, released man, the sinner, from anxiety about his own destiny, and thus enabled him to be mindful of the concern of others. Theological liberalism made a similar claim for its appeal to religious experience. In each case, the value became existential, dependent upon the capacities of each individual to have such access to what is more than himself.

The risk of subjectiveness here is evident. Yet simply to note this risk of subjectiveness is not sufficient to equate all such appeal to faith and experience with subjectivity. This is a point that neither Barthian theology nor religious naturalism has adequately acknowledged. Both Barth and Wieman reacted vigorously against the subjectiveness of the liberal, and sought to restore objectiveness to religious thinking by appealing either to revelation or to evidence. This is to detour attention from the existential situation with which both early Protestant and the theological liberal were basically concerned; and which, in the last analysis, is the point of mediation between whatever is objectively given and what is subjectively apprehended and received.

The folly of a sentimental dependence upon faith, or the illusion of an uncritical appeal to religious experience are not profitably corrected by the arbitrary appeal to evidence, except as something more than either of these follows. For if the sense of objective meaning is restored by the appeal to evidence, the capacity for adequately apprehending this objective meaning for man's own purposes is left uncalculated. In the one case the skepticism with regard to man's nature and destiny is left unrelieved. In the other case, something of the philosophic assumption that knowledge assures commitment, blurs the fact that the problem of human salvation still remains unsolved and, in a sense, unattacked.

Faith, then, is a precondition of thinking in all matters of serious consequence, especially upon ultimate matters, which gives some assurance of getting beyond sheer rational limitations of the thinking ego. That is, it provides a responsible relation to the ultimate concern on the part of the thinker which increases the probability of his response to such meanings or demands for meaning as may awaken religious discernment. This is tantamount to saying that a barrier stands between thinker and believer, between philosophic reflection and discernment—a barrier that is erected by the thinking ego itself and which disappears only as the egoism of attentive thought is tempered by recourse to an attitude of faith.

Again, in partial answer to the question, "What does appreciative awareness implied in the appeal to faith contribute to the theological task and to religious living?" I would say that it provides a condition of human response in which something creative can happen to man's total nature such that not only his habits of response can be transformed, but the very criteria which he envisages as being designative of the good may undergo radical change. Faith viewed as this openness to good beyond any definitive criterion of good, is thus creative of new insight, new vision that compels the reconstruction of criteria. It may do more than that, however. It may, by its very enlargement of vision and its imaginative appeal, elicit an effective response in thought, which is to prepare thought for commitment, for *knowledge with concern*, to use Kierkegaard's phrase. Whether or not thinking issues in *knowledge with concern*, determines its effectiveness, *i.e.*, determines whether or not the known result assumes a vital force or remains merely data of the intellect.

Protestantism, from Martin Luther down to Jonathan Edwards, has always implied that salvation is a problem of human affections, and not simply a matter of works or of intellection. One can, in fact, characterize the whole Protestant effort, including evangelical Protestantism and theological liberalism, as a movement to awaken in men and women religious affection which would transfer their lives from the orbit of themselves to the orbit of God. In this effort religion has been known to wallow hopelessly in sentimentalism and cheap melodrama. It is a commentary upon our Protestant plight, however, that our only corrective to emotional debauchery has been a rational reaction. Modernism can be said to be both a direct attack upon orthodox evangelicalism and an indirect restraint upon romanticism in liberalism. Religious naturalism continues the modernistic advance, but with more philosophical depth, having abandoned the sophisticated method of conceptualism. Religious naturalism has sought to escape from subjectivity and sentimental debauchery through the formulation of a criterion and the method of evidence. The disappointing result of this prodigious effort, I think, has become apparent. The criterion has been made clear. The evidence seems unmistakable.

Yet the capacity to embrace either of them as a guide to the educational process or as a motivation for religious living is not assured by the attainment of this secure knowledge. The difficulty as I have come to sense it lies at this point with which theology has always been concerned and with which Protestant theology, in particular, has been preoccupied: namely, the religious affections. Religious naturalism has clarified our sense of value; it has not been able to excite the mind toward that capacity for commitment whereby the philosophic quest might pass into religious devotion.

What, then, is the alternative to an exclusive concern for criteria? Must it be the relinquishment of all concern for criteria, evidence, and the like? Must it be a retreat to contemplation and to mysticism? Obviously neither of these is a solution. The solution lies in some kind of procedure in thought and action in which awareness and critical inquiry are continually kept in alternation. Critical thought should be able to sharpen the structure of meaning in which the sovereign good is visible and operative, but not to the point of being fully definitive. And the reach for absolute definitiveness may lead to an overreaching of the mind wherein the act of awareness is progressively minimized and eventually routed. This is the route to abstractionism and to an intellectualizing of religion in which the affective processes can play no significant part. The act of awareness, on the other hand, should progressively advance beyond the stage of sheer awareness to some degree of affection for the good that is discerned. This will be achieved in proportion as the redemptive good being discerned is recognized to be genuinely operative in human life—an actuality of experience—to which our emotions and active responses have relevance. The sense of a good not our own, yet imperative to our good as a never-failing source of grace and judgment, is precisely the feeling-tone which will awaken the affective regions of consciousness.

The solution, then, is in part a recovery of the orientation which Reformation Protestantism found in the appeal to faith. This orientation begins with acknowledging the grace of God in human experience as sovereign and saving, noting that this redemptive work of the Holy Spirit, offering forgiveness, has historical and symbolical meaning in Jesus Christ. Thus the Protestant appeal to faith rests back upon *the knowledge of Christ*—not as philosophic reflection derives knowledge, but as the total nature of man, his appreciative and affective powers, together with thought, discerns the redemptive good of experience disclosed in sacrificial love.

Now the validity of this Christian discernment that the tender working of sacrificial love is a sovereign and redemptive good can be rationally established. I think it has been so established at various times. Plato has given metaphysical formulation to such a notion. Spinoza has done so. Various forms of idealism including personalism have done so. I am persuaded that the metaphysics of Whitehead offers a contemporary structure of thought of great relevance and significance for Christianity, providing in fact the source of a new theology capable of giving cognitive structure to the sentiments of the Christian faith. A philosophical theology availing itself of this cognitive clarification and support can be a resource of immeasurable importance to religious Protestant thinking in a time like this. Only it must be made clear that the appeal to "the tendernesses of life" discerned in Christ has force in its own right as a persuasive and recreative element, redeeming "a world founded upon the clashing of senseless compulsions."

The insistence upon this fact has been the chief force of the Protestant witness. Its reluctance to embody this redemptive good in cognitive structures has followed from a sound sense of its authenticity as an operational fact apart from any attempt at conceptual clarity. The grace and judgment of God perceived in existential moments of beneficence or tragedy have been all too real to require elaboration. Thus the meaning of this gospel, it has asserted, does not wait upon intellectual defense or clarification.

What the Protestant thinker has often overlooked, however, is that the import of this gospel may be enlarged and made culturally more effective when given an adequate cognitive structure. Here, in fact, lies the chief weakness of the Protestant evangel. Its fear of all structures, preeminently of intellectual structures as being potentially idolatrous, has led it to minimize the rhythm of man's doing and to overstress the work of the Holy Spirit as if it were an operation without structures. The dynamics of faith have thus been represented as a superstructural activity in which man has been wholly passive and receptive. Faith as an act of awareness, albeit with penitence and humility, has been incapable of passing into a perception of goodness which, in turn, might be further defined and disciplined through critical inquiry. Thus the only Protestant alternative to idolatry has been a judgment of structures—a protestation against all cultural formulations whether in the realm of thought or of creative effort. And the only safe course for positive action, apart from judgment and reform, has been in the act of faith as an acquiescent response.

Granting that the redemptive good in experience, bringing grace and judgment to existence, affirms its own authenticity, and that its meaning does not wait upon intellectual defense or clarification, though its cultural effectiveness can be enlarged and enhanced by it, one must nevertheless acknowledge that a fuller meaning of its gospel does wait upon the nurture of sensibilities and affections such that this concrete good that is in Christ as tenderness and love can affect the hungers of men's hearts. If the Protestant appeal to faith as a primary response can be directed to this nurture of the human spirit, it may hold the key to resources within our human reach which can redeem our lives beyond any limits we are able to define.

In lifting up the promise of the Protestant appeal to faith I have not meant to urge it as an alternative to rational thought in theology. That is a familiar emphasis in our day; but I am not echoing that voice of theological reaction. Rather, I am urging clearer recognition of the force of the Protestant appeal to faith in so far as it awakens our effective response to the redemptive good that is in Christ. Whatever we do to reinforce this hungering and thirsting after the redemptive good through intellectual means will broaden the application and increase its relevance; for it will thereby integrate the religious appeal with the common discourse of culture. But our acknowledgment of this redemptive good, our appreciation of its qualitative meaning and force in a world that is ruthlessly indifferent to it, and our dedication to it as our ultimate concern—these are expressive of sensibilities in our nature which precede and follow the rational analysis.

In the working out of the theological task we shall have to go beyond the historical Protestant understanding of the interrelation of faith and reason, treating this concern, not simply as a problem of religious knowledge, but as a problem of relating affection to the act of knowing such that awareness of the source of human value may issue in faith and commitment to the sovereign God and thus offer a saving knowledge.

The Critical Stance in Thought 8

BY

BERNARD E. MELAND

Aʟʟ metaphysical and theological thinking proceeds from some decision regarding the human situation. Such a decision constitutes, not so much the starting point, as the fixation points, defining the bounds and the nature of inquiry; e.g., one who sees the human situation as presenting undefined, even limitless possibilities, both in knowledge and goodness, will set for himself unlimited goals of inquiry and of moral effort. The expectation will then follow that the powers of mind and of will are without bounds, except as man, himself, sets such bounds either through his own lethargy or his indifference to knowledge and goodness, or through some arbitrary decision to limit investigation or study. On the other hand, one who has come to see the human situation presenting certain clearly discernible limits in man, himself, say the limitations of creatureliness; or one who sees that man has limits which no education or human nurture can alter but for whom these limits give intimation of reality other than or beyond man's knowable world, will qualify the goals of his inquiry. He will regard the resources of mind, together with its logic, applicable to that area of experience in which structure can be designated or envisaged. Here he will seek knowledge, certainty of judgment, and clarity of decision and action. However, at the boundary of the human structure, where man's limits are discernible, and where reality ᴜother than man's knowable structure is apprehended, the human

93

mind will see, not knowledge, but intelligibility—i.e., an awareness of how it can convey meaning or goodness to the human situation. The goal here will be, not to inquire *into*, (for the instruments of inquiry with which the human structure is equipped are, by definition, not adequate to explore it) but rather to know how such a reality could be and how it could reach men. In other words, he will seek to acquire an intelligible relationship with what is beyond one's limits as a reasoning structure of mind. We do this, of course, in relation to other human beings when we deal with them, not as objects of inquiry, but as the mystery of a subject. To address them only with the facilities of inquiry that are peculiar to ourselves means that we encompass them within the structural forms of our own individuality. To address them as a subject beyond our structure means that we render ourselves open to an intelligible relationship by which we can be reached by what they in themselves really are. We leave ourselves open to fresh apprehensions of their meaning on their terms and through their initiative.

For one who is impressed by man's limits, and possibly by his predicament as a human being, and who sees reality only as it exists within those limits, no intimations beyond the boundary of man's limits will have any significant reality save as the subjective self creates its own world of meaning. Thus for such a one the goals of inquiry will be set solely within the existential path. Transcendent references as such, as well as immanent structures of meaning, will thus be assumed to be non-existent or irrelevant to authentic selfhood. Only the self can generate meaning if meaning is to exist, he will conclude.

Now once one makes such a decision, and establishes the goals of inquiry appropriate to it, one cannot cross over into another mode of inquiry which implies a different estimate of the human situat on. Nor should one ignore these basic decisions in presenting questions to anyone who has projected inquiry in any given direction. For example, to expect a philosophical idealist to answer questions raised by the existentialist, without reference to his initial estimate of man, is wholly unprofitable. Or to expect one for whom revelation has become a fundamental notion to speak in a way altogether persuasive to one for whom reason alone provides the categories and canons of understanding, is to court endless conflict in thought.

It may be that the most formidable barriers to grappling with problems of faith and culture lie right here: the difficulty to know the ground upon which we can clarify to one another the basis from which our deepest interests arise, and the path along which meaningful relationships regarding those interests can be established. T. S. Eliot once remarked that the difference between people who accept revelation and those who do not is the greatest difference there is between human beings.[1] This, I think, states the matter in the extreme, but it voices a condition of despair that must confront one when an impasse between opposing modes of discourse, based on this kind of difference, occurs.

The realism of our time, both with regard to the sobering events of history which have brought us psychically to the extremities of self-experience, and with regard to new resources of thought which have brought us fresh insight into the status of the human equation, has contributed enormously to lessening this impasse. To put it bluntly, we have come to know through the travail and tragedy of explosive events in history what *reality over reason* can mean. It has its terrifying consequences in so far as unreason in the human character during such volatile situations can release deadly violence and deception to destroy man himself. But the upthrust of reality over reason has issued, not only in unreason and in certain instances in an orgy of irrationality, but in the recreation of reason, itself. This has come about through chastening and judging experiences, on the one hand, and through the actual release into history, and into the experiences of human beings, of realities of goodness which were not of man's own making —occurrences born of a situation which no man had planned.

We have, in short, experienced in our time greater depths both of evil and spontaneous goodness. And this, in turn, has presented to us as living fact the valid spectacle of existence as being both volatile and dynamic, having as its character a degree of responsiveness to human forms and sensibilities that is in a measure manageable but, in large measure, is both creative and destructive beyond our control. Thus, a complacent trust in reason has been routed. Even the concept of order and of orderliness, so basic to the enterprise of science, has been radically qualified if not, as in some instances, given up altogether as a fundamental notion. The conditions of thought, together with the imagery shaping our fundamental notions, have been radically altered within our generation, compelling us to take a more sensitive as well as a more critical look at the works of the mind.

I mention this simply by way of saying that, for all kinds of reasons, some good and some bad, adherence to an uncritical trust in the discourse of reason has been challenged. Without acknowledgment of our human limits as reasoning creatures, and without recognition of dimensions of experience that soberly assert the fact of reality over reason, we cannot begin to use our reason critically, realistically or responsibly. This does not argue that we can be indifferent to the demands of rational judgment. The most disciplined expression of our own powers as human beings compels us to be assertive in making these demands. Only, the stance of the critical mind must change. It cannot hope to be adequately informed so long as it remains subservient to the demands of self-experience, and to the conditions of knowledge which its limited purview imposes. It is here that the relational character of the individual person becomes crucial in determining the conditions of knowing. The Christian understanding of man, as implied in the imago-Dei, sets individual judgment and inquiry simultaneously over against and in alliance with the deeper ground of man's nature as expressed in his being related to God and to other men. What this means is that open awareness, or appreciative awareness in the form of looking beyond self-expression to what is given in the relational ground is an indispensible dimension of the knowing experience. This is the sense in which faith deepens knowledge, judges reason, summons it to a sensitive level of function in which the larger freedom of spirit recreates it.

Except as reason becomes aware of the limitations upon its functioning and thus becomes attentive to this reach beyond the individuated structure of the self, it simply consigns the human consciousness to a monolithic order of meaning, where such a monolithic order of meaning envelopes the mind. The surprises of novelty, of intimations of judgment, of creative opportunities, of renewal of life offered through acts of grace and forgiveness beyond the self, simply do not come into view. Hence the order of freedom and spirit that transcends the mechanisms of the mind as well as the mechanisms of nature at the level of lower structure, can scarcely affect one's conscious experience. This, to my mind, is the most serious stricture one can make upon rational inquiry that ignores the appeal of faith; and on the other hand, this, in my judgment, is the most persuasive argument for alerting the mind to the reality of revelation. It is more than a matter of morals; more, even than a concern with ultimate destiny; it is a matter of illumining self experience. It is a matter of coming alive to the immediacies of experience in all their fullness as participants in the concrete ground of the creative passage.

All modern minds labor under serious handicaps in regard to this vision of mind and experience. For the prevailing emphasis in thought tends toward a monolithic order of meaning. The fear of supernaturalism, of losing the critical orientation of thought which liberal scholarship, in all areas of inquiry, established for the modern mind, give one pause when any such suggestion is made that we need to get beyond this monolithic order of meaning. Both fears, one must say, are well founded. The loss of critical insight and of disciplined inquiry, based upon this long established premise of one order of meaning, is a serious matter. One cannot cast these aside lightly or react irresponsibly to their proponents.

Yet the truth is altogether too vivid to ignore that we do live and move within a depth of relations that cannot be contained or wholly apprehended within this monolithic order of meaning. We do confront our own limits of structured experience as human persons, and we do encounter intimations of a sensitive order of reality that may not be grasped in the manageable ways in which we perceive observable events. In Tillich's words, we appear to be grasped by them. We appear to be participants in a depth of being that awakens in us a sense of our own boundary, and of an order of meaning beyond our perceptual world.

Now to one, for whom the notion of emergence has become a fundamental notion in interpreting the nature of structures, this sense of one's own boundary and of reality beyond one's definable structures, will not seem a denial of the critical orientation which liberalism and scientific inquiry bequeathed. It will appear, rather, to be a realistic and wholistic way of taking full account of the relations that point us beyond our definable structure. I do not mean to suggest that the notion of emergence explains or accounts for this mystery that attends us. I mean, rather, that it provides an imagery within the empirical order that affords proportion, restraint and a sense of awe appropriate to our creaturehood in which a sense of creatureliness is made possible. It serves the empiricist in a way that analogies, derived from numinous experience, served Rudolf Otto in formulating the idea of the holy.[2] The modern theologian would profit by following Rudolf Otto through his early studies of natural science in relation to religion[3] and to see the way his later concern with the idea of the holy stems from a persistent attempt to get beyond organic, then beyond ethical categories to account for the life of spirit. Otto's studies came at a time when emergent theory had hardly advanced beyond the vitalism of Hans Driesch. Even Bergson s work had not yet appeared when he published *Naturalism and*

Religion. It is understandable that he was to steer another course in pursuing the meaning of spirit and of religious awe. One can, in fact, speak of the work of Soderblom, Otto and John Oman as transitional attempts to go beyond the monolithic order of ethical and rational meaning which issued from the theological and philosophical writings of the liberal era. A dimension beyond these categories was apprehended which somehow had to be made articulate in rational and ethical speech without subsuming its meaning under them. What marks their work as distinctive in their period is that it remained conversant with these ethical and rational categories while at the same time it opened up in a general way a fresh grasp of the import of revelation. A new supernaturalism was implicit in their foundations, though a supernaturalism that remained attentive and responsible to a natural and empirical ground.

Paul Tillich's theology of symbolism may be regarded as a further development of this transitional effort to go beyond the ethical and rational order of meaning in liberalism and idealism. His thought carries other distinctive strands of reaction stemming from Schelling and Kierkegaard and thus moves within an existentialist view; but he clearly follows Rudolf Otto in establishing his symbolic or sacramental method. Otto and Tillich became persuaded that the depth of reality beyond reason can only be acknowledged, kept in focus as a sacred or numinous dimension of existence in which all life participates; but it cannot be concretely perceived. Mysticism thus became the route for Otto; religious symbolism, denoting the essence of culture, the route for Tillich.

Karl Barth who is also intent upon going beyond supernaturalism in apprehending this dimension of mystery in existence, has resisted both Otto and Tillich. He resists them on much the same grounds that he rejects Schleiermacher, namely that they translate into a permanent and pervasive *sensus numinous* what is a spontaneous and intermittent working of the Holy Spirit.

On the surface it would appear that Barth, in reasserting the doctrine of the Holy Spirit, is simply reverting to Reformation thought, especially to that of Calvin. Ultimately one may not be able to gainsay this judgment. However, it is possible that Barth is plagued with the same tantalizing hunch that has concerned radical empiricists since William James and that seizes the emergent thinker who sees the human organism and personality as being responsive to two quite distinct levels of freedom in the freedom to be self-assertive, and the freedom to receive and to participate in relationships. I am not attributing these notions to Barth; I am simply saying that, in his concern to restate a doctrine of the Holy Spirit, and at the same time to go beyond historical supernaturalism, he may very well be struggling with the same problem that has puzzled the radical empiricist in his attempt to understand the depth and complexity of the human spirit.

James, one may recall, remained poised at a point midway between naturalism and supernaturalism, unable, really, to resolve the dilemma in which he found himself. "The further limits of our being," he wrote in the conclusion to his *Varieties of Religious Experience*, "plunge, it seems to me, into an altogether other dimension of existence from the sensible and merely 'understandable world." (p. 515)

And again,

The whole drift of my education goes to persuade me that the world of our present consciousness is only one out of many worlds of consciousness that exist, and that those other worlds must contain experiences which have a meaning for our life also; and that although in the main their experiences and those that of this world keep discrete, yet the two become continuous at certain points, and higher energies filter in. (519)

James ultimately moved in the direction of mysticism, though he never could become wholly committed to it. Hence his tenuous "experimental super-naturalism," as he chose to speak of it, took on the semblance of numinous experience in the manner of Schleiermacher, Otto, and Tillich. Yet his restiveness with it, knowing that this more presents itself, not as a permanent and pervasive realm of being, but as intermittent visitations or incursions upon our own experiences, reminds one more of Barth than of Otto or Tillich.

Barth's Christocentric Theology may obscure this affinity with James at this point; for obviously this gives a focus to the latter's thought which James could not entertain. But I am concerned here only with the imagery of thought by which critical thought simultaneously takes account of realities beyond the structures of reason, yet seeks to avoid the magic of supernaturalism or the manageable divinity of mysticism. What Barth really seems to object to in supernaturalism is the assumption that the mystery of the "God-man" can supervene these earthly scenes in performing its miracles without the risks of embodiment. Embodiment means for Barth involvement in human structures, and thus ambiguity in the humanly conveyed Word of God. The Word as reality always stands over against the transmitted Word, even the Word conveyed through Scripture. Proclamation in Scripture and in preaching can never escape this embodiment in human form; nevertheless it points beyond this embodiment to the Word being proclaimed.

How strikingly this expresses the insight of emergent theory! There is undoubtedly more involved in what Barth means to say than what I am conveying. Yet, again, as a modern theologian struggling to recall his contemporaries to a sense of otherness, in countering the monolithic order of reason established by Hegelian idealism and modernism, he treads a path which, in its own novel and continental way, grasps at insights into the human situation comparable to those which are astir in emergent thinking and in a field theory of apprehensions where the energies of spirit are encountered and to which response is given.

The danger of employing the insight of emergent theory or

any of its related concepts, is that it may tend to over-simplify, or seem to simplify too readily, what in the nature of the case can only remain a horizon of faith and wonder for every man. At best, these analogical notions provide a stance, or a way of looking at ourselves and the testament of faith that would point beyond ourselves, such that the demands of our own inquiring spirit for intelligibility can be met within the limits that define our human structure in the very act of responding to the mystery and depth of existence, which is holy ground.

The critical stance in thought implies a critique of the use of reason as well as of every other form of human response in confronting the More of experience, or what comes to us as unmanageable mystery in our existence. On the other hand, the one thing that the critical mind cannot forget, however much it may strive to be responsible to what is beyond its own structured experience, is a sense of integrity in conveying its own authentic witness. This may seem to imply a contradiction of what we have been saying in behalf of open awareness and responsiveness to the depth of our relationship. It is important to see that the critique of reason in the interest of attending more fully and readily to the More of experience can never imply the denial of reason. Reality over reason is not the suppression of it, but the ordering of it in relation to what is primordially and ultimately sovereign over it. Yet the encounter of the human spirit with what is sovereign over it is such that this must mean more than sheer acquiescence. The suppression of reason, or the denial of it in the encounter of faith implies loss of authenticity in the human spirit which must mean loss of our humanness as well.

This heightened and alerted attention, which the disciplines of the mind provide, can render the human spirit both more resistant and more receptive to whatever in experience is · encountered. This means that its critical function is accentuated, sharpened and oriented for action. It can mean also, under favorable circumstances, that its appreciative capacity and response, and a maturity in exercising it, may also be increased. All of this is to argue that the resources of reason can greatly alter the dimensions of one's encounter with any datum or situation in experience.

If one applies this thesis to what has been called the *divine-human encounter*, one would see that the only way in which this can become a creative encounter is to have the divine initiative really engage the human structure in a real encounter of meaning, as it were—not a docile situation in which the human structure is nullified or trampled upon by the Holy God. The figure of Jacob wrestling with God is apt and relevant—perhaps a bit muscular, but suggestive, at least, of the tension appropriately involved in such an interchange. What it fails to convey, of course, is the capacity to receive the work of spirit when and if the transmutation of grace conquers. Nevertheless it sets forth what the saltier company of theologians have sought to convey, namely, that God has to work a bit if he is to get a good man down.

It is this kind of insight into the proper assertion of the human spirit that underlies such a suggestion as Tillich makes in saying that we are justified by grace through our doubts and through our skepticism as well as through faith.

But there is all the difference in the world between this kind of human assertiveness of a disciplined order of meaning and the human arrogance that assumes it has no opposition; that assumes that "man is the planet come to consciousness" and thus can throw his weight around. In an encounter one throws his weight against something with a readiness to be judged; with every risk of being overcome, or at least of certainly being countered. This creative conflict between different levels of disciplined orders of meaning is common to any instance of communication where a significant interchange is taking place. What issues from such responsible encounter between minds, between levels of disciplined orders of meaning, is a hard earned issue of the spirit—but accordingly significant. For it bears the illumination of a heigh-

103

tening and chastening experience in which orders of meaning have seriously confronted one another, and have engaged one another in communication under the stress and anxiety of a mutually serious act of witnessing.

Even when a victory of spirit comes to the human consciousness, wherein the mind is impelled to acknowledge the claims of the margin of sensitivity, tipping the human structure toward its ultimate lure, the spirited dialogue between faith and reason is not over. In fact it is never over so long as the person exists. This tension is an important element in the discipline of the Christian life.

Being open and receptive to the order of the holy, to the matrix of sensitivity which supervenes our experience, then, is not simply an act of acquiescence; but a struggle through and with the claims of our own authenticity, our own structure of meaning, toward that order of more sensitive meaning that is in God. And it is this encounter that constitutes the creative dialogue between faith and reason.

NOTES

[1]Baillie and Martin, *Revelation.*
[2]Otto, Rudolph, *The Idea of the Holy.*
[3]Otto, Rudolf, *Naturalism and Religion*, Tr. by J. Arthur Thomson and Margaret R. Thomson. London: Williams and Norgate, 1907.

By Bernard Eugene Meland
Associate Professor of Religion, Pomona College

T HE PROBLEM of how we know what we claim to know concerning the qualitative character of the vast exterior has presented one of the most baffling inquiries with which the human mind has undertaken to wrestle. Supernatural theories solved the difficulty simply by ascribing the active role of communicating knowledge to the divine order, and placing man at the receptive end. Plato, by identifying the reasoning soul with the divine world of ideas, resolved the problem even more simply, and his method has been the procedure in all forms of idealistic thought which have identified the mind of man with the mind of the divine. Whenever cognition is recognized to be a sensory act, or in any way dependent upon the senses, the problem of religious knowledge becomes increasingly difficult. It ceases then to be merely a matter of metaphysical reflection and becomes an intricate problem of psychology as well. In a discussion of religious awareness and knowledge, three problems present themselves. (1) What is the relation between awareness and knowledge? (2) What is the specific nature of religious awareness? (3) What may we say concerning the character and extent of religious knowledge in the light of these foregoing factors?

I

If we may assume the point of view that is commonly accepted among empirical philosophers and psychologists, that the act of knowing is the maturing end of perception, then the problem of knowledge and its relation to awareness narrows down to three basic matters: the sensitivity of the organism in response to stimuli; the nature of the activity, whereby undefined awareness passes into cognitive meaning or knowledge; and the character of the symbols employed in giving cognitive meaning to perceived events. Perception is basically an organic response, the nature and clarity of which depends upon conditions in the psycho-physical organism, and the character of stimuli to which the organism is habitually exposed. By conditions in the psycho-physical organism we would include both the physiological and the mental factors. An individual born with a sluggish reaction to stimuli, or with a vibrant aliveness to environment is predestined to embrace realities in one manner or the other. Every development within the organism making either for precision of response, or for fogginess (which in extreme forms may make for deception amounting to hallucination), shapes the course of perception. Likewise, every event involving attention imposes a conditioning upon the organism which in time may become accumulative to the extent of setting definite limits to sensation and awareness. Thus the established mores of a community, the routine of one's vocation or even avocations, tend to create a structure of response that becomes habitual and unyielding.

Through association we tend to build up a familiarity with certain stimuli, which in turn attaches emotional feeling to events in which such stimuli appear. Familiarity is not the only source of such emotional association, although it generally enters in some form to give appeal or persuasiveness to the event. Thus perception is conditioned by the kind of habituated experiences that give rise to emotional feeling impelling attention. But while the influence of such emotion is strong concerning ordinary men, circumscribing their responses, it is possible to achieve a measure of independence from such persuasion through critical reflection. Consequently the disciplined person is less likely to be limited in perceptions to the customary stimuli.

The point I am trying to suggest here is, that over a period of years individuals develop a certain kind of probable response to realities in environment. And this subjective outreach not only colors the character of things experienced, but it actually determines what may be perceived. For as James has said, "Just in proportion as an experience is probable will it tend to be directly felt." This point may be made more explicit by comparing familiar types of sensitivity. We generally contrast the prosaic and the poetic, the ruthless man and the person of feeling, the analytic person and the one responsive to unity and patterned relationships. Now, it is not accurate to say, as is so often assumed, that the one is less sensitive than the other—that the prosaic mind is less sensitive than the poetic type, or the ruthless antisocial person less than the socially conditioned person, etc. Certainly the prosaic person is inclined toward blindness to other forms. He catches immediate implications that aid the day's work. He senses the utility or the impracticality of suggestions and ventures. Where the poet might be oblivious to the engineering feat, transforming the desert waste into a thriving community, the man of a practical turn stands fascinated in a way that allows no incident of importance to escape his gaze. On the other hand, the poet's world of vision is an enigma to the prosaic mind. If there is contagion of feeling and elation, there is little exchange of meaning between them.

Similar is the contrast between ruthless and socially sensitive folk. Through habitual disregard for sentiment and sentient feeling, one can develop an immunity to the expression of pain or distress. The art of objective workmanship consists, to some degree, in remaining "stoic before the wincing eye," otherwise sentiment would deflect one from the necessary goal. Where this objective attitude is employed for other than helpful ends it assumes a ruthless character. One would not say that the ruthless person is less sensitive than the socially conditioned individual; rather, he is sensitive to a different area of stimuli. The thief, when he has attained organic consistency, is alive to the most subtle turns of events that announce his peril, because these are integral with the end he serves—himself; while the person of rare feeling for others may be indifferent to happenings that threaten his own safety.

This same element of contrast in perception appears in reactions of analytical and contemplative mentalities. Part of the conflict between science and philosophy, and between science and religion, arises from this contrast. What men see differs so widely by reason of their focus of vision. Over a period of years one can become so habituated to attending to specific facts and entities out of context, that the whole phenomenon of relationships may appear as but a vague background upon which specimens are pinned. Its dynamic, organic character may simply seem not to make a difference. The envisagement of pattern, or of subtle relations that unify or correlate existences, is a form of seeing that reverses the analytical process. The undisciplined, or common-sense, mind tends naturally toward this kind of seeing, but only to the degree that the seeing serves common-place existence. Common men are not attentive to unities and relations to the degree that marks the disciplined observer of the contemplative or poetic sort. Now between these two varieties of disciplined vision there is a vast difference in perceptual habits, and in things perceived. So extreme can this contrast become that the datum of one experience may appear as sheer illusion to t͟ e other.

The conclusion that this analysis leads to is, that awareness and knowledge are so related to the forms of feeling and attention that their character may be said to be in direct relation to the habitual associations and their persisting stimuli. The music lover, through continually hearing significant music, comes to be peculiarly aware of musical meanings and values. The lover of art, through constant observation of recorded genius, achieves a competency of perceiving and knowing art values. The skilled workman, by his continual association with tools and the shaping of materials, acquires a capacity for sensing and knowing defects and values of workmanship. Religious awareness and knowledge are similarly related to associations and persisting stimuli, bringing the realities of religious import into focus. One who never contemplates these may no more be expected to envisage their existence, or their significance of meaning, than one who never turns to music may be expected to be sensitive to that sphere of facts and meanings. There is point to the penetrating utterance: "They who hunger and thirst after righteousness shall be filled"—and only "the pure in heart" really "see God."

But the further fact is equally important. The character of that persistent outreach conditions the quality of awareness as well. If men are sensitized to discern religious meanings, they are also conditioned to see certain religious meanings, and to see them in a certain way. This fact throws important light, not only upon the varieties of religious experience, but also upon the varying views and emphases that enter into theologies and philosophies of religions. Every formulation of thought is an autobiographical utterance.[1]

Deriving knowledge from sense awareness, while a simpler and more reliable process than reporting insights, since it involves only the communication of meaning within a single nervous system, is nevertheless difficult at best. Although a child, before he has acquired the social symbols essential to conversation, may derive meanings in the form of a soliloquy as he responds to the exciting downpour of environing stimuli, the scope of meaning is obviously limited: hardly more than distinctions between pleasurable and undesirable sensations, familiar or unfamiliar events. The growth of social symbols, as the child takes on maturity, enriches the meaning of experiences. But

1. For an elaboration of this point see H. N. Wieman and B. E. Meland, *American Philosophies of Religion* (Chicago, 1936), pp. 11-14.

always the content of meanings is delimited by the vocabulary of meaningful symbols. Where experience surmounts the horizon of the obvious, or where there is an inrush of unexpected beauty or peril—a glimpse of a purple mountain, the tremble of mother earth, or an overpowering awakening to the slumbering strength of the sea—ordinary symbols of language may fail to elicit, or to record, meaning adequate to the experience. The emotionalizing of language, as in poetic description, is the attempt to stretch the garment of words to envelop the form of experience. Even to oneself, where experience is impelling, perception outruns the bounds of cognitive meaning. Always a penumbra of undefined awareness hovers about, giving us a sense of life that resists translation into knowledge. The prevalence of myths among early, uncritical people may be explained in part by the restless sense of wonder reaching toward meaning. Our continuing sense of mystery, when we contemplate existence as a creature experience, is the modern man's response to this surplusage.

If solitude leaves one baffled in confronting some moments, the attempt to communicate experience can only add to that bafflement. The mystic is not the only one to experience frustration in the attempt to communicate experience. His variety of experience accentuates the difficulty; but no one is ever wholly free from the dilemma. That we do not sense the difficulty simply means that we are easily content with an approximate communication of meaning. We let it go at that. For most conversation serves practical ends. When the ends are served, interest in the communication of meaning for that instance ceases. To the degree that communication goes beyond the mere give-and-take of the common life, and becomes appreciative, reflective, or charged with religious import, the difficulty of reducing awareness to knowledge presses upon one. The indescribable wealth of data in awareness exposes the impoverishment of language. I once heard neighbors of the late Rudolf Otto, in Marburg, puzzling over his health and mental condition because of his frequent remark, "Silence is the most profound form of speech." So senseless a statement, they thought, could only come from one whose judgment was failing, or being warped by mystical absorption. Sober reflection upon the relation between awareness and communicated meaning will readily disclose that Otto's statement, however abnormal to the common man, is both pertinent and accurate.

Difficult as the process may be, we do not hesitate to derive meaning from the moments of awareness that come upon us in rapid succession. That is because the course of the day's work depends upon our achieving some interpretation. Should demands be abated, one might conceivably exist in the state of suffused awareness, allowing the stream of conscious experience to play over his being without compelling peaks of meaning to arise. Day dreaming and sensuous awareness suggest such a state except when they tend toward indolence and insensitivity. There is awareness of this full, inarticulate sort in the passage that follows:

It was a fine day. The water was almost calm, the sky blue, a few clouds. I was lying on my back, my arms outstretched beyond my head. I was looking upward, just doing nothing. I could see nothing of the town or the boats or people, only the sky, a few clouds. The water was in my ears. Sometimes it splashed a little. I could feel, or seem to feel, the slight pressure of the ripples. A gull was above me, a great bird flying without motion. He was planing against the breeze, still, fixed by some strange tension there in space. Then I let go, somehow. I relaxed, settled down a little in the water. And I felt I was not anywhere. I was everywhere; I was always. I looked at the gull, at the clouds. I felt myself one with them as I imagined the gull felt himself to be. I made no separation. I was nowhere. I made no distinctions between myself and them. There was no distinction. We were the same. I cannot tell you how it possessed me. I was somehow drowned in them; drowned, or shall I say awakened from the particular dreams of life? Drowned in being; awakened to being? I do not know. I lay there forever, which I suppose was a few minutes.[2]

There can be no question but that this relaxed state of awareness yields a sense of knowing, although it can hardly be designated knowledge in any cognitive form. What is it then? It is, to be sure, the kind of knowing which the mystic calls intuition. To most mystics it is considered a special form of knowing that transcends sensory experience and reason. That it transcends reason is doubtless true, but only in the sense that its expanse extends beyond the focus essential to cognition. The mystic's error is more psychological than philosophical. Such awareness does not transcend sense experience, for it is above everything else thoroughgoingly sensuous. It is existence without tension. It is the opening of the organism to a maximum impact of data. It is the nearest the organism can come to being wholly immersed in the stream of events without losing consciousness of the stream, and of

2. Baker Brownell, *Earth Is Enough* (New York, 1933), p. 249.

the self's participation in the stream. When the mystic, upon emerging from such a rhapsody, struggles in vain attempt to make his experience articulate or meaningful, he is laboring with the task of engulfing the ocean in a tea cup. This wealth of sensuous knowing will not be thus contained.

Cognition, therefore, is not the act of giving definite form to this formless stream; it is rather bringing tension into the relaxed rapport with that stream. Cognition is becoming attentive to certain portions of the stream. It is focusing certain relations to the exclusion of others. It is an arbitrary reduction of the data for purposes of clearer envisagement. What the laboratory scientist does as a matter of specialized technique, when he extricates phenomena from their context for closer observation, the attentive individual, in the act of conscious reflection, does continually with the data of sense awareness.

To press this point too far, however, would be to falsify it. This is what the mystic seems to do, when he concludes from this observation that the rational process, or cognition, is the mechanizing of experience, breaking it up into artificial units. Cognition never actually extricates experience to the extent that the laboratory scientist extracts his phenomena for observation. The mind is an organic functioning, just as surely as is the nervous system in its less mental functioning. Its selection of data, therefore, never uproots realities, nor ignores completely the context of relation which floods into awareness though not into conscious attention.

At any moment one event of knowing may pass into a new event rising out of sense awareness without any break or barrier between the successions of cognitive events. And over a period of time these series of acts of knowing, in the normal mind, disclose an organic relationship that makes each event relevant, to some degree at least, to every other event of knowing. Thus the "life of the mind," taken as the accumulative, or total mental response of any one individual, presents a peculiarly qualitative functioning integral to the life of the organism. Yet by the very nature of its procedure, it imposes an instrumental structure upon experience, which is at once more expressive of meaning, and emptied of meaning. Both of these factors are important for an estimate of the knowing function. For this intensified meaning, while it yields clearer and more adequate understanding of the data in focus, excludes all meaning, or all possible meaning, relevant to the wealth of data outside of the instrumental structure brought into operation by cognitive activity. Thus the nature of the intensified meaning may give a clue to the kind of awareness and knowledge a mind is capable of, or apt to achieve.

Again the contrasts between the poetic and the prosaic types may be recalled to illumine this point. The poetic mind is one whose habits of reaction tend to bring into focus certain obscure relations in environing events that carry signal qualitative meaning concerning those events. This habitual reaction is due partly to a certain condition of sensitivity in the organism that predetermines perception; but it follows also from the structure of mind and impulse, arising as a cumulative condition from this persistent preoccupation with the obscure, rather than the obvious data of events. A *Sandburg* sees beauty in ugliness, where other people detect only ugliness, partly because of his sensitive response which catches much more of things than most people; but also because, after long years of such observation and discernment, he has become conditioned for attending to rare and obscure profundities in common things. A *Robert Frost* envisages and communicates the alluring sensuous quality of earth-life, partly because of the peculiar sensitivity of his perceptions, flooding his moments of awareness with the rich sounds and smells and shapes of growing things; but again, because through such preoccupation the total accumulative response of his organism has developed a *tropism toward* such data.

A prosaic mind not only may be devoid of the stimulus from environment, impelling such envisagement; it may be utterly unresponsive to the imagery even when it is communicated. But now it is important to recognize that the prosaic person manifests a kind of attention peculiar to the *set* of his organism, which opens up a field of data, and renders him responsive to a kind of stimuli which may never come to focus in the poetic mind. The contrast between the poetic and the prosaic mentality, then, is qualitative only in the sense that each embraces a content peculiar to its way of seeing. And this way of seeing follows from the focus of attention, which in turn goes back to the sensitivity of the organism, and the structure of mind and impulse resulting from habituated activity.

A similar characterization might be made of mentalities operating in specific fields and environments. There is an artist mind, a political mind, a commercial mind, a domestic mind, an academic mind, a laboring mind, etc. This is but a generalized, and not altogether accurate, way of saying that the intensified meanings, rising out of awareness are always related to, and to a degree, limited to the field of data in which mental response or attention takes place.

From this analysis of cognition in relation to awareness, certain minimum conclusions may be drawn concerning knowledge of that reality which is designated "God" in relation to our experience of that reality:

1. Awareness of God depends upon a kind of sensitivity which opens the organism to that area of data in which the "divine" reality functions. The common expression of this fact is that "only the pure in heart see God." This is but the poet's way of designating the nature of the stimuli which arouse men to the experience of God—the divine designating that operating reality, that developing order of relations that comes into visible or experienceable form to those whose order of living has the sensitivity of the pure in heart.

2. The meaning of the experience of God, as it comes in the solitary moment of awareness, is subjectively conditioned. No one escapes completely the limitations of the symbols which bring him meaning. Soliloquies are no less affected by this limitation than are conversations.[3] One's own mind and organic sensitivity impose impassable barriers, whatever the experience or the object of experience. The critically imaginative mind is less bound by this limitation than the uncritical and unimaginative one; for, by sensing his predicament, he may then refuse to be content with the symbols immediately available for interpretation. Where this corrective is active, men's views of God are less anthropomorphic.

3. When the difficulties of cognition are recognized, the effort to know God becomes properly tempered. On the one hand, doctrines concerning the divine which presume knowledge derived from cognitive meaning are seen to be excessive and presumptuous. The mind therefore assumes a humility appropriate to its capacity, content to derive such meaning as it may properly acquire. On the other hand, one acknowledges the persistence of mystery as inevitable. With the poet he confesses he "cannot apprehend," not being equipped with the

3. Conversation does involve a further complication attending the exchange of symbols, and the diversity of meaning in socially shared symbols.

organ of apprehension; or should we say rather, "with an adequate organ of apprehension"?

4. To the degree that awareness does yield cognition, however, men may strive for at least minimum knowledge of this reality *in their midst*. The sense of mystery is not impaired, but enhanced, where one undertakes to discern meaning, in so far as meaning may be derived. Here the empirical method may bring an advance upon the purely mystical, or purely agnostic approach to reality. When the empiricist is fully alert to the limitations of the cognitive process, he will not be tempted to profane the divine mystery with an arrogant use of the scientific method. On the contrary, he will employ it to bring such data as are within the human grasp of understanding into clearer focus. He will bring such cognitive tension into the experience of reality as will sensitize men to its meaningful operation in their midst. Worship may then become an act of devotion, that is intelligently directed toward God as a visible cause. Such knowledge of God, however meager or minimum, may lift the religious life out of the state of sheer sentimental attachment to a vague sense of God, into a more realistic venture of devotion to discernible value—the supreme value to which the heart is lured, and which the mind, with all its limitations, acknowledges and approves.

Unless I am misreading his meaning, the statement of Cornelius Benjamin, in his recent book, *The Logical Structure of Science*, would seem to validate this procedure of designating the religious reality by operations in the empirical order, which, according to a defensible theory of value, seem expressive of supreme value. His statement follows:

We are required to define the obscurely given occurrent through its relation to the realm of the clearly given, but we find that this relation is itself given only obscurely. Hence we replace the relation by the operation which is presumably its equivalent. We now have available all of the material in terms of which the obscure occurrent is to be defined. But since we wish to talk about this occurrent in advance of any clear awareness of it, we must replace the occurrent by a symbol for it; when an entity is not given clearly, we replace it by something which acts as its substitute and yet may be given clearly. Hence our problem is now to define the symbol for the obscure occurrent through the proper operational route. Immediately the suggestion arises as to whether we cannot define the symbol by that ultimately satisfactory method of definition, viz., the denotative method, or the method of pointing. But the denotative method necessarily fails in the case of obscure occurrents; they are obscure precisely because we cannot unambiguously point to them. Yet the ultimate meaning of our symbol must be found in some sort of denotative reference. If we cannot point to the occurrent itself, we can perhaps point to another occurrent which is clearly given and with which the obscure occurrent has known relations. This is the only possible method for locating it in the realm of the given; it becomes "reduced" to the given by virtue of its intimate union with the given. Hence, the symbol for the obscure occurrent with the clear occurrent is not unmistakably given, it is replaced by its operational formulation. We then define the symbol for the obscure occurrent content in the only way in method by directing the observer to a situation to which something must be done before he can experience the occurrent in question.

II

To become aware of the "clearly given" which, in minimum form defines "the obscurely given," however, one must be capable of religious vision. That there is such a thing as religious vision, in the sense that there is poetic vision or aesthetic vision, or inventive vision becomes increasingly clear. There is a way of viewing the world of relation and of events which brings into focus the operations that constitute the religious quality of existence. Conversely, there is also a way of viewing the world which excludes all awareness of the data that might otherwise give rise to religious knowledge. To carry this observation further, we need first to inquire into the data of religious awareness.

Any effort to define the data of religious vision will push one back upon the term, religious. I find the resolution of this problem aided by the realization that, just as the aesthetic vision is the focus of attention disclosing a pattern of relations which is called beauty, so the religious vision is a particular form of attention disclosing a distinctive pattern of relations.

What is the character of relations that becomes peculiarly apparent in the religious vision? It is the qualitative form of unity in life designated by the word "good." "Good" is a much used word in the vocabularies of theologians and philosophers, often with ambiguous meaning. It is important, therefore, in making "good" the basic word in defining the religious vision, to be clear about its meaning.

The Good, used in a nominative sense, may be distinguished from "good" used adjectivally. The former is a religious concept, the latter is an ethical distinction. There is a sense in which the two are coterminous (at least related), but given certain ethical suppositions, "good" may cease to have any nominative equivalent, being simply an expression of comparison as between relative conditions of satisfaction. If one speaks of "goods," referring to specified ethical judgment, the noun "goods" is still adjectival in implication, in that it denotes the collective interests or ends judged good at one time or another.

To speak of "the good" in a nominative sense is to pass from ethical observation to a standard, or a nominative criterion, for judging what is ethically good. This point might be sharpened if we digress long enough to observe its application in current thought. Many are sensitive to the antithesis between the type of thinking which loosely goes by the name of liberalism and the religious thought represented by Mr. Wieman, but few seem to have noted the basis of the tension. When Mr. Wieman's thought confronts religious humanism, the tension becomes sufficiently acute to reveal the dividing issue. This is simply because religious humanism is an extreme and forthright expression of what is implicit in liberalism, namely, relative value. Liberal theology has been sheltered from the chill winds of relativism by remaining reasonably moored within the haven of Christian tradition. Or to state it more aptly, it has avoided the logic of relativism by its anchorage to the historic Jesus. (Gerald Birney Smith once characterized this Christocentric form of liberalism as the last ditch of a receding orthodoxy.) One need only to observe the liberal's concern, insistent at times, to become clear regarding the mind of Christ, to see how utterly dependent he is upon this last ledge of the absolute. While he talks lustily about ends-in-view, and of value in terms of situations as they arise, the liberal covertly depends upon a theological assurance after all, which points him back to an historic ideal. Nevertheless, both liberal and humanist speak the language of relativism, and are quick to protest against any tendency in thought that suggests placing the criterion of value outside the flow of events within the social stream.

Now Wieman has sought to remain empirical, but has all along been concerned to place experience, and the judgments of experience, in relation to objective criteria in order to avoid, on the one hand, a relativism that tends to dissipate all discrimination, and, on the other hand, to avoid making absolutes of human desires and ideals themselves, lest all incentive or possibility of growth vanish. Thus "good" in Wieman's thought has assumed a nominative character in terms of a pattern of relationship. He achieves a qualitative unity in terms of the growth of connections that makes for the increase of mutual value and meaning in the world. This, I believe, is a verifiable condition of good, and may be shown to be the descriptive character which points to the quintessential core of the Christian concept of good.

The Good is both existent and potential. It is manifest in every operation that makes for mutual meaning and value. It is discernible in latent, or perhaps, incipient, form in the structures of inorganic materials. It is operative to a degree in every phenomenon of organism. It is more visibly apparent in the phenomena of personality: its growth and shaping, as well as the persistent processes established through habitual response. And it appears in varying degrees of control and effectiveness in the human personality: in the personality that is inhibited and frustrated, as well as in the one that is unified in its powers. To the degree that the personality integrates its life with the extensive environing reality, it takes on a fuller measure of this qualitative unity we call goodness. Goodness, as an operating unity, is observable in the life of a family, a community, and the commonwealth. A superficial glance will not reveal it, but discerning attention will disclose the silent, steady weaving of sentiments, hopes, and affections into an enduring enterprise of loyalty. Attaining the religious vision, then, is achieving the capacity to discern and to respond to this growth of connections that makes for mutual value in the world.

In one sense, the capacity to see this silent working depends upon the ability to think abstractly. For this working is process. And the envisagement of process is a highly conceptual achievement. Let us say that this sort of insight adds metaphysical meaning to the religious vision; but it is not to be confused with religious awareness. This metaphysical imaginativeness may stimulate the mind to religious awareness, and reinforce with logic what many are compelled to take *on trust*. Every faculty, in fact, aesthetic or philosophic, that helps to sensitize mind and feeling to this wider working, which is the good, contributes to religious awareness. But awareness of the good is a far more simple seeing. It involves being sensitive to growing things of beauty, flowers, trees, and nature's creatures. It is recognition of persons, of the fine feelings, sentimerts, love and friendship that bind men and women in common living and devotion. It is discrimination beween that which preserves and promotes personal living, and that which impairs and destroys the tissues of mutuality. Religious awareness is the envisagement of the active good in the world, in much the same way that the perspective of friendship is the focusing of good in a person. There need be no more blindness to error and evil in the one than in the other; but in each there is attentiveness to actual and responsive good. This simple form of apprehending the good is a kind of tropism, resulting from an inward compulsion. It is awareness arising out of the "hunger for righteousness." The theologian might call it "volitional"; the psychologist would call it "visceral." No matter. It is an organic response that accompanies strong desire for, and commitment to, the good. All insight of any profound proportion is born of a feeling after something, a yearning that impels to action and commitment. The feeling precedes the recognition. Scientific insight, in its most prosaic form, is the synthesis of vision and works, or shall we say, vision rising out of works. Whoever would see beauty must hunger and thirst after the beautiful. The capacity to respond to the stimulus, and to become aware of the reality, in each case, comes as a result of vision rising out of an incessant striving. We live the good life, therefore, not simply because we have beheld the good, but in order that we may *come to know it.* Or, to soften the contrast and state it more accurately, having beheld the good in part, we need to live for the good that we may envisage it more completely. And, as in the life of friendship, the awareness of good in the religious vision grows and matures with the experience of its object; which is a way of saying that living the good life leads one to a fuller knowledge of the good.

This would argue that the saint is more capable of the religious vision than men who have lived less worthily, however discerningly. And the vision of common men may be more clear and revealing than that of the metaphysician who feeds upon thought alone. There is danger in such an assertion. Men have been all too ready to repeat the stinging words, "foolishness to the Gentiles, but the power and wisdom of God to them who are called." Yet the truth remains that such insight as the religious vision yields can become apparent only when there is the will to discern, arising from the outreach toward what may be discovered to be good. Hence, the "plain man," with outreach and a sense of wonder, may apprehend significant meaning where the disciplined mind, unattentive to relations involving "value," would discern nothing worthy of attention.

This throws light on the relation between works and redemption, or between ethics and mystical experience. Character comes as a quiet growth, as imperceptibly as the acquiring of a stride, a stance, or a look of the eye. Life is lived for objectives, and that living imposes its own conditioning. Where life is lived for beauty, one achieves an absorption of self in the artist's role, which makes for rare perceptive powers peculiar to that role. Where life is lived for truth, one achieves absorption in the role of a philosopher, making for keenness of intellectual discernment. Where life becomes an unqualified commitment to the realization of the good, the same degree of absorption may be expected, making for awareness of spiritual meanings, peculiar to the pure in heart.

III

There remains the problem of determining the nature of religious knowledge that arises from awareness of the religious reality. Here I think some distinctions are necessary. Clearly there is a kind of verifiable religious knowledge, possible under certain circumstances where the religious data are observable, which is on a par with, or at least comparable to, scientific knowledge. In addition, there are various forms of *felt* insights that carry persuasion, if not conviction, yet which seem to elude every effort to give them factual basis or form. For lack of a better term I shall designate them by the phrase "emotive insights." They include:

(1) Ambiguous, but compelling feeling-states that presume a kind of knowing.
(2) The more refined intuitive form of insights that bring a sense of certitude.
(3) Inferred ideas on grounds of rational surmise.
(4) Inferred beliefs on grounds of moral interests.
(5) Inferred beliefs on grounds of emotional preference or necessity.

The troublesome question is, how shall we consider this vast amount of *felt-belief?* One procedure is to follow the suggestion of the logical positivists and say, as Carnap and the Vienna group ha e said concerning metaphysical propositions, that these intuitional and inferen-

119

tial ideas, like a lyric poem, have "no assertional sense, no theoretical sense"; consequently, they "do not contain knowledge."[4]

If knowledge is to be taken to mean verifiable knowledge only, this is certainly true. We need to be careful, however, in stressing this objective character of religious knowledge, that we do not overlook or minimize this area of certitude, so important to the religious man, which does not come within the verifiable pattern, yet which provides a kind of knowing. All cognition involves this penumbra of yet un-designated-fact, which hovers over the known as a promise of further frontiers. However, in respect to certain kinds of data—scientific data, for example—this yet unknown area is always before us as explorable, and as reducible to tested fact. While this sort of frontier of new facts is certainly involved in our knowledge of the religious reality, we may not assume confidence in our ability to carry the exploration to the degree of certainty sought in the sciences. This is because the datum of the religious reality, both in nature and form, transcends human vision. And this surplusage, while it cannot enter sensuous awareness to the extent that we may derive knowledge from it, nevertheless imparts profound overtones of significance which somehow leave us with the impression that we do know. That is, we feel we know more than we have a right to say we know. It is in relation to these overtones that the use of poetic language in religious utterances is justifiable as a means of grasping, in communicable symbols and with intuitive feeling, depths of meaning that resist definitive symbols and language. I am referring now, not to the super-empirical extension of reality (for that, to be sure, presents a mystery beyond resolution), but to the more-than-observable dimension of reality within this empirical order. This suggests that while the effort to develop a "science of God" is highly important to the task of increasing our factual knowledge of the religious reality, the concern to extend our poetic and aesthetic feel for that reality is equally imperative, in order that this factual knowl-edge shall be kept related to this wider area of significant operation. I feel the importance of the intuitive outreach too strongly to be willing to dismiss it completely from the area of religious knowledge. Something more than the logical positivist's procedure, therefore, seems necessary to deal adequately with this phase. While lyrical poetry, and even music, are clearly "expressional" rather than "asser-

4. Rudolph Carnap, *Philosophy and Logical Syntax* (London, 1935), p. 29.

tional" mediums, they nevertheless seem to create a condition of awareness whereby something more total than facts is brought to vision. I should be willing to say with Wieman that here we have undefined awareness which can yield knowledge only after it has been subjected to proper tests. But the fact that it may potentially yield knowledge—even though it may not be completely reduceable to observable facts, seems to make the logical positivist's statement— "they do not contain knowledge"—too extreme.

If this interest is kept in focus, however, I think there is some advantage in applying the distinction of the logical positivist to religious epistemology. One then keeps the search for factual knowledge concerning the religious reality cleared of the vagaries that attend the intuitive outreach, and thus provides a sound basis for a minimum of scientific certainty regarding religious beliefs.

What, then, is religious knowledge of the verifiable sort? It relates to all tested facts growing out of experiences, common, or especially projected, which express, demonstrate, or illumine the operations of the Good, defined as "the growth of connections making for mutual value and meaning." It is the knowledge of profound working that issues from the emerging life of the growing boy or girl. It is the knowledge of significant meanings rising out of friendships formed and nurtured. It is the knowledge of God resulting from the experiment of several people, undertaking to blend their desires, needs, interests, and activities into the organic unity of a home. It is the knowledge of God arising from observations of the growing cohesions and loyalties of corporate life, wherein society and individuals achieve a relationship of mutuality rather than of regimentation. In a word, it is a knowledge of the "clearly given" which points to the "obscure occurrent."

Prevailing conditions of evil may be equally revealing of facts essential to a science of God. For every situation of maladjustment involving frustration, or even dissolution of value, manifests the reality of God as a tragic imperative. Life proceeds this way! Dramatize it as you will, there appears to be a way of living that leads to life and more life; and the neglect of that way is death and dissolution. It is a hard truth, but it becomes increasingly inescapable the more one inquires into the process of growing up, the process of reaching fulfilment of life, the process of growth within cultures, and·· very possible phase of human relations. The social and biological sciences make its meaning increasingly potent, and the ignoring of it imperiling. For the sciences are continually adding to our knowledge of these silent forces within the Creative Order, shaping life's destiny and broadening the possibility for man's fulfilment. Religious knowledge at this point becomes indistinguishable from scientific knowledge. Or to put it more aptly, all scientific knowledge bearing upon the nature and operations of this Creative Order making for man's fulfilment, the ignoring of which results in loss of value and in dissolution, becomes religious in import, since it points the way to the kind of religious devotion that relates men healthfully to the empirical working of this reality.

In all these instances, envisagement of the empirical working of the religious reality may attain a certain degree of objective validation because, within the limits of observable operation, the criterion is verifiable in relation to the theory of value. Conceivably one could remain within the field of empirical data, making no effort to draw inferences beyond the verifiable observation that the good operates in human life. The manner of interpretation here will determine whether this empirical method in dealing with the religious reality is theistic or humanistic. If it is viewed as sub-human activity, conditioning human activity, or the accumulative response of human behavior, humanism is the most appropriate term applicable. If, however, these operations are viewed as but the minimum observable functioning of a wider working, whose meaning and scope is considered superhuman, theism is applicable.

Theism in its customary sense, however, would arise where one ventures to draw specifically homiletic inferences from these observable data concerning the vaster working of its operations. It is at this point, namely, where one moves beyond the empirical data to "legitimate" inference concerning the religious reality, that the subjective factor looms large. For here we have the kind of cognitive procedure (intensification of meaning) which not only must draw upon available meaningful symbols to give character to the inference, but must pursue those inferences along channels of thought, or within patterns of reflection, that make such extension of our knowledge of the religious reality intelligible and persuasive. Here we come upon one of the most common characteristics of the theistic venture: its personal and cultural coloring. Men's views of God, when carried beyond the field of empirical data, take on the characteristics relevant to the mental life of the individual thinkers, and to the cultural habits and outreaches in which such thinking is done.

This observation seems to suggest two things. First, the minimum conception of religious reality, based upon such observation as the field of empirical data affords, may transcend individual bias and cultural limitation of expression, since its condition of expression is not wholly dependent upon these subjective symbols, or patterns of meaning. Second, the effort to go beyond this minimum level of meaning to the basis of inference automatically restricts what is accomplished to the specific cultural area in which these inferred, extended characterizations carry persuasive meaning.

This conclusion may suggest the further observation that the concern to go beyond the minimum knowledge of God arises chiefly from a practical interest. And such conclusions as are reached are instrumental to the homiletic or institutional functioning of religion. The philosopher of religion, in so far as he seeks to relate his thoughts to the wider than personal or cultural area—that is, to think interculturally, will be impelled, either to hold to this minimum level of meaning, or to take but one step beyond the empirical field to acknowledge "the mystery out there," without presuming to give cognitive meaning beyond the minimum conception.

Organismic philosophy has brought back into religious thinking the stimulus to venture beyond the empirical area, and to designate, by way of metaphysical construction, a causal ground in terms of the larger organic unity, presumably to get beyond the subjective limitations upon religious epistemology, and to provide a way to interpret the extended areas of reality over religious responses. I do not see that this gets away from the view, however, that such knowledge concerning reality as is achieved by this method, continues to be of the inferential sort. Its advantage is that it provides a system of inference, making each step of the procedure more substantial and defensible. But even so impressive a construction as Whitehead's conception of the consequent nature of God seems to rest essentially upon emotive rather than rational persuasion. This does not discount its merit, but it designates the character of its merit, and the end it serves.

If the procedure we have followed here is valid, I feel impelled to conclude that such certainty as philosophy of religion is capable of

123

achieving concerning the nature and meaning of the religious reality must necessarily appertain to this reality's empirical working. We can know God and co-operate with his "Great Eternal Cause" as we are able to discern his working in our midst. What goes beyond this, becomes a venture of the mind prompted by the heart, and can be undertaken only with grave apprehension of the risk of illusion. Perhaps it is better to take this risk than to incur the opposite danger of losing that outer vista and the "further range." Is it not enough to acknowledge the Eternal Mystery, and to serve the present reality as it floods our awareness and experiences in the common life, keeping this acknowledgment always in focus through poetic contemplation, wistful wondering, and prayerful outreach? Philosophy of religion thus may explore the meaningful areas of the operations of the Reality we call the Good; our methods of religious living may increase our devotion to this creative working in our midst, and progressively improve our envisagement of this "clearly given"; worship will become preeminently[5] the adventure of orienting us emotionally to the vaster frontier, that "obscure occurrent" which presents the further range of this reality empirically known. Knowledge, devotion, and the attitude of wistful faith and outreach, keeping us sensitive to the over-plus of the empirically given, these seem to me to provide the bases for the religious relation with Reality.

5. I say "preeminently," because clearly worship has the twofold function of sensitizing individuals and groups to the implications of the "clearly given"—the reality of God in our midst—, and of increasing men's awareness of the "obscure occurrent"—that further range that may not be cognitively known, yet which may be apprehended and emotionally grasped through the poetic and aesthetic symbols of religious expression.

INTERPRETING THE CHRISTIAN FAITH WITHIN
A PHILOSOPHICAL FRAMEWORK

10

THE picture which the topic of this discussion quite naturally suggests is that of one attempting to compress his Christian affirmations within a rigid framework of propositions defining certain basic categories. I must warn my readers at the outset that I have no intention of attempting so arbitrary a task Ordinarily, in fact, were I not assigned to examine the possibility of interpreting the Christian faith within an acknowledged structure of thought, I should prefer, in setting forth my affirmations of faith, to have these conceptual matters work on more hiddenly.

I

That a philosophical structure of meaning underlies and informs my theo-.ogical discourse, however, I should never deny. There is no escaping such an ordering structure once the human mind

moves toward meaning and voices meaning through the symbolism of words or language No more can a man give voice to his religious affirmations and concerns without such structured reference than he can build a house without employing structural ideas and processes. The man building a house may never think of calling in an architect or even of discussing his plans with one. His house may then reveal the limitation of vision and imagination which his undisciplined attempts at design impose. He may, on the other hand, succeed in bringing to his building a degree of sensitive conception which will compel admiration, even from architects. In either case, processes by which structure and design are achieved will have been employed. Unawareness of these processes may or may not yield unhappy results. There is reason to believe, however, that, except in instances of unusually gifted craftsmen, some awareness of the discipline of structure will give better assurance of a disciplined result than complete indifference to such a concern.

But the analogy of building is not altogether adequate to convey the importance of structure to thought and feeling in formulating one's affirmations of faith. For here we are dealing with something more subtle than a self-conscious act.

* Bernard E. Meland is professor of constructive theology in the Federated Theological Faculty of the University of Chicago and one of the editors of the *Journal of Religion.* He is author of *Seeds of Redemp-. tion, America's Spiritual Culture, The Reawakening of Christian Faith,* and other volumes. His new book, *Higher Education and the Human Spirit,* will be published this spring by the University of Chicago Press. The present article was read at the meeting of the American Theological Society, Midwest Branch, in Chicago on November 14, 1952. The final portion of the article is a chapter in a forthcoming book entitled *Faith and Man's Destiny* to be published by Oxford University Press, Inc.

The structuring of the mind and of the bodily feelings is a deeply cultural process in which formative ideas, however adequately or inadequately acknowledged, have their way. A philosophic framework, implicit in the assumptions and in the spontaneous responses of a people, may persist without detection by those most active in employing their fundamental notions. The failure to lift up these formative ideas, or the refusal to do so, will not preclude a philosophical shaping of faith. It will simply postpone the discipline of attentive and critical consideration of the propriety and adequacy of these fundamental notions.

Thus, the archeological title, "Before Philosophy," when applied to the human adventure, is misleading; for in the elemental sense, no human speech or action has been without its philosophical structure and motivation. And, similarly, the theological insistence upon a biblical faith or a practical faith without reference to a philosophical framework is unrealistic; for the language of dedicated and inspired men, however simple, has been a structured speech, conveying, if only by indirect reference or by intimation, the fundamental notions which marked the limitations or bounds of their intellectual resources and, within those bounds, gave hint of the character and depth of meaning which their words contained. Thus the biblical witness, as it moves from the Pauline letters to the Synoptic Gospels and to John, discloses a shifting of philosophical presuppositions despite their common witness. The theology of Augustine is no less philosophically oriented than the more explicit philosophical theology of Origen and Clement of Alexandria. And the theology of the Reformers, however much they may have disdained the concern with philosophy, conveyed a decided prefer-ence for the Neo-Platonic premises of Augustine as over against the denatured Aristotelianism of St. Thomas. The liberal theology of the Ritschlians, who spoke out most vehemently against encumbering the discussion of religion with metaphysical problems, rested upon a scaffolding of Kantian and Lotzean timber. Apart from the Kantian *Critiques* and Lotze's *Microcosm*, the Ritschlian reinterpretation of Christian faith is hardly conceivable. It may be said, in fact, that the whole of the liberal era in theology down to the 1920's partakes of the Kantian *Critiques* and its subsequent revisions. All liberalism in its theological expression has, in some sense, been Kantian or Neo-Kantian. And the reaction against liberal theology from Kierkegaard to Barth moves within the same conceptual bounds. Yet, within these bounds, they make quite different philosophical and theological decisions.

It becomes apparent, therefore, that a philosophical framework is inescapable for the theologian, whether he chooses to acknowledge it or not.

II

What is not so clear is how one may best employ his philosophical awareness in formulating his theological judgments. I have steadily come to the view that one's philosophical orientation is not so much a system of ideas as a structure of meaning in which one's experiences occur and take on intelligibility. One's philosophy in this sense is initially a mode of perceiving events and of expressing one's self through language and only secondarily a formulation of propositions. In this sense, one is predisposed, through his early conditioning, to certain habits of thought which never really become uprooted or dissipated, despite one's maturing in thought. If these habits are not able to serve the mind constructively, because of a later shift in its perspective, they act as barriers or brakes to oppose or to temper the conscious intentions of the mind. To illustrate what I am saying, I should say that there lurks in the thinking of Professor Wieman the overtones of Calvinism and of Absolute Idealism, despite everything that he might do to assert his empirical method. However minimum his concept of God may be, it takes on a power and majesty that overrides all concrete goods. In contrast, I have become increasingly aware of the persistence of a Lutheran heritage in my thought processes despite all the intellectual somersaulting I have gone through. And this, in part, I think, has led me to prefer James to Royce and, before them, Schleiermacher to Hegel, Ritschl to Caird. Thinking upon these contrasts, I have been able to understand better the differences which distinguish me from Wieman, despite our affinities, and which, when applied to concrete experiences, set us upon different paths.

You will have decided by this time from my remarks that I am not the best spokesman for the topic to which I have been assigned. There is too much of the subjectivist speaking in me. Or, to put it differently, the inner landscape of memory and brooding, with its coloring and circuitous paths, make too great a claim upon me to permit a propositional faith.

Faith precedes and underlies the structuring of philosophy, in the individual as in the culture This is certainly true in my case. The biblical drama of redemption, from the Exodus to the Cross and resurrection of Jesus Christ, forms, the earliest chain of childhood images of which I have any conscious recollection. I do not know a time in my personal history when this imagery did not shape what thoughts I had concerning the beginnings of life and my own destiny. These tales held a charm for me in my childhood, as they undoubtedly have done for many children through the long years of the race. In this respect I was literally a child of the Christian community, whose mind and spirit was cradled and nurtured by its formative myth. Yet, like many who passed from a state of wonder and innocence to a reflective and inquiring mood, I found these tales becoming more and more of an enigma. The years of wandering in the desert of doubt and of disillusionment have their peculiar history in my case but in many respects are no different in their themes and transitions from those of millions of other youth who have lived through the critical years of growth toward maturity in mind and spirit.

My only point in intruding these observations is to suggest that childhood and Christian faith are inseparable in the structure of experience that forms my personal history; hence the problem of faith is as old and persistent in my thoughts as the reflective process itself.

I should have to say that I have come to a concern which the philosophical structuring of faith as an artist takes on discipline. The concern with faith has been prior. The *exercise* of faith has been prior. The disciplining of faith, in my case, proceeded along lines which could not, technically speaking, be considered philosophical. I pursued a course that sought more the disciplining of the human psyche, of participating in various ways in a discriminating response, of acquiring sensibilities and sensitivities which partook of discrimination, of judgment, and of awareness that opened the mind to a fuller appreciation of meanings and to understanding of a discerning kind. I cannot say what disciplines dominated in the shaping of my mind toward a concern with structured meaning. I know philosophy was present, though for a time very much in a minor role. There was literature, at times more dominating, especially poetry in so far as it sharpened, heightened, or penetrated meaning with its economy of words. Poetry for purposes of sheer sentiment was always something of an offense. Sentiment disciplined with a structure of meaning, however, had force of a deeper character, quickening the feelings with a creative fire that would light up the mind as well. There was art, particularly architecture, which conveyed the same structural concern. There were archeology and anthropology and the long trail through the history of religions and of cultures, seeking a pattern to this human response amid the vast variety of ritual and belief.

Philosophy, when it did come to assume a major importance, was like a summit view which came upon me quite accidentally and unexpectedly in these mental wanderings. And, being the philosophy that it was, it seemed to open up shafts of sunlight step by step until the whole, vast pilgrimage of faith stood forth against the horizon with vividness and with a scope that was as wide as the mind's eye could see.

I cannot say, therefore, that I reasoned from a philosophic premise to the Christian faith. Nor can I say that my understanding of faith rose out of the philosophical position I had come to assume. Even less can I say that philosophy now forms the framework of my faith. This seems too artificial, too mechanical, too arbitrary. My philosophical orientation is more in the nature of a structure of mind and feeling which forms the depth of my conscious experience and which brings to play upon the accumulations of experience, insight, and

brooding upon the problem of faith the full light of day, the sustained view, because the discrepancies, the broken meanings, the fragments of faith, the hit-and-miss turnings of thought which had no connectedness, no order, no symmetry, could now assume a pattern of relationships.

But now to speak more directly to the topic under discussion: My interpretation of the Christian faith within a framework of philosophy: I should have to say within a context of philosophy, within an orientation of thought which has been informed philosophically, illumined by the discriminations which the technical instruments of clarified vision can provide.

It would take too long to detail the dimensions of thought which have come to form the structure of my thinking, but I can indicate the nature of the perspective and point to certain fundamental notions which I know to be real in my thinking.

The perspective in which my thought moves is that which is being pointed up these days by what is frequently termed "the new metaphysics." This new metaphysics, which is simply the vew vision of the sciences imaginatively informed and elaborated, partakes of "field theory" in its various aspects along with the notion of emergence. In this it attempts to take seriously the revolution in thought which was initiated a generation ago by James and Bergson in reacting against Kant and Hegel. In rejecting Kantianism in favor of a more radical empiricism, this way of thinking moves toward a more forthright and realistic appeal to history and to experience. The concrete events of history, of communities, and of individual human "ves speak of the work of wonder in the creativity of God. Creativeness is no abstraction. It is the continual happening appearing in every moment of time. It is the most immediate and persistent occurrence, giving both actuality and character to events as they emerge. However impersonally one may speak of this happening in the technical discourse of one's field, the metaphysician knows that he is conveying through his abstract symbols truth about the creative moment which is charged with intimate and personal consequences. Man is not fashioned in a mechanism, a world machine; he is cradled and nurtured in a creative community of love which extends beyond the visible bonds of human relations, though in these human relations there is real God, real good not our own, at work issuing in grace and judgment.

Because the new metaphysics, giving to scientific categories their full and imaginative meaning, rises out of the living experiences of men in which decisions are made and where events of tragedy and triumph are forged, it finds an immediate rapport with the imagery and poetic symbolsm of the biblical writers. What this ancient lore sets forth through parable and poetry the metaphysician, atuned to the qualitative meaning of every concrete event, finds himself expounding in what he understands to be more definitive terms. The interrelating of these ancient and modern sources forms a continual dialogue in one's reflections.

The fundamental notions which are real to my mind are not so much propositions from which I reason as presuppositions which pervade my thinking and in which all propositions, ideas, and events of history take on vividness of meaning. These fundamental notions are as searchlights playing upon the data of the mind. Yet they are more than the illumination that proceeds from outward instruments; for in ways that are strange to me still they have become organic to my being.

They channel the way I feel toward ideas, the way I grope toward meaning, quite as much as the way I form judgments, make decisions in thought, or elaborate the meanings which are perceived. My statement of fundamental notions will undoubtedly overlap other analyses somewhat, though it is intended to be a more elementary characterization of representative features within this general movement of thought at points where they converge and at which they diverge from other historical formulations.

1. The first of these fundamental notions is that *events are primary.* Just as certain rational systems centered upon Substance as a primary notion, or upon Mind, Person, or Matter, the new metaphysics sees Event as having a primary status. This is a rather negative way of presenting the notion, for it appears that in such a perspective one is reducing everything to bare happenings, to process or behavior. In the sense in which the new empiricism means to employ the term, however, Event is highly compact and rich in meaning. This is because the ideas of immediacy and of concretion, or happening, which are associated with the term "event" carry far greater content of meaning than would be true in philosophies in which "event" is regarded simply as a segregated moment of time. In the perspective of the new empiricism, each moment of time is viewed as the creative passage taken as a total datum. What is said of each moment can be said of each emerging event. Event is thus to be taken, both in its elemental sense as the most primary notion, the simplest form of existence beyond which no analysis of experience can go, and in its ultimate sense as being inexhaustible: the bearer of all that is in miniature.

2. A second fundamental notion is that

there is a matrix of sensitivity in which all life is cast and out of which all structured events arise. This primordial source has been spoken of as the "Creative Event" or as the nisus toward diety. I choose to speak of it as a "matrix of sensitivity" in order to designate the quality and character of this creative ground of all existence It is present in every event in the sense that process is inseparably involved; only it is more than a constituent. Hartshorne has spoken of God as the "Inescapable Companion," meaning to suggest this same attending concern for the quality of spirit implicit in events. God in his concreteness is a sensitive awareness at work in every emerging event which accounts for qualitative attainment in existence: the emergence of you and me, of creatures all about us, of the glories of earth and sea, the emergence of mind and spirit, of cultures in all their complexity, discipline, and form. God's concreteness is an act within the process at every instance of creation, turning what would otherwise persist as brute force into events with direction, with capacity for a sensitive response, for selection, for decision; in short for feeling and sensibility in all their range of meaning. This infusion of a tender regard which makes for purpose and meaning is the creative act of God.

3. The third fundamental notion is *the social nature of reality*. The fact of sociality derives from God's intent as Creative Event in which individuals are created in community. Creation is a communal event, not only by virtue of a condition of mutuality in structures into which every emergent comes and which exists among all events, but because of the dynamic of the creative thrust which can be characterized as a persistent impulse of love within the power context of process, luring the individual events toward ful-

filment in the community of spirit, a structure in process of emergence in which love is dominant and regulative. Thus the social nature of reality applies both to the ground of being and to the goal of emergence in so far as one may speak of a definitive end of existence.

4. A fourth fundamental notion is that *relations are dynamic*. This notion unites the earlier notions in a way that underlines their interactive character. James spoke of relations as implying not only spatial connections but transitions as well. The transitive element he found to be a neglected factor; yet this element, he observed, is what carries the implication of meaning from this point to that. This was but a way of saying that a static reading of anything, of formal philosophic meanings, of words in a sentence, or of the elements of consciousness in the thought of a person, is a false reading of it—most certainly an inadequate reading of it.

5. The dynamic character of relations presages *the idea of emergence*, which is the fifth fundamental notion. Relations are thus seen to suggest not simply the notion of pattern but the interaction of structures in a way which makes for a subtle progression from lower to higher organizations of events. A binding factor, which is at the same time a thrust toward the advancing sensitivity of structures, is thus noted as a persisting horizon of mystery and promise attending each actualized order or structure.

I would not be able to convey the force of these notions for my interpretation of Christian faith were I not to mention two further notions. They are not in the nature of fundamental notions, as metaphysics might speak of them, but they are indispensable constructs for giving direction and intelligibility to the Christian faith as I have come to grasp its meaning. Perhaps I may speak of them as secondary notions.

The first of these is the structure of experience. The structure of experience, as I use it, might be defined as the persisting, living nexus of relations and residual meanings as they are presented in immediacy as actualized events. I can convey this best by citing a fact about the intimate, personal history of a people.

Every family group discloses two levels of history: the one they talk about and the one they possess more hiddenly. Letters, family albums, journals, and the like provide the tangible evidence of events now held in memory. Except for these mementos that fix a few fragments of the past, the personal history of individuals would, indeed, seem but a perpetual perishing. Yet this is not altogether true (and this points to the second level of history); for events live on in the sufferings and joys of those who, in ways remote or immediate, have been shaped by them. The past events of the family, those consciously cherished and those but dimly perceived, perhaps forgotten, live on in the character and disposition of the children now emerging and in the anguish or rising hopes of the parents for whom the past is now a living burden or a foretaste of joy.

The family history is one thing. This may be recaptured in festive moods that celebrate the passing of the years. The family character—this may be more. For it preserves as a present structure, subtly made manifest in a look of anguish or in a mood of expectancy, the uncommon workings of destiny which no celebration or historical review can apprehend. Thus actuality presents history in its stark, creative residue. It is here with the blessings and benedictions of God and with his wrath as well. Every community, every culture, likewise, carries as a living

burden or opportunity this survival character as a structure of experience which cannot easily be explicated or described.

The structure of experience gives form to our repeated valuations. It is impossible to get at the details of this accumulative valuation response, though of course certain memorable events or observations stand out in any period. And the history of events presumes to tell the story of this growth of the psychical structure. But, compared with the actual process of an evolving structure of experience, recorded history is a relatively superficial account.

It must be said, too, that the evolving structure of experience is not to be equated with the passage of events. Somehow all events enter into this emerging structure of experience; but something of all events partakes of a perpetual perishing which accompanies emergence.

The structure of experience is not merely accumulative. That is, it is not merely a blind appropriation of heterogeneous valuations. Rather, it simulates an organic unity at every stage of history. The struggles and crises of concrete events; the dedications and betrayals; and the discoveries, creations, and intellectual triumphs become the formative stuff out of which rises the persisting structure of experience within any culture. Great insight at any one point becomes creative in its influence beyond calculation. Stretches of insensitivity, with its consequent brutality and evil, likewise affect the accumulative valuations, not only in an additive sense, but in a transformative one. Within any given geographical environment, then, where human history has been in process, the present moment of time is laden with qualitative meaning so complex in character (being the accumulative decisions and resolutions of ages), so profound in implication for all existence and for all present events, that no living consciousness is equal to discerning its burden and its opportunity.

New generations come into an organic inheritance that is greater in depth and range than the perceptions of any living person. Thus they live in a context of feeling and awareness that is always beyond their grasp, emotionally or cognitively. They are not automatically bound by this inheritance, for they, too, are creative of its yet emerging structure in the way that all concrete events have influenced it. Nevertheless, all living persons carry within their conscious existence and in their perceptual nature something of the hidden drives and aspirations that rise out of this accumulative structure of experience.

Within our culture, the Christian faith is mediated through this structure of experience, rising from the accumulative valuations of the years that have been lived in which prophets and poets, the people's hopes and aspirations, destructive and redemptive forces, have been persuasively at work.

The other secondary notion which I consider essential to my interpretation is the dynamic and corporate character of faith, or faith as a social energy. This follows, of course, from the notion that relations are dynamic and that reality is social; but the force of its meaning came to me through cultural anthropology rather than simply as a derivative of philosophy. The gist of this notion is that in any culture, long before there are explicit attitudes of faith assuming theological refinement, there is a fabric of inexpressible meaning in living which provides a depth of incentive and of uncanny commitment to the ultimate ground of one's being and destiny. This feeling context within any culture is expressed in myth

and becomes the source of the poetry, song, and art of a people, as well as of its religious ritual. Out of this primal imagery come the sensibility and sensitivity of a people to feel after the intimations of the working of God as these become concrete in history.

This notion explains why the myth of a people is a creative drama extending over a considerable period, gathering into its story, as ever enriching themes and motifs, the decisive apprehensions which form into a pattern of hope or expectation. More specifically, this notion explains the relation of the Old Testament account of the Exodus, the Covenant, and the prophetic episodes to the Christian drama of redemption. The Christian myth is this total pattern of sensitive meaning, having its climax and summit in the Cross and the resurrection of the living Christ.

Fundamental notions, when they have become organic to one's structured experience, are as windows of the mind or, better still, disciplines of perception and awareness with which one encounters any event and in terms of which the imagination and interpretive powers are quickened. Whatever the mind, so structured, attends to, whether it be some perplexing problem in his immediate experience, the description of some past event, or the pages of scripture, it partakes of the imagery that is formative of meaning because of these disciplines of perception.

This is not to be viewed as the superimposing of a framework of philosophy upon the Bible. Rather, it is to be understood simply as the witness of the Word, reaching the structured mind in ways that are intelligible to disciplined perception. What is there in the Bible is itself actualized event, asserting its revealed world. What is there in the structured mind is the capacity to be both receptive and interpretive, even to be broken and re-created, by the witnessing word.

Now with this meager glimpse of the formative notions shaping my thought, let me turn quickly to the interpretation. The structured imagery which forms in the mind, informed by these fundamental and secondary notions, is that of conscious experience moving with an orbit of structured events, attended by an interpenetrating dimension of mystery.

III

That there is a dimension of mystery which continually attends our experiences, giving them depth of meaning and re-creative occasions, is a conviction that steadily takes hold of the inquiring person who confronts instances of sensitivity and spontaneity such as occur in acts of forgiveness, repentance, and love. This is a minimum conclusion to which emergent thinking comes as it analyzes the movement of faith in the life of the culture and in the human psyche. This re-creative life, though a mystery still, is a sensitive working which has been a resource of renewal and a source of judgment to human effort throughout the long years of cultural history among diverse peoples and places.

Any attempt to inquire directly into the nature of this redemptive good which reaches our human structures in transformative ways is doomed to disappointment. To this extent theologians who have insisted that God must come to man, that man cannot first come to God, have been right. For it is not in the capacity of any given structure to define or to observe as a datum the movement of spontaneous and creative meaning which intrudes with greater sensitivity and import upon its structural order. Some awareness of its emergent quality, of its judgment and transcendent good, may

be possible, though even this will require discernment and humility in the organism to enable it to be receptive to what is other than its habitual path of response and beyond its full comprehension.

The difficulties which theologians have confronted in dealing with this problem of God's coming to men are well known. When the matter is stated in its usual Protestant form, namely, that God, through the work of the Holy Spirit, prepares the heart and mind of those whom he chooses to have respond to his divine initiative, there is, to say the least, an uneasiness about what this can mean. It can be settled, as it has often been settled, by simply insisting that we must accept *on faith* what happens here, that to inquire further into the matter is to trespass upon holy ground.[1] In so saying, however, the Protestant theologian takes a decisive step toward dismissing the relevance of structured meaning, implying by this dismissal that God's work is without structure and thus fortuitous. The absence of a Protestant philosophy of faith and culture stems from this decisive act and its implications.

Now, to be sure, the structures which define and limit man's acts may not be generalized into a divine or absolute order, even when these structures can be defended as being "the highest we know," or as the ideal extension of man's best efforts. The fallacy of the Hegelian dialectic and of Absolute Idealism in general becomes clearer the more this matter is pondered. Likewise, the inclination of most liberal thinking to project its delineations of the ethical good into an affirmation of God's character must be regarded as an overreaching of the human structure. By contrast, the restraint of Kant in his reluctance to cross the boundary of the thing-in-itself appears humble if not actually perceptive. The readiness of the dialectical theologians of our day to stand with Kant on this point, however much they may press his formulation of faith back to its Reformation ground, and to counter all subsequent Idealism with their strictures upon its idolatrous logic, can be understood and defended as a proper sensibility. The scriptural warning that God's ways are not man's ways may not go unheeded by the theologian who would be concerned to give evidence both of discrimination and of proportion in his thinking. This is not simply a matter of religious concern; it is a matter of logic in its most subtle and sensitive form: knowing the limits of one's own logical structure, on the one hand, and, on the other, recognizing how the discernment of faith may enable one to peer through the glass darkly when these boundaries of the human structure are reached in thought.

Yet it becomes obvious, I think, that dialectic theologians, however discerning, cannot do more than repeatedly sound this warning. Theirs becomes a theology of negation for lack of a concern with structures or because of their readiness to dismiss all structured meaning as being man-made and thus irrelevant to the Word of God.

The mystery of depth or transcendence to which Christian theologians have persistently pointed can be spoken of in emergent terms without doing violence to Christian sensibilities. The effort to do so can accomplish two results: first, it can move our thinking suggestively beyond the impasse to which the Kantian *Critiques* brought theological thinking without issuing in an idealism that blurs the distinction between man and God; and, second, it can permit us to engage constructively in understanding the movement of grace and judgment to which the Christian gospel has borne witness. The conviction that this course

of inquiry could open up to us the meaning of the Christian witness and suggestively point up its directives for our time has led me to press constructive theology in this direction. In pursuing this course I have come to certain conclusions which I now set down as summary statements somewhat in the nature of a credo.

1. I believe God to be a reality of grace and judgment which both interpenetrates and transcends the life of man in the way that the hopes and judgments of a father transcend and intermesh with the life of his son. The imagery of parental care which the Hebraic-Christian faith has employed to convey the personal relationship between God and his creatures is sound so long as one does not employ the imagery to reduce God to human stature and thus to mythologize a meaning which really transcends man's mind even as it cradles and nurtures the whole of man's existence.

God stands to man as one structure of meaning stands to another. This is the import of the father-son imagery. The actuality here is, I believe, a matrix of sensitivity and meaning of subtle and vast dimensions, transcending our own— in fact, all human structures—which serves as the ultimate ground of our meaning and the source and center of all that we are and of whatever else we might become in the mystery of creation and re-creation.

God is a structure of infinite goodness and incalculable power. The empirical evidence of this fact is in the working of grace as a redemptive power which carries implications and consequences of judgment in situations of grief, remorse, suffering, dissolution, tragedy, and defeat, and in the creative experiences wherever a foretaste of fulfilment is attained. The historical witness to this fact of God's goodness and power within the Christian community is the biblical ac-.

count of the redemptive work of God in history and the continuing witness of the church to the good discerned in Christ. The confirmation of this empirical observation and the historical witness appears when one seeks to understand the primordial act of creativity metaphysically, wherein sensitivity and what seems to be an ordered concern transmute brute force into meaningful events. The metaphysical analysis of the creative act of God, implicit in every event of actuality, thus renders intelligible what is given more concretely in the historical witness and in present experience.

2. I believe God to be both hidden and discernible. What is hidden is the range and depth of the transcendent structure of meaning which is beyond our comprehension. Our human consciousness and sensibilities, with their limited structure, can only dimly apprehend this dimension of God's meaning. What is discernible is that measure of the concrete nature and working of God which reaches our sensibilities, awareness, and attentive minds. Specifically, it is the concrete working out of creative and redemptive occurrences as these touch our lives in events of joy and sorrow; in experiences of guilt, remorse, judgment, and forgiveness; in the lifting of grief; and in the summit vision of peace, in so far as the human spirit can rise to such fulfilment of meaning.

In my understanding of revelation within the context of emergence, the hiddenness of God refers to the fullness of sensitivity as a transcendent structure of meaning which nevertheless interpenetrates and subsumes every other structure. It is the "not yet" and "beyond" of all that is. It is not wholly remote, since it is immediate, ever present, and efficacious in every event or occasion. Yet it is a depth of mystery to which our structure of consciousness simply cannot at-

tend except in a mood of awe as in a holy presence.

What one says or does here will, in the nature of the case, tend to be an overreaching. So long as it is simply a straining appropriate to the reach of our structure, it need not be an overreaching. On the contrary, it may serve to deepen the sense of dedication and to heighten the mood, if not the meaning, of these events in experience in which the concrete work of God is discernible.

Whether one may presume to reach further into the hidden dimension of sensitivity and meaning in God is, to my mind, a serious and disturbing question. Thus I am led, on emergent grounds, to recoil from mysticism, if not to distrust it. At this point I would seem to converge toward dialectical and existentialist theologies, though my reasons would be stated differently. It would seem that I should be intrigued by the efforts of Gerald Heard, who sees possibilities of impelling the human structure to evolve toward a higher capacity for sensitivity through a more disciplined differentiation of consciousness.[2] To some extent I have been impressed by Heard, but I resist his magic on the same grounds that I distrust the mystic. To bring the human structure to its full capacity of sensitivity and dedication is, I think, our obligation and spiritual aim. But how far can we properly pursue this course without seeming to manipulate the creative process? At this point I find the proportion and the humbling response to God's otherness in Reformation teaching a welcome corrective.

3. I believe Jesus Christ to be the revealer of God and the mediator of God's redemptive work to men. By revelation I mean a decisive instance of a structure of meaning, more complex and sensitive in its relations, breaking with the force of disclosure and re-creative power upon a

more simple structure, thereby impelling it to a new level of awareness and sensitivity. Such an instance would be an encounter between the limited, human consciousness, together with its bodily feelings, and any intimation of a transcendent structure. The gospel story bears witness to such an encounter in the person of the Christ who, in turn, became the mediator of this transcendent structure of meaning within the human community wherever the witness was borne. This means to me that Jesus Christ, though human, embodied in his structure of consciousness the dimension of this transcendent structure and thus actually effected the work of God, not only in human events through the impress of his person upon them, but within the human personality in so far as this matrix of sensitivity which is God's structure could be transmitted and made expressive through human thought and feeling. To the degree that this interpenetration of sensitivity in thought and feeling occurred in the consciousness of Christ, a coalescence of structures occurred in which a novel advance of spirit was made manifest.

The antecedents of this emergent event lay in the developing moral consciousness of the Hebrew people, with its intermittent witness to the redemptive power of God in history, and, to a more limited, yet real, degree, in the developing rational consciousness of the Greek culture, with its persistent search for the sovereign, ethical good.

The sensitivity of spirit conveyed through the parables and narratives of the New Testament expresses a new dimension of goodness to which such terms as "grace" and "judgment," "repentance," "forgiveness," and "love" point. This transcendent good was not wholly unknown to the Hebraic and Greek cultures. Occasional and tenuous strands of its sensitive meaning rise like a mist from the recorded events and reflections of these two historic peoples, as in the more tender and decisive utterances of the prophets or in the more profound and sensitive reaches of Plato's anticipations. But in the gospels this sensitive meaning breaks upon the ear with a release and redemptive power that suggests its full creation as actualized event. The structures of moral and rational good are not denied or disowned, but they are re-created by this novel power of grace and forgiveness. The old structures are as stalks to this flower that is in bloom, whose beauty and promise break upon this company of troubled and disheartened men and women as a new horizon of hope, yet with demands and a counsel of judgment that is inescapable.

The revelation of God in Christ, then, became concrete, dynamic, formative, and impelling within the human structure and in a living community. This was a world event as truly as the atomic bomb, even though, like the release of atomic power, the facilities for its emergence first appeared in but one time and place.

As a novel advance within the human structure, this emergent life of grace and redemptive power has effected "a permanent revolution," to use a familiar phrase.[3] The culture of the West has never been the same since its innovation. And it continues to release men from their restrictive egoism as well as from the mechanisms of their own humanly contrived orders of logic and justice, enabling them to participate, in part, in this more sensitive order of meaning, despite the dominating frustration of their characteristically human structures. Thus the cruelty and folly of this human structure, tempered at times, to be sure, by a sense of virtue and idealized good, which at best is ambiguous and unstable, is continually under the judgment of this perennial innovation of spirit and within reach of its redemptive good as well. To have Christian faith is to affirm the reality of this redemptive power as a continuing and ever present energy of judgment and grace.

This grace and judgment, issuing from the transcendent structure of sensitivity and meaning which is God, reaches the structures of cultures through both mediated and immediate ways. As I see the matter, the revelation in Christ became a cultural energy in the West which assumed structure and dynamic power through the symbolisms and organizational witness of repentant and dedicated men and women, the emerging community of witness. Christ is therefore more than a memory in the minds of living Christians. He is the persisting structure of sensitive meaning which works at the level of cultural institutions and creative effort, pointing men to the real energy of grace in their midst. By whatever metaphysics one may designate this persistent force of the living Christ, one must acknowledge it to be formatively present within the mythos of our culture to which we bear witness in innumerable ways.

4. I believe the Holy Spirit to be real God. As Christian language has employed this term, the Holy Spirit is the immediate working of the concrete nature of God. It is the discernible and apprehendable working of God in human nature and events in so far as there is a direct and immediate encounter between God and man's present, structured experience. In saying that the Holy Spirit is real God, I mean to acknowledge that it is the actual working of God in human life; but in being discerned or apprehended its working partakes of the ambiguities of the human structure: i.e., its actual effects contend with the limitations,

in part to transform them, but under conditions imposed by the sensibilities, consciousness, and will of the human structure.

There are two reasons for this limitation upon the working of the Holy Spirit. One is that the "Comforter" is inevitably the power of God conceived in relation to explicit human needs and demands. This means that God, as Holy Spirit, stands to the human consciousness as the parent stands to the child. In the child's experience of the parent there is a focusing upon realities which are explicitly relevant to his needs and demands. The child is often oblivious to the nature of the parent in his fulness of meaning as a person. What this person he calls father or mother was before the child himself appeared or what each of them is in roles which are assumed beyond the family circle may be of little moment or as nothing to the child's world as it intersects that of the parent. At best it may be but an ambiguous fact of the past or of the remote present of which the child can make little sense. To be sure, much of the meaning of the parent, his hopes, his compulsions, his anxieties, all of which affect the child's present experience, are of a piece with the complex of mystery which supervenes upon what the child views as the actual parent. Yet the parent is known to the child and responded to by him through a role and within capacities which have been called into play by the demands of the parent-child situation. The analogy has its difficulties, but I mean to suggest that, similarly, God as Holy Spirit, God in his concrete nature, tends to be known and experienced within the human structure in terms that are defined and restricted by the purview imposed by men's practical purposes.

But the ambiguities of this encounter arise also from the structural limitations of the human consciousness by which

God is apprehended. Thus the visible working of God as known and experienced tends to be distorted or fragmented by the way that the human situation bends God to man's purposes and perspectives. To a considerable degree, then, the work of God in human life is subject to the limitations and obstructions of the human structure. God as Holy Spirit, a sensitive structure interpenetrating other structures, must work through such structures. Operationally, then, the work of God or the actualization of his purposes in human life can be no more than the yield of this interpenetration.

Shailer Mathews used to speak of Calvin's doctrine of the inner working of the Holy Spirit as an anticipation of the liberal concept of religious experience. This, I think, is what one would have to say within any one of the philosophic frameworks of liberal theology. The advance of process or emergent thinking over liberalism in its earlier philosophical orientations is indicated by the ability of the emergent formulation to recapture the objective working of God in this notion of Holy Spirit, while at the same time giving full account of its identity within the human consciousness and experience.

5. I believe that the work of Christ as mediator of redemption and the work of the Holy Spirit may be distinguished; yet they stand related. By reason of the work of Christ, the work of the Holy Spirit (as the concrete nature of God) actually reaches men and transforms them, if not by reconstructing their conscious lives, at least by quickening their sense of sin, their awareness of a good not their own, and, possibly, by impelling them to an affection for this good that is of God. Christ thus becomes the re-creative or redemptive energy within culture, in part because of the symbolism that arises about his life and work, in part because of the sentiment awakened within the Christian community centering in the revelation in Christ but also because of the persistent witness to him at all levels of human discourse. If one is to carry forward the emergent interpretation of the gospel, one must take this redemptive activity seriously. In doing so, one would be on the way to developing a cultural conception of revelation to which cultural anthropology could speak significantly.

One cannot speak of this cultural mediation of redemptive energy as the work of the Holy Spirit, for it is not the concrete work of God in its immediacy. It is, rather, the revelatory event of Christ continuing as a redemptive activity within culture and within the structures of human personality through the medium of witness, thereby providing conditions within the human structures for the working of the Holy Spirit as a direct and immediate interpenetration of the transcendent structure of sensitivity. Culturally speaking, this continuing redemptive energy, preparing men to respond to the work of grace as a direct impartation of the Holy Spirit, is the living Christ within the social organism.

This observation points us back to the resurrection as an inescapable facet of the Christian faith. The overcoming of death in the resurrection remains a mystery so far as its ultimate import is concerned. The recognition that Christ as redemptive energy survived the Cross is simply the discernible event within the human structure of consciousness. There is a hiddenness here, just as there is a hiddenness in God as transcendent. This is not to imply a "nonmaterial presence of some kind" or a nonmaterial order supervening upon what is discernible structure. It implies, rather, that just as the structure of meaning, which is available as explicit meaning to the human consciousness, moves continually upon a frontier of sensitivity that points to a more subtle and complex order of meaning; so every occurrence within nature and in human history carries adumbrations of meaning beyond its discernible dimensions. This is why we can speak of the height and depth of existence in intelligible terms, intimations of which do come to us in vivid encounters with God's concrete nature or with the witness to Christ's revelatory event. So long as this is true, we cannot properly truncate any event, least of all one so charged with intimations of emergent or transcendent meaning as the resurrection of Jesus Christ.

The import of this observation is to affirm the revelation of God in Christ as discernible and available redemptive energy within the culture in the form of a ministry of both grace and judgment and to live in Christian hope in the face of dissolution, death, and tragedy by way of affirming the openness of events in so far as they participate in the structure of sensitive meaning transcending the human frame of conscious existence.

6. I believe that the church is the self-conscious and continuing witness to the revelation of God in Christ. As such it is a cultural organism. It is the body of Christ through which the sensibilities of faith are mediated. The church is a distinctive and exceedingly precious instrument of grace, being the organic, cultural carrier of the revelatory event in all the ways that are suggested by a concern with doctrine, worship, pageantry, creative art, and the ministry of prophetic action as these persist through the care and dedicated labors of the believing community. In this sense, the church is the responsible bearer of the formative myth as it articulates the import of the revelatory event. To the degree that it is faithful to this obligation it remains the luminous center of its witness within the culture.

Yet, being a corporate expression of the human structure, however selective and dedicated it may be, the church is a fallible instrument of grace. Its failings have been enormous to the point of being an offense to the Christian faith. The evidence of this betrayal is clearly documented in the record of the church's climb to power and its struggle to cope with the issues of faith and culture in every generation since the inception of its role as a witnessing community.

The sources of these persistent failings are to be traced, in part, to the ambiguity of human goodness, however expressed: whether in the solitary efforts of individual men or in the corporate strategies of institutional enterprises. They are to be traced in part to the problem implicit in the relation of power and goodness and to the complexity of relating the demands of religion and culture, respectively. Yet the crux of the matter seems to lie basically in the indecisive character of the witness itself. The church, in one expression of its institutional role, has been prone to arm itself with the power of God and to assert its authority as an ambiguous voice of the divine, forgetting its frailty as a human structure and, by this very act of self-deception, becoming less and less perceptive of the quality of infinite goodness to which, presumably, it has borne witness. In this self-assumed status of a divine monarch, the church has wielded the power of its prestige over culture with little concern for or recognition of the sensitive working which is the essence of grace. And, conversely, where it has relaxed its authoritarian temper in seeking to serve as a community of believers, the church has dissipated both the power and the goodness implicit in its witness through an easygoing identification of piety with faith or of gregarious sentiment with the dedicated work of the kingdom.

The good that is discerned in Christ, that is disclosed in the revelatory event of Christ, exhibits a peculiar and even paradoxical interrelation of power and goodness. The power is a "gentle might" of infinite consequences, as the parables of the kingdom insistently portray. The goodness is a working of grace with inescapable intimations of judgment. To be equal, in some measure at least, to the task of witnessing to this good-not-our-own within the culture, the church must recover this sense of "the mystery of the kingdom," with its interplay of gentleness and incalculable power and its unrelenting message of judgment and grace..

That God was in Christ, reconciling the world to himself, thus becomes a formidable fact of history—a fact of overwhelming importance to each living man. It is the decisive event which sets all events and human structures in a radically altered perspective. For the structures of moral and rational good, the virtues of law and the logic of cause and effect, though not wholly canceled, are subsumed and transcended, even transmuted, by the spontaneity, the freedom, and the grace of forgiving love. As the act of forgiveness may transcend the impasse that has formed under the demands of causal connections and bring healing to the broken relationship, so the structure of consciousness in which grace and love are regulative transmutes and redeems the brokenness of men.

But this is a judgment upon us as well as the source of our hope. For this Kingdom of Good not our own, attending and transcending our every moment of existence, sets the limits and limitations of our structured human life in stark relief, exposing the depth of our human evil and revealing, too, the ambiguity of our human good. All have come short of the glory of God. All *will* come short. In this sense, judgment remains. But forgiveness implies a realistic understanding of this human predicament against the background of grace, not in the sense that all evil is tolerated but that man in his failure to attain the good, man in his shortcomings, will be accepted, when there is a contrite will to be so received, and that, in some sense, if one is to retain his sanity, he must accept himself as the forgiven man. Redemption is a social doctrine which removes the sense of guilt, the sense of failure and remorse in the penitent heart, without relaxing the hunger for righteousness and the love of goodness.

There is a goodness beyond our own efforts that works silently on in experience and in history to redeem us from the consequences that would otherwise follow were it not to intercede. In the midst of the evil that well-nigh overwhelms us, in the face of our human failings and the tragic consequences that tear at our hearts, there is a working of grace and of suffering love that confounds the measure of our days. For the God that was in Christ, reconciling the world unto himself, is the living God and the ultimate measure of our days.

NOTES

1. Cf. John Calvin, *The Institutes of the Christian Religion*, Book III, chap. ii, sec. vii, p. 496; also chap. xv, sec. ii, p. 197.

2. Cf. Gerald Heard, *The Eternal Gospel* (New York: Harper & Bros., 1946); see also his *The Ascent of Man* (1929), *The Source of Civilization* (1937), *The Third Morality* (1937), *Time, Sex, and Pain* (1939).

3. Reinhold Niebuhr ascribes the phrase originally to Trotsky. Cf. H. R. Niebuhr's use of it in *The Kingdom of God in America* (Chicago, 1937) and *The m_ning of Revelation* (New York, 1941); see also Bernard M. Loomer, "Neo-Naturalism and Neo-Orthodoxy," *Journal of Religion*, XXVIII (April), 89.

THE NEW LANGUAGE IN RELIGION 11

By *Bernard Eugene Meland*

Pomona College

Claremont, California

Much that is being written in philosophy of religion today is unintelligible to the lay reader. He may think it is because his mind does not follow deep thought readily. He may be right in his case; but not all of the difficulty is with him. Part of it arises from the radical change of meaning in the fundamental concepts of religion. For in its contemporary philosophical form, religion speaks a new language. It is the language of dynamic process. Its vocabulary is filled with words and phrases such as *interaction, creativity, environing activities, adjustment, flux of experience, empirical reality, growth, fulfilment,* etc. In this language, man's chief end is to grow and to fulfil his life upon the earth.

This was not the language of the *old time religion.* Our fathers spoke of change, but they mentioned the word with proud lips. "Change and decay in all around I see," they sang, "but Thou who changest not, abide with me." In this world of thought, man sought escape from the world of change, not fulfilment through its process. God, rather than being a reality in the creative process, was a being above and beyond the temporal scene of change.

I.

The preference for a static deity is a very old habit of thought in western philosophy. It goes back at least to Plato. Plato developed a theory of the universe in which the contrast between rest and motion became focal. Constancy and flux characterized for him two diverse realms. On the one hand, there was the world of every-day experience in which change and perishing were dominant tendencies: on the other was the realm of eternal forms or ideas which were changeless and fixed.

This changing character of the world of experience was for Plato evidence of its unreality. The changeless quality of the world of ideas was a guarantee of its genuine reality. In this view of the universe, Plato portrays God as an intermediary Being who rescues man's rational soul from the life of flux by influencing him to aspire to association with the static world of eternal forms.

Aristotle removed the stigma of unreality from the world of common experience, but he failed to give it genuine significance; for he identified God with Plato's Supreme Good, which remained, as in Plato's thought, distantly removed from these common scenes of flux and change. In Plotinus this separation was made more complete by a view of intelligence and a view of deity which could only lead to the conclusion that the divine realm was inaccessible to human intelligence. Augustine struggled to meliorate this estrangement by introducing into the Neo-platonic picture the Hebrew conception of a personal God of history, a deity with whom men might commune in person, provided they came within the orbit of His being. But the orbit of God was a static order above the world of change: and man attained identification with it at the price of becoming alienated from the world of experience.

We are accustomed to saying that in the time of Thomas Aquinas, when medieval theology discovered Aristotle, there was a sharp turning away from the Platonic tradition which had dominated Christian thought since Augustine; but we should not let this assertion obscure the fact that the revival of Aristotle in the philosophy of Aquinas did not eliminate Platonic elements which had persisted in the thought of Aristotle. One of these elements was the concept of a static deity, operating above the realm of change. To be sure, Aristotle's doctrine of *teleology*, which reappears in Aquinas, brought the world of flux and the eternal order into more intimate association than had ever occurred in the Platonic universe; but this did not alter the basic pattern of thought which placed deity outside the world of change.

The age of mathematical rationalism which produced the systems of Descartes and Spinoza returned the conception of deity to a static nature nearer to the mathematical pattern of Plato. For Spinoza, in fact, God was the mathematical order of the universe. "Whatever the difference between his God and the God tradition," writes H. A. Wolfson in *the Philosophy of Spinoza*, "Spinoza seems to say at the beginning of this new chapter in the *Ethics* that his God does not differ from the traditional God in the matter of eternity." It is true that Spinoza used the word *eternal* in at least three senses, but when applied to God, he, himself, said "Eternal" can mean only immutable.

Despite their differences, then, the generations of thinkers from Plato to Spinoza were influenced in their thinking upon God, and upon other matters pertaining to religious concerns, by one underlying assumption: That assumption was that the basic reality of the world was a mathematical reality. Until fairly recent times, all philosophic thought in the west subscribed to this mathematical picture of reality, and was therefore shaped by it. Hence the portrayals of ultimate reality have represented God as a static being, and the things of supreme value, as static, unchanging realities. The result has been, as Whitehead has said in *Modes of Thought*, that "the most evident characteristic of our experience has been dismissed into a subordinate role in metaphysical construction." Whitehead continues:

"We live in a world of turmoil. Philosophy and religion, as influenced by orthodox philosophic thought, dismiss turmoil. Such dismissal is the outcome of tired decadence. We should beware of philosophies which express the dominant emotions of periods of slow social decay. Our inheritance of philosophic thought is infected with the decline and fall of the Roman Empire, and with the decadence of eastern civilizations. It expresses the exhaustion following upon the first three thousand years of advancing civilization. A better balance is required. For civilizations rise as well as fall. We require philosophy to explain the rise of types of order, the transitions from type to type, and the mixture of good and bad involved in the universe as it stands self-evident in our experience."

The key to modern metaphysics is to be found in this concluding sentence of Whitehead's. The modern philosopher is concerned with the story of *emergents* and *transitions* and *fulfilments*. In short, with the story of process. And he is concerned with understanding the deep-lying spiritual problem that is raised by the inescapable inseparableness of good and evil discerned in a world in process. Hence the thought-climate of philosophy and religion has changed. Instead of a God who "changest not," the modern philosopher has come to know a God who makes all things new. And in that incessant creativity, he seeks to find the meaning of his own existence, and the meaning of all that is.

II.

This *temporalizing of the Chain of Being*, as Professor Lovejoy puts it, was one of the principal happenings in eighteenth century thought. Seeds of a new view of deity in the role of a Creative Power, he suggests, are to be found in the writings of Leibniz, Kant, Robinet, and Schelling. But they are only seeds. The new orientation of deity as a creative working in the temporal-spatial world was to develop increasingly in the nineteenth century, and to emerge as a great ground-swell in our own day.

Yet this development was to be overshadowed throughout the nineteenth century and the early years of the present one by a venture in philosophy in which basic reality was conceived neither as a static being nor as a creative participant in the world process. Between the era initiated by Plato and concluded, shall we say, by Spinoza, when deity was viewed as static being, and the very recent era, stands the Great Interlude—Idealism. The prophetic voice of this Great Interlude was Immanuel Kant. His *Critique of Pure Reason* cut through the steel strands that held together the mighty structures of the rational era. The falling of these rational towers of Babel rendered the objective

144

and the subjective worlds apart. Man was left with his own consciousness. The *thing-in-itself* hovered over him as a mysterious unknown, now become unknowable.

The agnosticism and subjectivism of subsequent years took its rise, there can be no doubt, in this decisive critique by Kant. But there was to rise from it also a most amazing development in quite an opposite direction. When Kant intimated that "the mysterious unknown, concealed behind the phenomena of sense, might possibly be identical with the unknown in ourselves," he opened up a path of thinking that was to lead to enormous speculative consequences. This was to lead to Absolute Idealism. Although Kant failed to carry out the implication of this seed idea, other German idealists, especially Fichte, and later Schelling and Hegel, were to make it the basis for their impressive systems of thought. Here the human ego became the key to understanding the Absolute Ego. In Fichte and Schelling the Absolute is still transcendent: but in Hegel, deity becomes completely immanent. As one contemporary writer states it, "If we mean by God the being transcending human reason, then Hegel is the most atheistic of philosophers since no one is more emphatic in affirming the immanency and perfect knowableness of the absolute." (Weber and Perry, *History of Philosophy*)

While Absolute Idealism may appear to be a further stage in "temporalizing the Chain of Being" it was not really so. Rather, it represents a departure from that tendency. One might even go so far as to say that when all things are considered, the world of deity swallows up the world of temporal existence in the philosophy of Absolute Idealism. All is resolved in the Absolute Ego; hence existences have no reality of their own, really. Every existent thing is but a facet of the Absolute.

One recognizes in the philosophy of both Royce and Hocking an earnest attempt to bring a more empirical content into the concept of the Absolute. This applies more particularly to the later stages of Royce's thought. Hocking's view of God as the Absolute Knower known directly through sense experience whose character gives reality to all social experience and to nature, brings Absolute Idealism to the threshold of Empiricism. It is the nearest, in fact, that any Absolute philosophy comes to a recognition of the empirical datum.

It would be an interesting study to trace through the turns of thought in philosophies which have reacted against Absolute Idealism in the sense of denying the Absolute Ego. What one would find, I am sure, is that in these instances, there was little more than a reduction of capital letters to small case letters all along the line, leaving the human ego the substitute for deity with accompanying postulates of Idealism concerning the human consciousness remaining. Is it possible that the religious humanism arising out of pragmatism and, for that matter, the humanistic emphasis that has always been manifested in the Instrumentalism of John Dewey, are but reactions against the concept of the Absolute Ego, without, however, any fundamental modification of the primary premise of Absolute Idealism? Instead of speaking of Religious Humanism as a *truncated supernaturalism*, we might rather speak of it as a truncated Absolute Idealism. This at least would get at the philosophical peculiarities of this position, and throw some light, I am sure, upon issues that now divide The Religious Humanists and the New Theists of the naturalistic group.

III.

Returning, now, to the main argument of our survey, if the seeds of the new orientation of deity were evident in eighteenth century philosophies, the forthright expression of this identification of deity with the temporal passage of events occurs for the first time in the writings of Bergson, and becomes full-blown as a naturalistic theism in the organismic philosophy of the British group, including Whitehead, C. Lloyd Morgan, Jan Smuts, and S. Alexander. In this country, development toward a naturalistic theism has come to fruition in the writings of Henry Nelson Wieman. A more detailed analysis of the rise of this new naturalism and its general outlook may now be given.

Prior to the nineteenth, century, naturalism was hardly anything more than a protest against the supernatural in the name of reason; or, in its sentimental form, a romantic effort to soften the shock of rationalism through emotional rapport with the world of nature.   The turn toward a genuine naturalism began with the writings of Lamarck, but did not significantly shape philosophical conceptions until the publication of Darwin's *Origin of the Species* in 1859.   During the decades immediately following this event, philosophical pictures of the world, based upon the evolutionary theory, began to take shape. These early naturalistic philosophies could not possibly go beyond the agnosticism of Herbert Spencer, for they were premature generalizations upon the newly discovered facts of the physical sciences.   The decade of the eighteen seventies might well, in fact, be regarded as the peak of the materialistic era.

The philosophical beginnings of the new naturalism, as Whitehead has pointed out in *Science and the Modern World*, date back to the closing decades of the nineteenth century when "the notion of mass was losing its unique preeminence as being the one permanent quantity."   Energy displaced matter as the fundamental concept.   Mass became a name for "a quantity of energy considered in relation to some of its dynamical effects."   At the close of the century, orthodox materialism, which up to that time had reigned supreme, was being rapidly undermined.

Whitehead attributes to William James the inauguration of the new stage in philosophy in the publication of his essay, "Does Consciousness Exist?", which first appeared in 1904 in *The Journal of Philosophy, Psychology, and Scientific Methods*.   In this essay, James denied that the word "consciousness" stands for an entity and insisted that it connotes a *function*.   In so doing, says Whitehead, James was challenging a conception of the mind which had been initiated by Descartes in his *Discourse on Method*, published in 1637, thus bringing to an end a philosophical period which had undergirded scientific materialism for two hundred and fifty years.   The full import of this decisive step away from materialistic naturalism becomes clearer when one realizes that with James, philosophy moved beyond the habit of thinking in terms of physical notions and entered upon an era in which physiology was to provide its basic language.

While James must be credited with initiating the method of thinking that was to create the new naturalism, the introduction of the physiological language into philsophy must be attributed to Bergson, whose memorable volume *Creative Evolution*, published in 1911, stands as the pioneer work in evolutionary naturalism. How close James and Bergson were in their pioneering thrusts in this direction can be appreciated best by perusing their exchange of letters. Bergson and James both reacted against the mathematical view of the world in favor of a philosophy drawn from concrete experience. Their differences doubtless arose, as Professor Perry has suggested in his *The Thought and Character of William James*, from the fact that James took Darwin as his scientific guide, while Bergson preferred to follow Lamarck. Bergson chose Lamarck rather than Darwin on the grounds that the former's view of evolution provided an explanation of the adaptation of organisms, enabling different parts and different combinations of causes to effect similar results. The explanation of this convergence of effects 1e found in an inner directing principle whch the Lamarckian nterpretation admitted, and which the Darwinian view did not. This no doubt accounts for the more subjective and mystical character of Bergson's thought, as compared with James' radical empiricism.

Bergson is best remembered for his exciting doctrine of the *elan vital*, and perhaps for his theory of the intellect, which made of mind little more than a candid camera; but more important than either of these, and more lasting in its impression upon modern p. :osophical and religious thought, was his concept of time, for which he used the term *duration*. It is common to amplify Bergson's meaning of duration by saying that he conceived of time as indivisible and thereby unmeasurable; but a more positive way of stating it is to say he viewed time as organic,a rich medium of multiple experience in which life spans were moving toward fulfilment, in which events of creation and dissolution were forever happening, and in which seasons changed, tides turned, and civilizations rose and fell with the imperceptibleness of growth itself. In fact, the term *growth* has come to replace Bergson's term *duration*, and rightly so; for it gives to this concept the dynamic and creative character which Bergson really intended.

The full import of this amplified view of time as duration and growth has not, it seems to me, been sufficiently recognized. Having become so accustomed to the pragmatists' dismissal of metaphysical reality in the empirical dictum, *reality is what it is experienced as*, which brings to mind a truncated view of reality, we are inclined to look upon every naturalistic theory of life as another form of truncation. Naturalism means ignoring the superstructure, so we assume. Or one says, empiricism is empiricism, however differently dressed. But this is not true. The empiricism of pure experience which arbitrarily ascribes boundaries to reality for philosophical purposes, as was done in pragmatism, is bound to lead to a humanistic basis for religious thought, in whch the reality *experienced* becomes, in fact, *human* reality, specified as the concourse of human minds, or the social environment. Dissatisfied with this humanly circumscribed reality in its truncated form, one might, as did James, hold open the possibility that the higher human phase of experience is "coterminous and continuous with a MORE of the same quality, which is operative in the universe outside of him, and which he can keep in working touch with, and in a fashion get on board of and save himself when all his lower being has gone to pieces" (*Varieties of Religious Experience*, p. 508). Or he may proceed to enlarge the meaning and importance of the human environment, to give it heroic dimensions, and to cherish it as a rare and precious spiritual fruition of earth forces in the vast and desolate spaces of cosmic wastelands. Empiricism in this truncated form has always led back to some compromised theory of dualism, or to a more rash relinquishment of superhuman meaning in the universe.

The empiricism which stems from Bergson's view of duration, and which finds formulation in the new philosophic amplification of growth, has abandoned this truncation view once and for all. It has always seemed to me that the chief significance of Wieman's work, especially in his book, *Religious Experience and Scientific Method*, lay in his giving decisive and clear expression to this turn of thought in empiricism. He cut through the rather insulated view of pragmatism and came to terms, head on, with the issue dividing naturalistic and supernaturalistic thought. One way of stating it is to say that he let go of supernaturalism in a way that enabled him to embrace a full-orbed naturalism. Hence, the tendency to shunt off metaphysical problems, with its truncating effects, so evident in pragmatism and humanism, has given way in Wieman's thought to a fresh and forthright empirical approach to the whole of objective reality as it impinges upon man's world. I think this comes out most clearly in passages in his *Religious Experience and Scientific Method* where he attempts to move beyond the position of William James. To the suggestion that in order to have access to the spiritual world we must turn away from the material world, Wieman exclaims, "No! That is the pitiful blunder that always leads to confusion—the path that leads out into the morass where nothing but dreams and will-o'-the-wisps can be found. . . If the spiritual is to be found at all," he insists, "it must be found in and through the material. The same senses that reveal the material must also reveal the spiritual. And, in fact, is that not very plainly the way in which we become cognizant of, say, other human minds which are spiritual entities, if the word spiritual has any significance at all."

One should not infer from this statement that Wieman's religious naturalism stems from the philosophy of Bergson. His religious thought may best be described as the confluence of the two streams of empiricism, issuing from Bergson, through the organic philosophies of Whitehead and others, and the empiricism of William and John Dewey. His repudiation of Bergson's anti-intellectualism indicates a fundamental divergence from his view; yet this should not blind one to affinities between Bergson's concept of duration and Wieman's use of the term growth. Both men see in the events of experience operations that carry mystical overtones, beyond the biological concept. While Bergson was content to leave the matter with a modified vitalistic explanation, Wieman is concerned to give the concept growth more definitive meaning in terms of sub-human and human operations, and operations that go beyond both these areas. But the pattern of thinking, in each case, remains the same, as distinct from that which underlies the philosophy of Dewey, Ames, and other pragmatists.

This observation may throw light upon differences that divide Wieman and Ames. Many noted a kinship between their views; yet each of these two men is aware that their positions do differ. Wieman senses in Ames a humanistic bent; Ames sees in Wieman's view a survival of the habit of spatializing deity. Both men are justified. For Ames' thought is essentially grounded in the humanistic soil of pragmatism, though he has sought to go beyond humanism, employing the conceptualist method for defining his theistic position. This has given him a concept of God which gives focus to recognized social values that have religious import, but a God that has conceptual meaning only, not existential implications; although, of course, the values so idealized do exist and genuinely affect the course of things. Wieman, on the other hand, as we have said, holds to the conception of a diety that is designative, a reality whose operations, in a minimum way, can be specified and recognized. Thus, while many of their terms are alike, and, in so far as fundamental human values are concerned, their religious interests converge, their philosophic positions differ markedly.

The spiritual, then, if, as Wieman says, it is to have any meaning at all, becomes the rich-fullness of experience that is ever potential with new meaning and new actualization as human life yields to the creativity that shapes it toward yet-unrealized ends.

This is close to the humanistic theism expressed in Dewey's *A Common Faith*, but it differs at the point where religious naturalism goes beyond pragmatism, namely, in the recognition of operations in this flux of experience, making for the actualization of value, which are more-than-human functionings, more than man's purposes, more than the fruits of human imagination. In *The Growth of Religion* (pp. 327-28), Wieman writes:

> "Growth which is creative synthesis is superhuman. The outcome of creative synthesis can never be foreseen by the human mind until after instances of the same kind of synthesis have been observed. It is never the work of human mind. It occurs spontaneously when the required conditions are present. All growth is of this sort. It is superhuman although men can and often do provide the conditions which are required for the miracle to occur."

Man's part in growth, according to Wieman, is to provide the required conditions under which growth might occur. Then, as a gardener, he waits in wonder to watch the miracle happen.

IV.

In a philosophy of Religion in which God and growth have become inseparable and indistinguishable, the language of religion not only takes on new words, but gives to old words new meaning. Religious naturalists have argued among themselves as to whether religious thinking is served better or worse by attempts to salvage old terms that have become freighted with precious meaning; or, whether religion would not be better served by striking out boldly, in the interest of clarity, to fashion a new language altogether. It is clear that they cannot avoid creating new terms. With what has the old religion to do with words like *concretion, creativity, the growth of connections?* One can find their counterpart in terms like *incarnation, creator, the work of love,* or *the Holy Spirit;* but what worlds apart in meaning! Much that is not meant becomes implied; much that is meant, is uncommunicated.

Similar objection may be made to clinging to old terms even where comparable meanings are more evident, as in the terms *God, sin, salvation, and prayer.* Wieman has argued for their continued use with some persuasion, saying that we are doing no differently here than we have done as a matter of course in other areas of thought. Have we abandoned the word Earth because we came upon the discovery that it is spherical instead of the flat disc the ancients thought it was? Have we ceased speaking of the Sun because, with the vanishing of solar faiths, we no longer ascribe powers of deity to it? No, we have continued to use these terms, adjusting our understanding of them to the meanings we now know them to have. So with these ancient words of the religious vocabulary: There must still be a word to designate that Reality upon which man and all life depends for its maximum support and growth. Whether or not we ascribe to it all that the ancients attributed to it, we may still call it God, says Wieman. There must still be a word to express that hideous and dark vein in man's nature that makes him recalcitrant and resistant to the growth of good. We may not wish to bring into our meaning the mythology of ancient lore, but we may still call this tendency by the age-old word, Sin. Likewise, there must still be a word to describe what takes place when this recalcitrance and resistance is overcome, so that men yield to the working of that creativity which is God, becoming transformed in character and purpose, and empowered with capacity to embrace a new life of meaning and value. It would be a mistake to suggest that by this experience one has become uprooted from the world of sense, and destined toward another world of spirit, as was thought in ancient times; yet the world Salvation, divested of this ancient meaning, may still express this new birth that transforms life and makes it new.

This is not the place to raise the question whether or not this procedure in religious naturalism is justified or sound. We are interested here merely to record the fact that while the new orientation of religious thought has given rise to a new language in religion, there is strong insistence in the direction of retaining old terms, enlarging their meaning, through explanation where possible, but more important, by associating them with activities and habits that accomplish the religious end that is sought.

Where this is accomplished satisfactorily, however, we have

a new language, whether we use the same words or not. That is to say, we communicate meanings that differ from the meanings of the older faith. Commitment to God, for example, becomes identification with an operation in this world of sense, superhuman though it may be, not disdain for these earthly hills. Being *saved*, yes, being *saved through grace*, implies being released to participate with fuller sensory powers in this wide, wide planetary life, not being resued from this earthly pilgrimage.

If, then, the result of our communication, when intelligently and satisfactorily achieved, conveys new meaning and accomplishes a new orientation for pursuing a significant life, the question arises, is anything really gained, or is something probably lost, by this conscientious effort to speak in a familiar tongue?

What is gained, obviously, is that it renders this new meaning communicable to masses of people for whom the new language would be utterly unintelligible. And this points to a familiar process, one that has generally followed upon the work of new prophets in religion where fresh insight has been disclosed: namely, the process of accommodation. In such adaptation, the new has been absorbed into the old in such a way that it ceases to be new, and becomes only a fresh and different exposition of the familiar theme. This has occurred over and over again in religious movements. It is what occurred in the rise of popular adaptations of religious innovations that resulted in Mahayana Buddhism, in popular Hinduism, and in the Catholic Christianity of common men. In all these instances, the fresh insight of a religious movement was accommodated to a social mind which could not, or would not, respond to innovation.

It would seem that wherever there is innovation in religious thinking, periods of accommodation follow in which new insights become clothed in a familiar language. There is some evidence that religious empiricism, in the new form that it is taking among theistic naturalists, is entering upon the early stage of such a period of accommodation. If this process continues, rapprochement between Christianity and the new naturalism might very well develop, and a new chapter in the growth of popular Christianity will have been written. The disturbing question that follows upon this suggestion is, Can the new language which has temporarily arisen, and which gives zest to creative thinking in religion, survive this accommodation? It has not done so in historic faiths. 'And this may indicate that language cannot continue or develop in any permanent way, even as tools of inquiry, apart from a cultus or some organizational group. Yet, if freshness of insight is to survive accommodation, if a sharp edge of inquiry is to persist so as to continue exploration along the new frontier of faith, the new language in religion must be kept alive. For in its defined meaning, and only through use of its clarified concepts, can a growing edge of religious truth be maintained.

Analogy and Myth 12
in Postliberal Theology

This is an occasion for which one can have only gratitude and praise; for it is a time for honoring the achievements of a colleague. But I sense an even more heartening cause for rejoicing as I hear some of the young theologians talk here in the Southwest who recognize a significant thrust toward a new focus of theological thinking in what their colleague, Schubert Ogden, has done. There are intimations of excitement, zeal, and dedication peering out from behind words they use in describing this event to others. There are signs that a movement of life is astir here, and that something of extraordinary importance to many who are present here is being observed and celebrated in this colloquy. This is what gives depth and intensity to this occasion; and we who have been brought in from other centers of learning to participate in this colloquy cannot fail to be caught up in the lure and zest of this creative ferment.

If I may speak personally for a moment, as one who shared in his earlier years of preparation and study, I must say that I enjoy a measure of pride and a great deal of satisfaction in the present attainments and promise of Schubert Ogden. I take this occasion to express my congratulations, and those of my university, his Alma Mater, to him as well as to his colleagues in Perkins School of Theology.

We are gathered here this afternoon, not simply to praise him, but to take seriously the words Schubert Ogden has spoken through this published work *Christ Without Myth*. There is, of course, no greater praise one can give one than to take his words seriously, to be moved by their stimulus, even to react and to resist their incitement, or to counter their claims upon us. It will become obvious to you that I have taken this work seriously, for it speaks to issues which have concerned me deeply in recent years. To illustrate to you how vitally I have responded to what Schubert Ogden has to say, I found myself, while reading the galley proof of this book, reading a paragraph and then writing a page, either in response or in reaction to what he had said. I had to give that up, for at that rate I could see that my paper would exceed the length of the book.

This book is more than a presentation and critique of another theologian's method.

It is a clarion call to reassert the claims of liberal theology within the range of insights now available to us, and in response to new demands and responsibilities which now make their claim upon us. The sharpness with which Dr. Ogden has focused the alternatives in contemporary theology, gives to the present theological task a vividness of purpose and direction which must immediately win our response and gratitude. Even when we take issue with the way he describes some of these alternatives, or the judgment he makes concerning them, we find the clarity of perspective which he has brought to the consideration of these issues significant and helpful.

The patient and meticulous manner in which Ogden delineates the one alternative that is central to his concern, namely, the theological method of Rudolf Bultmann, bespeaks his scholarly temper of mind. There is, to be sure, a vivid display of passion and intensity of feeling as he fends off Bultmann's critics. Like a hard running defensive back, Ogden blocks out one critic after another, enabling Bultmann to come within range of scoring. Then a peculiar thing happens. Just as you expect to see Bultmann crossing the goal line, Ogden turns and blocks him out. This would be strange behavior on the football field. In the theological field, however, this is not unusual. Somehow the critic in us always wins out, as he shall in the paper I am now presenting.

But Professor Ogden's criticisms of Bultmann rest upon so substantial an agreement with the alternative he presents that one must view this final maneuver at the goal line, not as that of negating Bultmann, but of carrying his theological method to a surer victory in establishing a basis for a post-liberal theology.

Since I am the first speaker in the colloquy, it is necessary for me to state briefly what is at issue in this book.

The problem centers around the phrase which Bultmann has made famous, "the demythologizing of the New Testament."

This problem comes to the front in Bultmann's theology because of his conviction, as Schubert Ogden has said, that "if theological work is properly pursued, it is neither speculative nor scientific in an 'objective' sense, but rather *existentiell*, that is, a type of thinking inseparable from one's most immediate understanding of oneself as a person." Bultmann is concerned "to unfold . . . the *existentiell* self-understanding implicit in Christian faith." Such a self-understanding, says Ogden, has a specific object and content. "It is a self-understanding that is realized . . . in response to the word of God encountered in the proclamation of Jesus Christ. It is always faith in the Kerygma, in the revealed word expressed in the New Testament and made concretely present in the proclamation of the church."

> If this understanding of the nature of theology is taken seriously, however, the contemporary theologian is faced with a fundamental problem. For him, just as for those to whom he speaks, the proclamation of the church in the conceptual form in which it encounters him in the New Testament and in the classical theological tradition, seems unintelligible, incredible, and irrelevant. According to Bultmann, any attempt at the present time to understand and express the Christian message must realize that the theological propositions of the New Testament are not understood by modern man because they reflect a mythological picture of the world that we today cannot share.[1]

We cannot share in this mythological picture, continues Bultmann, because we live and think within "the world-picture formed by modern natural science" and within "the understanding man has of himself in accordance with which he understands himself to be a closed inner unity that does not stand open to the incursion of supernatural powers."[2]

This sounds very much like the earlier liberal analysis of the situation, but it differs from the earlier liberalism in one fundamental respect. Earlier liberalism saw in the proclamation of the Kerygma itself a stum-

[1] *Christ Without Myth: A Study of The Theology of Rudolf Bultmann* (New York: Harper and Brothers, 1961), p. 24.
[2] *Ibid.*, p. 32.

bling block to modern man, and thus sidled away from its eschatological message, preferring to center upon the ethical dimension of Christian faith as this was expressed in the life and teaching of Jesus. Bultmann, on the other hand, insists that this proclamation of the saving act in Jesus Christ must be retained and restated within existential terms. Thus demythologizing is not a relinquishment of the mystery of the kingdom, but a translation of its meaning in terms consonant with man's present self-understanding.

The issue intensifies as one explores the implications of this last assertion. How does one translate the meaning of the Kerygma in terms consonant with man's present self-understanding? Does one allow the Christian message to coalesce with the philosophy of existence? Or does one hold to the centrality of the historical and saving act of God in Jesus Christ? Although the logic of Bultmann's thought seems to move toward the former, his decision is to affirm the latter. And this gives rise to the claim that inconsistency plagues Bultmann's exposition.

Now it is with a view to removing this inconsistency, and at the same time to support Bultmann's concern with retaining the Biblical witness, that Schubert Ogden proposes his constructive alternative, based upon the procedure of speaking of God analogically rather than mythologically. In this context, the appeal to the Kerygma becomes an appeal to the act of faith as being *a knowledge of* the universal love of God, concerning which a process metaphysics may provide analogical *knowledge about*. In this way faith and knowledge, Kerygma and the philosophy of existence, are correlated, and the seemingly irreconcilable tension between them is resolved.

II.

Before addressing myself directly to questions which are raised in my mind by the analysis of this issue in *Christ Without Myth*, I should like to record certain points at which I find myself heartily in accord

with Schubert Ogden. I do this, not simply to soften the barbed sting of the criticism which I shall offer later, but to say as decisively and as positively as I can at the outset that I am mainly sympathetic with the basic thrust and intention of this work. My deviations, I think, are more tactical than substantial; though of this there may be some question when my criticisms are fully stated. But now as to our points of agreement: One is Schubert Ogden's assertion that theology must be postliberal; it cannot be preliberal. It must continue to pursue its task within the critical disciplines that were initiated by liberal scholarship at the beginning of the modern period. Yet it must have a listening ear for voices that speak across the centuries from within more distant perspectives of Christian thought and experience. There is both decisiveness and openness in this scholarly attitude.

A second directive is that theology must be alive to its responsibilities within the culture at large, and be prepared to speak to its contemporary mind as well as to its issues. It cannot be content to withdraw into the sheltered compound of churchanity and to speak a language available only to those initiated into the mysteries of its faith. There are problems here, about which I shall speak later; but the thrust of this concern is one in which I heartily concur.

It follows from this as a third directive that theology will concern itself with the problem of intelligibility in ways that are appropriate to rendering the witness of faith available to modern men and women. There are issues here, too, and I think differences between us in the way we conceive this task, and possibly in the way we understand the claims of intelligibility; but at this stage of my presentation, let me say that with the intention of Professor Ogden's concern with intelligibility in faith, I heartily concur.

Consistent with this note of inclusiveness in matters of faith and culture, I find Dr. Ogden's stress upon the primordial love of God, and what this means for a doctrine of revelation and christology, singularly valid and refreshing. My own way of speaking of this matter is to insist that the doctrines of redemption and creation must be held together. Any tendency to isolate the doctrine of redemption will appear to set Jesus Christ above the God of creation, and to particularize the faith in Jesus Christ to such an extent that our primordial unity with all men through creation is disavowed. A great deal hinges upon this issue. And with the direction of Ogden's thought on this matter, with certain reservations about which I shall speak later, I find myself in hearty accord.

What this means for our understanding of revelation needs further elaboration than Ogden has been able to give in this book. For various reasons, which I shall make clear, I find it necessary to make more of the spontaneities and depths of history than Ogden has acknowledged, and thus I am led to lift up the notion of the New Creation in Christ with more emphasis than I find Ogden's doing in his analysis. That he has not stressed this point is of apiece with his tendency to assimilate the meaning of Christ to the more generalized interpretation of the love of God one finds in metaphysics, particularly that of Charles Hartshorne, wherein neither revelation nor Christ is finally necessary since what is conveyed through them is available through the metaphysical analysis of the meaning of love as it is understood in a fully explicated view of God. This is a point where things begin to pinch more seriously; but I still hold the basic understanding of revelation in Ogden's analysis to be valid, even though his explication and defense of it leave something to be desired theologically.

And finally, I am impressed by the slyness and cogency with which Ogden insinuates the appeal to analogy as an alternative to myth in the constructive argument. I shall have some critical things to say about this proposal, but let it be known that I am impressed by the adversary even as I seek to slay him.

There are other aspects of Professor Ogden's constructive emphasis which lead me to be encouraged by his contributions to what he and I together envisage as directives for a postliberal theology; but these may suffice to express my sense of kinship with what he proposes, and with what he cherishes as a vital concern of Christian faith in the present hour. And now we must turn to the critical phase of this paper wherein I shall designate the points at which I find myself in tension with the theological proposals of this highly significant work, *Christ Without Myth*.

III.

It may appear strange to some of you, as you read my paper, that one can concur with another scholar's intention and point of view as heartily as I claim to concur with that of Schubert Ogden, and yet be so decisive, possibly aggressive, in opposing him on specific issues. It has always been a conviction of mine that we disagree most intensively on particular issues with those with whom we agree fundamentally. Thus Barth and Brunner were hotly at one another; and Reinhold Niebuhr and Paul Tillich, so we are told, made theology interesting and vital at Union Seminary by the arguments between them, even as they supported and respected one another deeply. This is because a common vision opens up common problems upon which there are bound to be differences in judgment. Because the vision of thought is held in common, the issues involved in these differences that arise are felt with equal keenness and intensity. But where differences of this sort exist within a common vision, it is of the utmost importance that they be stated with candor and with forthrightness. For the strength and power of any community of thought lies in the integrity and openness with which basic differences are confronted and wit which they are dealt.

I have three questions concerning this work by Schubert Ogden; they relate both to Ogden's interpretation and defense of Bultmann's method as an alternative for modern theology, and to Ogden's own constructive effort. All three questions have to do with the adequacy of the conceptual imagery and presuppositions underlying the method of demythologizing, particularly as this method addresses itself to the present task of a postliberal theology.

My first question is, what is the image of the modern mind to which Bultmann and Ogden would have a postliberal theology address itself? Lurking behind this question is the further query, has Ogden really dealt adequately with the criticisms of those who have attacked Bultmann on the scientific imagery which he equates with the modern mind?

When one appeals to "the world-picture formed by modern natural science" as the common basis for understanding man and his world, do we not have to be more definitive and discriminating within scientific imagery itself than either Bultmann or Ogden appear to be? For the fact is, as modern men, we stand between two scientific visions of man and his world. As science is commonly understood, even among many sophisticated liberals today, the scientific picture of man and his world bears the image of a Newtonian form of orderliness in nature which readily lends itself to observation and description, and to the work of reason following from such direct apprehension of physical realities. It is, in fact, a world of orderliness based upon a conception of causality that allows no depth and freedom in nature, no discontinuities, no unforeseen variations, hence no inexactness or discrepancy in science. The ways of scientific method are sure and altogether trustworthy.

But the scientific vision of man that informs our most basic research is quite other than this. I refer to relativity physics and quantum theory, and to the revolutionary changes that have come into our scientific estimate of human thinking, and even into

areas of experimentation, revising one's understanding of scientific method. Bultmann seems to be making an oblique reference to these changes in saying that "the decisive thing is not the results of scientific thinking but its method." "Has the natural science renounced experimentation?" he asks. And Schubert Ogden adds, by way of amplifying Bultmann's statements, "However much the *results* of scientific research change, the fundamental *method* of science and the picture of the world correlative with it remain constant."[3]

Now we may be looking at different problems here, or have different considerations in mind; but from where I view the matter, Bultmann's own statements seem to evade the crucial aspect of change in scientific thinking affecting the vision of our world; and his position, as amplified by Ogden's comments, seem to me simply not to square with the facts, as one may glean them from hearing scientists talk among themselves. With the change of scientific vision in the present century there has come about a very radical change in the method of science, its being less a description of phenomena and the formulation of universal laws, and more a statistical formulation of probabilities and a venture in determining which of the many probabilities might be taken to be true to fact in this situation. And "the picture of the world correlative with the method of science" which is now in progress is vastly different from that picture of the world which Newtonian science throughout the nineteenth century and well into our own presented. So different is it, in fact, that I would venture to say that the realities of faith which were obscured by human formulations, and thus non-existent for the liberal mind of the nineteenth and early twentieth centuries, have become remarkably vivid and insistent in our time, thanks in large measure to the new vision of science. This vision has opened up to us the depths .

[3]*Ibid.*, pp. 33f.

and complexities, the discontinuities and indeterminacies of the physical world of nature. I have argued in a forthcoming work, *The Realities of Faith and The Revolution in Cultural Forms,* that the dimension of depth which has appeared in contemporary theology under the discussion of eschatology, has affinities with this new vision of science, if in fact it is not of apiece with it. The mystery of the Kingdom as an intimation of ultimacy in the midst of our immediacies, speaks a language consonant with this new epoch of relational thinking issuing from field theory and the complexity of any description of events that begins with relatedness. A post-liberal theology, we have said, must go beyond liberalism, not back of it. But it must go beyond it in scientific imagery as in every other aspect of its thought.

And now I come to my second question: How adequately have Bultmann and Ogden assessed the capacities of human thought in dealing with the realities of faith? Since a difference in estimating the shift in the vision of science affects one's views concerning the capacity of human observation and its formulations in reporting the realities of experience, one can assume that our views here would diverge somewhat. I sense in Schubert Ogden, especially, a degree of confidence in the formulations of human reason comparable to that of Professor Hartshorne, which I am unable to share. I take my cue here, not only from the critique of reason which the Christian doctrine of man conveys, but from the judgments of relativity science which quite openly place a different estimate upon the powers of human observation and reason in dealing with realities in themselves, than was true of science prior to radiation experiments and subsequent physical theories. The disparity which relativity science finds between man's measure of physical realities and realities in themselves has led to a notion of indeterminacy and depth in experience which would not have occurred to scientists of an

earlier period. But it is not indeterminacy in measurement alone that has intruded this notion. The vivid awareness of relationships, arising from field theory, has alerted the modern scientist to the complexity of the phenomena in nature to a degree that has made him cautious about employing his findings for any generalized law beyond the status of a working proposition.

Now the point toward which my remarks are intended to argue is that the canons of reason and observation within a postliberal theology must assume a far humbler role than was observed or exercised by an earlier liberalism. Where depth and complexity are taken seriously, in speaking of history as in speaking of physical realities, something other than appeal to logic, or even to the claims of observation, is involved. The appeals to logic and observation are important to sustain. They represent our most disciplined forms of utterance in dealing with the realities of experience. But they stand under the judgment of the very realities to which they attend. They appeal to these realities as metaphors to recall Whitehead's memorable statement, speaking of the words and phrases which philosophers use: "they remain metaphors mutely appealing for an imaginative leap." As such they are as words listening for a truth that is given, not as one defining or describing that truth.

It is interesting that Schubert Ogden should suggest, by way of finding a means of breaking through Bultmann's dilemma, that he ponder the relation between analogy and myth. I think this has real possibilities; though the danger here, as I see it, is precisely the one that befell Hegel, who assumed that metaphysical thinking was simply mythical thinking grown mature and sure of itself. What happens when this assumption is made is that what was once known as metaphor and as an approximation to meanings apprehended, yet deeper than our recognition of them, become manageable concepts and categories within the human framework of thought. Thus rationality takes over, crowding out the subtle discontinuities hinted at by the word analogy, and the tension between man's thoughts and what is other than man disappears.

This, to my mind, is the crucial problem confronting post-liberal theology: How do you employ such a tool of intelligibility as analogy in a way that preserves the tension between what is manageable and unmanageable in the deeper experiences of creaturely existence? Whitehead begins quite boldly declaring his recognition of the limits of human thought in his *Process and Reality*, saying, "Philosophers can never hope finally to formulate these metaphysical first principles"; but by the time his formulation of precise categories has been completed, one feels that confidence in the adequacy of these categories has noticeably risen, almost to the point of taking these forms at face value as being descriptive of the realities to which they point. By the time Whiteheadeans begin to distribute this new crop of fundamental notions, process thinking takes on the air of a new rationalism. Thus the demon dogmatism begins to plague us again. I have been a rebel among process theologians, protesting this very tendency to close the gap between manageable and unmanageable aspects of experience. My concern with myth has been motivated, in fact, by the realization that analogy as employed in metaphysics, appears unable to hold back the floodwaters of rationalism, once the tenuous "appeal for an imaginative leap" gives way to a more definitive mood of logical analysis. This may be because analogy stresses the note of continuity between thought and being, and does not stress sufficiently the discontinuity that exists. Myth, on the other hand, at least registers the shock of disparity between my thoughts as a human formulation and the reality that is other than my thoughts. I admit it is a weasel word, as Schubert Ogden's discussion in *Christ Without Myth* continually implies. Nevertheless, I would argue that we cannot dispose of it, any more than early man could dispose of it, in so far as we choose to be attentive to that dimension of existence which elicits our sense of creaturhood.

This brings me to my third and final question, Does the discussion in *Christ Without Myth* take adequate account of the nature and status of myth as a cultural form, and thus as an indispensable ingredient of history?

Let me say first that Schubert Ogden seems to me to be perfectly justified in insisting, against Bultmann's critics, that if they are to understand his effort at demythologizing, or to try to interpret it, they must do so within his terms, else confusion follows. Bultmann, says Ogden, employs the terms myth and mythology in the sense of "a language objectifying the life of the gods," or, as we might say, of objectifying the powers of Spirit into a supernaturalism, a super-history transcending or supervening our human history, thus forming a "double history." Now I agree to stay within these bounds of meaning as long as we are simply trying to understand Bultmann, or to interpret him; but the moment we get beyond these tasks to the larger constructive task of a postliberal theology, I want to take issue with this way of dealing with myth. I think Bultmann has adequately defined mythology in its classical sense. But I resist equating myth with mythology.

It may be pertinent to say that Bultmann, when he is speaking of myth, appears to be speaking solely within the context of classical philology and of the historical study of religions that has rested upon its research. Here there is concern with the term only as a conceptual medium for conveying the dramatic logic underlying historic mythologies. What is completely lacking here is the dimension of understanding which cultural anthropology and recent studies in the history of religions has brought to light, namely, that myth is more than a cognitive notion. I would argue that myth provides a deeper orientation in any culture than this kind of analysis assumes.

Myth reaches to the level of the creaturely stance which a people will assume in speaking of their existence. It affects and shapes, not only language, the mode of thinking and speaking, but sensibilities of thought, psychical orientation, thus psychical expectations. One senses this as one moves from one orbit of cultural meaning to another. Different myths have insinuated into the very historical heritage of the respective cultures a continuing fabric of meaning which has immediate and intrinsic intelligibility within that cultural orbit. It directs the way human beings normally think and feel, as one might say; but one really means it is the way human beings normally think and feel within that historic orbit of existence.

Now of this aspect of myth, Bultmann seems oblivious. At least he is indifferent to it, as when he writes that what should disturb his critics is "that philosophy all by itself already sees what the New Testament says."[4] Does this not overlook the fact that all thought occurs within a cultural matrix. Once the revelation of God in Jesus Christ became a concrete historical fact of western experience, there was no concealing it, not even from philosophers. Or to state it differently, no thinking or feeling of man's being within its orbit of meaning and experience was immune from its shaping. A philosopher may not say, "Jesus Christ is Lord." He may not even acknowledge the name, or think of it. He will still feed upon the sensibilities of thought that issue from its nurturing matrix. Thus to say that a philosopher, even when he is Heidegger, all by himself sees what the New Testament says, is to appear to have no sense of historical context; certainly not the kind of contextual sensitivity which the cultural anthropologist has come to understand and value.

Now it is possible to come to the Chris-

tian understanding of man's existence within the framework of philosophical terms and at the same time to be speaking out of the mythical orientation. Thus when a philosopher like Heidegger or Kamlah "sets forth in purely philosophical grounds a 'secularized' Christian understanding of existence," one should not assume that they are doing so independently of the Christian myth. To be sure, one can say, "But the actualization of the attitude to which they point is not dependent on the event of Jesus Christ"; but it does not follow that "revelation is unnecessary."

The confusion arises here because one assumes that philosophizing occurs in western culture without benefit of the Judaic-Christian mythos. This I would deny. The very way in which Greek philosophy is read and understood in Western thought is through the imagery and sensibilities of this primal mythos. How else does it happen that the problem of the One and the Many, or any philosophical analysis of the meaning of God, is plagued, or at least challenged by a concern with its implications for a personal deity? The indifference of philosophers to Christianity has nothing to do with their dependence upon a nexus of cultural meaning which, in subtle and unobtrusive ways, permeates every discourse that, of necessity, draws upon a given heritage of accumulative cultural meaning. The philosopher, George Herbert Mead, was acknowledging this when he wrote in *Movements of Nineteenth Century Philosophy* that the notion of Order which looms so importantly in modern science and philosophy was taken over from Christian theology. But in saying that he was not tracing the notion to its source; for back of Christian theology is the Judaic-Christian mythos, the primal source of all our fundamental notions in western experience.

Now what I am leading up to say is that mythology is expendable. This is the superstructure of myth, the literal and imagina-

[4]*Ibid.*, p. 69.

tive elaborations of these metaphorical responses issuing in myth. Mythology is expendable; myth is not.

Thus when I observe a meticulous and highly sensitive scholar like Bultmann proceeding with his method of demythologizing to interpret Christian faith exhaustively and without remainder as man's original possibility of authentic historical existence, and then making, as it were, a sharp turn from this procedure in his appeal to the saving event of Jesus Christ, by way of preserving the Kerygma, something demonic in me leaps up with glee, and I want to shout for joy. For it seems to me that, despite his equating of myth and mythology, in the field analysis, his own incurable and inalienable involvement in the Christian mythos impels him to make a distinction between the two. The metaphorical response to the saving act of God in history, that subtle and complex instance of attending to ultimacy in our immediacies, to the mystery of the Kingdom in the midst of historical circumstances, is thus seen to be a persisting and unexpendable witness to the very realities that inform and sustain our authentic existence.

Thus what others have noted and called a great scandal of inconsistency in Bultmann's method, strikes me as being singular evidence of his own remarkable sensitivity to the persisting truth of myth, as something *existentiell,* which somehow must stand over against the logic of demythologizing.

The corrective I would like to urge upon Schubert Ogden, then, is not that he abandon his method of process theology based upon analogical thinking, but that he consider some means by which he might avoid the inevitable drift of such thinking toward a closed rationalism, in which only man and his formulations speak forth.

The only concern I have here, really, is that we do not obscure the realities of faith or block them out of view by our human formulations—formulations which depend so exclusively upon resources drawn from present forms of experience for their intelligibility. Something that will continually register the shock of *reality over reason* is needed to keep reasonable men from becoming victims of their own mental enclosures, and thus open to the judgment and grace of the living God.

Faith, Myth, and Culture 13

CULTURAL ANTHROPOLOGY, by its persistent attempt to penetrate the façade of ritual and symbolic utterance among elemental people, has achieved an understanding of the mythical consciousness which can illumine all religious language and acts of worship. The anthropologist's grasp of the meaning of faith and worship has not always been so rewarding. Being insensitive to the complexity of the response to which he was trying to give interpretation, he was content to find plausible explanations for these acts and expressions by applying in direct fashion, methods of rational inquiry which often prejudged these events as having a certain kind of meaning or no meaning at all. The primitive was compelled to be some kind of philosopher; and in this role the simple religious man did not always fare very well. In fact, whenever the demands of rational inquiry have been imposed upon religious utterances without regard for the subtle and indirect qualities of their meaning, the religious mind has suffered by analysis. The prodigious labors of psychologists of religion, anthropologists, and sociologists of religion who, over the years, have sought to wrest from the enigmas of faith some intelligible explanation of religious conduct, have served largely to discount the importance of faith in civilized cultures. The attempt of anthropologists such as Frazer and Tylor to localize the irrationality of faith in the religions of early man by distinguishing between magic and religion, reserving the more respected word for the civilized faiths, was of short duration. In time, implications of superstition spread to religion in every form where the overtones of a living faith remained. Nothing short of a complete reductionism, leveling the poetic language of faith down to its lowest rational denominator, would suffice. Little wonder that one culture after another, in so far as its leadership succumbed to the pleas for modernity, sought to cast out the ancient myths and to establish society upon a purely rational basis. Religion reduced to its rational minimum was no match for logic or science.

A more moderate view of the role of myth and religious ritual appeared when the anthropologist abandoned his effort to find purely rational motives behind these expressions and sought, instead, to understand their function in the life of the community. Here the social scientist was able to point out the unifying force of myth in giving, as it were, some direction to the life of the people. Ritual, in repeatedly re-enacting the themes of the myth, could be accounted a stabilizing influence in society, conserving the cherished values by infusing them into the sensibilities of the people. Put in this form, the rationalization was tantamount to damning religion as a reactionary social force. The mixture of truth and error in this explanation made the judgment at least plausible to many and convincing to some.

The return of the philosopher to sociological and psychological concerns, and ultimately to the problems of anthropology, has probably been one of the genuinely scholarly advances in our day. This advance occurred quite accidentally. For generations the philosopher remained bogged down in epistemological inquiries, seeking to find a suitable answer to the question, How do we know? The query, What do we know? was an irrelevant question as long as the possibility of knowledge remained in doubt. Quite fortuitously, possibly by way of uttering a word of despair in the midst of this philosophical maze, some soul in distress asked, 'What do we mean when we ask, How do we know? How can we determine whether or not we know until we can be sure what meaning is?'

The effort to determine the meaning of meaning has led philosophers into labyrinths of technical inquiry which would seem to have bogged down the modern philosopher even more deeply than his predecessors who were obsessed with epistemology. However, two happy outcomes have resulted from the inquiry into meaning: (1) the philosopher has been pressed into explorations that have taken him into new fields of human thought and experience; and (2) the more discerning among the philosophers have discovered, as a result of these wanderings, that thought itself is a multidimensional happening. Its mysteries cannot be opened with one key; for thought is attended by a depth of feeling, signs, and symbolic utterances which exemplify resources of meaningfulness even when they cannot, on technical grounds, be said to have meaning. In the effort to fathom this complex occurrent, the efforts of philosopher and anthropologist have converged. For, like the anthropologist, the philosopher in search of an understanding of language and signs has turned to elemental communities where meaning has remained undifferentiated. Language, he has discovered in this context, is more than direct discourse. Even for practical purposes language is ceremoniously lived.

Out of this pursuit of the meaning of language and the use of symbols in action and in speech has come fresh insight into the meaning of myth both as a language and as a function of the culture in conveying to conscious experience something of the depth of awareness which would otherwise remain at the level of bodily feeling. It shall be my purpose in this chapter to recount important contributions to the understanding of myth, and to assess the significance of myth as a theological resource in the constructive task of conveying the meaning of the Christian faith to the present age. In pursuing this general problem, we shall be taking a step toward illumining the predicament of the liberal Protestant church; for a reconstructed liberalism awaits some grasp of the deeper dimension of faith which was relinquished in its zeal for clarification. The problems here, as I view them, are not simply apologetic inquiries. That is to say, they direct us, not simply to questions concerning the fashioning of tools by which to formulate some justification for the Christian faith in our time; but to such basic problems as the interpenetration of faith and culture, and the nature of the religious response as a creative act within history wherein man's inner life, the private world of thought and emotions, is brought into vital, serious play with what is ultimate and other than man. They press us further to consider the nature of religious discourse, both as symbolic expression in the wider, emotive sense, and as a form of communicating knowledge in the more definitive sense of reasoned understanding. In so brief an analysis we cannot hope to deal with all of these problems. Perhaps the best we can do is to summarize some of the findings of recent studies of myth and to show how they bear upon these three areas of problems. On the basis of these observations, we will be able to draw some conclusions about the constructive importance of myth in any theological formulation.

I

FAITH AND CULTURE

Without exception, I should say, recent studies of faith and myth see the problem as being, in some sense, involved in the issue of faith and culture. Among anthropologically minded philosophers such as Cassirer [1] and Langer,[2] this issue is given prominence; for it is clear to them that religious expression is, itself, a cultural occurrence, not only in the sense of partaking of a cultural coloring but in the deeper sense of giving voice to human hungers, anxieties, and appreciations which, in turn, exemplify and articulate the cultural psyche in so far as religious utterances achieve a consensus. Even theological interpreters such as Brunner [3] are compelled to acknowledge the relevance of the cultural issue in dealing with the total content of the myth and its corporate witness; although Brunner's insistence upon restricting the Christian meaning of myth to revelation in the decisive, Christological sense, causes him to take the problem out of its cultural context and to treat it as a concern to go beyond history and to speak with

[1] Cf. his *Language and Myth*, Harper, 1946; *An Essay on Man*, Yale University Press, 1944; and *The Myth of the State*, Yale University Press, 1946.
[2] Cf. her *The Practice of Philosophy* (1930); *Introduction to Symbolic Logic* (1937), and *Philosophy in a New Key* (1942).
[3] See esp. his chapter on 'Christian Mythology' in *The Mediator*.

dogmatic assurance from a point outside history. From such a vantage point, Brunner is able to dissociate Christian myth in its decisive sense from all non-Christian (what he calls pagan) myths. For the latter, from his point of view, are clearly immersed in the stream of history and thus bear all the limitations of the human mind and the human psyche. They are, in the last analysis, according to Brunner, the precursors of metaphysics.[4]

This distinction bears analysis because, upon its issue, both the meaning and the relevance of myth as a theological tool turns. If myth in the Christian sense is so wholly different from myth in the long range of human response to mystery, then the literature in cultural anthropology has no contribution to make to the theological use of myth. And if myth is to be equated with revelation in the radically super-historical sense in which Brunner uses the term, the bearing of the cultural context or of cultural history in general, to say nothing of the cultural pattern of response, is of no consequence to theological inquiry. I should argue, however, contrary to Brunner, that we have no choice but to acknowledge some continuity between mythical thinking within a Christian context and mythical thinking as it has occurred in non-Christian cultures. This is not to equate Christian and non-Christian myths; nor to relate them in any serial sense. It is simply to recognize that comparable human responses in the way of being expressive and creative lie back of the cultural motifs to which the various myths have given form.

Such an observation places myth at the psychical core of culture and generalizes it as a common feature of every historical experience within a geographical and ethnical frame. It makes of myth a characteristic, human response in any situation where the human psyche is awakened to a disturbing realization of an *otherness*, either in the form of a single object or power, or in the form of a total datum, affecting or determining man's present existence as well as his future destiny.

The cultural conditioning of the mythical response, however,

---

[4] The conception of myth as a precursor of metaphysics was developed by Hegel. A restatement of this point of view has been given with extensive elaboration by W. M. Urban in *Language and Reality*.

is inescapable. That is to say, the human psyche, being inwardly formed by the valuational responses arising from numerous events within experience, assumes a characteristic probability of response in keeping with these serial events. Psychic life, like vegetable life, thus partakes of a regional character which can never be completely obscured or canceled out.

This observation would suggest that the culture is always an exemplification of the structures of consciousness which are available within the region to initiate psychical responses as well as to express and to assimilate meanings. Sensitivity evidenced in creative imagination, in concern over human relations, or in the qualitative attainment of individual lives and in the group life, reflects the operation of processes within these human structures. The culture can rise to heights of sensitive creation and to sensibility in relations only to the degree that there are structures of consciousness available to carry and exemplify these happenings. Culture, I should say, is the creative work of God, made possible through his prior creation of these structures of consciousness, articulating the full psycho-physical organism.

Given these cultural determinants, we shall see that the character of the psychical response, its quality, its degree of sensitivity, both in the realm of feeling and in the area of expression, varies from region to region; from culture to culture. There is no universal human psyche; hence no universal human mythos. There is no common level of human, psychical response; hence no common level of mythical thinking; any more than there is a common level of creative expression. All cultures have historically manifested some capacity to be expressive in sensitive and creative ways; but there are marked variations among them, and in some instances the range of variation is vast indeed. It follows that no culture deserves to be neglected in the search for a full grasp of the psychical depth and outreach of the human spirit; for each culture exemplifies the concrete nature of God's working within the range of its available structures. But it is clear that some cultures deserve more serious attention than others when the concern is to focus upon the fullness of God's working within human structures.

Without attempting to appraise the degree of psychical superiority which can be ascribed to the Christian culture of the West,
it can certainly be said that it reveals a range and reach of sensitivity and of creative imagination which must place it high in
the human venture wherein God's creative working is exemplified.
The pivotal point, or the summit of this cultural creation of the
West is Jesus Christ. But Jesus Christ as a structure of consciousness in which God's intent and creative working are concretely
exemplified is not an isolated datum. Behind the Christ lies the
long history of the Jewish people. Their moral consciousness
which had been processed and refined throughout the centuries
of devotion to the Law became as a seed bed for a more sensitive
and appreciative consciousness in response to the working of God.
The prophets, we might say, were intimations of this emergent
in so far as they were in some sense sporadic efforts to transcend
the rigid mechanisms of the legal tradition. Yet, the prophets
were in a very real sense the fruition of the legal tradition; and
must ultimately be interpreted in the light of its claim upon the
Jewish people.

Christ stands to the moral culture of the Jews as love transcends the law. As over against the moral and the rational consciousness, the Christ exemplifies the appreciative consciousness
in which love is regulative. His structure of consciousness is the
ground from which spirit emerges as a novel event. The Christ
is at once the exemplar of the human consciousness at the level
of spirit and the innovation of spirit within the conscious structure
of man. He is the clear exemplication of the concrete work of
God in history, possibly the clearest; the clearest within Western
history without any doubt. Christ as the innovation of spirit and
the exemplar of man at the level of spirit constitutes a redemptive
consciousness among the structures of human consciousness
which are motivated ard, in large measure, bound by the moral
and the rational consciousness.

Christ as the summit of the cultural creation of the West is the
focal point of the Christian myth. This should not be interpreted
to mean that the Christian myth is to be equated with revelation
in the trans-historical sense described by Brunner. On the con-

trary, I should say, this summit vision points not beyond history but back to the formative events of history which have issued in this redemptive act; and to a further range of history which is to be seen, understood, and judged in the light of this redemptive act.

The Christian myth, then, is not one, decisive, isolated event; it is a pattern of events which has its luminous center in the Christ, but which begins in the earliest vivid awareness of God's creative work in history. The full pattern of the myth is to be found in the Biblical account wherein the drama of creation and redemption is delineated. This drama conveys the feeling tone of the culture with regard to its ultimate dimensions. Its details consist of apprehensions concerning God's intent for creation, the nature of God's creative activity in history, the nature and destiny of man, the interplay of tragedy and hope in human history, the facts of good and evil, and the attending operations of judgment, grace, forgiveness, and redemption.

These details of the myth have been variously analyzed and elaborated into Christian doctrine. They have been applied in liturgy, Christian art and architecture. They have been subtly woven into the literature and musical epics of the West. To some extent, their motifs have shaped the philosophy and ethic of the West. To a degree not commonly recognized they have influenced the political expressions of Western man. Deeper than we can discern, these primal notions permeate the feeling context of the culture in this present moment of history, giving the structure of Western experience its distinctive character.

II

THE NATURE OF THE RELIGIOUS RESPONSE OUT OF WHICH THE MYTH OF THE CULTURE TAKES FORM

The myth of a culture is a symbolic utterance of long standing, attesting to a persistent outreach in man toward what is ultimate in that which is other than man. This outreach varies in depth and in clarity of procedure. The clarity of the response is often in reverse proportion to the degree of depth which is achieved.

It is possible to detect certain periods in Western history when clarity and control have been sought in preference to every other form of orientation. Thus expressions of the religious response which early anthropologists were inclined to call magic conveyed a singular concern to bring the uncertain powers of this numinous experience within manageable bounds. The religious response in this context became a carefully developed technique of cursing and blessing, highly ritualized and corporately controlled.[5] In formalized and conventionalized periods of religious history, we see religious expression being reduced similarly to a minimum ritualistic response as a saving technique. In highly rationalistic periods the religious expression has been defined rather restrictively as ethical demands or agreements. In recent years we have seen the religious response narrowed down to a practical concern with religious energies comparable to the practical products of scientific research. We may say with some accuracy that in such efforts at clarification and control in religion, myth tends to lose its relevance and force. In its place, more precise and literal methods of thought and practice are sought.

Myth gains ascendancy where the appreciative moods of wonder, adoration, or praise are in dominance in recognition of an unmanageable datum in the objective event. Here the religious response is less a direct effort to use or to control the ultimate power discerned in the Reality not oneself, and more a readiness to encounter the fullness of the mystery as an Event of Grace and Beneficence, or as Judgment. The initial response in the mood of wonder or adoration may assume varying degrees of articulate form. In its lowest degree of conscious awareness it becomes a pervasive sense of unity with all being, as in certain forms of animism, and later, in nature mysticism. In its most articulate stage it becomes worship, or perhaps lyrical utterance such as we find in the songs of the Psalmist.

The mythical orientation is always one in which feeling takes priority over conscious attention or cognitive action. The feeling

[5] I have summarized and illustrated some of the features of this tendency in an article, 'The Development of Cursing,' in *The Open Court*, October, 1934.

orientation may be one of apprehensiveness, a shuddering before what is alien or unknown, as Rudolf Otto has indicated by his phrase, *the sense of the numinous;* [6] or it may be one of identity, an immersion in the deep ocean of reality, as the modern mystic has often described it. It may be of a third character: more dialectic in character, either in the sense of the encounter as Brunner describes it in a radically dualistic setting; [7] or in the sense of partial identity and partial discontinuity, as might be experienced in a situation which Whitehead has described as the *individual in community,* [8] wherein the bounds of individuality are noted and accepted in a cosmic situation which is dominantly social.

The religious response in this mythical orientation is thus a form of undefined awareness, a sense of knowing which must be taken to be a knowledge of orientation, or a knowledge by acquaintance — an inward assurance of having felt one's way into a situation. [9] Bergson defined this orientation in a way that appeared to have made it coalescent with instinct; so that creatures moving within a familiar environment without conscious awareness and without need of intellection appeared to be the most perfect mystics. Actually this was not his intention, though his formulation had difficulty guarding against this impression at times.

Suzanne Langer has helped to correct such an excess of animality in evolutionism by suggesting that what occurs in the mythical consciousness is not just an extension of this instinctual behavior, but a distinctively human response; continuous, to be sure, with the instinctive feeling of orientation, but having a creative and imaginative character which marks it as a distinctly human dimension. [10] Miss Langer has established that myth is a serious enterprise of people who are sensitive to the depth of their experience. Particular myths, she insists, can have symbolic force in a culture only as long as they persist as truth-bearers, undisturbed

[6] Cf. *The Idea of the Holy,* Oxford, 1923.
[7] Cf. *The Divine-Human Encounter,* Scribner, 1943.
[8] *Religion in the Making,* Macmillan, 1926.
[9] See James, *Psychology.*
[10] Cf. *Philosophy in a New Key,* pp. 138ff.

by literal inquiry. The moment the literalizing of their meaning is begun, their mythical force is dispelled; henceforth such meaning as their symbolizations support can persist only as metaphysical generalizations, on the one hand; and as epic poetry, or similar aesthetic expressions, on the other. This, however, is not her whole story. Langer has established also that the dimension of feeling which myth expresses and to which its symbols constantly refer, is not only a valid structure of meaning for the human consciousness, but an indispensable one if the distinctively human dimension is to be expressive in man. Relinquishing this reach toward symbolization at the level of feeling means literalizing experience in a way that lapses into pre-human or animal responses; which is to employ signs for direct, functional activity in the satisfaction of needs arising from a physical orientation in environment. Thus the effort to clarify experience by ridding it of non-functional signs or modes of expression which cannot be justified on the basis of direct discourse or communication of meaning, is judged by Langer to be a relinquishment of the humanizing dimension itself.[11]

Can metaphysics and epic poetry, then, succeed the appeal to myth? In a sense we can say that this is what happens in a civilization such as our own where the self-conscious attitude and habit have begun their work. The myths themselves cannot be revived as myths. They can be retained, on the one hand, in the form of poetic insights or parables to convey, within a disciplined emotional context, the valuations implicit in the feeling tone out of which these symbols have emerged. In this sense they remain motifs at the level of feeling, though in refined, and possibly, remote form. On the other hand, they can be retained in the form of abstract generalizations which a metaphysics might provide. The metaphysics, in this case, becomes a source of authentication in the way in which the feeling context initially gave authenticity in direct form to the valuations. The authentication is of a different order, being of a discursive nature. As such it cannot replace the emotional force of the original impact of the myth. Nevertheless, the metaphysics in combination with epic poetry or the musical

[11] Ibid. pp. 20ff.

177

epic may provide a civilized equivalent of the aboriginal orientation such that the mind will be both tempered and deepened by feeling, and the feelings structured and disciplined as a directive of human drives and impulses.

The retention of myth in this sophisticated form is not wholly secondary in its effects; for it can be the nurturing matrix of fresh and original mythical impulses. This simply means that the feeling context of culture, being active and continually formative, generates deep emotions of a direct and spontaneous sort, authenticating the valuational responses of modern man at the level of sensibility where judgment is immediate and unrationalized. In this awakened state of sensitivity, human consciousness may reach a depth of feeling which will enable it to appropriate the valuations of the myth as an original impulse, thus giving these valuations the force and authenticity within the modern consciousness of knowledge by acquaintance.

The process here is comparable to the emergence of creative art in the matrix of a disciplining tradition. The retention of the cultural myth, through a fusion of metaphysical and poetic, or aesthetic, effort, is similar to the retention of art forms as a nurturing and accrediting medium. Through this medium, the valuations of the persisting structure of experience are carried forward into the emerging moment, thus bequeathing to it the promise of character. Character, whether in art or religion, in individual or in culture, is a qualitative attainment that issues from the creative happening wherein past attainment and the novel event are somehow made to coalesce, or in some sense to achieve an integration. Character is always threatened from two sources: one, from the pressure of tradition which threatens to suppress or to frustrate creativity; second, from the insurgence of the passage into novelty which threatens to dissociate itself from the nurturing matrix. Qualitative attainment results to some degree, however, in spite of these overreaching or rebellious tendencies; and the metaphysical explanation of this occurrence is the creative work of God which presses upon every emergent event the possibilities of past attainment; or bends the persisting valuations to the opportunity of creative emergence. The work of God in this creative passage is always either enhanced or obstructed by the facilities of structure and response which include both the habits of individuals and the corporate barriers in policies of institutions available in any period of creativity. God does not work in a vacuum. He works through the available structures of the culture. Thus the beneficence and wisdom of man are not in vain. Neither is his evil working and folly without irreparable loss.

Although Reinhold Niebuhr's characterization of myth presupposes a dualistic imagery comparable to that of Brunner's thinking, his insights int · the truth of myth help to convey the indispensable character of myth as a primary mode of the religious response.[12] What is Niebuhr's view of the truth of myth? Niebuhr insists that myth is a mode of apprehension which grasps the depth dimension of experience as it is given in the inner nature of any organic form of existence and pre-eminently in the existence of man. Description, he points out, is able to delineate the external, visible features; and the full account of any living organism from within this perspective can depict it only as mechanism. The essential unity of the event or being can only be discerned and articulated through an imaginative form of cognition which is the mythical method.

In man's experience this inner core of being which resists ready comprehension is to be understood best in the exemplification of freedom and transcendence. These two facets of man's depth dimension exemplify man's spiritual capacity to go beyond the sheer mechanistic level of cause and effect and to participate in a world of decision, choice, sin, and responsibility; and ultimately in redemption. Freedom is man's capacity to break free of the causal chain within history; transcendence is his capacity even to go beyond historical experience itself and to participate in super-historical dimensions of living. Because this dimension of depth is at all times present and operative in man's experience, and forever interpenetrating the events of history, it is a dimension of historical existence in the most realistic sense; not simply an imaginative perspective for contemplation. Time, man's days,

[12] 'The Truth in Myth' in *The Nature of Religious Experience,* J. S. Bixler, ed., Harper, 1937, Chap. VI.

the cultural process, rise and fall within a rhythm that partakes of this total actuality, even though the describable events cannot convey the full importance of its momentous passage.

Myth, that is, permanent myth, myth that is as true today as in the primitive world, is the mode of apprehension by which this total actuality is seriously envisaged and encountered. Christian myth (the drama of creation and redemption evincing man's relation to a Creator and to a Redeemer, and the ambiguities of man's nature, held in tension between good and evil) is such an effort through dramatic imagery to glimpse and to probe man's total actuality. In Niebuhr's judgment, it is the most adequate and the most expressive myth for achieving this orientation within existence.

In my judgment, Dorothy Emmet brings us nearer than any of the writers we have considered to a contemporary understanding of this feeling orientation in which mythical thinking takes place. Because she sees it as an elemental condition of the perceptive act whenever consciousness is confronted with events of import which are at once intelligible, yet beyond immediate comprehension, her conclusions seem less inclined to make of myth thinking an outmoded response which must now be replaced by metaphysics or some other form of sophisticated symbolization. Her view of perception in what she terms 'the adverbial mode,' a pre-animistic orientation in which we meet environing reality with a full, bodily response ('a responsive state of the organism in *rapport* with or receiving shocks from its environment'[13]) prepares the ground for conceiving of mythical thinking as following from a condition of responsive awareness, as she calls it. Responsive awareness, as Miss Emmet uses the term, I understand to imply in part what I would mean by appreciative awareness. Hers is a more active term and thus in some instances expresses better the nature of the religious response in such an encounter. Appreciative awareness means a reaching out toward reality beyond the self and thus is never as passive as the term would seem to imply; but it strongly inclines toward receptiveness

[13] *The Nature of Metaphysical Thinking*, London: Macmillan & Co. Ltd., 1946, p. 61.

to that to which it atteɪ ʹs. Yet this act is not passive either — not sheer acquiescence to what is encountered; but a creative act of acquiring unto oneself real meaning of another self or of another object through a process of exercising empathy and identification in a circular movement which returns this feeling-into-another-center-of-existence to one's own self-orientation.

With the conception of perceptual experience to which Miss Emmet holds, such responsive awareness takes place in a context of depth or of relations which makes its rise less a cognitive act, in the usual sense of a subject attending to an object outside of itself in which all the hazards of isolation and the means of communication enter in, and more a matter of the organism, deeply involved in this nexus of interpenetrating relations, rising toward a self-conscious status. Responsive awareness marks a sort of threshold between the deeper levels of communal existence, to which the bodily feelings give fuller report, and the towers of the mind that rise from this nexus of relations in more solitary, reflective awareness. Thus Miss Emmet writes,

> If something like a 'pre-animistic' stage underlies experience, we do not start from projective modes of our consciousness, or analogies of our own activities, on to a world beyond us. We start from consciousness of ourselves as arising out of a *rapport*, interconnection and participation in processes reaching beyond ourselves. Such feeling is a pre-condition of self-conscious experience . . .
>
> Knowledge is only possible where there is some actual situation of relatedness together with conscious awareness of relationship.[14]

It will be seen then that the situation in which myth-thinking takes place is thus a perceptive horizon of consciousness in which bodily feelings, conveying the nexus of relationships, and conscious awareness, attentive to solitary concerns, merge; and, in fact, interpenetrate. The religious response is thus bi-polar, involving, on the one hand, a genuine concern for individual destiny; and, on the other hand, a responsive awareness to that which is more than the self, out of which ultimate demands arise.

[14] Ibid. p. 65.

III

The Nature of Religious Discourse

It remains for us now to inquire into the third area of problems concerning the nature of religious discourse. Here the concern is to understand (a) the function of symbolic expression as a language of myth; and (b) the nature of theological discourse as an intellectual interpretation of myth.

By symbolic expression in this instance I mean the use of religious symbols through the media of the dramatic arts, poetry, and music for expressing or conveying especially the depth of feeling through which the ultimate demands of being are mediated. Such symbolic mediation will vary in the degree to which it holds feeling and awareness of meaning in a creative unity. Where feeling predominates to the neglect of a concern for meaning, symbolic expression lapses into sentimentalism. Where the concern for meaning is over-stressed to the neglect of feeling, the result may be an arid formalism. Here the relevance of the aesthetic discipline to religious expression is made evident. It is the indispensable source of control and discrimination in the blending of feeling and meaning, giving both power and pointedness to religious expression. Such symbolic expression is, in Suzanne Langer's sense, the highest form of humanizing activity; for it addresses both mind and the bodily feelings to demands which extend the human reach toward symbolization.

Theological discourse as an intellectual interpretation of myth must be differentiated from theological inquiry which is addressed to discursive problems. The latter is pre-eminently analytical in nature. It would include, for example, thinking upon the relation of theology to philosophy or to cultural issues arising from political, educational, or economical situations within the perspective provided by the valuations of the myth. Here the theological perspective or, we might say, the religious vision in the form of theoretical affirmations, is brought to bear upon various issues as a criterion of criticism. The witness of the faith is made to speak as a directive of culture in terms of possibilities of good or evil; in terms of motivation with reference to choice or decision in relation to good or evil; in terms of judgment bearing upon conditions within such areas arising from choices and decisions in regard to good or evil.

Theological discourse as a mode of inquiry into the meaning of myth, on the other hand, partakes of a more subtle and indirect use of language. Theology under this aspect should be conceived of as being midway between art and philosophy. If worship is viewed as a form of the fine arts, theology as an interpretation of myth should be seen as having direct affinity with the arts. It should, in fact, be allied, as a mode of disciplined criticism, with art criticism and with literary criticism in so far as these are conceived to be directly responsible for illumining creative effort, disciplining its expression, and thus enhancing its communicable force.

The theologian in his attempt to lift the themes of the myth, or the full drama of redemption, to a more explicit, cognitive expression, is constantly caught between two demands which tend to be antithetical in purpose. The one is discriminating thinking of a more direct sort, requiring analysis and the searching out of implications; the other is relational thinking of a perceptive sort, requiring the use of analogy, metaphor, and parable. The theologian is constantly seeking to achieve penetration of meaning in relation to a vast orbit of related meaning. His language, if analytical, is never simply scientific. He must use the sciences in a way in which the scientist cannot be expected to employ them: namely, in a context which shocks the understanding with surprise implications because of the juxtaposition of scientific fact and poetic vision. His language, if relational, is never simply metaphysical; for he operates at a level of imaginative thought which, as yet, has not yielded to extensive abstraction. He must use metaphysical concepts in a way that enlivens these bloodless abstractions with the vitality of concrete existence. His language, if aesthetic or poetic, is never simply poetry; for he seeks to interpret and to communicate mythical meaning with more direct, cognitive concern than the poet can exemplify. He must make use of poetic imagination and poetic expression in a way that turns the indirect assertion into immediate alliance with direct inquiry. Theology, in its function of interpreting myth, thus carries forward two seemingly contradictory modes of inquiry: the one, definitive with a view to explicit clarification; the other, imaginative, with a view to insinuating the fuller range of meaning implicit in the adumbrations of experience which can never be fully borne by explicit language.

IV

From our analysis of these three areas of problems, we can see that myth, both as a concept and as a content of seminal meaning, is a constructive tool by which the depth of the cultural experience can be theologically envisaged and organically related to worship and to religious inquiry. Within an emergent perspective, myth is seen to be a symbolic method for seizing upon the tenuous intrusions of the psychical thrust within history and within the cultural experience, wherein the creative movement of the life process toward the new order of events can be discerned. But myth, being the symbolic carrier of the deeper sentiments of the culture, pointing at once in a mood of judgment to the current, creatural limitations of man, and in a mood of grace and forgiveness to the redemptive activities of God in history, is also the source and the nurturing matrix of the most profound sensibilities of man. Without its resources, and without its nurture, the heart may literally be *hardened*, the mind made arrogant, and the spiritual outreach of man altogether atrophied. Myth, therefore, is indispensable to a profound orientation of the human psyche in our culture, and the source of our most discerning theological insight.

MYTH AS A MODE OF AWARENESS AND INTELLIGIBILITY 14

Bernard E. Meland / The University of Chicago

The assumption that myth is a mode of response expressive of a pre-rational and pre-scientific age, and therefore not pertinent to modern times, has become commonplace within disciplined circles of thought. People of primitive times are spoken of as "children of the human race" who, by way of appeasing or communicating with a spirit world, indulged their fantasy in playfully projecting events and practices of their work-a-day world into rites and symbols appropriate to mythical discourse. The race came of age, it is said, when reflection and inquiry acquired sufficient proportion and influence in human communities to put to rout such notions of fantasy and feeling, replacing them with critically established judgments of fact and belief. The initiating of this age of critical reflection in the West is commonly ascribed to the subtle and taunting art of questioning exercised by the Athenian seer, Socrates, in dispelling the folk-beliefs and fantasies of his countrymen. Though Socrates, as a consequence of his acts, was to meet death by being compelled to drink from a cup of hemlock, his critical legacy was preserved for posterity as a philosophical witness in the *Dialogues* of his student and disciple, Plato; and later rendered more orderly and structured in the metaphysical writings of Aristotle. This Grecian legacy of critical inquiry was to undergo successive stages of metamorphosis at the hands of subsequent seers of the Mediterranean world, notably Plotinus, Augustine, Bonaventure, Aquinas, and the Renaissance Humanists. And it has continued, in either its Platonic or its Aristotelian mode, to influence, if not to shape, subsequent developments in Western thought.

By the sixteenth century, however, a new legacy stemming from innovations associated with the names of Copernicus, Kepler, and Galileo, was visibly forming. The thrust of this new legacy of critical inquiry issuing from concern with scientific method through experimentation was given a decisive turn in the writings of the British essayist and philosopher, Francis Bacon, writing in the sixteenth century, in which he harshly criticized the earlier legacy of Plato and Aristotle as being "the corruption of philosophy by superstition and an admixture

of theology,"[1] which, in his judgment, could only be described as refined fantasy given speculative extension. Bacon rejected all such
reflection, heralding the experimental procedures then emerging, addressed to the processes of nature, as being the only reliable course of
inquiry appropriate to the new age. From such inquiry, Bacon envisaged emerging a *Novum Organum*, a natural philosophy, designed to be
the mother of all sciences. Through the knowledge accruing from such
inquiry Bacon envisaged the whole of the natural universe and its creatures being placed in the service of humankind. John Dewey, in *Reconstruction in Philosophy* (1920), proclaimed "Francis Bacon of the Eliza-
bethan age . . . the great forerunner of the spirit of modern life,"[2] and
devoted an entire chapter to expounding his innovating stance.

What had been anticipated as a visionary stance in Bacon became
an orderly world-view in the natural philosophy of Isaac Newton with
the publication of his *Principia* in 1687, initiating the era of Western
thought that was to elevate the scientific outlook above every other
perspective as being definitive, and thus authoritative for inquiry, beyond every other mode. Immanuel Kant, through his *Critique of Pure
Reason* (1781) and his *Critique of Practical Reason* (1785), effected a
detente between the two legacies, though the two procedures were set
forth as independent modes of inquiry with different fields of concern,
and with no communication or rapport between them. In Hegel's absolute idealism, however, the philosophical legacy, as an all-embracing
mode of inquiry, was given more audacity; and, during the closing years
of the nineteenth century, under the stimulus of ardent Hegelians in
Europe and America, the philosophical legacy seemed amply restored,
looming even more assertive in that context as a rival of the scientific
outlook. And in American thought, notably in the writings of Josiah
Royce and his followers, philosophical inquiry in the mode of absolute
idealism was to become a vigorous alternative to scientific inquiry,
paving the way for the spirited rivalry between Science and the Hu-
manities in higher education.

What was implicit, both in the philosophical legacy and in the
scientific outlook, was the presumption that human inquiry and reflection could be disciplined and perfected to the extent of embracing the
whole of reality in a structure of precise knowledge, thereby displacing
the anguish and illusion of childish phantasies as represented in myth
and in the vast legacies of religious belief stemming from such origins.
Hegel is said to have made this assumption explicit in claiming metaphysics to be the modern person's mature alternative to myth.

---

1. *Bacon Selections*, edited by Matthew Thompson McClure (New York: C. Scribner's Sons, 1928), pp. 305ff.

2. John Dewey, *Reconstruction in Philosophy* (New York: H. Holt and Company,
1920), Chapter II.

I.

In so far as disciplined inquiry and reflection in the modern age is represented by the eras of thought expressive of Bacon, Newton, and Hegel, one would have to say that science and philosophy have clearly displaced myth, and have tended to discredit all symbolic modes of expression which are unable to claim the precision and clarity of meaning provided by science and philosophy in their respective modes of inquiry. And they who continue in our time to hold to either of their formulations of the problem will persist in regarding myth obsolete in a scientifically or philosophically mature age. For contemporary scholars and scientists who see the present perspective as having gone beyond the assumptions of Bacon, Newton and Hegel, the question concerning the appropriateness or relevance of myth in our modern discourse cannot be resolved that readily or summarily. The crucial question today in its preliminary form is, to what extent has the Newtonian or the Hegelian vision of the world been shown to be discredited or at least misleading by developments in the sciences and philosophies since the turn of the century? Clearly the Newtonian and the Hegelian perspectives can be said to have spoken for the modern age through the nineteenth century. What has happened in disciplined inquiry within scientific philosophical fields alike since the turn of the century, however, would seem to suggest that *a new modern consciousness* has emerged, for which neither Bacon, Newton, nor Hegel speaks.

What looms on the horizon of modern, disciplined thinking, stemming from discoveries in sciences and philosophies as represented by nuclear science and language analysis, presents far less claim for the definitive authority of science or philosophy with regard to a total vision of experience than was projected by that earlier stage of the modern consciousness. Nuclear physicists, themselves, have, in effect, relinquished the role of natural philosophers in the sense embraced by Newtonian science, insisting upon recognizing the limitations of scientific inquiry as defined by its own tentative procedure in projecting formulae in the hope of realizing some measure of success in their expectations. The magnitude of their success, as evidenced in the atomic bomb and flights to the moon, has tended to create a public opinion in behalf of scientific inquiry virtually restoring authority attributed to it in the Newtonian age. Yet scientists themselves, more knowledgeable about their efforts, and more modest in estimating their method, have rejected such acclaim, recognizing the tenuous and limited character and application of their explorations, given the new vision of the *mysterious universe*. Language analysts, speaking for one phase of modern philosophical inquiry, have concurred with this modest stance of the scientist, observing, as did Ian T. Ramsey in *Models and Mystery*,[3] that we can no longer employ either scientific or philosoph-

3. Ian T. Ramsey, *Models and Mystery* (London: Oxford University Press 1964), pp. 1-21.

3. Ian T. Ramsey, *Models and Mystery* (London: Oxford University Press 1964), pp. 1-21.

187

ical language in the definitive mode exercised by nineteenth century understanding of Newtonian science or philosophy, namely, as "picture models" of the universe. On the contrary, what we have in each instance of scientific discovery or philosophical judgment are "disclosure models." The mystery of the universe and of our lived experiences, so this observation contends, exceeds the reach even of disciplined inquiry.

III

What to do with this penumbra of mystery that attends or confronts all disciplined inquiry, and which invades our presence periodically with surprise, or, on occasion, with consternation and concern? Many disciplined and realistic minds of our time have preferred to "bracket" all such intrusions of unmanageable intimations of meaning, and attend solely to what can be confidently addressed or explicated. This would certainly seem a sensible procedure. It is, however, but a variation upon the one commonly pursued among various disciplines in the "twenties" in which it was said, "We know nothing of beginnings and endings," by which they meant to imply that disciplined inquiry is attentive only to what will respond to observation and precise deduction. That dictum, however, assumed that all immediate experience and its data could be expected to respond in this manner. In view of the changed perspective impelled by the modern consciousness, which recognizes that our immediacies within experience are by no means transparent in all respects to the critically inquiring mind, disciplined thinkers can no longer employ that glib retort of "the twenties." What is resorted to instead is a distinction between manageable and unmanageable areas of inquiry within immediate experience, and a decision to opt for a manageable course, letting the penumbra of undefined awareness hover about as a horizon of inquiry, serving to temper or restrain judgment; but not to intrude upon it as a constituent of inquiry itself. This, in effect, has been the procedure most common in disciplines where there is a sense of what the new modern consciousness speaks of as "the mystery of the universe" and of all experience, including the mystery of existing itself.

Since the time of William James, however, there have always been those who have been lured into contemplating this "MORE" in the very act of pursuing disciplined inquiry, partly on the assumption that inquiry cannot really be critical except as it is in some sense attentive to the MORE; or at least mindful of it, and to some degree concerned to sustain its impact upon thought, if only as a horizon of inquiry.

In recent literature the word "depth" has tended to replace the notion of "the MORE." The import of this change in language is to convey this "MORE" as being a dimension of what can be more vividly attended or apprehended; rather than, as James intended in his "experimental supernaturalism," "a realm of other Minds bordering upon our human consciousness in ways we but dimly apprehend." The effect of these changes in stance has been to reopen the subject of myth and to view it as a mode of human response to dimensions of experience that are possibly more subtle and sophisticated than nineteenth and early twentieth century anthropologists, as well as philosophers and theologians, represented it to be. In fact, symbolic discourse, itself both scientific and philosophical, has come under review afresh as being kinds of symbolization designed for specific purposes, chief of which is that of abstraction. Abstraction, whether designed along lines of philosophical or of scientific models, tends toward a common end: to render experience, or the data of experience, manageable within a given disciplined discourse. And, when manageability is made foremost in importance, something of indefinable importance in experience as lived is relinquished, or rendered inoperative as a contributing source of insight, namely understanding, or even truth concerning the way things are in the total passage of events within each moment of immediacy. Once this penumbra of undefined awareness attending every instance of precise, disciplined inquiry takes hold of one, intent upon reflecting upon the way things are in their depth of awareness, along with abstracted vistas of manageable data, concern to consider the import and the role of symbolic discourse other than abstraction is full upon one. And this is not by way of abandoning disciplined discourse for undisciplined modes of attending these depths of awareness, as in esoteric or evangelical modes of reverie, bent on occultism. It is rather to explore more critically modes of attending the subtleties of sensitive awareness arising from response to *the textured quality* of these lived experiences. And, as quickly, one senses that all disciplined discourse may not be subsumed under abstraction. There are levels of responding in giving expression to undefined awareness, ranging from sheer indulgent feeling and sentiment to the most subtle, restrained, and discerning responsiveness to what is being attended. The latter may come about as an achieved art of responsiveness through practiced discipline, or as a natural gift simply and continuously expressed.

IV

Now this review of developments in the modern consciousness is by way of asserting that we have moved beyond that earlier stage of the modern consciousness initiated by Bacon and Newton into a stage that is more temperate in its claim of exact knowledge concerning the universe and the life of humankind, on the one hand, and, on the other hand, more sensitive to dimensions of experience and reality which can be only marginally apprehended, but which can have important bearing upon all that we are and do. To some degree, it is assumed, these dimensions or depths of marginal awareness may be explored, and conceivably brought within range of our competence and explication. Yet, the bland assumption that was so widely held as late as the nineteen twenties that it was only a matter of time before the whole of reality could be so domesticated has clearly subsided. Not only has the limitation of tools of inquiry been more realistically appraised, but the illusory character of disciplined inquiry, itself, has been made apparent when the fallibility of our human forms and symbols is not taken adequately into account.

What has pressed this problem to the fore within certain philosophical and theological circles, notably among process theologians, taking their cues from James, Whitehead, and others such as Teilhard de Chardin, has not been the usual theological claims concerning man's fallibility as creature, but persisting insights from an emergent way of viewing life's experiences, a mode of thought which developed among British biologists and philosophers a generation or more ago under the influence of Bergson's *Creative Evolution*. Much of this mode of thought has passed into history; but what persists as a formative influence today is the recognition that, like any other natural structure, the human structure is limited, being definitive and expressive of a specific level of emergence, yet bodying forth within the human psyche a sense of prescience that impels a creatural thrust beyond its limited structure, giving rise to sensitivities, modes of awareness, yearnings which, in the language of S. Alexander, intrude "a nisus toward deity" in the human structure inherent in, but not of a piece with, its own structure. This formulation of the human structure and its prescient dimension has the effect of reasserting the creatural stance as being more readily attuned, and conceivably responsive, to "the MORE," or the depth of these immediacies of existence than the exercise of the sharpened intellect in critical, disciplined inquiry, where the latter proceeds with unawareness of or indifference toward that dimension of human existence. However this is judged, it is clear that some account of the creatural stance is being taken seriously at various levels of philosophical and religious inquiry. As mentioned above, it was implicit in the work of William James and Henri Bergson, and was given explicit formulation by emergent philosophers. Alfred North Whitehead, at the time that Bergson's influence was at its height in England, was too preoccupied with his own work in mathematics and the philosophy of nature to heed the urging of his emergent colleagues to read Bergson, though he read James with care and much appreciation. Later, however, he was to get around to Bergson. In *Process and Reality*, he was to produce a philosophy of organism which, in a way, gathered up into cosmological form the basic insights of the new physics along with this earlier lore of mathematics and biology, and thus, in effect, became the leading exponent of a process philosophy that subsumed much that had gone before into the shaping of a new modern consciousness in science and philosophy.

What is distinctive about Whitehead's work, apart from the way he summarily gathers up new, formative insights of the sciences and philosophies pertinent to a post-Newtonian perspective, into a structured cosmology, is its sensitivity to the tentative and experimental character of intellectual reflection upon the mystery of existing. The bodily event, expressive through existing and perceiving, carries within it depths of awareness that can be only partially and tentatively formulated in conceptual terms. Always the effort to formulate the conceptual vision is called back to the prior event of perception, and, by that course, to the primal event of existing. The audaciousness of Whitehead's own formulation of a conceptual system in *Process and Reality* may lead one to overlook this sensitivity in Whitehead; but it is there, and it is basic to an understanding of what he has put forth as a generalization upon these lived experiences.

There is implicit acknowledgement in both James and Whitehead that the creatural stance represents a primacy which no conceptual response in disciplined form can claim or emulate. It is a bit like returning to the act of concretion, itself, to address this primal point of origination. And, whenever this acknowledgment is made, it reverses the procedure commonly followed or assumed in rational systems where reason tends to designate, and even to dictate, the form and status of the reality so apprehended. Where the creatural stance is given weight as offering a primal perspective upon the realities of experience, the note of realism intrudes in decisive ways. And this is to see every created event in the context of the Creative Passage, itself, or of the ground of Reality, as we say. Although Whitehead, as interpreted in much of process thought today, would seem to reverse this procedure, I believe a careful reading of the empirical stance underlying his reflective cosmology would support the kind of realism I have indicated.

V

Phenomenologists, too, have been busy altering the record of reflection left by Hegel, and even Husserl, with regard to the primacy of the creatural stance. And this has taken the turn, first of modifying the conceptual character of intentionality in a way that embodies it more explicitly in the structured elan of experience as lived;[4] and then of attending more explicitly to modes of response more expressive of this primal reality than a conceptual mode conveyed through intentionality can effect. Interestingly enough, wherever this kind of revision has occurred in phenomenological literature, recourse to the mythical mode has been sought, as in Eliade's several works,[5] and, more recently, in Ricoeur's later writings dealing with the symbolic language and idiom of mythical discourse.[6] It could be said that modern phenomenologists have been more concerned than process philosophers and theologians to reaffirm and to explore the relevance of mythical discourse. And this

---

4. Cf. Merleau-Ponty, *The Phenomenology of Perception* (Paris: Gallimard, 1945).

5. Mircea Eliade, *The Myth of the Eternal Return* (Paris: Gallimard, 1949); *Myths, Dreams, and Mysteries* (Paris: Gallimard, 1957; London: Harvill Press, 1960); *The Sacred and the Profane* (New York: Harcourt, Brace, 1959); *Myth and Reality* (New York: Harper & Row, 1963).

6. Paul Ricoeur, "Philosophy and Religious Language," *The Journal of Religion* 54 (1974): 71-85.

derives in part from the original stance of their mode of inquiry: phenomenology having been from its inception in the work of Husserl, more attentive to the logic of thought as experienced than of experience as thought. Nevertheless there is within the legacy of process thought (I prefer the caption "empirical realism") a richer vein of what may be described as empirical sensibility, derived in large measure from the writings of William James. While this vein of the process heritage has been less to the fore in recent years than that of conceptual clarification, as pursued by Charles Hartshorne and a younger group of Whitehead's interpreters, it persists as a resource to be explored in the light of the conceptual advances made possible by these Whiteheadian scholars. Were this to be pursued, process thought, I am confident, would deepen in its understanding of the conceptual notions now employed as they relate to experience as lived. Conceivably, as a consequence of availing themselves more readily of this legacy of empirical sensibility, process theologians might find increasing rapport with current scholars among phenomenologists in their efforts to reinterpret and reassess the import of myth as a contemporary mode of symbolic discourse. The process legacy, I am confident, has much to contribute to the empirical understanding of the lived experience which phenomenological inquiry has not been able to convey, and, in fact, will not address since the focus of interest, influenced by its methodology, precludes it. On these grounds interchange between the two modes of inquiry may be severely limited; yet this need not preclude their mutual awareness and possible interplay of insight and judgment.[7]

Within the modern context, then, the symbolic discourse of myth, in one of its aspects, is to be understood as conveying tentative and explorative ways of acknowledging, denoting, or expressing the subtleties of wonder and surprise; or even intimations of experienced, but unnoted, depths of the Creative Passage within the commonplaces of human living. Whatever token of meaning or hope these occurrences may evoke concerning what may transcend these existent moments to give hint of what could pertain to the mystery of not existing, myth in this modern sense is not to be understood as being exclusively concerned with transcendent or projected meaning or expectation, in the sense implied in the *eschaton*, or the end of time. On the contrary, myth addresses these depths within the immediacies of existence as being a horizon of data and efficacy relevant to inquiry; though it may be inaccessible or unmanageable within modes of inquiry prescribed by the various recognized disciplines. Myth is, as we have indicated, expressive of a language of surprise and wonder, of subtle, even wistful apprehension of what is implicit in such events of surprise and wonder,

7. I have pursued this interplay between these two modes of inquiry in an essay, "Can Empirical Theology Learn Something from Phenomenology?" in *The Future of Empirical Theology*, edited by Bernard E. Meland (Chicago: The University of Chicago Press, 1969).

illumining the creatural stance of man—in these modern times, as in
more elemental stages of human history.

But another aspect of mythical discourse is equally pertinent:
myth has always been expressive of what inheres as a sensibility and
apprehension within the structure of experience that moves into every
moment of immediacy within any culture as a distillation from past
events and experiences. I have spoken of this pre-conscious or vaguely
conscious dimension of historical experience as the *mythos* of a people.[8]

Historians of religion have been increasingly attentive to this dimension of any cultural history, viewing it, not as an esoteric intrusion
from without the cultural history, but as an accumulative and persistent
expression of funded sensibilities which somehow are made expressive of
insistent valuations, deterrents, or behavioral tendencies among a people. These funded sensibilities declare, as it were, the legacy of faith
in terms of motivation and restraint, cherished meanings and incentives,
giving shape to the cultural ethos and intention of a people. This
legacy may not be ignored within any period of a culture's history
without loss to the qualitative overtones of its communal experience
and expression. For, as a qualitative dimension of the historical experience, it is even more formative of a people's psyche, style, and mode
of expressiveness than traditions established more formally through
institutional acts and precedents. Yet this legacy of sensibility and
shaping is continually susceptible of a reshaping in societies, especially
where *living forward* is attended by impulses to *think forward*. But the
kind of thinking forward that is best suited to such a role, both in
being sensitive to subtle nuances of such experiences of change, and
commonly available in idioms and responses of feeling, is that which
occurs in narrative vision, or reflective reverie and probing, as in art,
literature, and drama, or other media eliciting a creative outreach or
response. Where there is an atmosphere of spontaneous participation in
creative expression through narrative, imaginative reverie or surmise,
resources of creative outreach and change are more readily at hand to
adapt these depths of motivation conveyed through the mythos to what
is continually emerging in cultural experiences as a farther or innovating range of experience. Direct attack upon such subtle issues of
change or reconception in the culture's mode of experience, as in moralistic reform or simply didactic moralizing, can be self-defeating, and
generally is so. And it has the further defect of generating within a
society a "closed morality" (Bergson) that defeats or obstructs such
creative change, thus rendering the mythos moribund. In large measure, the health of cultural history turns rather subtly upon its freedom
to be expressive in the imaginative mode in ways that can transmit its
inheritance of feeling and sensibility to emerging moments within the

---

8. Cf. Bernard E. Meland, *The Realities of Faith: The Revolution in Cultural
Forms* (New York: Oxford University Press, 1962). Also, "Christian Legacy and
Our Cultural Memory', The American Academy of Religion Proceedings, 1970, p. 25ff.

structure of experience in a confrontation that intermingles persisting sensibilities and an open awareness toward change. Moral zeal and pragmatic concern with the commonweal can seldom effect such a creative transition; for their bent of interest tends to be addressed to more coercive and restrictive ends.

The creative mind and spirit, however, expressed through imagination, wonder, creatural yearning, as expressed in the arts and literature, are rarely given the opportunity to be socially renewing or redemptive in modern societies. In societies ardently committed to past valuation; or, conversely, to new valuations presently being established by radical reform, creative art is generally considered suspect. At best, where there is pressure to seem tolerant of individual capacity and expressiveness, creative expression in the arts and in literature is generally tolerated as a concession to individual initiative. Yet imagination, wonder, and creatural sensibility appropriate to such expression are rarely esteemed in modern societies as having social value. Rather, their media tend to be viewed as modes of escape from serious concerns or involvement; or as ways of indulging individual tastes in leisurely pursuits, or as entertainment.

The nub of the issue, therefore, involved in the query concerning the relevance or import of myth as a discourse in modern times, and its relation to science, comes down to a proper or adequate assessment and esteem of the art of wonder and open awareness in the context of exercising disciplined thought and action in addressing the serious ends of modern life.

Bernard E. Meland / University of Chicago

One of the methodological limitations that has often been ascribed to
an empirically or phenomenologically oriented theology is its seeming
reticence in speaking of the reality of God. Modes of thought employed
in classical philosophies of Being, or in recent forms of Absolute
Idealism, have been less plagued with such reticence since the system,
itself, in each instance made vivid how one was to think of God: that
is, as Absolute Being or as Absolute Mind. To the degree that
reflection moves more closely to the realities of experience wherein
something approximating specification of meaning within the experienced
or lived events is expected or demanded, simply to give the assurances
of logic concerning the ultimate reality may not suffice. Does what is
affirmed in language square with realities as experienced or lived?
     The reticence implicit in Schleiermacher's theology with regard to
the reality of God is well known. The feeling of absolute dependence
in man was the nearest he was to come to an explicit apprehension of
such a reality; but this was enough to suggest the numinous presence of
God. And an emerging God-consciousness in the men and women of his
congregation was sufficient evidence of their encounter with that
reality. The same reticence appears in Rudolf Otto's The Idea of the
Holy; and the restraint evidenced in Paul Tillich's doctrine of God was
such as to impel some of his philosophical colleagues to pose the
question, "Is Tillich an atheist?" Restraint in such matters is often
taken to mean negation when, in fact, it may imply quite the opposite.
To be sure, any reluctance to express conceptually what is implicitly
affirmed carries some degree of skepticism with regard to historic or
traditional formulations already affirmed. Yet this is more apt to
imply a skepticism with regard to the formulations, themselves, or with
the effort to conceptualize a reality so profound and unavailable for
thought; though it can imply as well a kind of reverent caution against
believing too readily what is not easily formulated. Such reticence,
in turn, may express sheer skepticism concerning the reality itself; or
it may indicate a stance of open awareness toward reality with a
sufficient degree of trust and waiting to pursue these depths of
experience more rigorously and patiently. In his book, The Skeptical
Approach to Religion,[1] Paul Elmer More undertook to defend skepticism
as an appropriate dimension of the reverent and discriminating mind.

---

1. The Skeptical Approach to Religion (Princeton: Princeton
   University Press, 1934).

People believe too much, too easily, he argued. They become offensive to the discriminating mind in their zeal to lay violent hands upon matters which really should evoke more reserve and a sense of distance. In another essay, entitled Pages from an Oxford Diary, he wrote:

> The fool hath said in his heart there is no God, yet after all, is there a God? One thing is certain: despite the innumerable essays of pagan and Christian rationalists, reason has never been able to prove to its own satisfaction the existence of a God. And what reason cannot demonstrate, the "fool" has some excuse for rejecting.[2]

Despite his skeptical approach to religion, however, More was by no means indifferent to the reality of God, or in any way insecure about the fact of that reality. I. common with Christian humanists of all ages, he chose to affirm that reality and to pursue its implications for human destiny. What he did deny and openly decry is the philosopher's or mystic's expectation that one could come upon knowledge of God. On these grounds he turned his back upon all modern quests for God and took his stand with the traditional Church in affirming God.

He was, along with Irving Babbitt of Harvard, the leading exponent of Classical Humanism among American men and women of letters a generation ago. Unlike Babbitt, who despised and openly "hated the Church,"[3] Paul Elmer More embraced its tradition with a moral zeal, preferring to call himself a Christian Humanist. Humanist, here, meant not disbelief in God, but an ardent belief in the human spirit, following from a presupposition of affirming God.

Rudolf Otto, in quite a different way, cautioned restraint in conceptualizing the Holy. One comes upon the idea of the Holy, he argued, as a kind of distillation from various numinous moments in experience. It is a sense of The Wholly Other, awakening a feeling of awe, mingled with a deep sense of unworthiness, and evoking a creature feeling. Otto was elaborating the sense of the numinous in experience, which he claimed Schleiermacher had re-discovered.[4]

One will recognize in Rudolf Otto's approach to the Holy an element that appeared also in the theology of Paul Tillich, who acknowledged Otto's influence. For Tillich, too, the idea of the Holy was appropriate; but to venture beyond this presupposition, except in symbolic terms, was for him to violate that propriety. Thus Being-Itself, which was Tillich's one literal assertion pointing to the reality of God, must be considered comparable to, and in some sense informed by, Rudolf Otto's idea of the Holy.[5]

---

2. Pages from an Oxford Diary (Princeton: Princeton University Press, 1936).

3. Paul Elmer More in his essay on Babbitt in On Being Human, recalls Babbitt stopping before a church in North Avenue, and with a gesture of bitter contempt, exclaiming, "There is the enemy! There is the thing I hate!"

4. Religious Essays (London: Oxford University Press, 1931), Chapter VIII.

5. I am aware that the ontology of Schelling is more determining in

Behind all these men stands the gaunt and cautious figure of
Immanuel Kant with his restraint in attending to the thing-in-itself.
Kant, in effect, set aside all rational arguments for the existence of
God by demonstrating how inaccessible this thing-in-itself is to the
reasoning mind. In lieu of knowledge of God or of a reasoned argument
for God's existence, Kant affirmed belief in God as a necessary idea
and as a practical postulate. One might say that this resolution of
the problem of God was in direct response to the skepticism of Hume.

The skepticism of Hume, in fact, hovered like a low-hanging cloud
over the whole of the liberal period. And its shadow is nowhere more
evident than in liberal attempts to deal with the problem of God. The
weakness of the liberal's skepticism lay in the fact that it did not
retain the note of tension and restraint which the skeptical attitude
normally and properly provides. Instead, liberals tended to find in
the human equation, including the humanity of Jesus, all that they
regarded necessary to their religious needs. In this way, the
dimension of the holy, the quality of otherness was progressively lost
sight of. Christocentric liberalism, which made the historically human
Jesus the center and norm of its theology, may be said to have been the
essence of the liberal's faith. This turn of liberal theology reached
the summit of Christocentricism in the assertion that God must be as
good as Jesus. "We believe Him to be so," commented one American
Ritschlian, "but if compelled to choose between believing in Jesus and
believing in a God who is not as good as Jesus, we will choose to
believe in the historical Jesus."

The shock of Schweitzer's Quest of the Historical Jesus, in
undercutting the premises of Christocentric theology, opened the way
for a new period of skepticism in liberal thought, reaching even to the
liberal's belief in the historical Jesus. The loss of this
transcendent norm left the liberal fiercely dependent upon human values
and human ideals. And once disillusionment with this Christocentric
summit was expressed, the descent to humanism was swift and resolute.[6]

The appeal of humanism is not to be denied. Once one has been rid
of the idea of God and of the problem it creates, to say nothing of the

---

Tillich's system. I am suggesting only that Tillich's use of the
religious symbol in pointing to the Holy in ecstatic moments of
experience or history partakes of Otto's analogical method.
6. One will see in the theologians of "the Chicago School," especially
in Shailer Mathews and Gerald Birney Smith, an attempt to steer a
middle course between Christocentricism and Humanism. Both men had
been attracted to Ritschlianism in their earlier years, but
relinquished it as they developed a more explicit socio-historical
method in which the sciences played a determining role. Mathews
continued to correlate what he called "generic Christianity,"
centering in the New Testament witness to the historic Jesus, with
his scientific modernism, but G. B. Smith was impelled to abandon
dependence upon an historic norm and instead sought recourse to
what he called "a mystic experiment in the natural environment."
Cf. Shailer Mathews, The Faith of Modernism (New York: The
Macmillan Co., 1925); and G. B. Smith, Current Christian Thinking
(Chicago: University of Chicago Press, 1928), especially Chapter
IX, "The Modern Quest for God."

whole theological enterprise and the problems it creates, one can breathe free air again. It is like unburdening oneself of a heavy weight, or like breaking free of the old world of inhibitions and restraining sensibilities, and of entering unencumbered into a new country.

What humanists overlooked, however, and in a way chose to ignore, is the limitation of the human structure. There was a bent of idealism at work within their mode of thought, magnifying the role and status of reason, and of human value, beyond its bounds.[7] The religious humanism of that period, in fact, was a truncated idealism--Absolute Idealism shorn of the Absolute. The humanist simply collapsed the inflated Ego which Hegelianism had blown up into an Absolute; yet the powers of idealization remained as functions of human imagination. The function of creative imagination itse'', in fact, was given the connotation of deity.[8]

The Religious Humanism of the nineteen twenties and after represented a more spirited, non-theistic view than was common among Christocentric liberals who had capitulated to the view that the logic of liberalism led to humanism. The latter accepted their plight reluctantly, and sought to salvage their legacy of faith within a perspective of idealization impelled by devotion to the historical Jesus, and by recognition of the ultimate worth of that which is "highest in man." The religious humanist, on the other hand, whose mood and spirit was more akin to that of the radical deists of the seventeenth and eighteenth centuries than of twentieth century theological liberals, found a sense of release in being rid of the idea of God and of being unencumbered with old-world inhibitions and restraining theological sensibilities. This mood of release is reflected in the spirit of inquiry evident in the work of Max C. Otto, who zealously affirmed his disbelief in God by way of affirming man.[9]

In some instances religious humanism took the form of a truncated idealism, as in the philosophy of John Dewey. Dewey employed the word "God" in A Common Faith;[10] but, in doing so, he meant to lift up the significantly creative function of the idealizing process at work in man and society. It becomes a moot point in that context whether one is expressing theism or humanism. Because of the way theism was commonly understood, Dewey dissociated himself from any implication ascribed to his position which might identify him with that tradition;

7. One of the most cogent arguments countering modern humanism will be found in Charles Hartshorne, Beyond Humanism (New York: Harpers, 1937).
8. To test this assertion one should first read Feuerbach's Das Wesen des Christentums, 1840 (What Is Christianity?). Cf. Harold Hoffding's rendering of Feuerbach in A History of Philosophy (London: Macmillan & Co., 1924), Vol. II, pp. 276ff, an excerpt from which appears in American Philosophies of Religion by Wieman and Meland (New York: Harper & Brothers, 1936), pp. 254-55; and then read John Dewey, A Common Faith (New Haven: Yale University Press, 1934).
9. Cf. Things and Ideals (New York: Holt, 1924); and (with Wieman and Macintosh) Is there a God? (Chicago: Willett, Clark & Co., 1932).
10. (New Haven: Yale University Press, 1934).

hence he preferred the company of humanists. His use of the word, "God," was really but a manner of speaking to express vividly and emphatically his esteem of the act of creative imagination which could impel unqualified commitment to creative advance in human thinking and in devotion to social ends. It was understandable that Wieman was to find affinity with what Dewey had written in A Common Faith and to assume that what Dewey had set forth was expressive of what he was about in presenting "a working idea of God." Dewey, however, rejected that implication. In retrospect, it appears that Wieman was right; for in Wieman's later works, beginning with The Source of Human Good, in which the notion of God is set forth as a four-fold Creative Event, the affinity with Dewey has become clearly persuasive. Wieman, himself, said in his later years that, as he looked back over the years, he found that he had had more in common with Dewey's concern than with that of any other contemporary philosopher.

II

In its minimal form, the implication of affirming God is to acknowledge the dependence of man. However negative this may seem as a basis for affirming God, it is nevertheless a pervasive notion throughout all literature concerning belief in God. It can be detected in the biblical literature from Genesis through the Pauline epistles. It is re-echoed in Augustine, and in much of Reformation thought, especially in Luther; it is clearly evident in Schleiermacher and in modern theologians from Barth to Wieman and Tillich.

The sense of human dependence is the beginning of piety. There is nothing particularly noble about that notion. In fact, piety, stemming from the initial perception of dependence, has often taken a rather crass and depressing form, setting the human being in so servile a relation to deity as to rob him of any sense of human dignity. It is this aspect of piety that has aroused sensitive human spirits to decry all religions of piety as being unworthy of man's higher impulses and to appraise it as essentially degrading in its effects upon the human spirit.

As an alternative, these sensitive minds have argued for a religion of spirituality that sees the beginning of religion in an impulse to relate oneself with God in a common venture of spirit.[11] The one has stressed the weakness and depravity of man, requiring the redemptive power of a higher reality. The other has stressed the ideal aspects of man, his more sensitive yearnings, his will to pursue the higher good.

When these two aspects, piety and spirituality, are held apart, each tends toward a dissipation of what the other holds to be important. Piety, devoid of this impulse toward spirituality, depreciates the human will to the point of regarding it wholly impotent and incapable of higher motivations. In fact, all such motivations are dismissed as being a form of idolatry, identifying the finer human

---

11. Cf. George Santayana, Reason in Religion (New York: Scribners, 1905); and Walter Lippmann, A Preface to Morals (New York: Macmillan, 1929).

feelings with rebellion against God. Ultimately all idealizations of the human spirit and aspirations get cancelled out as being opposed to the worship of God.

Spirituality, on the other hand, when it develops a contempt for piety, loses both proportion and realism regarding human nature. It is this tendency that gives credence to the pietist's claim that such spirituality idealizes man and ultimately equates him with God.

Now this is where dependence upon typologies goes astray. For to choose between these two types of response to the reality of God would mean to pass over or to pass by the most discerning and most mature forms of witness to the reality of God. For these have been sensitive and responsive to both aspects--not in the way that either expression of faith has appeared as a typology, but in a way that has held the two aspects in a creative tension as inseparable and counteracting dimensions, appropriate to the complexity in which the life of faith is pursued.

No affirmation of God partakes of the realism of the Christian witness that passes lightly over the limitations implied in the notion of our dependence and the consequent ambiguity, even the evil and frailty, of the human situation. This is a prerequisite to understanding the real peril and tragic import of human existence, as well as the import of affirming God's otherness and the sense of the holy. Man and God stand in a Contradiction that sets the problem of Creation, and which makes creation incomplete apart from redemption.

Yet no affirmation of God partakes of the poignancy and beauty as well as the sensitive depth of the Christian witness that overlooks, or relinquishes over-readily, this yearning of the human spirit which dares to equate its vision and hunger for goodness with the ultimate venture of God. This is a prerequisite to understanding the meaning of freedom in God and of freedom in man. It is essential also to understanding the communion and companionship between them, which follows from the fact that this freedom in relationship exists, is respected, and is accepted as the badge of our authenticity as creatures who were created good, despite our every denial, despite even our individuation, and our alienation.

But these statements serve only to define the climate in which the Christian witness concerning God occurs. They do not get at the question, How real is this affirmation of God? Does the Christian witness really affirm God literally and unmistakably?

This I take it is the most difficult question to resolve regarding the Christian witness to God's reality. The issue comes down to the nature of the affirmation--not only whether it is literal or symbolic; but whether it implies doubt as well as certainty and to what degree; whether it rests upon an act of faith or upon evidence, and to what degree.

We are back again to the question that opened our discussion: The question as to how far skepticism is appropriate to any witness concerning God. Contrary to what might be commonly supposed, the Christian witness concerning God does move very close to the skeptical attitude. That is to say, any tendency to take belief in God too casually, or to make belief in God an easy matter of demonstration; or to seem to know too much abc · God, is bound to be opposed by sensitive Christian thinkers.

Where the spirit of the Old Testament has pervaded Christian thinking a pronounced sense of distance and restraint in speaking of "the Most High" has been in evidence. To be sure, there is a qualitative difference between this kind of reverent skepticism, accompanying belief, and the audacious disbelief that simply disavows God's existence on the grounds of insufficient evidence. The former is always an assertion of belief, in the mood of a prayer that invariably ends, "Help thou my unbelief."

There is, however, something approaching kinship of spirit between the two kinds of skeptics. It is as if each had assessed the burden of belief alike, as being more than the mind can bear; and as if each had taken a common measure of "the mind's allegiance to despair."

III

It is often argued that the representative Christian affirmation of God is not an act of mind, but an act of will. If left to the mind, so it is said, skepticism would inevitably triumph. The balance in favor of the act of faith is due to a will to believe against the impulse to doubt. I think one cannot fail to feel the force of this position, however unsatisfactory one may judge it to be.

The point here turns upon a vast body of discussion having to do with the mystery and greatness of God, on the one hand; and on the other hand, with the limitations in human nature and its capacity for apprehending such a reality other than itself. The most aggressive efforts to bring the reality of God within human comprehension have occurred, obviously, during those periods and in those situations in which man has placed a high estimate upon the powers of human reason.[12] The restraining efforts, amounting at times to an aversion to acknowledging God on any grounds other than the act of faith, have occurred when reason, itself, was under threat of devaluation.[13] In between one finds restraint emboldened by some effort at a minimum designation of deity to which reason can give its seal of approval, or by a method for apprehending God, appropriate to His nature, which will justify a correlation of faith and reason.[14]

The question as to whether belief in God implies a literal response to something definitive and concrete, or a symbolic response to a reality beyond definition or designation, turns upon one's estimate of structures and relations and upon one's estimate of the ultimate effect of such relations upon the ontological dignity of God.

It was interesting to note how shocked Tillich could become over the question, Does God exist? This was simply the wrong question to ask, in Tillich's judgment. God as Being itself was for him a presupposition of all existence, but to ask does He exist was, in Tillich's view, to assume Him to be an object along with other objects, i.e., to have relations and to be explicitly affected both by these

---

12. Cf. the Greek theologians Origen and Clement of Alexandria, Thomas Aquinas and the Scholastics, Descartes, Spinoza, Leibniz, Hegel, Royce, Whitehead, and Hartshorne.
13. Augustine, Luther, Calvin, Kant, Kierkegaard, Barth, Niebuhr.
14. Schleiermacher, Schelling, James, Bergson, Wieman, Tillich.

relations and by the structure through which his concern and intent are actualized. To Tillich this was blasphemy, while to Wieman and Hartshorne it need not be so at all. This was so because the logic of Tillich's system required him to view God as the ground of all structures which can never be actualized or made concrete except as it is made transparent through ecstatic instances when revelation occurs: "The Gestalts of Grace," erupting into conscious experience or into historic moments of the Kairos, presented for Tillich a semblance of God appearing concretely in history. And the appearance of Jesus as the Christ, bringing forth new Being, was for him a decisive instance of God as essential nature taking the form of existence without incurring the fall. But all this was in the nature of symbolic discourse, rather than literal description; for it amounted to employing structural imagery to represent a vivid truth of essence and existence, or to render us aware of this truth which, in the nature of the case, cannot be brought to the level of descriptive occurrences.

Wieman's attack on this problem moved in quite a different sphere. He dissociated himself both from the underlying skepticism in Christian faith concerning God and from the symbolic response to God as Being or as reality transcending the human mind. To Wieman, both the skepticism and the act of faith in the Christian witness present a problem to be solved. The ambiguity underlying each and persisting in each, he was convinced, leads to possibilities of illusion and idolatry. "God is more than we can think," he acknowledged; yet God is not beyond our thinking in every respect. Except as we employ a minimum of perception and thought, he argued, we have no way of knowing whether we encounter God or some illusory object of our own making or idealization.

Wieman's definition and description of the dynamic structure of events to which he attributed the meaning of God as creative event, was his attempt to grasp in minimum form the criteria which give empirical certainty, within this limited scope, that what is being attended to and worshipped is really God--the reality creative of good and worthy of our supreme commitment.[15] What is perceived, Wieman asserted, is not all that inheres in the reality of God. For the fullness of God's reality is abundant beyond anything the human mind can perceive or think. But the minimum certainty which such a criterion affords, he insisted, enables one to give himself with complete abandon and trust to this Abundance of Good beyond our reach or grasp.[16]

Hartshorne would seem to be nearer to Tillich than to Wieman in the sensibilities of his thought concerning God. For he means to speak of the reality of God in the ultimate and inclusive way that has characterized historical theism. Yet Hartshorne manifests the same insistent concern evident in Wieman's work to have explicit assurance concerning the fact and reality of God that motivated Wieman's

---

15. A full discussion of these criteria is given in Wieman's The Source of Human Good (Chicago: University of Chicago Press, 1946), esp. Ch. III.

16. Cf. "The Absolute Commitment of Faith," Christendom 2 (1937): 202-14. This essay is important for an understanding of how the dimension of depth enters into Wieman's thinking upon the nature of God. It is one of the few places where this aspect of his thought is fully discussed.

thinking. The routes by which Wieman and Hartshorne have sought specificity and certainty in their understanding of the reality of God have differed. Wieman sought to develop "a science of God," that is, a working formula by which the data of a structure of reality worthy of commitment and devotion could be specified. For Hartshorne, on the other hand, demonstrating the layers of perfection became imperative, and this has become an absorbing task for him through the years.

Wieman's concern to particularize the meaning of God for purposes of verification led him to turn away from most of the problems concerning God to which metaphysics and theological inquiry have generally addressed themselves., His procedure thus took on a singularly empirical character that excluded, not only the notion of fullness of meaning such as may be implied in a term like Being or Norms of Being, but rational inquiry that undertakes in any way to go beyond experienced or perceived events in the exposition or explanation of God's meaning. Hartshorne, on the other hand, has sought to appropriate both the scope of a philosophy of Being in his philosophy of Becoming and the concreteness of empirical theology. He has done so by insisting that "The most general abstractions from experience are still experiential, they cannot refer to what is just not experience, to mere matter, mere being."[17] By this means he came to the assertion that cosmic being is cosmic experience. God thus assumes a concreteness of character in Hartshorne's thought which seems to partake of an empirical orientation comparable to that of Wieman's; yet it has the metaphysical reach of Tillich's theism.

This dipolarity of Hartshorne's theism, and the consistency with which he pursues it, may be said to be the distinctive characteristic of his thought. In so far as Tillich's Logos Christology can be assimilated, or be regarded as being integral, to his metaphysics, his reflections upon God could also be said to participate in a dipolar mode of theism. It is apparently on these grounds that Hartsorne, in commenting on "Tillich's Doctrine of God," heartily welcomed him as "one of the rapidly growing company of dipolar theists."[18]

IV

The revival of a dipolar mode of theism in recent philosophy and religious thought has been attributed to Alfred North Whitehead.[19] Here both the juxtaposition and the interplay of essence and existence are given a modern rendition within the processes of the natural universe. Working within the philosophical tradition, Whitehead, in effect, confronted inherited cosmologies as given in Plato's Timaeus and the writings of Seventeenth Century scientists and philosophers (Galileo, Descartes, Newton and Locke) with the advance in knowledge represented

17. Man's Vision of God (Chicago: Willett, Clark & Co., 1941), p. 346.
18. The Theology of Paul Tillich, Charles W. Kegley and Robert W. Bretall, eds. (New York: Macmillan, 1952), p. 166.
19. Cf. J. E. Boodin, Three Interpretations of the Universe (New York: Macmillan, 1934), p. 41. See also Charles Hartsorne and William L. Reese, Philosophers Speak of God (Chicago: University of Chicago Press, 1953), pp. 278-79.

feelings with rebellion against God. Ultimately all idealizations of
the human spirit and aspirations get cancelled out as being opposed to
the worship of God.

Spirituality, on the other hand, when it develops a contempt for
piety, loses both proportion and realism regarding human nature. It is
this tendency that gives credence to the pietist's claim that such
spirituality idealizes man and ultimately equates him with God.

Now this is where dependence upon typologies goes astray. For to
choose between these two types of response to the reality of God would
mean to pass over or to pass by the most discerning and most mature
forms of witness to the reality of God. For these have been sensitive
and responsive to both aspects—not in the way that either expression
of faith has appeared as a typology, but in a way that has held the two
aspects in a creative tension as inseparable and counteracting
dimensions, appropriate to the complexity in which the life of faith is
pursued.

No affirmation of God partakes of the realism of the Christian
witness that passes lightly over the limitations implied in the notion
of our dependence and the consequent ambiguity, even the evil and
frailty, of the human situation. This is a prerequisite to
understanding the real peril and tragic import of human existence, as
well as the import of affirming God's otherness and the sense of the
holy. Man and God stand in a Contradiction that sets the problem of
Creation, and which makes creation incomplete apart from redemption.

Yet no affirmation of God partakes of the poignancy and beauty as
well as the sensitive depth of the Christian witness that overlooks, or
relinquishes over-readily, this yearning of the human spirit which
dares to equate its vision and hunger for goodness with the ultimate
venture of God. This is a prerequisite to understanding the meaning of
freedom in God and of freedom in man. It is essential also to
understanding the communion and companionship between them, which
follows from the fact that this freedom in relationship exists, is
respected, and is accepted as the badge of our authenticity as
creatures who were created good, despite our every denial, despite even
our individuation, and our alienation.

But these statements serve only to define the climate in which the
Christian witness concerning God occurs. They do not get at the
question, How real is this affirmation of God? Does the Christian
witness really affirm God literally and unmistakably?

This I take it is the most difficult question to resolve regarding
the Christian witness to God's reality. The issue comes down to the
nature of the affirmation—not only whether it is literal or symbolic;
but whether it implies doubt as well as certainty and to what degree;
whether it rests upon an act of faith or upon evidence, and to what
degree.

We are back again to the question that opened our discussion: The
question as to how far skepticism is appropriate to any witness
concerning God. Contrary to what might be commonly supposed, the
Christian witness concerning God does move very close to the skeptical
attitude. That is to say, any tendency to take belief in God too
casually, or to make belief i. God an easy matter of demonstration; or
to seem to know too much about God, is bound to be opposed by sensitive
Christian thinkers.

Where the spirit of the Old Testament has pervaded Christian thinking a pronounced sense of distance and restraint in speaking of "the Most High" has been in evidence. To be sure, there is a qualitative difference between this kind of reverent skepticism, accompanying belief, and the audacious disbelief that simply disavows God's existence on the grounds of insufficient evidence. The former is always an assertion of belief, in the mood of a prayer that invariably ends, "Help thou my unbelief."

There is, however, something approaching kinship of spirit between the two kinds of skeptics. It is as if each had assessed the burden of belief alike, as being more than the mind can bear; and as if each had taken a common measure of "the mind's allegiance to despair."

III

It is often argued that the representative Christian affirmation of God is not an act of mind, but an act of will. If left to the mind, so it is said, skepticism would inevitably triumph. The balance in favor of the act of faith is due to a will to believe against the impulse to doubt. I think one cannot fail to feel the force of this position, however unsatisfactory one may judge it to be.

The point here turns upon a vast body of discussion having to do with the mystery and greatness of God, on the one hand; and on the other hand, with the limitations in human nature and its capacity for apprehending such a reality other than itself. The most aggressive efforts to bring the reality of God within human comprehension have occurred, obviously, during those periods and in those situations in which man has placed a high estimate upon the powers of human reason.[12] The restraining efforts, amounting at times to an aversion to acknowledging God on any grounds other than the act of faith, have occurred when reason, itself, was under threat of devaluation.[13] In between one finds restraint emboldened by some effort at a minimum designation of deity to which reason can give its seal of approval, or by a method for apprehending God, appropriate to His nature, which will justify a correlation of faith and reason.[14]

The question as to whether belief in God implies a literal response to something definitive and concrete, or a symbolic response to a reality beyond definition or designation, turns upon one's estimate of structures and relations and upon one's estimate of the ultimate effect of such relations upon the ontological dignity of God.

It was interesting to note how shocked Tillich could become over the question, Does God exist? This was simply the wrong question to ask, in Tillich's judgment. God as Being itself was for him a presupposition of all existence, but to ask does He exist was, in Tillich's view, to assume Him to be an object along with other objects, i.e., to have relations and to be explicitly affected both by these

12. Cf. the Greek theologians Origen and Clement of Alexandria, Thomas Aquinas and the Scholastics, Descartes, Spinoza, Leibniz, Hegel, Royce, Whitehead, and Hartshorne.
13. Augustine, Luther, Calvin, Kant, Kierkegaard, Barth, Niebuhr.
14. Schleiermacher, Schelling, James, Bergson, Wieman, Tillich.

by relativity physics and modern mathematics. Within this revised modern version or vision of the cosmos he addressed himself to the age-old inquiry concerning the reality of God, addressing himself as well to the inherited symbolism of essence and existence. From this line of inquiry he projected his dipolar view, differentiating between the <u>primordial</u> nature and the <u>consequent</u> nature of God. Whitehead's projection of the primordial nature of God carries the connotation of being purely abstract; yet one needs to recognize that his detailed characterization of that primordial nature, conveying what is implied in every instance of concretion, points up processes that are visibly creative of concrete occasions and situations. For creativity is seen as being incessant and diversified, yielding richly textured modes of events and circumstances, individuated and communal, sharply contrasted yet complementary, or at least implicitly related. The source of insight from which Whitehead envisaged and depicted these creative happenings is an aesthetic order of relations distilled from his own research and that of modern physicists and related fields of inquiry. In the consequent nature of God, this primordial Source of all that exists is portrayed as a living presence; and thus concerned as participant and companion within all creation.

Increasingly I have felt that what is distinctive and impelling in Whitehead's formulation of the meaning of God, beyond what he provides in updating the dipolar imagery, and in employing and interpreting the contributions of modern science within a new cosmology, stems from his insistence on reconceiving the implications of the term "Order", and the consequences he was to derive from that reconception. His announcement of this reconception was made explicit in <u>Religion in the Making</u> when he wrote:

> The metaphysical doctrine, here expounded, finds the foundations of the world in the aesthetic experience, rather than--as with Kant--in the cognitive and conceptive experience. All order is therefore aesthetic order, and the moral order is merely certain aspects of aesthetic order. The actual world is the outcome of the aesthetic order, and the aesthetic order is derived from the immanence of God.[20]

For, as he had observed earlier, "God is the measure of the aesthetic consistency of the world."[21] These observations are followed by a further one:

> The birth of a new aesthetic experience depends on the maintenance of two principles by the creative purpose.
>
> 1. The novel consequent must be graded in relevance so as to preserve some identity of character with the ground.
>
> 2. The novel consequent must be graded in relevance so as to preserve some contrast with the ground in

---

20. <u>Religion in the Making</u> (New York: Macmillan, 1926), pp. 104-05.
21. Ibid., p. 99.

respect to that same identity of character. . . .

All aesthetic experience is feeling arising out of <u>the</u>
<u>realization</u> of <u>contrast</u> <u>under</u> <u>identity</u>.[22]

Contrast under identity, which is an aesthetic symbolism, is the key to
the meaning Whitehead gives to the concept of relations as he employs
it in various contexts such as God and his creatures, or that of
relating human beings to one another, as when he writes, "The topic of
religion is individual in community."[23] This is not to be understood
simply as a social conception of realities; rather it conveys or
implies conceivable tension and dissonance appropriate to the contrasts
within an imagery of correlation appropriate to their identity. The
aesthetic imagery does in fact imply a tensional correlation of the
themes of dissonance and coherence, as contrasted with a rationalistic
or moralistic imagery oriented solely toward resolution in an imagery
of coherence.

A decade later Whitehead was to say,

The distinction between logic and aesthetics consists in the
degree of abstraction involved. Logic concentrates attention
upon high abstraction, and aesthetics keeps us close to the
concrete as the necessities of finite understanding permit.
Thus logic and aesthetics are at the two extremes of the
dilemma of the finite mentality in its partial penetration of
the infinite.[24]

It may be pertinent to add that within the "space-time" imagery
employed in Whitehead's metaphysics, wherein awareness of the
processive character of spatial dimensions is consonant with the
temporal passage being spatially structured, the aesthetic vision of
relations would seem especially illuminating, if not imperative. This
is made evident both in the abstractive envisagement of creativity as
expressed in Whitehead's conception of God as primordial, and in the
concrete envisagement of God and His creatures in his view of God's
consequent nature. In fact it is implicit throughout Whitehead's
discussion of relational themes, as in his "doctrine of prehension" and
in his "reformed principle of subjectivity." In both themes the
principle of "contrast under identity" is vividly exemplified.

---

22. Ibid., p. 115.
23. Ibid., p. 58.
24. <u>Modes of Thought</u> (New York: Macmillan, 1938 [paperback, New York:
G. P. Putnam's Sons, 1958, p. 84]). The fact that these
observations and judgments appear in lesser works is no reason to
ignore them as being irrelevant to Whitehead's major works; for, as
Arthur Murphy has pointed out in his essay, "Whitehead and the
Method of Speculative Philosophy," <u>The Philosophy of Alfred North
Whitehead</u>, Paul Arthur Schilpp, ed. (New York: Tudor Publishing
Co., 1941), the primacy given to aesthetic experience permeates the
whole of Whitehead's metaphysical system as expounded in <u>Process
and Reality</u> and <u>The Adventure of Ideas</u>.

Whitehead's use of the aesthetic imagery is again exemplified in the way he employs the concept of God's primordial nature. Although presented as a presupposition of creativity, the primordial nature is not dealt with wholly as abstracted. For, consonant with his imagery expressive of aesthetic order, there is implicit in Whitehead's procedure a readiness to discern, in the new understanding of physical and relational occurrences within the universe, substantial grounding for the abstractive notions that are advanced within a philosophy of organism. His presentation thus becomes a matter of pointing to rationally defensible grounds for acknowledging the Source of creativity, and conceivably for illumining a long-standing symbolic idiom expressive .of a primordial and continuing Source of all that exists. While this primordial Source is differentiated, it is not dissociated from what pervades experience or existence as a Consequent and living Presence within all creation. And this is again to express symbolically--though with implications that are to be taken quite literally as being expressive of sensibilities, attentiveness, and "caringness" in the processes of reality--"a tenderness which loses nothing that can be saved," and "a wisdom which uses what in the temporal world is mere wreckage."[25] These are poetical, even mythical symbolisms, employed by Whitehead quite consciously to convey explicit implications drawn from an organismic cosmology as contrasted with that of sheer mechanism.

My own reflections upon the reality of God have drawn heavily upon the imagery and sensibilities of Whitehead's exposition of his organismic cosmology, especially as they relate to modes of awareness in exploring the relational theme, which I have found to be basic to his philosophy of theism.[26] The fact that I have given special attention to addressing the orientation of human awareness and its outreach, which can enable one to be responsive to that "which is more than we can think", is not to be interpreted simply as mystical or empirical in approach, implying a rejection or dismissal of abstractive considerations. The abstractive, however, tends to be provisional in my reflections as being instrumental toward generating degrees of intelligibility in projecting religious awareness and wonder appropriate to the dimensions of the problem of reflecting upon the meaning of God.

25. Process and Reality (New York: Macmillan, 1929), p. 525.
26. Cf. Seeds of Redemption, Chapter IV (New York: Macmillan, 1947), pp. 49-70; The Reawakening of Christian Faith (New York: Macmillan, 1949), pp. 98-125; The Realities of Faith (New York: Oxford University Press, 1962), Chapter V; Faith and Culture (New York: Oxford University Press, 1953 [paperback, Carbondale: Southern Illinois University Press, 1976]), Chapter VIII; and Fallible Forms And Symbols (Philadelphia: Fortress Press, 1976), Chapter IV

THE SENSE OF WONDER 16

What we have hitherto called omniscience is better thought of as an infinite power of wonder. Knowledge is static, a stone in the stream, but wonder is the stream itself—in common men a trickle clouded by doubt, in poets and saints a sparkling rivulet, in God a mighty river, bearing the whole commerce of the divine mind.[1]

THESE lines from Charles Morgan's fascinating book, *The Fountain*, strangely echo the words of the late Charles Bennett, taken from the posthumous publication of his Lowell Lectures:

The thing that strikes one most about the mystery of religion is that it is foreign to the native air of our minds, that it is opaque to human intelligence. It is certainly grasped, yet it is not understood; if it reveals itself, it also conceals itself from rational comprehension. . . . It is as though in religion we came upon some surd in experience, some nonrational factor; and more and more I find myself coming to sympathize with that paradoxical assertion of the mystic that if God is to be known he must be known in "a cloud of unknowing." [2]

What, then, is this sense of wonder—this sense of the unseen order "supervening upon, shining through, and transfiguring the seen"? It is not enough to dis-

[1] Published by Alfred A. Knopf. Reprinted by permission.
[2] *The Dilemma of Religious Knowledge*, edited by W. E. Hocking, New Haven, Yale University Press, 1931, p. 10. Reprinted by permission of the publishers.

miss it as an illusory hang-over of a supernatural mood that has passed. The sense of mystery still persists among those who are sensitive enough to become aware of it, and who find occasions to encounter it. Let one saunter off into the great pine forests in northern Michigan. Or let him exile himself from man-trodden trails and take to some seldom used mountain path that leads on and on toward staggering heights. Let him impinge himself against uncivilized horizons where only clouds, trees, and the water's edge commune. Thrust close to these open frontiers of the world of nature does something to one's emotions, and the experience lingers with alluring inquiry. Calling it nature mysticism or æsthetic temperament classifies it, but it does no more than that. It does not get to the heart of that experience of creature-feeling, of solitary affinity with the vaster expanse of reality.

He who has walked out under the stars and looked with wistful wonder at those distant worlds, unreachable, and then recalled that

> Far out beyond those starry boundaries
> Still other worlds the telescopic eye has seen—
> More distant than those neighboring heav'ns,
> Galaxy upon galaxy of twirling planets
> Rolling in infinite space!
> Age-long and ageing!
> While gaseous breath takes up the pace
> To form new worlds in ceaseless creativity,

has found himself uttering:

> What mystery!
> What of these worlds upon worlds

That move in endless vastness
Through timeless time?

If the supernatural has been lost to us because of science, the natural world which the sciences have recovered in penetrating the distant spaces only returns us again to the mood of mystery when we try to apprehend its immeasurable immensity. If mysticism is, as Havelock Ellis has defined it, the "joyful organization of an emotional relationship to the world conceived as a whole," then modern man, once he glimpses this universe around us, may find himself going mystical.

There is a baffling problem here, however. What more than an emotional aghastness at vast and strange environings is this sense of wonder? No one who has undergone the experience will be content to leave it there. There is a feeling of intimacy that arises when contemplating the vast universe around us which takes the whole experience out of the realm of æsthetics and makes it deeply religious. It is a feeling of solitary affinity with this expanse of reality. Schleiermacher long ago called it "sense of dependence." I am inclined to agree with Rudolf Otto's criticism of Schleiermacher that sense of dependence is too conceptual a term to describe the experience. It is more what Otto calls a "creature-feeling." But the basic problem is not one of terms. The urgent inquiry is, has this sense of wonder, which issues in creature-feeling, objective validity? Or is it merely an illusion of the senses?

Rudolf Otto contends for its objectivity, saying that

"The creature-feeling is itself a first subjective concomitant and effect of another feeling-element which
casts it like a shadow but which in itself indubitably
has immediate and primary reference to an object outside the self."[3]

As we follow Otto further to discover more about
this *other* feeling-element which casts it like a shadow,
we find that the "mysterious object" is beyond our
apprehension and understanding, not only because of
our circumscribed knowledge, but because in this mysterious object we come upon something inherently
"wholly other," whose kind and character are incom-
mensurable with our own, and before which we therefore recoil in a wonder that strikes us chill and numb."

Thus we are led again to the walled-in conclusion
that knowledge is a stone in the stream, and that the
purpose of a contemplative life is simply to develop
the faculty of wonder, that we are to receive the kingdom of God as a little child with wonder and great
faith. I take it that this is clearly implied in Otto's
characterization of the "wholly other." I have too great
a regard for Professor Otto's discerning mind and
deeply sensitive, religious temperament to turn away
from his words lightly. Yet, I must confess that this
conclusion leaves me baffled. I may be a victim of
Westernized epistemology, but I find it difficult to sub-
mit to the absolute, irreconcilable dualism in cognition and perception which Otto's statements here
demand.

[3] *The Idea of the Holy*, New York, Oxford University Press, 1928,
p. 10. Reprinted by permission of the publisher.

Charles Bennett undertook to deal with this problem in *The Dilemma of Religious Knowledge.* As I understand Bennett, he would say that the religious worshiper's grasp of the real world is objectively valid in the same sense that the poet's portrayal is authentic. He draws a distinction, to be sure, between "grasping" reality and "understanding" it. And here he strongly resembles Rudolf Otto. Yet, there is a marked difference between the two. Bennett's article on "Poetic Imagination and Philosophy" (*Yale Review* Vol. 20) throws light on his position here. Poetry, he points out, is not merely a symbolic or sensuous embodiment of philosophic truth, nor merely an *aspect* or *version* of truth; neither is it simply a medium for arousing subjective emotions. Poetry is a serious art. *The poet is one who has stood in the presence of reality and the effect of his poem, if it succeed, is to usher us into that same presence.* This gives us a clue as to what Bennett means by the "non-rational factor" in religion. It apparently is the same non-rational factor that he finds in poetry: not contrary to the rational, however, in Otto's sense; not absolutely different in kind, to the point where there is no meeting-ground, for Bennett goes on to plead for an alliance between poetry and philosophy. Philosophy and poetry should not be left in separate worlds, he urges, concluding with this inimitable sentence:

The poet, we will grant, catches the music of the spheres; let us not prevent the philosopher from trying to set words to that music.

This seems to me suggestive of the relation between the worshiper and the theologian. For the worshiper also catches the music, perhaps the vaster music, of the spheres. And while he emerges with a stammering tongue, unable to bridge the gulf, religious worship and religious knowledge should not be left in separate worlds. Let us not, then, prevent the theologian from trying to set words to the worshiper's music.

The question has been raised whether or not simple, undefined awareness of religious experience does actually exist psychologically, since the reactions in such awareness are determined by a prior "set" of the organism, part of which is the ideational background of the one who has the experience.[4] This view is prompted by Dewey's statement that the organism, in the presence of stimuli, is not passive, but active, and that its responses are determined by antecedent conditions of the organism. To be sure, all perceptual experience is conditioned by a prior *set* of the organism, and therefore the meaning of that experience (for the experiencer) is to a large extent pre-determined. Yet, we must not lose sight of the fact that immediate experience has a *forward* as well as a backward look. According to the Gestalt interpretation of human behavior, during that experience, objective environings are active as well as the organism, for all such experience involves two active agents. And there is *interaction* between the two, not simply a dual activity. Consequently, when past experience functions in pres-

[4] See the article by E. E. Aubrey in *The Journal of Philosophy*, October, 1930.

ent experience, it only *partially* defines the meaning of the object. Contact with new environings often does something to the organism which completely upsets that *prior set* of the organism, and thus paves the way for redefinition of meanings and reorganization of tendencies and patterns.

A further fact is that the activity of the organism is by no means constant and consistent. At times the degree of attentiveness is high, and at such times the effectiveness of the organism as a conditioning influence in defining meaning, is particularly marked. But in moments of relaxation the activity of the organism, although it does not completely subside, decreases in intensity, and thus becomes more susceptible to outer influences. There is, then, an alternation of emphasis: at one time, the aggressiveness of the organism is dominant; at other times, the impact of the environings is dominant. When the organism is mentally active, the influence of its own prior set is most determining; but when the organism is relaxed before the inflow of environing events, the impact of those objective stimuli becomes particularly disturbing, even effecting revolutionary transformation in the emotional and mental set of the organism.

Thus it seems that while simple, undefined awareness of religious experience does not exist in the sense of being empty of ideational influence, this influence is less defining and less active at times than at others. And further, there is a condition of awareness in which those ideational factors, although present, are measurably disturbed, if not transformed utterly, by the influx of new stimuli. Definition, in that case, may actually follow awareness, rather than precede it.

The relation between mystical experience and religious insight is a compelling problem. Coming back, then, to our earlier conclusion that the theologian may put words to the worshiper's music, what kind of words may they be? How specific is the cognitive result? I shall relate three examples which may help to illuminate this point. One is from Margaret Prescott Montague's article, "Twenty Minutes of Reality," which appeared in *The Atlantic Monthly* some months ago:

> It happened to me on a day when my bed was first pushed out-of-doors to the open gallery of the hospital. . . . It was an ordinary cloudy March day, almost a dingy day. The branches were bare and colorless, and the half-melted piles of snow were a forlorn gray. Colorless little city sparrows flew and chirped in the trees. Here, in this everyday setting, and entirely unexpectedly, I caught a glimpse of the ecstatic beauty of reality.
> I cannot say exactly what the mysterious change was, or whether it came suddenly or gradually. I saw no new thing, but I saw all the usual things in a miraculous new light—in what I believe is their true light. I saw for the first time how wildly beautiful and joyous beyond any words of mine to describe, is the whole of life.
> Once out of all the gray days of my life I have looked into the heart of reality; I have witnessed the truth; I have seen life as it really is—ravishingly, ecstatically, madly beautiful, and filled to overflowing with a wild joy and a value unspeakable.[5]

Here we have religious awareness so vibrant with

* Reprinted by permission of the editors of *The Atlantic Monthly*.

the experience of reality that the individual shrinks from interpreting it; not because she questions its cognitive implications, but because there is so much meaning that to try to put it all into words only limits and mars that immense significance.

Another example is the religious experience that came to Havelock Ellis, while a youth, which he records in his book, *The Dance of Life*. One memorable day Ellis chanced to read James Hinton's *Life in Nature*. In contrast with the usual book on biology of that day, this book went beyond the explanation of the world as an orderly mechanism, and saw in it a vital life, full of warmth and beauty—something which the heart as well as the intellect might accept. The effect of this insight, says Ellis, acted with the swiftness of an electric contact. The tension was removed. His whole attitude toward the universe changed from that of hostility to one of confidence and love. In Ellis' own words, he had entered a new world.

In commenting upon this experience, Ellis says, "I had not gained one single definite belief that could be expressed in a scientific formula or hardened into a religious creed." Yet, the theoretical implications were there, even though Ellis did not articulate them to himself. For it was awareness of a world such as Hinton described, in contrast with the one that Strauss and others had presented, that *set him off* and fused his "opposing psychic tendencies in delicious harmony" and changed his whole attitude toward the universe. And while he was not conscious of any specific beliefs issuing from that experience, that single glimpse of the universe satisfied his intellectual wonderings. In his own words, "the primary exaltation subsided into an attitude of calm serenity toward all those questions that had once seemed so torturing."

Our third example is taken from J. Middleton Murray's "spiritual autobiography" recorded in his book, *God*. Following the war period, Murray had undergone a gradual debilitation of spirit, partly the result of war disillusionment, but due more directly to the tragic illness of his wife. When, finally, his wife's death did suddenly come and his despair was complete, he left society to be "really alone." He gives this account of an experience that came upon him during his solitariness:

Then in the dark, in the dead, still house, I sat at the table facing the fire. I sat there motionless, it seemed, for hours, while I tried to face the truth that I was alone. . . . Slowly and with an effort I made myself conscious that I was physically alone. . . . At last I had the sensation that I *was* in my hands and feet, that where they ended I also ended, as at a frontier of my being, and beyond that frontier stretched out vast immensities, of space, of the universe, of the illimitable something that was other than I. Where I ended, it began—the other, strange, terrible, menacing. It did not know me, would never acknowledge me, denied me utterly. . . .

What happened then? If I could tell that, I should tell a secret indeed. But a moment came when the darkness of that ocean changed to light, the cold to warmth; when it swept in one great wave over the shores and frontiers of myself, when it bathed me and I was renewed; when the room was filled with a presence, and I knew I was not alone—that I never could be alone any more, that the

universe beyond held no menace, for I was part of it, that
in some way for which I had sought in vain so many years,
I *belonged*, and because I belonged I was no longer I, but
something different, which could never be afraid in the
old ways or cowardly with the old cowardice.[6]

This mystical experience gave Murray a kind of
certitude that unified him completely and restored
him to a mental health he had not known in years. "It
impelled me into a course of action," he writes, "which
in a sense I still follow; it set my mind upon a chain of
thinking which I have never relinquished; it restored
me to life of the kind I value; and, indeed, it has occu-
pied me ever since."

We may draw these conclusions from our observations. One is that the mystical experience, while it in
itself comes as a vague, emotional stirring, suffused
with the feeling of great importance, is not without
cognitive activity. The glimpse of total meanings is so
overcoming that specific and derived meanings remain
entirely in the background. But the experience of
glimpsing great truth in this sense of seeing reality
synthesized, serves a cognitive function. It *settles* intellectual inquiry! It may not yield specific answers; it
simply enables the individual to outgrow intellectual
stress at those points.

Another point of importance is that in giving certitude of a kind, such experiences unify the emotions
and the intellect in a way that assures buoyancy. On
this point, J. Middleton Murray has said explicitly

[6] *God*, New York: Harper & Brothers, 1929, pp. 28-29. Reprinted
by permission of the publishers.

what both Havelock Ellis and Margaret Montague have intimated—namely, that the real value of the mystical experience is that it brings a kind of unity to mind and heart which previously did not exist. In the ordinary thoughtful person there is an inward division due to the incessant opposition of heart and mind, a condition which can be overcome only by a change in the quality of the universe as known by the mind. "The Universe known by the Mind must be, or become, such that the Heart can be satisfied with it." The mystical experience effects that change. Where once thought and emotion were at war with each other in their evaluations of the universe, they become one and indistinguishable in the new kind of consciousness which follows the mystical experience.

A further conclusion is that while the subject of such an experience may not derive specific meanings from these high moments, they are derivative. Another interpreter may have failed to get all the meaning packed into Margaret Montague's twenty minutes of reality, or in Havelock Ellis' instant response to Hinton's conception of the universe, or in Middleton Murray's solitary awakening; but he could have interpreted them—as discerningly, at least, as one can interpret any second-hand experience.

But more important still is the fact that one who undergoes such an experience may find himself coming upon the cognitive implications of that experience gradually and continually throughout the rest of his days. For years later, his moods and thoughts may be but the dénouement of that one mystical moment.

One glimpse of reality synthesized may keep his mental reactions active ever afterwards, distilling meaning, and creating new meaning through discovering significant relations between these several progressively discerned meanings. In religious awareness, as in the poetic experience, the moment may be too full of emotion because of the tremendous perceptual grasp of things, too charged with stirring feeling or elation, due to the great wealth of potentially meaningful stimuli, to yield clear understanding of what is experienced *at the time it is experienced*. Even in our most commonplace experiences, we respond *consciously* only to a limited margin of things perceived. Later, as emissaries from the Unknown, unheralded thoughts—we call them intuitions—break in upon our consciousness and stir up our reflective processes. The wider margin of what was earlier perceived has just come into focus. What is true of commonplace experiences is more significantly true of these rare experiences under great sensitivity. One must live with the experience awhile to become aware of its meanings and insights. Even then, unless one's analytical and reflective powers can rise to the height of his religious or poetic sensitivity, he may never adequately interpret his vision.

One may not, therefore, dismiss all mystical experience as mere emotional indulgence that prejudices reflection. In some cases the mystical experience may actually be perspective-giving illumination. It may actually yield a new focus of reality, visible only under conditions of heightened sensitivity when the organism is serenely open and receptive to its environings, and peculiarly attentive to the relations that unify the details. The genius of the artist or of the poet lies in his appreciative grasp of objects. He envisages beauty, hidden to the prosaic eye, because he is aware of the *relations* between objects which reveal balance, proportion, and shading. The prosaic eye is out of focus for such delicate discernment. So with the mystic who responds appreciatively to the vast realities of the cosmic order; he envisages profoundly significant aspects of the total world order, obscured in common observation, because he is aware of the relational side of realities, revealing order, objective, and quality in the universe.

In summing up our observations concerning the sense of wonder, then, I am inclined to believe that this mystical awareness, commonly called religious experience, is no mere subjective trick of the emotions when our mental guards are off duty; but is a valid experience of objective realities. Whether one insist upon some occult meaning here, or accept it simply as implying psychological adjustment to objective conditions, the fact stands that a new and healthful relation between subject and object ensues. And the reality, so far as we are able to tell, gets its validity in the integrity of that relationship. Furthermore the religious vision, like the poetic vision, may be interpreted in philosophical and theological terms. The practical difficulty of actually interpreting hilltop experiences does not seem to me to be a convincing objection, any more than the practical difficulty of attain-

ing the religious vision discredits it. Both undertak-
ings require great sensitivity and discernment. It is
this difference in capacity to wonder and to respond
to subtle stimuli that divides "common men" from
poets and saints and other rare individuals who have
broken the bonds of tradition and habit sufficiently to
respond to subtle happenings and to hear the vaster
symphony of the spheres.

About some things we shall always be agnostic in
our honest and thoughtful moments. For the mystery
of simple existence opens into profundities that defy
solution. But healthful living demands only working
hypotheses. And if, through our sense of wonder, our
gropings may eventuate in tentative certitudes that
unify our vision and energize our efforts, we shall be
discerning enough of that mystery to live confidently
and to live well.

THE APPRECIATIVE CONSCIOUSNESS

IN so far as these essay present a constructive philosophy of education, they center in a concern with the appreciative consciousness. This emphasis, I insist, offers a distinctive focus of human values and the method of thinking assuring their envisagement. The appreciative consciousness stands alongside of the moral consciousness and the rational consciousness as a principle of selection and as a regulative principle in educational criticism. The rational emphasis had its origin in Aristotle. Aristotelianism is a model of intellectual architecture and has served as such for all subsequent philosophical analysis in which a mathematical conception of universal order has been assumed. The moral consciousness as an organizing principle in knowledge, religion, and art arose with the critical philosophy of Kant. Here something of the premise regarding a universal order persisted, but being inaccessible to the human consciousness, as Kant thought, it was not reducible to a rational understanding. The moral consciousness, thus, provided a basis for affirming certain regulative ideas upon which the religious and the metaphysical ventures might proceed. The era beginning with William James and Henri Bergson initiated a third organizing principle in thought and experience which I have chosen to call the appreciative consciousness. This principle rejects, in effect, the premise of a given, static universal order and seeks to come to terms philosophically and religiously with the creative character of the world.

Because of the pervasiveness of the Kantian perspective in modern educational theories within higher education and its significance as an organizing principle in liberal religious thought, we might note some of the features of this emphasis. Kant addressed himself to the problem of inquiry in the various fields of human interest. Being a scientist himself, he was naturally concerned to assure the possibility of scientific inquiry. This he did through his analysis of the knowing process, showing the conditions under which knowledge arises and the way in which understanding is related to such knowledge. Being persuaded that knowledge began with the stimulus of sensory experience and that reason following from the categories of the understanding could not establish a metaphysic or provide a rational basis for religion, he set to work to establish the practical reason, based upon the assurance of the moral worth of the person, as the technical instrument of truth and value in the higher reaches of human culture. On the basis of the practical reason one could argue on grounds of moral necessity that belief in certain controlling ideas was justified. Such ideas, for example, as Freedom, God, and Immortality, appeared to Kant to be necessary postulates.

It is remarkable how pervasive this appeal to moral faith became as an organizing principle in matters pertaining to the human spirit. The labors of liberal theologians following Albrecht Ritschl, or of literary leaders like Coleridge and Matthew Arnold, as well as of philosophers of various Neo-Kantian shades, literally created an epoch of thought-centering authority in the moral consciousness.

This Kantian episode was in one sense a reformulation of the Protestant spirit. Kant, himself, was conscious of reasserting the Protestant faith, and theologians following in his path were quick to recognize in his critical philosophy a rational justification of the appeal to faith as it had been expressed by Luther. Kant was, in fact, often referred to as the Protestant philosopher, as representative in this role as Thomas Aquinas had been in exemplifying the Roman Catholic faith.

The affinities were more than theological; they were cultural. That is to say, they revealed a common grasp of human values that defined the human spirit pre-eminently in terms of the moral consciousness. Whether one is dealing with the age of Calvinism, pietism, or theological liberalism, the moral measure of value and the moral concern about the individual appear as dominant motifs. Somehow the restrictiveness of the moral ideal, as well as its discipline and zeal, characterize all three stages of the Protestant mind.

While reacting against the Kantian perspective, William James remained in part committed to it; for he perpetuated the appeal to moral faith in his will to believe. The affinities between this method of resolving the metaphysical dilemma posed by the problem of evil and that of Kant's practical reason have been noted many times.[1] Yet, too much should not be made of this affinity; for the solution was one of a number which James essayed. His method in his *Psychology* took another turn. His *Varieties of Religious Experience* suggested still another possibility. And his later *Essays in Radical Empiricism* and *A Pluralistic Universe* opened the way for a radical departure from all three solutions.

I

Implicit in James's *Psychology* and in his radical empiricism was a view of conscious experience that was to become formulated philosophically by Bergson as duration.[2] Neither James nor Bergson, taken by himself, focuses the formative notion back of the appreciative consciousness as sharply as when they are taken together as reacting to a common vision. Bergson's discussion of time provides a helpful clue and establishes the feeling-tone for the approach to meanings which the appreciative consciousness implies. Time, says Bergson, is of two kinds: time that is thought, and time that is lived. Time that is thought is easily spatialized, for it implies a simple projection from any fixed point as one might attempt in mathematical construction. The future envisaged in such a temporal pattern need not involve fundamental differences in meaning from point to point. It implies, really, that reality is given at any fixed point and can be projected by carrying out some scheme of prediction or application of criterion. Bergson points to various philosophies of determinism and to theologies of design as exemplifying this conception of time. His words for these philosophies and theologies are "mechanism" and "finalism." They are radically different in certain respects; but in respect to their use of time, they are alike.

Over against time that is thought, there is time that is lived. Time lived is of a radically different sort from time thought in that it is subject to no easy projection. Too much is involved in the creative moment by which the temporal process moves into the future to allow for easy spatial projection. The *not yet* is a real mystery in the sense that it cannot be deduced from *what is. What is* bears upon the future eventuality; for the past persists in some form to give character to the emerging event. Nevertheless, time will make a difference since the creative passage means the advance into novelty. Each moment is very old; yet in its matrix there arises constantly something new. This sense of the flux of events involving both constant change and the persistence of past attainment appears in James's discussion of the stream of thought[3] and of his notion of pure experience.[4] It is more vividly discussed in Bergson's *Creative Evolution.*[5]

This formative notion of the radically novel event in time that is lived, simultaneously focusing the past and the future in the present moment, was to be fully developed in subsequent philosophies of emergence[6] and to become characterized as creativity or creative event in the works of Whitehead[7] and of Wieman.[8]

Now it is in the context of this fundamental notion which we have been elaborating that appreciative awareness assumes metaphysical import. For in this context it is simply the creative response in man which relates him seriously to the creative passage and to the emerging events which ensue. One can call it by various names: "receptiveness to the novel event and to its interweaving with connections which transmit past attainment," "attending with wonder the mystery of emergence," "becoming sensible to the import of the creative event," etc. None of these formulations quite gathers up the complexity of meaning which is implied in the appreciative consciousness since it is concerned simultaneously with past qualitative attainment, and the mystery and possibility of the new. However one may phrase it, one must see that this response is as crucial to an understanding of the metaphysical reality within this context as the rational attitude is in Aristotelianism, or as moral faith is in the Kantian perspective.

We may elaborate this notion from another side of its meaning, centering upon its psychological aspect. Here James was especially discerning, particularly in his analysis of the significance of the fringe of consciousness and in his delineation of the stream of thought with its consequent feeling of tendency.[9]

There were various facets to James's psychological interpretation of mind as a stream of thought; but its chief differentiation from earlier theories was its dynamic or activistic character which was, at the same time, given a voluntaristic emphasis. Where hitherto the conscious process had been represented in a somewhat mechanical fashion as the association of impressions or ideas rather passively received, James presented it as an active teleological process. Mind he acknowledged to be of a piece with the biological organism, partaking of its moods and its physiological drives, as well as of its peculiar organization of impulses. Furthermore, being, as it were, the luminous center of a living organism, the mind of the individual person was looked upon as being continuously at one with a vast, dynamic resource of ever changing meaning. This hardly expresses the matter adequately, for it is impossible to convey the really fluid character of this conscious process, which rushes through time and space like a river in a canyon. And then one realizes that the figure of the stream succeeds in conveying in a measure *only* this fluid character. There is more to be conveyed: there is the constant shading of the luminous stream—now everywhere luminous though with a quiet glow, as if the whole content of continuous meaning were being borne to a conscious level; now darkened everywhere save for a sharply intensified luminous point as if the full conscious intent of the person had become fixed and concentrated upon some one tiny point of attention.

Always the conscious span of thought reaches to subliminal depths. For James, this depth was neurological. Like Whitehead, he put the burden of memory upon this sensitized organism, impressing the events of past moments, its tragedies and tears as well as its joys, upon the delicate nerve endings which somehow take up the passage of history into the organism. Thus for James, as for every natural empiricist who has followed in his steps, the organism became the bearer of precious cargo. All that man has been through the aching years of childhood, youth, and adulthood is curiously engraved like a line of symphonic melody upon a waxen disc. Place the needle of attention upon the disc at this or at that point and a stream of familiar meaning, long buried in our depths as it were, comes forth into conscious awareness. This states the matter too mechanically, to be sure; but some such analogy is needed to convey both the immediacy and the depth of accumulative meaning which lives on in the organism as incipient conscious event. It would be fair to say that for James, mind was not some one thing among many in the organism which might be designated in the brain or in some portion of the brain, but the whole organism seen as a psychical body—dormant at times, but at any instant ready to be roused into action as conscious awareness. And it was always more than a mechanism of the moment—an instrument for attending to some immediate interest—for it carried along this slumbering past, the treasury of memory which lay hidden and unobtrusive until aroused in the sensory depths of the nervous system.

Again, for James, mind was a selective activity. Mind, he would say, has its passive aspects: There is a brooding quality of thought which drinks in the environing scenery as a placid pool mirrors the trees at the water's edge. But even these serene moments of contemplative thought have their origin as well as their fixation in some form of interest. Always the stream of thought has some focus, however distended; though usually it is sharply focused, impelled by desire or by sensory disturbance of some kind in a way that brings the whole organism into focus as a conscious event.

The volitional basis of thought was one of James's distinctive emphases and colored all that he said about conscious experience. Not only is it what brings the whole organism into play in the act of awareness, but it is what gives individuality or character to thought. It makes thinking self-assertive in a deeply organic sense.

It was because of this restrictive, selective character of the thinking process that the doctrine of the fringe was of such importance to James; for it was in the concept of the fringe that the rich fullness of the stream of thought was preserved and accentuated. The fringe contained not only the outer range of stimuli which could not come to view in the focused attention, but "the feelings of tendency" and of direction as well—the transitions which, because of their subtle nature and of our habit of fixing upon conclusions (substantives), fall out of view. The fringe was also for James the threshold of the unconscious, as it was then conceived, behind which the abundance of accumulative valuations resided as a pent-up resource of attendant meaning, providing the feeling-tone for each new experience. Thus, in any span of conscious awareness, the accompanying fringe imposed a vagueness upon thought. In the interest of clear thinking, the logician as well as the practical person was disposed to cancel out these vague areas of thought. Precision in either form would seem to dictate a sharper course of attention. James was making the point, in various ways and with various approaches, that the reach for clarity through such indifference to the subtleties of relation implied in the fringe is precisely what has given us a false, mechanized conception of intellect. It is what has abstracted mind from its organic context, thereby creating the mind-body problem. Furthermore, he argued, it is the tendency to abstract mind which has led to setting mind above the body-life as a supervening activity, creating illusions of a transcendent ego, a phantom of mentalism which bears only incidental relations to the body-life. All of these devices, James contended, are forms of illusion or of distortion which have resulted from too thin a view of the conscious activity, ignoring the subtleties of the fringe.

What was sought by Kant in his proposal of the transcendental ego was an organizing principle of consciousness. James claimed this procedure to be a thoroughly artificial effort, dictated by rational need, precisely because the empirical circumstance was inadequately discerned. By being attentive to the transitive relations—that is, to the full content of conscious experience—James saw the empirical alternative to the transcendental ego. It is to be found, he argued, not in the area of abstract intellectualism, but in the feeling of relations.

The doctrine of the fringe has implications beyond these technical matters concerning the nature of the mind and of the self. It opens up the whole problem of perceptiveness in thought as over against precision in thought. This matter has had relatively little attention apart from a few poetic minds among philosophers and psychologists who have sought to justify either poetic perception or mystical awareness.[10] In its traditional context, this problem was quickly resolved by appealing to the mystical method of intuition. All rationalist emphases of whatever kind have been efforts to combat the intuitive method or to counter the possibilities of illusion and the insecurities attending such a method. Neither in these expositions of intuition nor in rational protests against the mystical method has the issue of perceptiveness really been confronted. James, in his emphasis upon the fringe in conjunction with his conception of the stream of thought, offered, in my judgment, the most impressive justification for sensitive awareness in thought which is to be found either in philosophical or psychological literature. Bergson, to be sure, presented a case for it too,[11] reviving the word "intuition" for designating that kind of penetration of inner meaning in contrast to descriptive analysis which simply conveys the external aspects. James, however, was able to get at the matter in a less arbitrary way. I will not say that it was a more discerning way, although one might make a case for that, too; it is, rather, a way which reveals the inside of all descriptive analysis or of logical exposition to be a rich texture of feeling and relations which not only greatly extends and enhances the defined meanings achieved by rational effort, but actually discloses the pits of illusion which befall the rationalist when he goes his stubborn way independently, seeking exact and precise formulations.

A vaster stage was set by James in his later works for conceiving the interplay of the many streams of thought against a backdrop of pure experience.[12] By this effort, James, in my judgment, was anticipating what the new metaphysics has come to designate the "social nature of reality" or the "interrelation of events."[13] Specifically, he was countering the prevalent dichotomy between subject and object which was implicit in the act of the conscious mind contemplating any object. Things and thought, he argued, are not two different existences, but one event seen under different relations to pure experience. To suggest his point more vividly, James cited the dual function of paint as one instance. He wrote,

"In a pot in a paint-shop, along with other paints, it [paint] serves in its entirety as so much saleable matter. Spread on canvas, with other paints around it, it represents, on the contrary, a feature in a picture and performs a spiritual function. Just so, I maintain, does a

231

given undivided portion of experience, taken in one context of associates, play the part of a knower, of a state of mind, of 'consciousness'; while in a different context the same undivided bit of experience plays the part of a thing known, of an objective 'content.' In a word, in one group it figures as a thought, in another group as a thing. And, since it can figure in both groups simultaneously we have every right to speak of it as subjective and objective both at once."[14]

The conclusion to which James came in his analysis of consciousness was that "Consciousness connotes a kind of external relation, and does not denote a special stuff or way of being. The peculiarity of our experiences, that they not only are, but are known, which their 'conscious' quality is invoked to explain, is better explained by their relations—these relations themselves being experiences—to one another."[15]

The intent of this analysis of consciousness, showing the interpenetration of things and thought, was undoubtedly to demonstrate that the meaning of consciousness itself is found in experience. "Searching for a meaning in terms of experience," as Perry has stated it, James "found consciousness, like the knowing subject, to consist in a peculiar relationship among the terms of experience."[16] To formulate its meaning in this way was but a step toward saying, as Bergson had said, that the depth of knowing occurs, not in this "external relation," but in an immediate feeling of the inner stream. And this, in fact, is what James was to say in concluding a discussion on the contrast between percept and concept, preparatory to launching upon a metaphysical inquiry into the One and the Many:

"If the aim of philosophy were the taking full possession of all reality by the mind, then nothing short of the whole of immediate perceptual experience could be the subject matter of philosophy, for only in such experience is reality intimately and concretely found. But the philosopher, although he is unable as a finite being to compass more than a few passing moments of such experience, is yet able to extend his knowledge beyond such moments by the ideal symbol of the other moments. He thus commands vicariously innumerable perceptions that are out of range. But the concepts by which he does this, being thin extracts from perception, are always insufficient representatives thereof; and, although they yield wider information, must never be treated after the rationalistic fashion, as if they gave a deeper quality of truth. *The deeper features of reality are found only in perceptual experience. Here alone do we acquaint ourselves with continuity, or the immersion of one thing in another, here alone with self, with substance, with qualities, with activity in its various modes, with time, with cause, with change, with novelty, with tendency, and with freedom.* Against all such features of reality the method of conceptual translation, when candidly and critically followed out, can only raise its *non possumus*, and brand them as unreal or absurd."[17]

In stating the matter thusly, James had gone the full way in his revolt against conceptualism and in establishing his constructive case for perceptive awareness.

It is instructive to place alongside of James's analysis of consciousness the following characterization by Whitehead:

"Consciousness is that quality which emerges into the objective content as the result of the conjunction of a fact and a supposition about that fact. It passes conformally from the complex object to the subjective form of the prehension. It is the quality inherent in the contrast between Actuality and Ideality, that is, between the products of the physical pole and the mental pole in experience. When that contrast is a feeble element in experience, then consciousness is there merely in germ, as a latent capacity. So far as the contrast is well-defined and prominent, the occasion includes a developed consciousness. That portion of experience irradiated by consciousness is only a selection. Thus consciousness is a mode of attention. It provides the extreme of selective emphasis. The spontaneity of an occasion finds its chief outlets, first in the direction of consciousness, and secondly in production of ideas to pass into the area of conscious attention. Thus consciousness, spontaneity, and art are closely interconnected. But that art which arises within clear consciousness is only a specialization of the more widely distributed art within dim consciousness or within the unconscious activities of experience.

"Consciousness is the weapon which strengthens the artificiality of an occasion of experience. It raises the importance of the final Appearance relatively to that of the initial Reality. *Thus it is Appearance which in consciousness is clear and distinct, and it is Reality which lies dimly in the background with its details hardly to be distinguished in consciousness.* What leaps into conscious attention is a mass of presuppositions about Reality rather than the intuitions of Reality itself. It is here that the liability to error arises. The deliverances of clear and distinct consciousness require criticism by reference to elements in experience which are neither clear nor distinct. On the contrary, they are dim, massive, and important. These dim elements provide for art that final background of tone apart from which its effects fade. The type of Truth which human art seeks lies in the eliciting of this background to haunt the object presented for clear consciousness."[18]

Except for peculiarities of expression and emphasis, it would seem that Whitehead and James are at one in deciding for a depth in immediate awareness which conscious experience as an attentive act can never attain. Perceptiveness in this form is thus not simply the vague portion of conscious thought; it is the more deeply involved orientation of the human psyche in which the report from experience is both full and concrete. To the degree that this psychic relationship is thought to merge with a primordial sensitivity in nature, the report goes beyond mere prehension or feeling and opens up profound metaphysical and religious questions concerning the ultimate character of this depth discerned in concrete experience.

Now it is true that James entertained the possibility of a panpsychism comparable to that of Fechner's[19] which gave intimations of a community of other mind, or higher consciousness, toward which these complex relations of human minds presumably tended.[20] This tendency in James led the more sober naturalists like Dewey and later, Wieman, to steer away from this preceptive course and to set up danger signals as warnings against the route of Ulysses.

Wieman's procedure in his early work, *Religious Experience and Scientific Method*, was to stress the importance of appreciative awareness as a fructifying and nurturing medium of thought but to insist that its contribution was ambiguous, if not suspect, except as it was submitted to the tests of observation and reason by which knowledge might be distilled from its vague intimations. Wieman, thereby, while not ignoring the perceptive quality of thought implied by the fringe and the importance that it bears to discursive thinking, practiced a reductionism by which this More was compelled to yield to exact findings. The consequence was, even so, a richer quality of rationalism than, say, the rationalism of Descartes or of Kant, and a more unwieldy sort, as well. Yet, the meaning of the fringe and of the feeling-depth in consciousness was essentially lost to Wieman's thinking. Its implications were virtually cancelled out. This way of stating it, of course, exaggerates the dissociation of knowledge from the depth of awareness; for actually Wieman's thought, even when it means to be precise, is suffused with overtones which can have meaning only as one refers back to the moment of immediate awareness in which the penumbra of meaning impinged upon critical reflection. Wieman is no different in this respect from other radical empiricists. His way of relating depth and precision, in fact, strikingly resembles that of Dewey's. And this recalls affinities between Wieman's use of concepts, purged of emotive attachments, and Dewey's instrumentalism. It may be said that Wieman, in seeking an empirical certainty in religious faith, has fashioned "working ideas" of God and value after the manner of Dewey's instrumental method of inquiry.

As to Wieman's affinities with Dewey in relating awareness and critical thought, I am reminded of a footnote which Dewey appends to a discussion of "the underlying unity of qualitativeness' in an essay on qualitative thought. He writes,

"The 'fringe' of James seems to me to be a somewhat unfortunate way of expressing the role of the underlying qualitative character that constitutes a situation—unfortunate because the metaphor tends to treat it as an additional element instead of an all-pervasive influence in determining other content."[21]

This comment makes clear that Dewey is aware of the suffusion of meaning which persists even in one's efforts at clear and exact thinking. And one might add that one of the distinguishing features of Dewey's mode of analysis of situations is this retention of feeling-tone. Yet, I am not convinced that Dewey deals adequately with this fullness of meaning to which the notion of the fringe refers. I should agree with Whitehead when he observes that "that portion of experience irradiated by consciousness is only a selection. Thus consciousness is a mode of attention. It provides the extreme of selective emphasis."[22] To the degree that one presses conscious attention into channels of critical analysis or into instrumental procedures for regulative purposes of discovery, as both Wieman and Dewey would insist upon doing in pursuing knowledge, this selective emphasis is accentuated.

One need not treat this "underlying qualitative character of a situation as an additional element" as Dewey fears. It is simply a dimension of depth, less luminous with conscious intent, yet profoundly relevant and operative upon thought in the way that the bodily feelings, for example, influence mind, or that the feeling context of cultures shapes the conscious activities of a community.

This sense for the concrete richness of content in any moment of consciousness and the tendency or habit of the mind to cancel out what is not definitive in order to fix upon precise meanings led

James to suspect any rational effort which presumed to simplify the data. Bergson's suspicion of the intellect rested upon a similar observation; though his concern involved differences which need to be kept in mind.

In dismissing the rationalist's direct efforts the problem of wresting meaning from this suffused awareness remained for both James and Bergson. It was this concern that led Wieman to resist their analysis of perceptive experience. The sense of the vague has played an important role in Wieman's thinking, despite his wariness in regard to untested awareness. His first book, *Religious Experience and Scientific Method*, is a particularly fruitful work for exploring its implications in religious thought. Wieman had distinguished between knowledge by acquaintance and knowledge by description, meaning by the former what James had intended by these two phrases taken together, and by the latter what Bergson undoubtedly meant to oppose as intellectualism. Acquaintance, Wieman argued, gives knowledge that is immediate and deducible from experience. Description yields conceptual knowledge which has no relation to experience, as in formal logic or mathematics. Wieman's concern was to show that religious experience is knowledge by acquaintance rather than by description. But all knowledge of this sort, he pointed out, is suffused with an undefined awareness. In fact, he continued, one can say that all knowledge arising from perception is bathed in an ambiguous content of immediate awareness. Before attention sharpens the object and fixes one's gaze, there is an uneasy grasp of an ambiguous datum. Such awareness is not knowledge, Wieman insisted; but it may yield knowledge if the tests of attention and analysis are applied.

It was here that Wieman came into conflict with Bergson's view of instinct and intuition; for Bergson had claimed a great deal more for the realm of undefined awareness than Wieman was willing to concede. With Bergson such awareness implied an inner orientation which afforded immediate understanding—a kind of understanding, in fact, which could be achieved in no other way except by such inner orientation. James, in my judgment, stood midway between Bergson and Wieman on this point, tending more toward Bergson than toward Wieman in his appraisal of the importance of "the vague," as he phrased it, in giving amplitude to the knowledge of events. Yet his sense for the importance of the definitive route of experience in matters of communication or in shared experience led him to give due weight to the claims of exact knowledge. His way of resolving the issue was to recognize the variations among individual or subjective tracks of common experience and to insist that in the communication or interchange of meanings only the outcome of the train of thought, where it assumed the form of external expression, was apt to be relevant and reliable. The inner scenery, with its devious paths and singular delights, which were enjoyed as subjective experience, could be employed in communication only at the risk of befogging the issue or beclouding its meaning. Nevertheless, the fullness of the meaning thus communicated depended in some degree upon recourse to this inner orientation since this is where some hint of the organic context or concrete actuality of the abstracted or distilled idea would be given. [23]

That the inner grasp, incommunicable and irrelevant to the outer meaning, was knowledge of a sort, I think James had no doubt. At least it yielded understanding to the one who possessed it—a feeling-orientation which enabled one to act with greater surety and zest than his explicit knowledge might seem to warrant.

The doctrine of the fringe, along with James's analysis of the perceptive ground of thought, stands as a warning against an over-reaching exactness in thought—not in the precise sense in which theology has often suspected the reasoning mind, nor with the same implications with which the Protestant reformers in particular held philosophy at a distance, but with similar apprehensions. There is, after all, a certain affinity between the Protestant appeal to faith and the radical empiricist's emphasis upon appreciative awareness.[24] Each, in its distinctive way, points to a *more* that is excluded by the reach for precision and to a *less* which must inevitably follow from the illusions of rationality where reason becomes assertive, mechanizing, and over-abstracting in its effect.

In James there is the basis for a perceptive kind of thinking which opens the way for receptiveness to the rich fullness of experience such that the tyranny of the rational ego is tempered, if not routed, and for an understanding of such awareness in relation to disciplined attention such that a measure of precision appropriate to the circumstances of thought is achievable and thus sensitively sought.

The constructive efforts of Whitehead, in so far as they bear upon an understanding of the process of knowing, may be considered an extension of James's own efforts to establish the perceptive dimension in thought. And his metaphysical writings will be seen to be an attempt to generalize this notion of "relations" beyond the amorphous stage of James's radical empiricism. Whitehead's concern with

the various grades of feeling along with his recognition of the mutuality of relations between events can be considered an attempt to
state, more objectively and with greater rigor, the notion which
James tried to convey in such terms as "feeling of tendency" and
"feeling of continuity." Where James found terms within an imagery that borrowed from introspectionist psychology even as he
struggled to express them more functionally, Whitehead appropriated the imagery of the new physics with its fields of energy. Whitehead was thus able to visualize a structure of relations and of tendencies or feelings to which a more definitive intellectual procedure
could apply. In acknowledging his indebtedness to Bergson, William
James, and John Dewey in the preface of *Process and Reality*,
Whitehead wrote, "One of my preoccupations has been to rescue
their type of thought from the charge of anti-intellectualism which,
rightly or wrongly, has been associated with it." The phrase "rightly
or wrongly" intimates that, in Whitehead's judgment, anti-intellectualism might well have been attributed to the empiricism of
James because of the way in which he formulated his fundamental
notions. Yet, the meanings which were there to be grasped, and
which James had certainly seized upon in terms of conscious experience and, later, of pure experience, could be stated intellectually,
Whitehead believed, if one retained in one's formulation the fullness
of the context as objective event, as seen, for example, in a structure
of relations, even as one probed the inner meaning of these relations
as feeling. When one moves into contemporary philosophies of con-
textualism, as formulated, for example, in Stephen Pepper's *Aesthetic
Quality*, one sees this clue being seized upon in the attempt to express the meaning of quality as structured events which elicit certain
depths of feeling because of definable relations.

In applying this notion to logical method, Whitehead insisted upon
holding in awareness the adumbrations of thought and experience
(which is but a more contextual way of speaking of the fringe) even
as one focuses attention in the act of precise inquiry.[25]

II

The issue which emerges from this discussion as an insistent problem is the validity and the degree of value which one is to assign to
the appreciative consciousness that is so weighted on the side of subjective experience; charged with a fullness of meaning, richly concrete, immediate and vital; yet so inaccessible, even resistant, to the
mind bent upon definitive ends. The first observation which occurs

to my mind in confronting this issue is, How seriously is one to take the metaphysical truth which stares out from the analysis of experience by radical empiricism: namely, that reality is unfinished; that time makes a difference; that relations extend every event indefinitely, even making each event inexhaustible? It would seem that within such a perspective the very phrase "exact knowledge" is but a manner of speaking—a studied compromise, as it were, to enable one to take a fixed view when, in the nature of the case, all fixity is lost or, in any case, mobility has come to assume a priority of meaning. Mobility is the basic category in the sense that creative change is a perpetual happening. Fixity is a quality of change in the sense that past, present, and future are in some sense connected. There is a persistence of identity. The structure somehow endures though it is its very nature to undergo continuous transformation.

Within this perspective, "definitiveness" is perhaps a more suitable word than "exactness." "Exactness" harks back to mechanism or to finalism where time makes no difference. "Definitiveness," though often employed as a synonym for "exactness" or "precision," does not imply all that these terms mean to convey. "Definitiveness" means simply a designative structure of meaning. Amid overtones and adumbrations which shade into indistinguishable tones of the environings, there is a luminous center, a point or an organization of points which provides a manageable focus of meaning. Thus a person, whose full meaning could never be gathered into a tangible datum such as a physical organism, which bears the person's name, can be dealt with definitively, as the law must deal with him, as if he were wholly defined by this *corpus*. Likewise the indescribable complex of events and relations which comprise a national culture can be definitively envisaged within the bounds of a map or symbolically designated by a flag or by a coat of arms, and encountered on definitive terms of relationship through an ambassador or some other representative company or responsible officials of state. Countries can clash through the physical encounter of their armies or through the intrigue of their secret agents. Thinking definitively is always motivated by some functional purpose. The object in such instances is not to understand the person or the object, but to deal with it. Under such circumstances, the penumbra of mystery and meaning which radiates from the clearly defined event is ignored, set aside as if it did not exist. Only the luminous center, the manageable core, matters. The fringe might be acknowledged. The realm of undefined awareness might be noted as an aesthetic datum, having possible

meaning to the appreciative mind or to the mind unfocused upon the
immediate task at hand; but to serious thought which pursues an end,
leading to action, it appears irrelevant, if it appears at all.

Pragmatism, especially as it developed through Dewey's instrumental philosophy, was a singular effort within the perspective of
radical empiricism to achieve definitiveness by defining truth functionally, i.e., within the restricted range of some instrumental end.
This was paramount to allying philosophy, and religion as well, with
science and industry, and to equating experience with practical experience, i.e., with experience directed to ends in action. In narrow-
ing the range of truth to such verifiable meaning, philosophy, education, and religion joined science and industry in nullifying the truth-
value and thus the relevance of appreciable meanings—meanings
which give range and qualitative import beyond the specific function
in focus.

Now the tendency, where some concern was manifest to rescue
the appreciable meanings from oblivion, has been to cite the two
sides of life (mechanism and spirit), or the two rhythms of existence
(fertility and utility), or the two realms of being (the world of
action and the world of contemplation). While the intention in each
instance was to reserve a rightful place for the appreciative functions of life, the outcome has been to make it possible to drive a
wedge between the appreciative and the active interests of man, and
thus to dissociate, e.g., art from serious action or reflection from
functional concerns, or, as it appears in certain educational situations,
to make disparate and unrelated, appreciative awareness and critical
thought. It is high time that this dichotomy in all its forms be repu-
diated except as a distinction in emphasis and procedure and that the
appreciative consciousness as a constant and indispensable companion
and resource of critical thought be acknowledged.

The appreciative consciousness as a regulative principle in thought
can best be understood as an orientation of the mind which makes
for a maximum degree of receptivity to the datum under consideration on the principle that what is given may be more than what is
immediately perceived, or more than one can think. That is to say, in
the appreciative consciousness, there are no preconceived premises
that the categories are at hand with which to exhaust the meaning of
this object, or that what is being attended may be reduced to some
structure already known and defined. Call it what one will: intellectual humility, wonder, reverence, or simply open awareness, some
such mood is essential to the orientation of the mind we are describ-

ing. The reason for such a mood is metaphysical in its initial basis. The full meaning of the datum is not given. Nowhere is there a preconceived pattern, a static order to which this object or event can be readily referred in the sense, e.g., that mathematical principles may define or describe a prism, a rectangle, or a cylindrical object. Patterns, categories, criteria, useful as they may be for pursuing definitive meanings, are held to be approximate, tentative, subject to revision as the creative passage continues its route toward possible ends.

Furthermore, what is given in any object stands in a context of mystery which always defies precise formulation. The actual is always pointing beyond itself, not only to the possible (which is its future occurrent) but to its hidden aspect however actual (which is its obscure occurrent). Whether one is speaking of some happening, a person, an institution, the living community, or of God, one is dealing with an inexhaustible event, the fullness of which bursts every definitive category.

A sense of the-more-than-the-mind-can-grasp as well as a sense of expectancy concerning every event, knowing that creativity is occurring, that time is real, attends every act of cognition where the appreciative consciousness is operative.

The appreciative consciousness, then, takes as its starting point the mystery of what is given in existence. Metaphysically, this could mean the total datum. Practically it would mean the rich fullness of the concrete event with all of its possibilities and relations, imagined or perceived. The thing, in and of itself, apart from any instrumental or functional purpose, any rational or moral preference, becomes the object of inquiry. Thus receptiveness to the datum envisaged becomes the initial conscious response. The datum with all its mystery is received in wonder. The objective event is enabled to declare itself. The consciousness attending the datum is thus subjectively enriched by the intrusion of novel relations into its stream of previously structured experience.

Yet the emphasis is first upon awareness of the object itself and secondarily upon identification with the attending consciousness. What does this person, this culture, this event have to say? What do they mean, of themselves, and to themselves? This is the first query. Complete relinquishment of vested interest and a readiness to be broken in upon by the new experience or by the novel event characterizes the initial step.

There then follows, as the second step of cognition within the appreciative perspective, the act of identification. The consciousness attending the datum receives the communicated meaning within the limited frame or structure of the perceiving mind. Here we encounter a problem similar to the one that led Kant to formulate his critical theory regarding the forms and categories of the mind, insisting that while knowledge arises in experience, it is formed by the imposition of the categories of the mind upon the raw stuff of experience. What happens in every act of cognition is that the fullness of meaning attending any datum is funneled into some conscious experience and made part of the internal stream of thought which has been structured in a given way through a process of symbolization by which every conscious mind internalizes its objects. To a considerable degree the act of cognition implies the fragmentation of meaning, i.e., the appropriating of the rich fullness of actual meaning within the restricted range of some partial perspective. This is true whether one is speaking of any simple form of symbolization in the private experience of the individual or of more disciplined forms of cognition, as in the co-operative inquiry of scientific or logical research.

Identification, however, implies more than a cognitive appropriation of the meaning of the object within a given frame of symbolization; it implies also sharing to some degree its feeling-context. Now this may be something more than the inner knowledge by acquaintance of which James and Bergson spoke; although it quite obviously includes such immediate rapport. It may extend beyond the subjective act of feeling into the event and assume the nature of real discernment into the solidarity of events: a penetration of the realm of internal relations where the *me* and the *it* find their common ground. This act of feeling into a situation or into an object, the full meaning of which one cannot grasp, is an important aspect of cognition itself. It may be that it holds the key that would have unlocked the door which Kant found to be concealing the thing-in-itself. Schleiermacher seemed to be grasping for this key in his emphasis upon feeling as a more subtle approach to relations with the Infinite.[26] He apparently thought he was simply finding a more agreeable detour around Kant's formal rationalism in taking this course; but actually he was taking account of the deeper dimension of the cognitive process which Kant seemed to ignore. Kant was too much impressed by the limitations of the human consciousness to be sensitive to these subtle strands of feeling, giving thought its deeper orientation. Had he noted these features of consciousness as limitations he might have been more concerned to deal with this problem of orientation. Instead, he represented them as distinguishing marks of the personal consciousness, unvariable forms implicit in the conscious ego by which the reason impressed its identity upon experience. There was something of the bias of personal idealism at work here, elevating the human consciousness to an absolute status. What Kant had arbitrarily formulated as the categories of the mind can be equated, in part at least, with what the modern psychologist recognizes as structures of meaning which arise within every individual consciousness in the act of symbolization whereby the growing consciousness is individuated. Cognitively speaking, every individual is contained within a given sequence of assigned meanings which define his structure of personality. At the level of communicable symbols or consciously assigned meanings, in terms of which his rational discourse takes place, he knows experience only within this partial perspective which his living experience has itself formed throughout the succession of moments of awareness and activity defining his conscious life. But a more elemental dimension of his personal self attends his conscious experience: that which has been less individuated by the assertive consciousness. To be sure, the body, with its specific sensory equipment, is individuated. It is, in fact, the physiological basis of what occurs as individuation at the conscious level of experience. But it is also less individuated than the conscious mind in that it pursues its own course in accordance with the substratum of involuntary impulses. What is sometimes called "the wisdom of the body" is the psychophysical activity of the human organism which operates below the level of consciousness and without its aid or interference. Mind, though the highest order of structure that is operative in man, is also the least reliable, the most unpredictable, imposing upon the human organism, through freedom of imagination and thought, a precarious superstructure which is at once man's route to glory and his path to almost inevitable folly.

The "wisdom of the body" is not enough to pilot man's life; for it is, after all, a structure of physical and psychical activity which is only faintly atuned to the higher reaches of man's organism. It operates as a ballast, however. It has the soundness of all elemental things where the regularity of seasonal operations is observed, unperturbed by reckless innovation. Its proneness toward regularity and soundness, however, tend to make it resistant to the creative drive in man's nature which expresses itself at the conscious level of experience. Nevertheless, it is what preserves and continually recreates the conditions essential to the existence of the organism and is thus somewhat in a parent-child relation to the conscious mind. In the last analysis, this psychophysical structure is the bearer of its life, its meaning, and its duration. The vital energy that rises to psychic heights in creative effort, moral courage, or rational discourse has its source in the intricate workings of this body-life. The track of memory, which assures the persistence of identity to the conscious self and which gives range and depth to conscious experience, is this complex of finely grooved lobes which connect mysteriously with nerve endings that radiate throughout the body.

Apart from providing a durable and dependable context of sensory operations out of which the finenesses of the human spirit emerge, the body is as a threshold to the deeper stratum of organic being. Through its perceptive powers and through responses even more subtle than these, it literally relates the individuated life with the fuller context of living, both in the realm of nature, including the deeper creative passage, and in the social matrix.

This does not mean that mind, in its deeper concourse with events, is reduced to a sensuous level of feeling; rather it implies that the human self, when it becomes totally atuned to the fullness of being which reaches it through the structure of experience that cradles each conscious life, thinks and feels with its body. The whole of the self is awakened with a wide awareness which renders the organism perceptive to a high degree. Mind is deepened with feeling and heightened with a psychic quality of animal alertness. The senses are quickened and sharpened with a conscious concern which is our peculiar form of alertness. Body and mind thus become suffused in a way that renders each highly receptive and responsive to the other, and to the stimuli which reach the organism in direct perception.

To be sure, mind and body are not two different entities, but two different dimensions of the one organism. Each is a distinctive emphasis, as it were. Consciousness can become so acute in a high degree of attentiveness that the whole organism will seem to be operating as an intellect. At other times, the mental powers can be so completely out of focus that intellect will appear to have become completely absorbed into the bodily senses. This alternation is due to the varying kinds and degrees of stimulation determining what shall fix the organism: either in conscious attention or in sensory absorption.

The state of perceptive awareness we were describing earlier is neither one nor the other of these processes but a unifying of them in a way that brings the conscious organism to its maximum degree of sensitivity.

We begin to see the difference, then, between sheer thought, sheer bodily sensation, and sensitive awareness. Thought which is a conscious train of images following serially from a high degree of fixed attention is the intellect operating with a minimum of bodily intrusion. In this process, the body is bent toward conscious awareness. The fixity of the mind narrows the range of attention and thus lessens its perceptive powers. All is spent for this moment of fixed attention. An acute and incisive attack upon the datum under observation is possible in this act of attention because the mind is at its maximum state of discipline as intellect. It so happens, too, that under these circumstances the play of individual limitations is most readily operative; for in attentive thought the human ego is assertive. The full force of the structured mind achieved through symbolization is brought to bear upon the datum. It is understandable that Kant should have spoken of the categories of the mind as being imposed upon experience. In this act of cognition individuality is both sharpened and asserted.

Sheer bodily sensation need not occupy us long in this part of our discussion. It is readily recognized as the fruition of the sensory apparatus responding to stimulus, either from within the organism or from without it. This, to be sure, is no simple or single track response. The senses are interrelated; and the bodily responses operate as a community.

Sensitive awareness is the bodily senses becoming consciously alerted without being tunneled into a narrow channel of fixed attention. It is the intellect widening and extending its depth and range to the level of feeling without losing its conscious focus. Thus it is properly referred to as being more profound than thought, and more disciplined and directed than sheer sensation.

Whether or not Schleiermacher meant to insist upon this kind of subtle and full blending of intellect and sensation, which we have called sensitive awareness, in his stress upon feeling, one can only conjecture; but I should be willing to hazard the suggestion that, in resisting Kant at this point, he was seeking out the deeper trail that leads in this direction.

My concern would be to try to avoid the pitfall of conceiving of this trail as leading away from rational thought or of emptying wholly into the darkened well of feeling; as I think both Schleiermacher and Bergson might be accused of doing. Again James appears to be the safer guide, though he leaves much to be desired in amplifying the meaning and condition of appreciative awareness beyond the cognitive event.

Two dimensions of the method of appreciative awareness have thus far been given: (1) the reach toward the object in, and of, itself as a genuine datum, unaffected by the intrusion of the conscious ego—a feeling into a situation with a maximum degree of psychic distance—(2) the appropriation of the object, relating it to the conscious ego, implying both its fragmented form through symbolization and its undifferentiated form as discerned in experience where the merging of events in their ultimate feeling-context is noted.

A third step of cognition within the appreciative perspective is discrimination. This is the act of noting the vivifying contrasts which differentiate the datum and which set it apart as a distinctive event. This act is analytical; though it does not involve extricating the datum from its context. The assumption which guides appreciative awareness is that an event is never properly known apart from its context; for the relations are as real a part of its meaning as the internalized core. Thus analysis within the perspective of the appreciative consciousness must take the form of examining the parts with a full sense of their function and of their relational aspects. This amounts to saying that the quantitative and the qualitative features of any datum are held in juxtaposition as being, not only interrelated, but mutually qualifying. Any attempt to understand the one apart from the other falsifies the meaning of the datum.

On first thought, this sort of analysis would seem to be a muddlesome procedure. How can analysis of any datum take place if there is not some degree of dissection or extrication? The answer can only be that the kind of knowledge which is sought through that form of analysis wherein the datum is first extricated from a context and then dissected into its multiple parts is not the kind of knowledge that is sought here. This raises the question, Are there different kinds of knowledge? I would answer that if there are different kinds of analysis, or different circumstances under which analysis can proceed, then there are at least different degrees of knowledge or, perhaps, different dimensions of knowledge. The knowledge derived from analysis of an organism which has been rendered inanimate may be somewhat similar to that which is achieved when the organism is living; but it is of a different grade. It is anatomical or structural, chemical or physical. Knowledge of behavior and of the subtle interplay between the physical and the psychical structure is simply not available to the analyst working upon the corpse. It will be objected, "But this is simply a difference in the data that are known. It is not a different grade of knowledge." I should reply that if the difference between the levels of structures is a real difference, as emergent evolution makes evident, then something of this radical difference applies to the process of inquiry as well, and to the results that ensue. There are different levels of inquiry, different orders of inquiry. The method applicable to data in which no psychical behavior is explicit is not wholly relevant to data where the psychical organization of functions has become, not only evident, but dominant and controlling. Furthermore, a method that is informing at the level of psychical structures where no assured condition in the form of a matured cortical mechanism is given for the play of imagination and of creative insight is not wholly relevant to that level of data where these conditions have come to fruition in personal and communal form. They are relevant to some degree. The study of physiology and of psychology based upon physiological processes is informing for a knowledge of personality to the extent that the personal structure has subsumed the psychophysical structure or organism; but to press the knowledge so derived to the extent of compressing personality within the confines of these psychophysical data is to reverse the process of emergence. It is to deny the creative happening wherein the novel event of personal life has appeared.

The fact of structural evolution by which a new degree of complexity and of creative organization of parts occurs within the psychophysical organism, giving more range and subtlety to its operations, compels a similar differentiation in methods of inquiry for exploring meanings at these various levels.

I am not ready to follow T. E. Hulme[27] and others who insist that the difference between biology, psychology, and sociology, on the one hand, and religion and ethics, on the other, is so great as to create two wholly different orders of being; but I am confident that the customary procedure in liberal-arts quarters of making the transition between biology, psychology, and sociology and the concern with the more subtle play of sensitivities in which spirit is discerned, a simple and direct line of inquiry is equally unsound; and it opens the way for oversimplifying the spiritual dimension of man or for canceling it out altogether.

It is this oversimplification of the transition between structures that has led to the insistance that there is but one kind of knowledge, meaning knowledge that is derived through the direct scientific

method of descriptive analysis. Recognition of the creative emergence which has set each succeeding structure above and apart from
its predecessor does not involve the denial of the relevance of cruder
and more direct methods of inquiry which are applicable to lower
structures; but it does imply an insistence that these cruder procedures become allied with a more sensitive kind of inquiry which
takes account of, and which operates within, the range of the new
emergent. This means that there will be as many different degrees or
dimensions of knowledge as there are levels of structure.

Now analysis within the appreciative perspective is that form of
disciplined inquiry which is peculiarly relevant and rewarding in the
realm of data where relations and creative possibilities form the essential stuff of meaning. For here the evident aspects of the data,
while giving clues to more hidden aspects, are often superficial and
transitory. The depth of meaning lies, not in these readily observable
or measurable features, but in what operates more hiddenly, either
as a long-range influence reaching out from the past, or as something
too tenuous to be embodied—expectations, hopes, or more imminent
possibilities rising out of existing structures though as yet not explicit or recognizable except to the most discerning mind.

The positive import of our analysis is that the appreciative consciousness, because it attends to the dynamic character of events
and relations, to time that is lived, elevates perceptiveness to a place
of prime importance in the art of thought. In this context, in fact,
perceptiveness assumes the kind of primacy which precise calculation
acquired under Newtonian physics, where the motions of mechanism
and the exact principles of inviolable order provided the clues to
both method and imagery.

Perceptiveness acquires this importance because, in the dynamic
and unfinished situation which the creative passage provides, the
incalculable and immeasurable dimension attending every moment
turns out to be the most formidable factor to be taken into account.
Except as this dimension is envisaged, reality is simply not apprehended! When this dimension is ignored, facts turn out to be illusory. Except as some recourse to this dimension is sought, truth is un-
attainable. And without such recourse, knowledge becomes as chaff.

We need to be clear, however, about the relation of this immeasurable and incalculable dimension to the structural order that is observable. It is not an indifference to structure or the absence of a sense of
structure which impels the mind, so awakened to this incalculable
dimension, to look beyond measurable results. It is, rather, that struc-

ture is seen in a different light, say, than Newtonian science presented it. Where, in the Newtonian context, structure meant mechanism
or an order of meaning which was permanently given, so completely,
in fact, that mathematical science could describe, measure, or predict
its character, structure as seen from within the appreciative consciousness is organic in character with implications of emergence,
hence attended by hidden or barely perceptible, even unpredictable,
possibilities. Structure and possibility thus form a simultaneous feature of the measurable and the immeasurable aspects of any event.
What is measurable is inseparably related to the immeasurable, and
vice versa. These stand in a dynamic context of interpenetrating
orders of meaning. The appreciative consciousness thus attends to
every event with a twofold awareness: (1) with a sense of fact and
structure and with a recognition of the descriptive procedure which
these elicit; but (2) with an even livelier sense of the intimations of
meaning transcending fact and structure to which the measurable
order of meaning points, but never wholly contains or exemplifies.
These intimations turn the appreciative mind to a kind of seeing
which is often falsified or denatured by an arbitrary separation if its
function from the order of fact and structure. Thus it is made into
a special form of intuition or act of faith that sets aside empirical and
rational inquiry as being irrelevant to its deeper knowledge. But this
kind of seeing must be rescued from these doctrinaire procedures
and be given a recognizable status within the educational experience
as a mode of discernment that is opened up to any sensitive mind in
the act of inquiry where the organic and dynamic character of situations and events is taken into account.

It will be understood, then, why the appreciative consciousness
seems to suggest a mode of awareness that implies the denial of
measured meanings or the discipline of attending to facts. It has
parted company with that mode of inquiry that deals with structures
in a purely mechanical way, or that pursues knowledge as if it were
simply the tabulated results of descriptive processes which isolate
and measure observable data. But it has not parted company with
these structures or processes. It has simply enlarged the scope of inquiry to accord with the dimension of the data which each structured event is known to present. And this is to add to the discipline
of observing facts, the more perceptive concern which is exemplified in the act of discernment.

III

Almost any datum will illustrate the truth of what I have been saying; but the appraisal of happenings within a community will suffice to make it vivid. People are assessing the life of a community all the time. Those who have lived in it a long time have usually come to a stereotype assessment: it is a unique community for some reason or other; and it ranks along with the best of the country's smaller towns. Naturally it exceeds the excellence of the cities, for it is free from the pressures that oppress and from the daily grind. It is free, too, from the alien influences of undesirables who cluster about the larger centers. Then, too, so this estimate runs, this town affords a man a sense of security in his ability to help control the public policies, and in his access to numerous friends who are his neighbors, all of whom call him "Bill." This is a commonplace characterization of the good life in a small community. It is expressed in various ways by various people; and it can be heard on any street corner, in men's furnishing stores, in the barber shop, and in the office of the town paper. The newcomers in town also have their version of it. "It's good enough as towns go; but it's not the only town on earth. It isn't as far along in some things as the last town we were in. People aren't as friendly either. There's a lot of smugness here. The oldtimers seem to think it's the only place on earth. Well, it isn't; not if you've been around."

Then there are the fully intrenched citizens who have become assertive in the name of what the town has always stood for. And there are the newcomers who are convinced that the town has real possibilities if only the sticks-in-the-mud could be routed and some new methods could be introduced into its civic affairs.

Every town is plagued by contradictory sentiments and appraisals which tend to generate rival social forces, making for deep-seated cleavages and often more serious open hostilities. In time, the social analyst may be brought in to assess the situation. The analyst is free from bias, so everyone says; and so he himself acknowledges. He is interested only in facts. With technical procedures of population survey, questionaire analyses, and statistical measurements, he is soon able to tell the more advanced, civic-minded citizens just where the town stands: its population distribution and trends, its dying and growing edges, its religious and social groupings, its economic stratifications, its tension points as well as the type of tensions that exist. Reduced to charts and pin points, the community appears

250

much more manageable than when these facts lay lurking in the inarticulate minds and moods of its puzzled population. Thus the social engineer, fortified with facts, goes to work to alleviate the frustrations, or to create more; to release the tensions, or to compound their corporate effect; and to create community, or to dissipate whatever natural, unconscious communal sentiment had heretofore existed.

I do not mean to caricature the serious effort to apply modern social intelligence to the problems of the community, but to suggest that even such competent inquiry into the meanings that are operative falls short when it seeks to deal with vital human forces with statistics and graphs. They are aids to any effort to understand the data; but, in themselves, they do not illumine the powerful as well as the highly sensitive drives which are at work in the social organism, forming, on the one hand, ambiguous resources for good or ill, and, on the other hand, subtle, almost inaccessible resources of insight or of pathological resistance to understanding which can mount in might as they become accumulative and consolidated through the strange maneuverings of the lonely and the estranged who seek their own kind of solidarity. The novelist, and sometimes the humorist, has often proven to be the shrewdest analyst of social ills and frustrated hopes particularly if he has been a resident of long-standing in the community with which he is concerned. This is because he brings to his study of the social process, not only a normal amount of literary astuteness, but a high degree of perceptive curiosity and sympathetic understanding with which his mind weaves in and around the frail remains of unheralded tragedy strewn along the path of representative men and women whose personal history he has chosen to delineate. Within this area of delicate data, he searches out the motives of people's actions through successive years of failure or success. He penetrates the region of people's hopes, fulfilled and unfulfilled. And whatever tapestry of meanings he may succeed in portraying in the final writing of his story, he is able to convey, within the limited scope of his narrative, a high degree of understanding into the human situation: the kind of perceptive grasp of the data which is inaccessible to methods of graphs and figures.

Often the sage of the community who has remained free from the commonplace illusions and biases of the old-timers, and whose dreams of empire have been in a deeper vein than those of prospector or financier, has been able to serve the community periodically as its prophetic analyst. His looking back into the history he has helped to create has not been solely an indulgence in reminiscence, but an appraisal as well: a measuring of actuality against dreams and, perhaps, a persisting thrust toward hopes yet unrealized. In such minds, charged with the emotion and energy of a purposeful participant and equipped with a vital imagination as well, the full force of the appreciative analyst is felt.

Such resources of the appreciative consciousness exist to a far greater degree in communities than is generally known; but they are not as articulate as the less discerning kind. Sometimes they find their way into journals or letters, and thus become known to later generations as a fresh source of insight into circumstances which have historically shaped their lives. These resources of the appreciative consciousness have been difficult to organize, sometime difficult to assess because the facilities for such inquiry are difficult to systematize, even more difficult to establish on any consistent basis. Hence, these resources operate as an aesthetic horizon of feeling and reverie, communicating their insight through artist, poet, and the occasional sage. But it will be seen, on a moment's consideration, that the kind of analysis in which these resources come into play is a serious instrument of reflection, too important to be relegated to individual, casual expression in art and song or in occasional ceremonials. It is a form of thinking, or a level of thinking, which can be awakened and nurtured just as surely as discipline in logical analysis or precision in scientific thought can be achieved within the educational process.

Appreciative awareness has been associated so exclusively with the aesthetic and the poetic temperament that its spiritual force in the wider, cultural, or simply humanizing sense has been obscured if not lost altogether. As a regulative principle in thought and action it can be sharpened to imply the disciplined effort to go beyond one's self through such capacities as empathy and the nurture of sensibilities may provide. Technically, this is precisely what is implied in appreciation wherever it is extended. In art appreciation one understands that the difference between the act of appreciating any creative effort and the more commonplace egoistic response of the museum prowler who knows only enough to say, "I like that!" or "I don't like that!" lies in this capacity to get beyond one's self, to grasp, with some degree of understanding and sympathy, the meaning and intention of the work that is being observed. This act of appreciation does not imply the complete relinquishment of one's own powers of discrimination. On the contrary, it requires a high degree of discrimination. Nor does it cancel out judgment and decision regarding worth. What it involves is the employing of one's critical faculties in a context that is mutually informing and corrective: i.e., a situation in which one brings to bear upon the object or the event the full play of one's critical powers, being receptive at the same time to what is given in this object such that one's critical powers may also stand under judgment in the very act of appraising the work of art. How else does the critic grow in sensitivity and discrimination except as he profits by his continual association with competent, creative effort, exercising his judgment in relation to it?

It is true that art criticism suffers like all other acts of judgment from lapses into egoistic reaction. The art critic is as susceptible to the failings of the human ego as any other individual. Yet the discipline of art criticism, when it is practiced with discrimination within an informing perspective, remains a valid blending of the subjective powers and psychic distance, which is to compel the valuations of one's own subjective experience to seek a wider reference in the good that may be beyond one's self.

Now this principle is as applicable to politics, religion, education, and other phases of the common life as it is to art appreciation; for it is simply an orientation of the human ego which defines the range and receptivity of its attention and feeling. The person in whom the appreciative consciousness is feeble or inactive will, by every conscious and purposeful act, impress the limited and circumscribed meanings of his own valuations upon whatever he encounters. He will confront and know other people, not as persons in their own right or in the relationship of a community, but as so many individuals who may be instrumental to his own ends. Other people thus become simply extensions of his own ego. Specifically, a parent devoid of appreciative awareness in confronting his child will envisage the child, not as a person in his own right, but as *his* child—a life dependent upon him and thus responsible to him, a life which may somehow fulfil his own ends. Similarly, a child deficient in appreciative powers on confronting his parents or any other adult will see, not a world of human mystery beyond himself to enjoy and to understand, to which he can become helpfully related, but a possible refuge in time of trouble, a source to draw upon, a comfort to compensate for his own insecurity, and nothing more. And, when denied this egoistic attention, the child, or even the college youth, will contrive defenses against those who exemplify qualities superior to his own.

Citizenship is meaningless to the person deficient in appreciative awareness; for government and community can signify only a place and means of one's own support and well-being. Political leaders and holders of office are simply the keys that unlock or close the doors upon coveted power. Taxes, civic movements, and the community chest are but obstacles to one's capital gain.

Education suffers without some stirring of the appreciative consciousness. To the student, the educational process becomes either a hostile or a beneficent force, depending upon grades and the personal attention of the professors; to the faculty, a means of professional success or frustration, or an assurance of vocational security with its dubious rewards.

Without appreciative awareness, religion can degenerate into a pathological concern for salvation from sin. The envisagement of a good not our own, the beauty of holiness, the glory of God for His own sake—these are nonexistent to the shriveled soul that is shaped by the tyranny of his own impulses and fears.

The appreciative consciousness begins in a recognition of the metaphysical fallacy which inheres in the concern for fixity, and issues in an art of life which sees beyond the appeal to one's own securities. It is a principle which casts out possessiveness as a criterion of value, whether it be the exaggerated concern for exact understanding, in which the world is reduced to the confines of one's own mind, or the assertiveness of the unrestrained ego which can understand value only as it is absorbed into the purview of one's own valuations.

Precision, analysis, comprehension, and form are not alien to the appreciative consciousness; but these are but means to an end, not ends in themselves. And as such they are tentative and subject to revision before the great on-going mystery in which our lives are cast—a drama of existence in which wonder, inquiry, and the appreciative mind play the creative roles.

Finally, the appreciative consciousness must be seen as a disciplined, co-ordinated working of the mind and sensitivities in a way that embraces the relevant and decisive factors in a situation, however clear or unfocused these factors may be. In parting company with the insistent concern to attend only to clear and distinct ideas, the appreciative consciousness is motivated by a reconception of the realities we experience, and of the nature of truth pertaining to these realities. It is in the complexity of meaning, arising from the interrelation of facts and forces, which arrests its attention. For it is by apprehending the signs and intimations which are constantly occurring within this complexity that one comes upon the truth of any situation. These signs and intimations are always of a transitive and relational character. They are discerned, not in the noting or measuring of fixed facts, but in the attending to the process wherein facts are moving toward new facts or toward a new status by reason of other facts or other circumstances. They are discerned, not in the single entity, but in the pattern of relationships which forms the depth of every event or experience, and thus contains the resources which point up the tendencies and possibilities in any situation.

The appreciative consciousness is the indispensable guide to understanding any problem, situation, crisis, or impending peril, as well as to dealing constructively with events of scope or of imaginative proportions. For the facts of crucial importance in any such situation are always relational within a dynamic context. The wrong decisions generally proceed from an inadequate grasp of the moving and changing status of facts and relationships. What was unanticipated overwhelms the calculations; and the unexpected happens, often not because the facts gave no hint of the outcome, but because there were no eyes to see or to attend to these relational and transitive factors that formed the pattern of emerging events and which generated its movement. The right decisions, on the other hand, more often than not, proceed from some degree of alertness, and possibly aptness, in sensing the moving drama of relational factors. Usually one simply says that he played a hunch. Actually, one has been moved to play the hunch because of the intimations of meaning which appeared on "the fringe," or which loomed as a faint vista when the facts which were known came to be fitted into a pattern of related meanings.

There is nothing mysterious or uncanny about these situations or decisions. Nor is recourse to the appreciative consciousness a mysterious or mystifying act. On the contrary, it is the soundest sort of realism in dealing with family situations, with community crises, or with any problems in society of a complex character. For once complexity is acknowledged to be the actual status of any living or dynamic situation, denying the complexity, or ignoring it through measures of simplifying the data in order to assure exact scrutiny, can only lead to a false perspective, idealizing the implications. In a world of complex meanings, plagued by forces of incalculable possibilities and of ambiguous intent, there can be no realism of judgment or of understanding except as facts are seen in their relations and in their condition of becoming, and in terms of the intimations of meaning which these relations and tendencies imply. This is the realism of the appreciative mind.

18
RELIGIOUS SENSITIVITY AND DISCERNMENT

WHY some people are responsive to a religious stimulus and others not, and why religiously responsive people vary so enormously in the degree and character of their concern, are problems which have provoked considerable inquiry among psychologists and philosophers of religion. William James, seeking a reply to these questions or to questions like them, found a partial answer in his distinction between the healthy and the sick mind.[1] Subsequent inquiries into the nature of religious behavior, particularly as it appeared in various forms of mysticism, pursued this clue with even greater precision,[2] some concerning themselves chiefly with the pathological manifestations of religious experience.[3] Except for the expositions relating the religious life to the social expression of human values, one might reasonably claim that the net result of this prodigious effort to get at the psychical root of the religious response has been to characterize the person who has become alive to the urgency of ultimate issues as being, in some sense, a sick soul, or at least as being somewhat abnormal compared to the healthy-minded individual who has been able to take life in stride, unperturbed by problems of destiny.

Religious concern as a normal manifestation of the human response has seemed difficult to maintain in the face of this persistent bias that tended to identify health of mind with an unreflective absorption in well-being. To be sure, theologians and philosophers of religion had entered the field to state some psychological values of religious living.[4] While these were carefully reasoned expositions, matured in their grasp of psychological facts, they nevertheless bore a common limitation as an offset to the long line of publications in the psychology and history of religion in which religion had become suspect: they were avowedly normative, while the earlier studies had presumed to be descriptive in method. The excellence of their analyses, the balance of their judgments, their measured conclusions, could not effectively counter this underlying suspicion that an apologetics for religion was being advanced, howbeit a sophisticated apologetics.

257

The contribution which this normative literature made to the functional understanding of religion was impressive in its own right.

Richard Cabot's insight into the conditions which produced spiritual fatigue and their consequences for human behavior in ordinary experiences of living advanced James's analysis of religion as a source of psychic energy along constructive lines and provided a kind of psychological apologetic for religion of genuine merit. Cabot's book, *What Men Live By*, became indispensable reading both for the student of religious psychology and for the professional religious worker as the shift in attention from theology to psychology of religion progressed—a tendency which had begun to manifest itself at the turn of the century, following James's memorable work. Hocking's principle of alternation advanced a similar argument and took on force as one viewed religion in the context of absolute idealism, although his insight was in no sense confined to that metaphysics. Religion, Hocking contended, is wholeness. Activity is fragmenting. To be engaged in a continual round of activities is to reduce consciousness to the bare events of immediate and repetitious stimuli and, ultimately, to lose sight of the farther range of meanings altogether. Worship, he argued, recovers the perspective in which the whole of things is envisaged, bringing man's partial experience into accord with the vision of God. Conversely, worship, if persisted in to the exclusion of concrete experience in the world of facts, becomes abstracting, dulling the sense for precision and for practical demands. Fertility and utility, two dimensions of conscious experience, Hocking insisted, must be sought in alternation if the human mind is to continually renew itself.

Rufus Jones found the contemplative act of prayer and worship a means of access to the depths in our consciousness in which spirit is made articulate and reinforcing. Jones, thinking out of a mystical form of absolute idealism, commonly known as spiritual monism, conceived of the human consciousness as having levels of religious awareness. The attentive consciousness, fixed upon outer events, was, of necessity, withdrawn from the deeper issues of its life and thus represented the person at a more superficial level of consciousness. The subconscious mind, free from the distractions of outer stimuli, was seen to be attuned to the inner self, wherein spirit in man communed with the Infinite Spirit at the depth of all existence. Our minds are like an iceberg, said

Jones, in part rising into view, but four-fifths submerged. The spiritual quality of conscious existence depended upon recourse to these submerged depths wherein spirit dwelt as a quiet pool.

Wieman saw religious living as a problem-solving adjustment of human consciousness and will, by which man was rescued from the life of illusion and made responsive to the sovereign good in existence. Worship, he viewed, as a stage in this process, an act of orientation and conscious commitment; but living continually in a mood of openness and responsiveness to the demands of the sovereign good, he regarded equally imperative.

Horton found in the doctrines of the Christian faith the affirmations which assured mental health. Christian belief and religious living were thus justified, not merely by the logic of their position, but by the therapy of their practical results.

The suggestive insights that have come from these several analyses of religion as a psychological act of worship and religious living have been of great importance to recent religious thinking. And their practical benefits may be of far greater significance than one is able to estimate. Yet, as an interpretation of the religious response, say in the basic creatural sense of providing clarification of its elemental importance to man, none of these analyses ever really seemed decisive. For all their reasonable persuasion and valuable insights, they did not grip one with a conviction that religious sensitivity or religious discernment was an indispensable creatural response like eating and drinking, breathing and sleeping, or that it figured as prominently in the category of human responses as political and economic activity.

In fairness to these normative studies of religion, one should, perhaps, recognize that they reflected the practical mood of the period in which they appeared, which was apologetic in the pragmatic sense. Pragmatic value in religión, as in industry, carried a conclusive note. To be able to demonstrate or prove the practical importance of religion in an age that had become self-consciously pragmatic was tantamount to rescuing religion from the discard. In academic circles, this new apologetic could prove religion intellectually respectable. In popular circles, it could demonstrate that it had some practical importance.

Neither of these motives reaches a sound theological basis. In fact, neither can claim a theological basis if by a theological concern one means inquiry into issues of human destiny in terms of their ultimate bearing.

I am convinced that a defense of the religious response, whether on psychological or dogmatic grounds, does not contribute to the kind of understanding of religious sensitivity which makes it irrefutably a normal functioning of the human consciousness. Such understanding is immensely important and needs to be pursued either as a science of religion, independent of practical considerations, or as a concern for aiding the differentiation of consciousness in human beings and providing for its nurture, by which that dimension of greatness in our human capacity may be enlarged and fructified.

I would offer no apology for the religious response any more than I would seek to defend scientific curiosity or aesthetic enjoyment. Like them, it is a fruition of human consciousness under certain circumstances that opens up its datum to the human mind, eliciting various kinds of reactions: joy, dread, adoration, wonder, moral zeal, love, integrity, good will, reassurance, apprehension, hope, resignation to the tragic sense, a renewed will to live, dedication to an envisioned good, and devotion or even relinquishment in the pursuit of that good.

I

What is the nature of this elemental human response? Pathology, to be sure, is sometimes present in it; but beyond its pathological aspects, what is this response of joy and adoration and wonder, this persistence in integrity, hope, and goodness, often in the context of an acknowledged tragic sense?

I think psychology of religion, both in its descriptive and in its normative explorations, has contributed to this study; but I believe they have failed to lift up the most significant meaning of religious sensitivity as it applies to our creatural existence and to the individuation of consciousness by which the psychical self achieves spiritual emergence.

Religious sensitivity has to do, first of all, with our attachment to life as creatures. This defines the most elemental condition of our existence. It concerns, next, those developing sensitivities and sensibilities through which we engage in the apprehension and enjoyment of the qualities of experience. These qualities of experience derive from various grades of relationships which the human creature bears: his solitary moods that accentuate his self-awareness; his companionships and more general human associations in which his subjective life is made integral with other human beings, even reaching the concept of the community; his awareness of, and devotion to, the source of all life, awakening him to the sovereign meaning of all life. There are various ranges of sensitivity implied in these relationships, and, accordingly, they represent different degrees of complexity in human discernment.

Conceivably, the child is peculiarly a victim of his solitary compulsions, his subjective life. Infancy suffers from inadequate differentiation of consciousness and from unformed sensibilities to actual qualities in the environing world. The meaning of his life as an individual waits upon development in these areas of response. The conceptual problems that arise with the capacity to abstract concrete meanings and thus to conceive relationships may not intrude upon his tender consciousness. Life, for him, is a succession of concrete objects, not even held together by an active memory, nor set in an orderly sequence projecting future events. Slowly the pattern of existence is perceived; but at this level, no reflection upon the human problem is likely. Religion, in so far as it has any reality at all, is a psychical fact of attachment to life, carrying innumerable possibilities for developing qualitative distinctions in experience which give rise to personality structure and character.

The religious response in the child, then, takes the form (1) of an animal assurance, an unreflective sense of being accepted, thus being released from whatever degree of undue apprehension the child's psyche can comprehend (love as a religious reality is learned in this organic sense of solidarity); (2) of an intermittent sense of disorder, arising from inner cravings rejected or from disapprovals, registered in ways that even a baby can understand; and (3) of an awakening empathy, presaging the whole order of relatedness that can rescue the infant from his solitariness and give him the normal craving for human company, even the hunger for union with all of life, which is implied in the ultimate concern of religious faith.

These seminal sensitivities emerge and develop in response to very concrete happenings in the child's life. And their nurture beyond childhood depends upon the stimulus that will hold the datum of the good (which assures qualitative existence in consciousness) before the consciousness, such that consciousness individuates in response to these felt demands, and acquires hungers and affections, impelling the person to embrace voluntarily the good of life so discerned.

Religious sensitivity awakens out of preoccupation with the facts and meanings that define life as good. Without the incentive to say life is good, without the impulse to praise life, the religious response cannot emerge—save as a retreat from existence. Religion as a retreat from existence, which may develop into disenchantment with life itself, bears a negative relationship to the religious response. It has often been lifted up as religion par excellence, particularly in cultures where the existing world has been regarded as an evil that must pass away. Dread of the world, the complete depreciation of mortal existence, can only be looked upon as a diseased estimate of the life-process, atrophying the elemental creatural outreach that would otherwise result in relationships.

To insist that life is good, however, without inclination to acknowledge the horror and evil that attends existence, would likewise be a defective religious sensitivity. Religious sensitivity implies an accompanying dread, or at least an apprehension, in part the result of an incomplete orientation in the world, but more deeply the realization of one's own limited powers to comprehend existence—an uneasiness that grows out of misgivings with one's self and recognition of the likelihood of one's being at odds with what is ultimately right and good. There is nothing pathological about this apprehension. In fact, the absence of it would suggest a hint of incipient pathology in the same way that lack of a proper uneasiness in the child when confronting strange situations would be considered abnormal by an observing psychiatrist.

Fear in excess becomes morbid; but fear as expressive of a proper awareness of conditions with which one must come to terms is normal in the child as it is in the adult.

These matters are not to be reversed, however. An exaggerated sense of the tragic quality of existence to the exclusion of the affirmation that life is good obstructs or routs the creatural response that is basic in religious sensitivity. There is real illness in the psychic life of a person when this condition arises. James's studies of religious experience expressing this kind of psychic illness remain a permanent advance in delineating the religious response.

The "sick soul," while manifesting pathological symptoms, must be characterized as "religious" because of the character of his anguish, and because of the process issuing from his response, to redeem his situation. There is a reaching toward the good, in this process; and this reaching provides a tenuous attachment to life, even though the disturbances of his psychical nature render his sensory capacities incapable of religious perception. Another way of saying it is, the sick soul has promise of a religous restoration by reason of his anguish and concern, which in themselves can become creative agents. If the illness of spirit develops into a state of complete rebellion against the good or passes into a confirmed state of cynicism and denial of the good, then the religious capacity of the person is seriously impaired. The redemptive forces cannot affect his psyche because his total nature is unresponsive, in fact, unreceptive, to the appeal of life's good.

When this happens to the individual, discrimination in perceiving the interplay of good and evil in existence vanishes, or is greatly reduced. Perceptions of good are routed, or so minimized as to exaggerate the perception of evil. Life's events, and one's own existence, are read in the light of this supervening dread or distemper. The resolution of life's issues is thus on the side of despair, and may possibly reach complete pessimism. Just as fear and joy exist concomitantly in normal existence, so the acknowledgment of goodness in life and of the tragic sense occurs in tension in the discriminating response to existence evidencing religious sensitivity.

The emergence of religious perception and sensitivity in the growing individual is marked by an advance from concrete feelings of good and ill that are personally experienced, to discernment that arises from reflective judgments which disentangle the general situation from the particular. Here a refinement of religious perception begins to take place, altered toward greater complexity by the conceptual power of the person. This conceptual power enables the individual to discern more subtle and complex evidences of good. It also provides him with an imaginative ability to anticipate implications or to project immediate concrete data and relationships such that every immediate good, concretely envisaged, takes on greater scope and significance.

To the degree that this refinement of religious perception develops in the individual, he is made more responsive to objective conditions of good and is thereby increasingly delivered from the compulsions of his subjective nature which, in infancy, tended to rule his life. A greater stability and objectivity in the face of crises is thereby made possible in the adult in whom such refinement of perception occurs. Injuries to self, loss and pain subjectively felt, are not generalized into universal evils. This is the discriminating consciousness gaining control over subjective compulsions.

Growth of religious sensitivity also brings to the individual a kind of vision that adds to his competence in discerning and appraising the meanings of existence as they present themselves. It gives fuller

orientation to his life—perspective we call it—for, being delivered
to some degree from egoistic desire and from the circumscribed
vision which egocentricity imposes, his thought and feeling find a
wider range of appreciation and understanding.

Such vision and receptiveness toward appreciable data actually
lifts one to a new level of understanding. The world, in itself, comes
into view. People as authentic persons take on character. The community as a social reality is envisaged. Purposes and possibilities,
however intangible, become motivating. The long range of human
meanings takes on significance. What is of ultimate worth becomes
a present concern. In this view of things a fundamental notion like
that of *God* assumes reality, and the destiny of man in relation to
such a fundamental notion is seen to be of greater moment than
the satisfaction of desire.

II

This matter of religious vision, or of sensitivity in one's envisagement opening up to the mind significant data bearing upon human
destiny, is a more subtle problem of human personality than is commonly assumed. It is closely allied to the valuations which form
the structure of personality over a period of years as well as to the
bent of mind which gradually becomes fixed under the stimulus of
habitual attention. I have dealt with this matter at some length in
an article on "Religious Awareness and Knowledge," a brief excerpt
from which may help to illumine the present discussion:

"Through association we tend to build up a familiarity with certain stimuli which, in turn, attaches emotional feeling to events
in which such stimuli appear. Familiarity is not the only source of
such emotional association, although it generally enters in some
form to give appeal or persuasiveness to the event. Thus perception
is conditioned by the kind of habituated experiences that give rise
to emotional feeling impelling attention. But while the influence of
such emotion is strong concerning ordinary men, circumscribing
their responses, it is possible to achieve a measure of independence
from such persuasion through critical reflection. Consequently, the
disciplined person is less likely to be limited in perceptions to the
customary stimuli.

"The point I am trying to suggest here is, that over a period of
years individuals develop a certain kind of probable response to
realities in environment. And this subjective outreach not only
colors the character of things experienced, but it actually deter-

mines what may be perceived. For as James has said, 'Just in proportion as an experience is probable will it tend to be directly felt.'

. . . .

"The conclusion to which this analysis leads is, that awareness and knowledge are so related to the forms of feeling and attention that their character may be said to be in direct relation to the habitual associations and their persisting stimuli. The music lover, through continually hearing significant music, comes to be peculiarly aware of musical meanings and values. The lover of art, through constant observation of recorded genius, achieves a competency of perceiving and knowing art values. The skilled workman, by his continual association with tools and the shaping of materials, acquires a capacity for sensing and knowing defects and values of workmanship. Religious awareness and knowledge are similarly related to associations and persisting stimuli, bringing the realities of religious import into focus. One who never contemplates these may no more be expected to envisage their existence, or their significance of meaning, than one who never turns to music may be expected to be sensitive to that sphere of facts and meanings."[5]

Religious vision, then, arises from a structure of human consciousness in which perceptiveness has quickened the mind to be attentive, not only to a wide area of facts and intimations bearing upon human destiny, but to certain kinds of data in ordinary experience which offer some clues to the ultimate meaning of man and his destiny. It thus involves a process of perceiving data and of attending to meanings.

The character of events which becomes peculiarly evident to religious perception is a qualitative occurrence in life to which the word "goodness" may be properly applied. "Goodness" is an exceedingly difficult term to clarify. Without some base from which to work the word can be made quite meaningless. In the context of this discussion the word "goodness" will be understood to convey a quality of meaning which points the human emergent beyond its own ambiguous perfections to intentions implicit in occurrences which move God-ward. This quality is not dissociated from natural or human structures, for its operational route is these very structures which give actuality to meaning. One could speak of it in the way in which the emergent philosopher has spoken of any novel meaning which appears in a structure where a new complexity of relations gives intimation of new meaning in process of forming but which in its present state is but incipient in character. "It does not yet appear what it shall be." Enough appears, however, to indicate that a quality not wholly its own is emerging from the structure. Goodness would then be to the human structure what psychical activity would be to the physical existence in a structure of mechanism.

Goodness derives its essential meaning, then, from these intimations of a higher-than-human working within natural and human structures. God, being qualified by his goodness, as Whitehead has phrased it, exemplifies a certain character of relations to the world and to the human community. These relations express a concern for meaning and for conditions which are creative of this meaning. God's goodness may thus be viewed operationally as his participation in events which move toward qualitative attainment. This is what is implied in the creative act of God.

III

The reach toward clarification of this profound happening within the structures of the world is always met with some degree of frustration, for quite obviously the human mind, in pressing for understanding of this qualitative happening in events, is struggling to envisage what exceeds its sight. Yet the human mind does catch intimations of its working in acts of beneficence or of judgment which arise in situations and in relations between human beings, often in conjunction with situations of extremity involving, for example, such responses as remorse, repentance, and forgiveness. These acts reveal a sensitivity at work in human beings which can radically transform both the individual and the situation in which the persons's life is cast. Often a situation of conflict between people, it may be between parent and child, reaches such an impasse that the two life-streams seem to seal up against one another. They cannot effect a complete insulation from one another once they have been interpenetrative. Each bears the burden of the other's life in his own structure of experience. But a sufficient degree of hypnosis is effected in the mood of alienation to enable each of them to pass by on the other side so as to avoid any direct encounter between them. This condition of concealment may continue until one or the other is moved to a sense of the tragedy of the relationship. Such a momentary glimpse of the total meaning of the situation may be enough to enable one to break through the fortress of the ego which pride has reared, and with this one swift, penetrating glimpse, the citadel may crumble. For in such instances, the redemptive act works swiftly or it does not work at all. This instantaneous escape from the self-contained view is enough to start the deflation of the ego which may then begin in remorse to move toward repentance and reconciliation. The repentant act elicits a response of forgiveness. The forgiven state, in a way, changes no single fact. The lifetime of unintended injury may not be undone. Time being real, effectual, will not turn back; and it may not be in its power to heal. Yet forgiveness transforms the tragedy of time that has been lived into a situation which makes tragedy acceptable and accepted. The injury no longer rankles. Relations are no longer strained. The individuals are no longer estranged. The healing that cannot alter conditions in fact does alter the perspective in which the facts are borne. Thus the transformative power of the repentant heart releases both a healing and a creative force into the relations between the two people.

In situations which press men and women to a sense of their extremity, where the resources of self-help seem spent or unavailable, these recreative and healing events break in upon human relations, often spontaneously as if unanticipated, to transform a situation of defeat and despair into hope.

Again, intimations of goodness come in situations where abundance presses upon conscious experience. This, too, is a form of human extremity in that it becomes a joy too great to bear. The cup runs over. Joy is a welling-up out of gratitude for grace which abounds. The capacity for joy accompanies the capacity for appreciative awareness not only in that such awareness opens up the world of meaning to the receptive consciousness, but it also releases the bodily feelings from possessive demands which would otherwise intrude an acquisitive outreach. The peril of selfhood is thus, in effect, removed or at least diminished as the bounds of the self are extended.

The movement of the human psyche toward ends not its own in this appreciative way awakens a sense of identity with other life or with other events. This, too, is perilous, as I shall soon point out; nevertheless it is the route to that summit of experience where the vision of God and the vision of man converge. In this orientation of the psyche love, as an outward movement toward people and toward the Source of all goodness, is made increasingly controlling in contrast to that condition of self-love which separates people from one another by its inward movement toward the many egocentric foci. In the one instance, the relations which bind life together are acknowledged and made the resources of living; in the other, the relations, if acknowledged, are resisted and, where possible, severed. More often, however, where the look of the self is selfward, the relations go unnoted, though by no means unencountered.

The movement of the psyche toward identity with other life is not, psychologically speaking, a relinquishment of the self. The center of sensory organization within the personality structure of the organism remains as an individuated channeling of meaning. Only the bodily feelings become transformed in their automatic responses by the appreciative consciousness which receives the good of the world as its good. The identifying marks of goodness move God-ward and other-men-ward instead of simply selfward.

The emotion of joy is a response, then, acknowledging the fullness of life's meaning and a confession of one's incapacity to receive its fullness or to hold even a portion of it for any extended period of time. The cup runs over.

IV

Joy as an emotion can be intelligible only to the consciousness which is capable of an outward movement toward an experience of identity; for the movement selfward can yield no such sense of the fullness of life. The demand for self-satisfaction is insatiable. Self-seeking may subside for moments at a time, as hunger and passion and similar cravings may be assuaged. In this sense, satisfaction can be achieved. The rhythms of the body are formed by its rising and receding hungers. But a vast gulf stretches between sheer bodily satisfaction and the emotion of joy. They are not comparable either in dimension or in level of meaning.

Now a problem intrudes here which is often magnified into a stumbling block for those who would hold body and spirit together. What I have just said about the contrast between bodily satisfaction and joy will seem to border upon asceticism with implications of self-denial and especially denial of bodily satisfactions. I have no intention of asserting either of these denials to an ascetic degree. Certainly I would insist that any concentration upon bodily satisfaction such as is implied in sensuality, in whatever form, aggravates the demands of the self in a possessive sense. The line between bodily delight and sensuality is often a very thin one; nevertheless there is a proper demarcation between participation in the bodily senses and indulgence which enslaves the spirit of man. Bodily delight, which, of course, includes many forms of self-satisfaction, can be consonant with the outward movement of the psyche in the sense that community or the interrelation of life, when it is a genuine correlation of interests, becomes an instance of *individuals in community*. Such community, in which the concrete goods are acknowledged and accounted for, is of a greater complexity of relationship, carrying a higher degree of qualitative tension than the communal form in which individuality is canceled out or in which sensory capacities are obscured as in asceticism. Solitary asceticism and mass society have one basic trait in common: both have relinquished the creative tension between the living center of the sensory self, which fosters individuality in the bodily feelings, and the demands beyond the self. There is a truncation of spirit whenever this tension is destroyed or obscured.

There is a further reason why bodily delight may not be depreciated in deference to the emotion of joy. Any perception of goodness giving rise to such an emotion invariably manifests itself to the individual as a bodily feeling; and the persistence of its meaning as a recreative force of the personality is made possible by its retention in the bodily feelings. There can be no sharp dichotomy, therefore, between the sensory self and some "higher" self or between the self and the not-self, even though the distinction is made between a pattern of responses within the individual which moves self-ward and one which extends the individual's concerns appreciatively beyond the self.

V

The outward movement of the human psyche, leading to identity with the full range of life and meaning, enlarges the scope of sensitivity, making one responsive to a greater range of appreciative awareness; but in so doing, it also increases the range of pain and suffering. It is in this sense that joy and sorrow are concomitant experiences. The extension of the range of feeling is inevitable where identification with other centers of living or concern occurs. Thus the problem of evil mounts as a feeling-event in proportion as the appreciative consciousness extends its reach.

It is at this point that the perception of goodness falters. For even in the individual consciousness which has won its way to an awareness of meaning beyond the restrictive bounds of the self, the vision of meaning in which both good and evil are encountered will invariably be more attentive to events of evil than to events of goodness. There are several reasons why this will occur. For one

269

thing, evil, more often than not, releases bizarre and violent configurations of destruction and pain, as in the earthquake or the
blinding storm; while goodness may come into one's path with the
quietness of sun and of gentle rain. The import of evil, or better,
the urgency of judging and denouncing evil, impresses even the
religiously sensitive person as a topic of greater significance than
the designation of goodness. A subtle influence motivates the choice
of emphasis here. Even the person concerned with religious meaning is susceptible to the appeal of power over goodness. And the
denunciation of evil yields an illusion of power in the name of
goodness. Thus if one can champion goodness with a feeling of
power through fighting against evil, he is apt to choose this course
as being more suited to his reforming zeal, leaving to poets and
mystics the more gentle and ambiguous art of perceiving the good.

To be sure, a further motive often enters in. Metaphysically,
some would hold, the goodness of God can be approached only
through negation of evil. The good is not given in structured events,
they would contend. If it appears, it comes as a grace that is given
on God's initiative. One will know when this decisive event occurs
for God, himself, will make it known. This conception of goodness dissociates the goodness of God from the events of common
goodness so sharply as to leave no alternative but to define the religious act as the perception of evil. The perception of goodness,
in this perspective, could have only idolatrous connotations.

Against both this indiscriminate identification of power and goodness and this extravagant abstraction of goodness, I would argue for
a religious discernment which attends to the qualitative events
within the concrete structures of experience giving intimation of
God's grace and goodness.

A greater degree of discrimination in religious discernment is demanded, however, as perception of evil and perception of goodness
crowd into consciousness to counter one another or to create a disturbing tension which is not readily resolved. The tendency of the
human mind to want to balance accounts between conflicting
forces and to give intellectual allegiance to whatever figure survives
below the line as debit or credit causes it to cancel out the creative
tension between good and evil and thus to be oblivious to real differences. Lurking beneath this habit of mind is, again, the insidious
inclination to capitulate to survival power, even to worship it. What
prevails in the balance of forces is thus accounted right whether it
be good or evil.

The discrimination which religious perception tries to make here
is one that dissociates the mind from inevitable allegiance to sheer
ambiguous power without dissociating power and goodness. This
implies a purer vision of goodness or, rather, a perception of goodness which is committed to meaning and quality rather than to
sheer force; which is a way of saying that goodness and whatever
prevails are not accounted synonomous. Goodness if it is a quality
of meaning remains good whether or not, in the balance of forces
and tendencies, it prevails under any given circumstance. Purity of
religious perception consists precisely in this capacity to perceive
goodness in the complexity of events where evil abounds. It is not
an act of ignoring evil, but an act of realistically holding in view,
under vivid contrast, both good and evil as they operate in concrete events. The resolution of the conflict between good and evil
is not wholly the work of man; nor is it wholly in his hands. This
raises the troublesome question as to how far, and in what sense,
men may fight the evil they apprehend and fight for the good
which they cherish. One who makes an easy resolution of this problem will be overlooking the creative character of events as well as
the ambiguity of men's valuations and affections. In a creative situation, good and evil intermingle, often to the human perspective in
indistinguishable form. The ambiguity here arises from the tension
between novel and persisting value and from the differences in the
way men assess the claims of novelty and of persistent events. Creativeness demands an interrelating of these facets of meaning; but
only the creative act, itself, can effect the transition through which
interrelation occurs. The habits and fixations of men tend to line
them up on one or the other side, impelling them either to a stubborn resistance toward novelty or to champion novelty for its own
sake, thus countenancing ruthlessness toward all created goods.

These seemingly opposite characteristics among people, the one
impelling people to cling steadfastly to what is given, the other
pressing individuals toward innovation, have a common basis in the
tendency to equate goodness with what one personally cherishes
and in which one finds his own sense of security. Basically this is an
egoistic drive which ignores the note of judgment upon one's self
and leaves the reconstructive forces, which are objective to one's
existence, uncalculated. Generally, the person for whom the past
and its fixed meanings offer the greater degree of security will
identify God with past values and set him at odds with creative
change; while the individual whose sole security lies in the promise

of the future will define God exclusively in terms of novelty or creative change as the breaker of patterns, the creator with a nailed fist. In both instances, God is made in the image of one's own valuations which, in turn, have been defined by one's intimate sense of need and desire.

The resistance to creative change in large part arises from the conviction that change, itself, is but a manifestation of transitoriness and that changelessness is, in itself, the basic good. A metaphysics of long standing underlies this conviction—one in which *the good* can be mathematically delineated as an eternal structure. The commitment to novelty also arises from a basic conviction—the conviction that sheer process is a sovereign source of good; thus whatever issues from its occurrence is good or is better than the structure through which it has broken in its advance toward the novel event. Emergence in its profound meaning is never simply change; it is re-creation or reconception. It is a transformative occurence in which the elements of an older structure are thrust into a new order of relations. The new is never the polar opposite of the old. Each stands in a formative relationship, the one qualified by the other. The old can never be the same once the new structure has actualized some portion of the possibilities which were implicit in its existence. The new, however different it may appear at the moment of emergence, moves out of a context which is always the receding past. It bears in its organic being the accumulative and transformed residue of whatever past has preceded its actuality.

Now the perception of good as over against evil in this creative passage of events becomes difficult in proportion as one is inflexible in either direction. Goodness then tends to be defined in relation to one or the other point of fixation. Yet the good is always in the act of qualitative attainment wherein emergence wrests from past structures the qualifying influence which can be assimilated into the new. Where value cannot be so assimilated, it forms as an accumulation of obstructive energy registering defeat in every subsequent act. Having dissociated itself from the ongoing stream in which creative meaning is being fashioned, it has no part in the creative purpose itself. Its defeat thus becomes increasingly evident as its own dissolution of structure occurs in its every act of resistance. On the other hand, where partisans of novel advance remain indifferent to this qualifying event wherein the increment of persisting value is assimilated, their very thrust into novelty has the same dissipating effect. Its resources are highly contemporary; thus the dimension of its meaning is meager. It lacks depth and quality which only time and its creative passage can bequeath. At best, such a thrust can boast but a seasonal triumph which must be readily dissolved as soon as its meager resource of energy and insight is spent.

VI

Religious discernment is always an act of awareness in the midst of creative advance; yet it is not always preoccupied with the moment of change. It is a process of attending to persisting features of quality which rise from experience, attesting to the goodness of existence in the form of a fruition of creative change. This is one source of generalized notions such as mutuality, love, tenderness, forgiveness, beauty, order, truth, and peace. The concrete occurrences of these qualitative meanings is always a process, a happening having to do with relations and qualities of response arising from these relations. But it is their nature to have enduring effects in the sense of eliciting subsequent processes with affinities for these qualities and of giving direction to processes such that the goodness of existence which has become actual by reason of their occurrence persists, both as a qualifying effect upon all processes and as a matrix of meaning which generates new events in kind.

These generalized notions, therefore, are not just abstractions of the mind. They are, as it were, distillations of quality from concrete occurrences which, in becoming cumulative, give a sort of texture to experience within the relationships in which such events persistently occur. Thus they live on in events. In this form, they are effective as overtones and depths of experience which add a dimension of feeling to the experiences of people who live within such a relationship. Anyone who has achieved some measure of this depth in experience in living with people or with some person, or in relation to some place, will recognize immediately the persisting quality of goodness to which I am pointing.

These overtones elicit from the group life, itself, a consensus of meaning and valuation by which a society or a culture comes to a common understanding of such general notions as truth, beauty, love, order, and the like. Thus it may be said that while the individual philosopher may arrive abstractly at a definitive conception of these terms through arduous analysis, the group as a whole, or people living within the common experience of the group, come to have a sense for these meanings and these values in concrete terms, by acquaintance one may say, through the life they have lived together. This fact will help to explain why such general notions take on a cultural coloring. It is often assumed that these notions are nothing but predilections of the culture. This is a half-truth. They will always assume some cultural character when they are encountered in concrete form, for they are actual ingredients of some context of living-experience. Abstractly they can be distilled from any culture or from many cultures. Concretely they exist as overtones of some actualized meanings or values within events which have been known and felt by actual people within a given pattern of living.

Once these overtones and depths of experience, to which we give the names "beauty," "love," "order," "community," etc., form within a given relationship they have the force of actuality even though they may not always be designable or measurable; for they generate the quality of meaning which enters into every experience-able occasion within that relationship. The presence of these overtones and depths of experience is what gives reassurance to the human psyche—at times amplifying and heightening the intellect's grasp of discernible meanings, at other times serving as a ballast when the mind moves toward despair. When we have discerned the import of this feeling context, much of which envelops the structure of events with an imperceptible fullness, we will have penetrated to the empirical basis of faith.

The Significance of Religious Sensibility and Wonder in Any Culture 19

One conclusion that is being drawn from the present turn of events in modern cultures, where secularization has been a dissipating force, is that all historic religions have been rendered obsolete. I shall undertake to deal with that judgment later. A second, more serious observation which is being made today is that religious sensibilities and the sense of wonder are no longer relevant to a technological civilization. The posture of man generally presupposed in such sensibilities and response, it is argued, no longer obtains now that man has aggressively addressed himself to exploring every conceivable aspect of reality and is so successfully opening up hitherto concealed areas to human enterprise, turning its energies and resources to the use and betterment of mankind. Ethical values, appropriate to the conduct of affairs in the human community, it is conceded, can be seen to be imperative; but sensibilities or responses expressive of anything more than this would seem to be incongruous with what a technological civilization implies.

This judgment is by no means a recent one. It is at least as old as the scientific attitude stemming from Francis

Bacon. And it has motivated much of educational theory as well as social and philosophical reflection since Positivism became a generally accepted world-view among educators. What is recent about it is the widespread assent to it among moderns, young and old, following from the magnitude of scientific achievement, and thus the vividness of its contribution to every sphere of life. It is this that has enlarged the public image of science as a benefactor of mankind, and, conceivably, as the source of its salvation.

No discerning person will brush aside this judgment lightly. I must say, in all honesty, that it is a judgment with which I have lived during all of my mature years as a student of religious history and philosophy. I have confronted it, pondered and probed its meaning for modern man and his cultures, at times feeling the force of its claim, but more continuously sensing the shallowness of its understanding of man in the full dimensions of his being.

To put it bluntly, this judgment that religious sensibilities and wonder are no longer relevant, now that we have entered upon a technological civilization, overlooks the basic fact that, despite all the accomplishments of men in the exploration and use of his natural environment, the posture of man with reference to the ultimate dimensions of his existence, as marked, for example, by birth and death, has not changed. The context of human existence still presents to each of us a sense of something given, to which we are related in elemental ways. However far we develop and use our human powers, we do not slough off this elemental condition of being creatures of a Creative Process that is not made by us, not really influenced or altered by us in anything that our sciences or philosophies undertake. It is given as a primordial fact of our existence. We can obscure this sense of creatureliness, block it from view, proceed with the business at hand without thought of it, and, in our sophistication, we can disavow it. But this changes nothing except our attitudes and states of mind. The realities of existence presented by this elemental fact of creaturehood persist as ineradicable circumstances of this living context.

Let me pause at this point to make a distinction which I think may be helpful to our discussion. In speaking of the significance of religious sensibility to any culture I am using the term "religious sensibility" in a rather restrictive and specific sense. If one assumes that by religious sensibilities one means simply the characteristic feelings or responses of those who are sensible to what concerns religions, our confusion will be confounded. If, however, one takes religious sensibility to imply responsiveness to what ultimately claims man, supports and judges his ways in the light of this primal context, one will be looking beyond religions as such, and beyond all human responses evidencing such behavior to the sovereign good that is the source of all religions and that stands in judgment of their human ways.

When one distinguishes between religious sensibilities and the religions, one is implying, of course, that not everyone who manifests religious sensibilities is a participant in some religion. And, on the other hand, one may imply also that not everyone who does participate in the overt forms of religion is expressive of religious sensibilities in their most discerning sense, or in a sense that renders such a response relevant to the cultural life of a people. I am talking, you see, about a kind of response that is appropriate to every human being, regardless of his faith or culture, by reason of his participation in a primal context that is given in existence.

But now I move to a second observation. Not only is there a primal context in which our lives are cast, there is a specific context, a particular dimension or level at which our creaturely existence occurs—the human structure, it is sometimes called, as differentiated from all other natural structures. This fact, that we are in a sequence of evolving structures, and that we constitute one characteristic structure of life at a specific level of differentiation, implies both the range of our possibilities and the limitation under which we exist.

Now let us note parenthetically that, while the human structure has a distinct set of facilities consonant with its level of emergence which are peculiarly its own, it retains certain other features which mark its solidarity with antecedent forms of life: a bone structure, internal organs, a blood stream and a vascular system, etc. This body-life of man is a miniature repository of much else that antedates the animal structures. The sea water that flows in our veins, carrying salts and minerals, giving substance and seasoning to our internal workings, recalls our identity with the prehistoric deposits of rock and soil, and our continuing solidarity with this wondrous environing nature.

Yet, mind you, the human structure is dynamic in nature. It is not just a static repository of substances derived from antecedent forms; nor is it an arrested level of existence in every respect. It is volatile and eruptive with psychic disturbances, some of which arise out of its own sensitivities as a psycho-physical organism, but not all. Some of these disturbances give outlet to anxieties, wonderings, and outreachings that are expressive of what William James once called our tropism toward the More of existence.

Religions have been quick to mythologize this More of existence that seems to supervene our characteristic structure; thus we have fully elaborated accounts of its nature. Unfortunately, these accounts are so varied and contradictory that, to discerning and critical persons, they tend not to encourage confidence in the fact of this more ultimate ground of sensitivity. The truth is, we have only marginal apprehensions of it, such apprehensions as our limited structure of life affords. Yet these apprehensions are sufficiently acute to alert us to the tenuous intimations of a level of sensitivity reaching beyond our attained level of existence.

Thus, we may say, man as an organism has a natural history; but as an emergent spirit he appears to be within an orbit of existence that points him beyond his characteristic, structural attainments, to a "thither-side" of his presently evolved structure. Accordingly one may speak of man as having his representative structure as human being, i.e., the facilities of personal existence that are native to his level of existence, and this outreach toward something More that evokes responses in him.

With this general view of our existence in mind, we may be able to come to a sharper understanding of what is involved in religious sensibility and wonder. It is, first of all, a capacity in man to be aware of himself as being a creature at one level of existence, and thus mindful of certain structural limits. To put it baldly, certain explicit senses (five in number) give him access to a certain range of occurrences. These can be magnified and subtly differentiated in fantastic ways, as we have seen in these latter days of radio and television. How much farther parapsychology will extend this sensory range of the human being we have yet to learn. Yet the basic sensory limitation remains.

More positively, I have intended to suggest that this religious sensibility and wonder appears as a capacity in man to be tenuously and intermittently aware of yearnings or intimations transcending his structural existence. In my *Realities of Faith* I undertook to establish a working concept of the reality of spirit as man's relational ground with whatever constitutes this More of existence. In that discussion I quoted John Donne's familiar line, "No man is an island," and then commented that, On the contrary, every man *is* an island; but islands are not what they appear to be,

279

isolated bodies of land. When one probes the shoreline one finds that, at a deeper level, every island is related to a land base that extends to a mainland and that unites each island with other islands in the sea. Now I cannot build a philosophy on a figure of speech, but this figure of the island and its relationships may help to make vivid a philosophical claim that proceeds quite naturally from the conception of man's emergent structure. And I use it only for that purpose. I subscribe, as you can see, to a metaphysics of internal relations which, in turn, has affinities with the modern vision of relativity physics. This will come out more clearly later.

A sense of wonder, therefore, is not just a vacuous outreach toward a great empty Nothingness, but an expectant and somewhat apprehensive openness to what is envisaged in this relational ground. All firm concepts of such a ground are hazardous, and probably misleading; but I am insisting that we have intimations of its meaning in concrete relations which are sufficiently discernible to give us a sense of what such an ultimacy can mean. One such intimation is the notion of context, which I mentioned earlier—the context of each individual existence marked by birth and death. There is an entrance and an exit defining the visible bounds of concrete existence, which can suggest to the critical mind either Nothingness as a context, or a Creative Passage in which life is given and in turn received. By this point I mean to suggest only that there is a dimension of the Given in our existence, an aspect of it which is not in our hands to command, and which has not been shaped by human hands.

Furthermore, I would hold that our relational ground is intermittently discerned in the relationships that hold us in existence. These are numerous, but the ones most revealing are those in which a good that is not of our own making comes into our existence as a grace that is given. In moments of dependence, when the grace of another's concern for our well-being or the grace of an affectionate relationship reaches us, we are made aware of such a good not of our own making. To be able to receive such grace that is given in existence gives some inkling of what transpires at more primal levels of our existence which we cannot observe or consciously attend.

Now as I said earlier, the fact of this wider dimension of the human spirit can be brushed aside in our sophistication as modern people. And it is quite understandable that many of our contemporaries should choose to focus upon the clearly marked traits or features of our presently emerged structure, taking these characteristic human capacities as being defining and normative of the human person and his order of life. One can establish an impressive order of life on this basis. Most of our workaday world proceeds on this basis. Certainly our political and economic spheres of society conduct affairs within this clearly defined orbit of existence. Much of educational theory and practice proceeds within this delimited dimension of our humanity, and the tendency to follow this course is accentuated wherever education is directed toward competent and successful living in a technological age. Even certain modern forms of religion may be found which settle for this representative human dimension of life, and thus they seek to formulate regulative and directive measures for assuring a responsible and morally rewarding human existence on this basis. Religiously speaking, they are saying that ethics is enough.

It may not be improper to speak of these orders of life, which consciously confine their commitments to the characteristic and representative structure of man, as forms of voluntary isolationism; that is, as ways of looking at man and his community in isolation from all other structures of existence, and thus to ascribe autonomy and ultimacy to man simply as man.

Perhaps you can see, then, from what I have said thus far, how the problem of secularization takes on added dimensions in this context. You will recall that, in speaking of the modern state, we differentiated between a secular state that conceived of its secularization as being constitutive, and one that viewed secularization as instrumental. The one became closed and inhospitable to everything save what served its immediate ends; the other sought to pursue its urgent and immediate ends within an open society, responsive to criticisms and judgments which might arise within its society, and able to negotiate when dealing with the differences that inevitably emerge. Speaking now in the terms which we used in commenting on the modern secular state, this human isolation, when it is asserted in all spheres of the culture, limiting the orders of life to this representative structure of man, imposes upon the culture a secularization that presumes to be *constitutive*. It tends to render the total cultural outlook within its purview hostile to whatever would transcend the human community. Now it can be argued, much as we argued in discussing the modern secular state, that the political and economic life of man must proceed as secular activities, uncomplicated by the nuances of religious sensibilities and wonder. Ethical values, looking to the exercise of just and orderly processes and to the integrity of human relationships, will certainly be imperative; but more than this need not be required—except one thing: a policy of openness and toleration toward those enterprises of man that do pursue the meaning of man within a larger orbit of existence.

In all other enterprises, however, the arts, education, philosophical, religious, and even scientific inquiry, such isolationism, implying a constitutive secularization of modern culture, will act as an unnecessary and detrimental closure upon the culture. Their function, in each case, does not demand that they be secular, either in a constitutive or in an instrumental sense in the way that other processes of society might or do. And their role as cultural disciplines, nurturing and expressing the human spirit, and extending the range of its possibilities under the limitations of its existence, would be immeasurably enhanced were they to remain open toward this total reality with a sense of wonder. Needless to say, the cultures in which the creative, aesthetic, and reflective disciplines could be attuned to the full dimension of the human spirit, and free within a secular state to exercise these functions, would likewise be enhanced, if not actually blessed.

But it is probably oversanguine to expect that these critical disciplines will readily respond to such an appeal. It may not, however, be either utopian or uncritical to insist that, when these disciplines, in their zeal to be heard or to be decisive, make their secular disavowal of religious sensibilities assume the finality of a dogmatic claim, they relinquish the right to be known as a critical discipline, concerned with critical inquiry, and become instead another form of apologetics for a constituent secularism.

Now what has been distinctive about the historic religions has been their openness to a dimension of reality beyond the human sphere of existence. We need not elaborate upon the various ways of acknowledging or responding to this vision of reality. Much of what is conveyed through formal and doctrinal statements or ceremonial practices rests, as we have said, upon mythological constructions which must be taken to be the poetic and dramatic extension of primal insights or intuitions. The philosopher of religion and historian of religion will be attentive to the rich tapestry of

283

mythological creations as creative expressions of the human spirit, and as possible indices to what is basic in the human response to the ultimate dimension of existence. While he will not take the full doctrinal and ceremonial history of any religion as being the inevitable and final expression of this primal religious sensibility, or of the profound sense of wonder that inheres in or underlies its religious forms or exercises, he will value them, along with the institutions that currently convey them, as being the present carrier of that primal response within that particular culture, and as being its persisting, motivating mythos. In saying this, you will see that I am distinguishing between myth and mythology. The latter is an explicit ideological projection of this sensitive awareness into an imaginative and dramatically creative lore, either as a direct expression of the creative impulse or as a didactic means of explicating and propagating the witness of faith arising from these primal sensibilities. Myth, I would hold, is not to be identified wholly with mythologies. Rather, it is the persisting sensibility and sense of wonder, abstractly referred to by Rudolf Otto as "creature-feeling," functioning within any culture or community of people as a dimension of depth in their existence. It is, in short, the historical and deeply organic expression of what I earlier termed "the tenuous intimations in the human structure of a level of sensitivity, seemingly reaching beyond its attained level of existence." The persistence of this sensitive awareness of what is at work in the human structure, motivating and impelling it beyond its own ends and capacities, is what keeps the individual organism and the communal life alive to the full dimension of its existence and meaning.

Thus while mythologies are expendable, myth, as a persisting expression of this primal response of sensitivity and wonder, is not. For our human rendering of what is involved or meant by the primal creaturely response is constantly subject to modification and correction, or reinterpretation, as cultural history proceeds and as cultural forms and the idioms of thought and speech change; but the sensibility in man, giving current history to the primal response as a sense of wonder and anticipation of the fullness and depth of his creaturely existence, is an elemental capacity in man that persists wherever man is left free to be open to the total range of his organic existence.

We noted a moment earlier that cultural man, through studied and disciplined effort, can shunt off these tenuous intimations of sensibility and wonder beyond his own structure; and through neglect or habitual indifference to them, can establish a life-order that is neither motivated nor consciously qualified by this sensitive range of spirit open to the human structure. The common life, thus shorn of this appeal to sensitivity and wonder beyond its own norms, or of sensibilities that can render man responsive to it, will suffer a deficiency of spirit that will become delimiting, progressively enclosing its norms and purposes within the demands of the cultural experience. Man's experience then becomes the sole measure of his ways. Men so committed to becoming characteristically human may thus be made statically human: that is, a community closed within those established concepts of moral good that the cultural experience can achieve and sustain. What is lost from this social vision is the sense of judgment or challenge that can come from a transcendent measure, or from a sense of limitation in the human structure which will forever keep one open to and inquiring about the validity of human forms and formulations.

In one respect, both the humanistic decision to adhere to the characteristically human dimension of existence and the procedure of religions to mythologize the transcendent outreach and live rigidly within these doctrinal definitions tend to come to the same thing. Each of them, in its own way, encloses man within the forms and fantasies of the historical culture. In both instances the religious sensibility and sense of wonder, expressive of the primal response, tends to be lost sight of, and, as a consequence, the resource of judgment or corrective in its transcendent reach beyond all creatural experience is made nonexistent. Without such a resource, self-criticism and openness to judgment of the ways of one's religion or one's culture tend to atrophy or to disappear altogether. This has been the story of our historical religions as well as of humanistic ventures presuming to counter their claims.

The will to look beyond cultural norms, and to establish a world outlook in faith or in politics has, on the other hand, generally followed the course of emptying thought and policies of all cultural coloration, including its religious biases; and this has meant not only secularizing the international ideal, but also abstracting it from all concrete involvement in the sphere of cultural differences. Internationalism, or what is at times called *universalism*, thus assumes a strangely artificial character as a vision of man deprived of all concrete references, and dissociated from cultural involvement or commitment.

The look beyond cultural norms need not imply this disavowal of cultural involvement and commitment; any more than being attentive to dimensions beyond the human structure need imply a disavowal of our humanity. It need recognize only that cultural assessments and interpretations of experience are limited, and thus fallible, just as the human structure, as a distinctive level of emergence, is limited, and thus to a degree fallible, liable to the errors of its limitations. Yet, within these limitations and fallibility, both cultural experience and the human structure are capable of creativities in thought and act which are expressive of its indigenous character, and as such, are not only valued outlets of self-expression, but valuable contributions per se to the total drama of existence. These human creativities within any culture are to be cherished, nurtured, and sustained, but they are not to be absolutized any more than the human structure itself or the mythological renderings of the primal outreaches among religions are to be absolutized. Holding all of these creativities and formulations answerable to a higher level of sensitivity, or at least open to judgment, even as we cherish and sustain them, can enable us to look beyond these structures, even as we participate in them, and promote their indigenous goods amidst the differences of other cultures, other religions, other creatural forms.

Furthermore, the very spirit of mind expressed in holding one's own creativities and formulations subject to the judgment of a more ultimate level of sensitivity can enable one to be critical, yet measured in one's response to the historical religions that arise within one's own culture, even as one acknowledges and cherishes the truths they affirm, even as one participates in a religion as one's own resource and witness of faith. To have people in any religion who can exercise this kind of critical acumen, even in the interpretation of doctrine and moral judgments, is an asset to religions as well as to cultures.

In what we have said thus far, we have sought to identify the scope and quality of the religious sensibility and wonder we envisage and the contribution it can make to the vision of a people, giving openness and outlook to the culture as well as a critical sense in attending to its own creativities and judgments.

Where there is outreach beyond the human structure, the religious sensibility and sense of wonder arising from it can contribute to modern cultures in other ways. It can actually bring into the common life resources of a kind that appear as a surplus of goodness which comes into existence out of the relationships that hold men in existence. The Christian religion has spoken of this surplus of spirit as *grace*. The Bhakti devotion in India, going back to the Hindu philosopher, Ramanaja, presents a similar characterization of it. This resource of grace is an empowerment of life and purpose that is not of one's own calculating effortfulness, not at one's bidding or command, but comes as a gift, as one says, where there is the capacity to receive what is given. The capacity to receive what is given implies an orientation of life, a stance, if you will, that is itself expressive of religious sensibility and wonder. It implies, first of all, that something can only be *given to me*, for it is not mine to command. This goes back to a very old premise: "The earth is the Lord's, and the fullness thereof." That is one expression of it. You may recall many others. This premise stands as a restraint upon the energetic drive of modern men and civilizations, bent on getting what they want, and upon the so-called enterprising spirit of modern man and civilizations stemming from the time of Francis Bacon and the Industrial Era of the West, when initiative and enterprise in compelling nature and the processes of men's labor to yield up their goods was first vigorously asserted as a principle around which to organize scientific and political activity. Cultures in the West have become addicted to this stance, and have fortified it in some sections of the community with moral directives, sanctified by religious doctrine.

What has given cultures in the East, prior to this recent period, a sense of spiritual superiority over the West stems in part from their instinctive response of aversion to this spirit of unrestrained enterprise. Yet, at the same time, they have recognized their own physical inferiority to the driving power of the West; and, for a time, they suffered under the imperialistic extension of Western control. But the ironical fact is, so it would appear at least, that, having been released from the imperialistic control of Western powers, Eastern cultures, one by one, seem to be relinquishing the premise that once gave them a sense of spiritual authority, and instead they are adopting the spirit of aggressive enterprise to remove or to correct their social ills.

On the surface this turn of events would appear to be a clear instance of secularizing the cultures of the East, not only imbuing them with a spirit that is alien to their history, but causing them to forsake historical guidelines that are indigenous to their religious traditions. I dare say that some of the resistance that one detects among reactionary groups in Eastern cultures to this so-called Westernization of its life stems from this kind of analysis of the modern situation.

Yet it requires but a moment's pause to realize that to dismiss as secularization those programs of action and reform that are so desperately needed to bring hungry men and women the bread and rice they need to sustain life is simply to enhance the word secularization. We are confronted here with a paradox. The paradox may be more apparent than real, but it nevertheless evokes profound confusion in present-day thinking on the crisis in modern cultures. The paradox seems to be that the cultures of the West, with their spirit of initiative and enterprise, stand under the judgment of the age-old religious premise, common to East and West, but more consistently sustained among Eastern cultures; yet to assure its people life in a time of unprecedented need, the East must avail itself of this spirit of enterprise, and thereby incur the risk of spiritual regression.

As in all paradoxes, this one conceals discrepancies of logic upon which the terms of the contrast are built; only in this instance, they are not discrepancies in the logic of thought, but in the logic of history, as it has been lived both in the West and in the East. If the spirit of human initiative and enterprise in the West has tended to obscure the primal religious premise that the earth is the Lord's, and that to this Ultimate Ground we are beholden for resources of grace, the response of the East to this primal premise has wreaked its own form of cultural havoc. In the words of one of the most revered statesman of the modern age, the late Jawaharlal Nehru, who in his lifetime was bent on revising the course of action in India, this response of Eastern cultures has been to encourage a spirit of fatalism, the cultural consequences of which have been lethargy and indolence in coping with the practical problems of human livelihood. When applied to specific situations, these observations may appear very wide of the facts. As generalizations upon the prevailing moods of West and East, however, they speak a truth that is sobering beyond anything we can presently imagine.

It would be audacious of me to presume to find a way through this modern dilemma, the issues of which have challenged the best thinking of statesmen and seers of both East and West. Yet I have been impelled to apply every energy of thought I can muster to contribute whatever earnest reflection can bring to bear upon it, hopefully to break through the impasse in some slight respect. To that end, I invite you to consider one insight that appears to me to be relevant to the discussion. It has to do with the way we conceive of man, or more particularly, the way we conceive of man's relation to whatever is considered divine. The basic premise which I offer, as a ground for reordering our thinking about man, and for revising his response to the primal religious premise, is this: The conception of man as being related to a higher order of sensitivity does not disavow the propriety of man's individual initiative and creativity. It does, however, imply a condition of dissonance in the relationship between man and the transcendent Good which at one and the same time affirms man's freedom to be creative and assertive, as well as his need to be responsive to the judgment of the level of sensitivity that transcends and cradles his human structure. Put in traditional terms, man's commitment to God does not nullify the command to exercise man's human powers of creativity. The dissonance arises from the interplay of authentic centers of selfhood, in which freedom of self-expression is acknowledged and the freedom to receive another's expression is affirmed.

Neither the typical Western mind nor the representative Eastern expression of religious and cultural thinking, in my judgment, has adequately acknowledged this complexity in their concepts of the divine-human relationships. Both, in a way, have assumed that divine transcendence implied domination of the human spirit, either on the ground that the divine, being other than man, stood in a relation of judgment toward man, or on the ground that man, being less than God, was therefore subservient to Him. Consonant with this premise, the will to freedom in the West has generally implied man's alienation from the divine, and in proud but sensitive Westerners, for whom the authentic existence of selfhood has meant life itself, such a state of mind has led either to a forthright disavowal of the divine dimension or to a form of pragmatic humanism which, for all practical circumstances, dismissed this dimension from consideration in human affairs. In the East, subservience to what was deemed divine superiority has left the will of man docile and accepting of conditions imposed. Insofar as the East has partaken of the spirit of Western humanism, and has sought to elevate the human spirit, it has felt duty-bound to equate its human idealism with ultimate goodness itself, and thus has tended to merge divinity and humanity. Interestingly

291

enough, except for the most recent efforts in Neo-Hinduism, this high valuation of man has not turned Indian thought to the task of improving the plight of man in his present existence; rather it has led it to explore the intricacies of the human mind and spirit on the assumption that it was thereby exploring divine dimensions of existence. Spirituality in the East, particularly in Indian thought, has thereby come to imply every kind of esoteric manifestation or exercise which could lay claim to being another facet or nuance of personal existence.

Those, in turn, who have been awakened to the need of more direct dealings with the practical concerns of human living have been léd to disavow all such preoccupations with mystery and mysticism, as did Pandit Nehru, and to address themselves to these social tasks on a scientific basis in defiance of any appeal to spirituality. In this, modern Indian secularists have joined hands with the Western scientific humanists to rid the world of all obstacles to a scientific understanding of human problems, out of a concern to attack them directly on this basis. It is no accident, I think, that the writings of Bertrand Russell have been so widely read in India. He speaks for a formidable group of Indian minds who have dispensed with spirituality as Indian thought has conveyed it.

We see, then, that both East and West have tended to view this relationship between the human and the divine as being one, either of subservience or resistance, conformity and identification, or rebellion and alienation. Conformity and identification have led to the concern to re-enact the divine life in man, to the neglect of man's human initiative in expressing his distinctive structure of existence. Rebellion and alienation, on the other hand, have led to a determination to assert or to pursue the human dimension of man with indifference toward divinity, or any transcendent dimension. This pattern of subservience or rebellion, determinism or freedom, in religious thinking about God and man has precluded any notion of a negotiable relationship existing between the structure of man and the transcendent. Yet it is precisely this kind of relationship that most accurately defines the interplay of divine and human structures. God, as a goodness not our own, has an integrity of structure that is what it is, a level of sensitivity and grace that stands unshaken or unmoved from divine purposes by the foibles and follies of man. Yet one can say He is moved by what we are and do in the sense of being responsive to us in His acts of judgment and grace. Man as a creature of God nevertheless has an integrity of structure that is what it is, a level of sensitivity functioning within the limits of its emergence, yet with an authenticity appropriate to its being. Man, too, is relational, yet solitary and individual. This is the complexity of his being. One can say he is made for God, for other men, and for himself. This is the formula that best expresses the interplay of the relational and individual aspects of his existence. As a conception of man, it expresses the dissonance that inheres in his existence as a given fact. He is possessed with a freedom to be himself, and, as a creature of God with a divine intent, he is obligated to pursue this freedom to fulfill that intent. Yet he has access to a freedom to be more than himself, free to be in relation to other men and creatures, and to be in relation to God. The true state of our humanity is defined by the demands with which these dissonant relationships confront our existence. And our negotiation of them is what ultimately characterizes our nature and destiny. The British-American philosopher, Alfred North Whitehead, was pointing to this truth of existence when he wrote in *Religion in the Making*, "the topic of religion is individual in community." This is a resolution of the issue which does not destroy the dissonance of relationships.

293

When that dissonance gives way, either to rebellion or to acquiescence, both freedom and responsibility are impaired in man; and the stature of man as a free, yet related being, deteriorates.

I would hold, then, that the source of much of our difficulty in retaining religious sensibilities and a sense of wonder in the modern era, or of relating them to the concerns of a scientific and technological age, roots in the fact that religious thinking has been dominated by a pattern or mode of thought which inevitably causes all such sensibility and wonder to issue in a piety of subservience. The humanist tradition in every age has been a proper protest against this kind of docility that denegrades the human spirit and the structure of its existence. But the folly of humanistic thinking has lain in the tendency of its protesting to move invariably toward a truncated, ethical view of existence which has disavowed the response of religious sensibility and wonder in man.

A proper relationship would seem to be one of genuine dissonance, rather than one of subservience in which one seeks to come to terms with the ultimate measure of life in the context of pursuing with seriousness and appreciation the known values in our human creations. In the Jewish and Christian Scriptures there is a story of the patriarch Jacob, wrestling with the angel, which I would suggest is an apt parable of the relationship between the human and the divine. And its meaning would imply a vigorous assertion of the human equation, even in confronting the measure of this ultimate good not our own. I would put it this way: In any encounter between the human and the divine, it takes a bit of doing on the part of God to get a good man down. Dissonance in this context is expressive of a serious and genuine encounter between concerned and qualitative levels of existence.

Yet, we are to do all this, not in lieu of our critical inquiry, but in the context of it; not in lieu of pursuing the completion of our human creations, but in the context of it.

Eventually this would bring us around to saying that, in acknowledging the transcendent aspects of our being as a structure of sensitivity in which our lives are cast, we do not deny or disavow the freedom of man to employ initiative and enterprise in attacking problems of well-being. Spirituality is not the denial of our materiality, not the denial of our body-life or of our humanity, but the summoning of it to be itself and more.

In this brief résumé of a working conception of man, I have meant to give the rationale for asserting that, in acknowledging the transcendent aspect of our being as a structure of sensitivity in which our lives are cast, we are not necessarily denying or disavowing the freedom of man to employ initiative and enterprise in attacking problems of well-being. On the contrary, we are suggesting that this effortful program of reform and renewal can be enhanced by religious sensibilities which alert man to resources of the spirit that inhere in relationships, and that can bring to bear upon these effortful labors, energies of grace "which can do for man what he cannot do for himself."

I come, then, to some judgments about the significance of sensibility and wonder in any culture. Religious sensibility, as we have been employing it, has to do with the response of wonder and sensitivity to what inheres in the human structure as in intimation of A-More-Than-Human-Reality, to which the human structure is related as creature to ground, and toward which it has instinctive outreaches. Sense of wonder is its elemental expression, issuing simultaneously, as the anthropologist, R. R. Marett, has observed in a response of apprehension and "vital joy."[1] Its mature

[1] R. R. Marett, *Faith, Hope, and Charity*, London: Macmillan, 1932.

and seasoned expression will be a steady openness of mind and spirit toward possibilities of goodness and meaning, transcending man's own measure of good. Sophisticated levels of existence can find common ground with what is less sophisticated in proportion to the individual's capacity to exercise this maturity of judgment that partakes of the elemental outreach. To the degree that the sophisticated person cannot do this, he dissociates his mode of discourse from the more common levels of humanity. And to the degree that one cancels out, from one's intellectual and cultural concerns, all semblances of sensibility or response which would convey a sense of wonder consonant with creatural innocence in the presence of life's mysteries and the exigencies of existence issuing in both good and evil, one forfeits a significant quality of one's humanity. The Christian scripture quotes Jesus as saying, "Except ye become as a little child, ye cannot enter the Kingdom of Heaven." This, I think, could be claimed as a true anthropological statement. Put in more explicit terms, Except one can retain something of the childlike wonder and innocence of elemental people in the presence of life's ultimate mystery, one is shut off from the depths of one's own being, and of life's meaning. For the claiming of these depths waits not on our own initiative in inquiry so much as upon our capacity to receive, in wonder and sensitivity of feeling, what is being conveyed to us in such moments of awareness.

Secondly, the presence of such sensibilities in men has a leveling effect, in the good sense of that phrase. That is, it creates a ground common to all wherein the primordial equality of our humanity can be envisioned, and where acknowledgment of limitations appropriate to the human structure can be made sobering and edifying. Man needs the elation of sensing the innate possibilities of his human creativity, but he needs equally as much the sobering and restraining effects of confronting his creatureliness. Whether this takes the form simply of seeing oneself as an individual in the context of the Species, as Feuerbach was insistent upon doing,[2] or of confronting the edge of one's being in ways that open up a wider horizon of transcendence, the reorientation of selfhood that can come with recalling this primordial dimension of existence can be both heightening and restraining in its effects upon the human psyche.

The common bond of creaturehood is at least preparatory to a sense of solidarity in relationship, either as human beings cast in a common lot and confronting common possibilities and perplexities or as beings in relation to a common source of human good, from "whence cometh their help."

It is true that, in morally awakened religions, the formulations of what God expects of man, as directives for human living, tend to lessen acceptance of the human condition, and thus tend to abound in moral censorship rather than in social sympathy or human kindness. Yet, when the crises of life come, or when human need or suffering becomes acute, the resources of sympathy consonant with religious sensibility are evident, and are generally expressed with generosity and a wholehearted sense of solidarity.

The absence of this resource from any culture becomes a major human catastrophe, as in Nazi Germany, or in instances of war or in mass uprisings when men encounter one another, not as fellow human beings, but as objects of hate, or simply as impersonal symbols of the enemy that is to be destroyed. Yet the absence of this resource can be felt in societies in times of peace through the impersonalization of institutional life and the mechanization of the processes of society in which human persons tend to lose their identity as persons, and the humane response is displaced with auto-

[2] Ludwig Feuerbach, *The Essence of Christianity* (1841). Paperback edition in English, New York: Harper & Row, 1957.

matic mechanical action. The magnitude of this mechanization in present-day technological and industrialized societies
accentuates the possibility of dissipating this resource of human sympathy, and of thereby imperiling its humanity to a
critical degree.

Thirdly, it may be said that such sensibilities in any culture provide a resources beyond the egoistic drives in a society, and thus contribute a restraint upon them. A moment
earlier we spoke of the limitations of the human spirit that
can arise from its total absorption in the human structure,
with no reference in values beyond the norms and measures
of its own formulations. This limitation of the human spirit
stares out from the corporate transactions of society wherein
motives of self-interest or gain, on the individual or group
basis, tend to prevail. Where effort has been made to regu-
late or to elevate the tone of these transactions, the procedure has been to extend the concept of self-interest to embrace common interests, as in co-operative associations, or
even in the United Nations. On the surface this reconception of the motive of self-interest would seem to be only an
enlargement of the basis of interest, thereby bringing the
self into accord with other selves. Self-interest, so it would
seem, is thus made convivial or social without lessening the
self-centeredness of the motive. In a sense this is true, but it
is also true that this very act of relating one self to another,
and of taking account of a horizon of interest, with its responsibilities that extends beyond the immediacies of one
structure of existence, is of a piece with the movement of
spirit in man that can reach beyond the human structure itself. It is but a step beyond the co-operative envisagement of
common interests and goals to what Buber has called the
I–Thou encounter, wherein spirit arises in man at a more
sensitive level than in these utilitarian acts calculated to
bring about a larger social good. Yet it is a step not easily

taken. For this requires a contemplation of the *other* in and for itself, which implies a radical subsiding of egoistic drives in man. This relinquishment requires a degree of abandon or of trust in the bond of relationships that is not readily available to men steeled for action and accomplishment.

As one pursues this notion of relationship among individual selves, especially in a context in which individuality has assumed a high degree of freedom and self-consciousness, one will be led to see that one important path leading into the life of the spirit lies along this way: that is, that spirit as a good not our own, or as a resource of grace, is in relationships, not in any kind of relationship nor in every relationship. For relationships can turn in on themselves and become simply the human ego writ large, as in nationalism, or in tribes and clans. But wherever the fact of man's relatedness can summon them to acknowledge a good not their own, or the good of another, which simultaneously stands as good in its own right to be nurtured and cherished or as a resource of grace for other men when the occasion demands —wherever this can occur, the cultures of men can be called blessed. And in this kind of fabric of human relationships, the culture of the human spirit is significantly assured.

The Mystery of Existing
and Not Existing 20

Bernard E. Meland

Death establishes a common fate for every living thing, and thus gives a decisive character to our dependence upon God and our unity with all His creatures. It opens the way to the participation of this finite life in the infinite life of God.

—Daniel Day Williams[1]

By definition, existing and not existing would seem to be polar opposites; yet this judgment of their relationship may be purely impressionistic. Existing is so clearly an overt act of manifesting visible and expressive qualities of identity and behavior that, by contrast, it would seem, *not* existing could only mean the cessation or dissolution of such qualities of identity and behavior; hence, the negation of existing. In speaking of this contrast as impressionistic, I mean to direct attention to dimensions of depth pertaining both to existing and to not-existing which, in effect, may alter our understanding of relationships between them.

Existence and "Depth"

In the context of human inquiry made imperative by our understanding of the limited function of our forms and symbols, an horizon of incalculable data looms as a relevant dimension of experience. In that context, the mystery of existing as an inescapable depth and overtone of our understanding intrudes a persisting horizon of awareness, which somehow gives new dimension to understanding itself, along with intimations of resources which cannot readily be dismissed or ignored wherever critical inquiry is ventured.

The word "depth" in this context is not intended as an evocative term. In fact, it becomes misleading when it is so understood. That it has evocative power may not be denied, especially when the force of its epistemological import is made clear. What is basic in the notion of depth, as I mean to employ it, is the recognition that relations are experienceable and actually experienced, forming a substantive part of the continuum of experience as lived. This is a point initially made by William James in his *Psychology*[2] against the view of Hume. An accompanying insight, which James made insistent in his radical empiricism, is that perceptual experience is a richer event than conception can possibly be, in that it provides every occurrence of awareness with a "fringe" implying a *"more,"* much of which persistently evades conceptualization. These insights were to be given more explicit formulation as abstract notions in Whitehead's philosophy of organism, in which "concrescence," or the textured character of experience, was advanced as a key notion. Within that perspective, every event (including every person) is envisioned simultaneously in terms of its individuated concretion as a novel event, and the communal ground in which the individuation occurred. "Individual in community" thus became Whitehead's formula for expressing the nature of each concrete event, including each person. But this "textured" character of every event, as S. Alexander and others were to suggest, carried with it overtones of a prescient awareness of a future thrust of occurrences already implicit in the existing structure. This was the emergent theme in this philosophy of organism. Thus every person was seen as holding in tension within its immediate existence, a persisting structure of experience, bearing along past valuations with a restless bent toward novelty as a futuristic motif.

Depth, in this sense, then, is contextual, relational; and simultaneously so in a spatial and a temporal sense. The relational or contextual ground of all existence is dynamic and ongoing. The notion of depth thus provides a perspective upon every single or individuated event or person that illumines the context in which each "lived experience" takes place. That perspective, in turn, provides a resource within and beyond that which each individual in itself initiates or represents, as well as a source of judgment or caution toward what is individually enacted with indifference toward that relational ground. Yet a valid correlation of each centered existence and its communal ground is simultaneously one of individuation along with being communal, implying an appropriate degree of dissonance along with a communal response. Sheer subservience of the individual entity to its communal ground is thus viewed as a breach of the contextual occurrence. For any resolution that implies relinquishment of the authentic, novel concretion of the individual within community would be false to what is crucial in the creative event itself.

Similarly, in speaking of the mystery of existing, I intend more than to evoke a mood of wonderment or apprehension about that event, though both responses are appropriate. I mean, rather, to lift up implications of the dimensional character of each concrete occurrence as this applies to each human experience, particularly the depth of immediacy in each such experience.

The mystery of existing, with its experiences of joy and sorrow, fulfillment or defeat, is the vivid empirical datum which evokes inquiry. The bare event of existing is the most immediate and enduring fact of experience, and thus the most immediate empirical datum. Yet this bare event of existing rarely, if ever, presents itself to our conscious awareness. For the sensory responses in each individual, and the quickening of conscious meaning that follows from such psychical and conceptual interaction, clothes each life-span with a plethora of images, giving to each moment of existing its own self-conscious experience. And this can be a complex of feelings and valuations expressing intermittently a heightened awareness of the joy of living, or an aggravated sense of anguish, anxiety, and despair; or, possibly, a persisting experience of ennui in response to its deadly routine and futility. Normally an intermingling of these moods and valuations characterizes human existence.

The sheer event of existing, however, is deeper than consciousness, and deeper than anyone's sensory awareness of it. It opens into an ongoing stream of interrelated events, simultaneously enjoying or enduring this fact of existing.

Each event at whatever level, as we have said, appears to be held in existence through a structure of relationships that is integral to its own act of existing, and to circumstances creative and supportive of its existing. The history of natural structures is thus a serial accounting of the various nexus of relationships that have accompanied this "coming into being and perishing" of the many existing events throughout nature. Our human existence in each instance subsumes much that has preceded the human being in this emergence of natural structures. It contains, within its own structural emergence, tendencies and sensibilities that are responsive to this depth of relationships which supervenes it, and more. The *more*, in this instance, is not just this sequence of subhuman structures, but the ever-present interplay of *creativity*, *sensitivity*, and *negotiability* that give dynamic possibilities to each nexus of relationships, imparting to each event a creative intent, enabling it to live forward and to participate in the *elan* of existing.

The limits of our human structure preclude our having full understanding or steady awareness of this depth of mystery that has brought us into existence, and for a time, holds us in existence as humanly conscious beings. Thus, our existing as immediate occurrences takes place with but marginal awareness, and often with relative indifference, to the penumbral occurrences that carry and give intimation of the Ultimate Efficacy attending all existence.

Existence as contingent. As we have implied, all existing is fraught with peril, as well as with possibility and promise. The peril of existing derives in large measure from the surd of insensitivity that intrudes upon all relationships with varying degrees of defeat and destructiveness, ranging from the anguish and evil of isolated existences among individuals, to explosive encounters between individuals and groups. As an empirical datum, this surd of insensitivity appears to derive from pathological conditions within the human structure itself, and conceivably among other structures within nature. There is no assurance, however, that this surd of insensitivity is confined to conditions within these created structures. Speculatively speaking, there is the possibility that it may extend to conditions accompanying creativity itself; that it impairs the creative process; or, in any case, sets obstacles to the creative act, thus persistently offering a threat to that act, as well as to conditions consonant with it, as is implied in the terms "sensitivity" and "negotiability."

To the degree that this peril assumes ontological proportions, say, as an abyss of disorder and irrationality, or as an aggressive distaste for or disregard of creativity, it becomes a threat to the Ultimate Efficacy attending existence, as well as to existence itself. I see no way of affirming or disavowing such an ontological peril categorically. But the tendency of my thought is to assume its possibility, to the extent, at least, of acknowledging that the creativity, sensitivity, and negotiability that bring meaningful and redemptive events into existence do so at a price—at the price of an ultimate encounter with suffering and anguish, consonant with qualitative attainment. Thus our anguish and suffering, while pertinent to the conditions that attend our structure of existence, may not be peculiar to our situations as created human beings. It may be analogous to, if not a counter part of, the strain attending creativity itself, in its encounter with an ultimate surd of insensitivity.

The imagery of *the Suffering Servant* in the Judaic-Christian legacy, which in the Christian story becomes the *Suffering* Christ, is an oblique, though penetrating, reference to this inherent surd of insensitivity and tragedy at the core of existence. The *pietas* of Christian art, depicting Jesus on the Cross, was a graphic reminder that it was God, the incarnate one, who suffered—not God as He is in Himself. For the conception of God as immutable, implying His being impassible as well, precluded associating the Godhead with suffering in such a direct and concrete manner. One of the radical revisions in contemporary theology, notably among process theologians, is its repudiation of the notion that God is unchanging and immune to suffering. *Divine relativity*, as Charles Hartshorne has expressed it, is at the heart of our thinking about God.[3]

So much, then, for a minimal sketching of the mystery of existing as an empirical datum.

Death as Experience

The mystery of existing is exceeded only by the mystery of not existing; and this is to confront the inescapable fact of death. Here one comes to a strong sense of the limitations of critical inquiry in the area of theology and philosophy. Except as these disciplines can break through their conventional format of inquiry to enable the inquirer to assume the stance of a humbled human being confronting the mystery of existing and the more devastating mystery of dying, such inquiry may go far afield, both in what it offers as illuminating that event, or as consolation and support in the experiencing of it.

The task of the constructive theologian in confronting this query is made acute by the very nature of his concern; namely, to address the more elemental question within the legacy of faith which underlies the tradition of doctrine to which the systematic theologian speaks. The systematic theologian tends to be concerned with conveying a viable rendering of doctrine bearing upon the problem of death and the hope of survival beyond death. This generally takes the form of speaking to the resurrection-experience. But if faith itself is problematical for the constructive theologian, the legacy of belief and its various doctrinal interpretations are rendered even more unavailable as a guide or resource for inquiry. In effect, the mystery of not existing is then full upon him. To be sure, that legacy of belief is not wholly ignored or set aside. In the language of phenomenology, it is "bracketed," or held in abeyance as a witness of belief with an attitude of critical reserve and questioning, as are the legacies of belief or other religious cultures. The stance of the constructive theologian with regard to this issue, however, is not that of the historian of religion. Nor is it the stance of the philosopher of religion, who may review the legacies of the various faiths comparatively or abstractly, either by way of vivifying the rich texture of religious belief, or of detecting an underlying kinship in reponse to a basic, human outreach or concern. By contrast, the constructive theologian, while attentive to these other modes of inquiry and research, approaches his inquiry within the legacy of the creatural response that is expressive of his cultural history and witness. In this respect he is, like the systematic theologian, within "the circle of faith," as it were; though the circle was widened to include the larger orbit of meaning which speaks through our own lived experiences. Both existentialism, speaking from within a phenomenological inquiry, and empirical realism, speaking within a process imagery, address the issue in this manner. Yet both are attentive, in their way, to the witness of faith that speaks from other cultural orbits of meaning, in so far as they are critically, existentially, or empirically available to them. At no point is the elemental stance of the creature lost sight of. Such flights into abstract reflection, which simulate an over-view, extricated from creatural existence, can be helpful only as a vision upon experience imaginatively projected. Yet their value is not visionary when they are brought into some accord with, or subjected to, a critical encounter with experience as lived. The vital stance of creaturehood thus looms large in empirical realism. All reflection or inquiry that moves abstractly or imaginatively beyond that pivotal stance must be regarded as secondary, though by no means irrelevant or necessarily misleading.

Where one is thrust back to such an elementary stance, the impulse to keep the issue of the ultimate horizon open may be accentuated. This will be especially true when the shattering experience of death is intimately encountered, as in the loss of the one beloved. The sheer fact, for example, that this person who meant more to one than any other human being, and whose presence was cherished above every other experience, has vanished, will mean to the person surviving that the past now holds more of the reality of grace and meaningfulness than any future occurrence can provide. It might mean, on the other hand, that these immediacies now upon one, shattered and desolate though they seem, somehow contain and body forth this meaningful reality of grace and beauty, vigor and strength, that was known and experienced in the living presence of that person, though under circumstances not readily apprehended or imagined by those yet living. To succumb to the first alternative would mean relinquishing meaning in life, if not life itself. Baffling and incredible though it may seem on first confronting it realistically, the latter opens up possibilities of heightening, and of making more vivid, a judgment that the immediacies of our experience carry within them depths of ultimacy and import that exceed our conscious awareness. The latter supposition, to be sure, opens the door to all kinds of mythological and mystical mumbo-jumbo, and would seem to be a turning-back upon the stance which can assure critical security of judgment. I regard this, however, not as a collapse of critical judgment, but a tempering of the audacity implied in the wilful enclosure of the mind within an assertive system of thought, in humble response to pressures of reality within the lived experience, to which such a system may not readily or adequately speak.

The meaning of being. The relational ground in existence at once gives more empirical warrant than was hitherto available for attending seriously to the events of our immediacies as being genuinely expressive of the full measure of realities that pervade our existence. At the same time it supports the acknowledgment of the limited purview of every natural structure (including the structure of human being) in attending to those immediacies, accompanied as they are by a depth that cannot readily, if ever, be consciously apprehended or perceived. It is in this sense that we are justified in saying that the lived experience, or experience as lived, is a deeper, richer event than experience as thought or consciously attended. And this limitation of conscious thought is not overcome simply by appealing to disciplined measures of observation and reflection. Nor does it follow from this predicament that what cannot be thought does not exist. That is the illusion, I believe, that has deceived empiricists and sent them back into the company of rationalists and idealists. The import of taking relations seriously, ontologically or psychologically, theologically or sociologically, requires us to affirm that reality exceeds thought and, to a considerable degree, eludes it.

This is not to revert to supernaturalism in any form, "experimental," "piecemeal,"[4] or otherwise. It is to emphasize our empirical realism, fully cognizant of its relational ground. It is empirical realism, acknowledging that these realities are experienceable, though much that is experienced as lived exceeds the bounds and capacities of thought. Thus reason as we know it is a function of our humanly defined natural structure, with all the potentials and limitations appropriate to that level of emergence.

Given that emergent and relational quality, naturalism itself, as expressed in empirical realism, takes on dimensions which may not be wholly circumscribed by such rules of reason as science or logic prescribes without making the human structure at its specific level of emergence expressive, without remainder, and of reality itself as lived. This would amount to a wilful enclosure of reality and its meaning within the human structure. It would be a limited, if not an arrogant, vision to which the sensitive inquirer should not subscribe.

The alternative, it seems to me, is to pursue our sciences and our rational inquiries with full attentiveness to their limited purview, and thus with openness to reality as lived, or as it persists within dimensions beyond our present ken or manageability. Many scientists, in so far as they embrace a post-Newtonian understanding of their universe and discipline, seem to have no hesitancy about pursuing this course. Philosophers and theologians, on the other hand, many of them committed to a universal mode of rationality which, they assume, speaks through human reason (thus foretelling or forecasting a coherence inherent in the human world of experience which must somehow be found and articulated), seem more resistant to such marginal inquiry. They are thus indifferent, often hostile, to the open adventure in thought or experience which appears to be our only critical and disciplined option.

Reconciliation With Death

In assuming this stance in response to death, one must be prepared to endure a great deal of frustration—frustration which arises from the persisting anguish of the situation despite the passage of time; frustration, that gnaws at one as he reflects upon what seems a cruel disruption of a life intent on living forward, frustration over the opaqueness of the broken situation immediately upon one, with no sure thrust toward its resolution or acceptance.

Yet one learns to live with such anguish, with the sense of being bereft. One may not become reconciled to it, either psychically or theologically. And one may resist such efforts at theological reconciliation either because of their pat-ness, or their utter lack of empathy with what has really happened in such instances of dissolution. This may, in turn, lead one to look upon the many historic ventures in contemplating a myth of *the eternal return* in the form of the hope for resurrection, with more patience, rapport, and understanding; not that one will be persuaded by these things intellectually, or impelled to succumb to their lure on other grounds; yet one will recognize in them an elemental yearning and resistance to what happens in death which concurs with one's own experience of death's deprivation.

In an effort to evoke serenity and acceptance of the irrevocable fact of death, some have chosen to speak of death as culmination. I, myself, have often spoken of it this way. Yet, in many instances, death is not culmination, but disruption—sheer, unexpected intrusion with a tragic sense of life unfulfilled, with an extended chain of despairing circumstances for those who survive the loss. When one has finished out one's years and is prepared to relinquish one's labors to those better able and suited to pursue them, the event of death is clearly one of culmination, and can be celebrated as such. Yet, even in such instances, the extinction of an identity so vividly and concretely experienced and enjoyed is at least a surd that will not readily dissolve.

There is, to be sure, what some have spoken of as "the economy of death," by which is usually meant nature's way of eliminating or disposing of the burden that the prolongation of life would impose, as well as the provision of new configurations of experience for generations to follow. Professor Williams stated this point succinctly in saying, "Even death has its place in the service of God. It is the way life makes way for more life."[5] The social economist will carry the argument still further, pointing out the sheer necessity of death as a way of preserving a livable social economy in any culture. These observations seem highly acceptable as generalizations of the phenomenon of death in the abstract. And they will help socially-minded human beings to place their own demise in a perspective that enables them to accept relinquishment more readily. Accepting one's own death on these terms seems to me to present no serious problem. In confronting the death of one beloved, however, such a perspective is of no more help than theological or philosophical generalizations.

There is also, in some instances, an humane aspect to death. When, for example, the dying person arrives at a judgment, from endless cycles of suffering and meaningless persistence, that release is imperative, it would seem that he or she should have the right to relinquish life, and thus be released from interminable suffering. Medical ethics (as well as the legal code, of course) is an obstacle to this kind of humane act. Or, again, when the personal presence of an individual has receded, or has dissolved into sheer, vegetative existence, with the result that the medical act of keeping the patient alive becomes an incredible burden upon others, death would clearly seem to be an act of release. All such conditions may render the explicit occasion of death acceptable. It does not, however, alter the fact of death inherent in the process of deterioration. It remains a problem to the one who intimately confronts the loss of that personal presence.

Death and its possibilities. One might assume, from this stubborn stance of being unreconciled to the fact of death in its intimacy that one might be impelled to attend to various speculative inquiries concerning life beyond death; specifically, to pursue the Christian doctrine of resurrection more assiduously. The truth is that many are not. One can continue to live on in trust, open to possibilities exceeding our rationally or empirically defensible views of existence or non-existence. To press beyond this elementary stance, so it seems, would be to try to think and to presume beyond our structure of experience: Neither our structure of experience in and of itself, nor our imaginings which transcend that structure, offer any warrant for speaking definitely or confidently on that issue. It does not follow, however, that one so disposed has only to rest on his oars with a cynical or stoical attitude of "Come what may!" while awaiting his own dissolution. Quite the contrary! The mystery of dying, as well as the mystery confronted in witnessing the dying of one whose very life has been one's own life, may pose a question which, though it might never be resolved for us as a conceptual problem, may be contemplated "as through a glass darkly," within the structure of the life of our sensory experience. To come to any such glimpse of what could be, or can be, that could amount to something more than a projection of experience, as lived, we must first sense, acknowledge, and take seriously, the limits of our structure as creatures; that is, to feel the full, existential depth of what it means to be held in existence. The mystery of that event of existing might then bring to mind a vivid sense of not existing, were it not for what is presently operating as a resource of grace and recreative power within the Creative Passage that sustains life. Such a resource presumably could have ways of sustaining further, even beyond the event of death, whatever has been attained within the identity of each such created event—other than that of emptying all created good into "an eternal treasury of good," expressive only through the Creative Event itself, which is God. All possible occurrences of resurrection, transmigration, or other modes of transcending the event of death, rest ultimately upon this redemptive creative resource within the Creative Passage, and the power it wields in the ultimate passage of events.

It is here that I am led to regard the ultimate issue of existence and non-existence as being more of a problem than Christians, Hindus, Buddhists, and other world faiths, have acknowledged or recognized. For invariably, within these historic formulations, the ultimate act beyond the drama of existence tends to be made consistent with the way existence itself has been understood. Hence, the episodes or stages of an after-life, following upon any given span of existence, tend either to be re-enactments of the life-span as known, or conversely, one posed in sharp contrast to what has been known. In either case there is an implied projection of what is presently given in history as a measure of what is beyond the given. What has become increasingly insistent in my own reflections during recent years, is that the creative matrix itself tends to suggest that coherence, taken by itself or comprehensively, tends to be a false motif. It is at least a misleading motif when it is employed to project beyond the span of existence we have known; for that is to subsume whatever might emerge beyond death under the structure of meaning of "what has been or now is" as an available rationality within experience.

This vivid sense of existing, and the mystery of its occurrence is, to be sure, the threshold through which all else follows as reflection upon what could conceivably extend beyond existence; beyond, that is, each person's existence. No reflection, it would seem, can be profitable as bearing upon this ultimate issue of life and death except as it stems directly from this immediacy of lived experience. Efforts to transcend this concrete matrix in ways that ignore its focal role can have only the value of wishful or mythological musing. What this statement means to affirm is that such redemptive or resurrective power which might bring about drastic, renascent change in the lived situation now entering death, is an efficacy presently within the vital immediacies themselves, an efficacy that has persisted all along as a depth of those immediacies, however marginally attended.

To live forward in death, therefore, is consonant with the act of living forward in life; that is, assimilated to the depth of existing in some dimension and with some vivid concrete effect. It is to participate, as well, in the life of God, which provides the creative matrix for all lived experience.

To speculate beyond that concrete mystery of the Creative Passage, that is, to ask how consciously they who have entered death form the depth of our immediacies (or participate in it), is to reach beyond our structured existence in a way that abandons the focal orientation of the inquiry. And this simulates a way of transcending it. However, in so far as we attribute to this depth of our immediacies the creative and redemptive qualities expressed in the affirmation of a Creative Passage (having the tender, negotiable and redemptive efficacy of a good not our own, an inherent Creative goodness we call God), this depth of ultimacy within our immediacies will itself be the bearer of that concreteness which, as we say, endures or lives forward in death. This may seem to be only a variation on Hartshorne's theme of an eternal treasury of good;[6] but I do not mean it precisely in those terms. For the concreteness that lives forward in death is not a deposit of value accrued, but a continuing thrust of concreteness which, in ways we may not surmise, persists within the Creative matrix of our lives in God. The mystery of this concreteness that lives forward in death may be experienced by those who persist within life only as a presence, a depth of memory with hope of "an eternal return." To be sure, this in itself gives no indication or measure of the depth or reality of such a presence. And to pursue its reality within the terms of our critical disciplines offers no sure insight, for such disciplines are not formulated or prepared to address so imprecise an inquiry. The imprecision here is of a piece with the emergent quality of events which, while participating within the existing structure, at the same time intrude, a prescient quality of a "not yet" that is incipiently present. What is beyond our comprehension may not be made the subject of reflection without inviting deception or fantasy; but this need to imply that it is beyond our awareness, our wonder, and perchance, our waiting.

Meanwhile, there is a concreteness about the persisting, living presence of the one who has entered death which can be assimilated to the lived experience of those who survive, not simply as a haunting memory, or personal reminder of the desolation this death has wrought, but as a depth of intentionality in individuals (or in a community) who provide, in their identification with that life-span as it is recalled, and their cherishing of it, continuity with the ongoing stream of existence. How to carry this life, that has physically ended, into the future as a participating presence, then becomes an empirical inquiry. An obvious answer to such a query would be something like enabling its qualitative attainment to live on as a continuing presence with the enjoyable and decision-making events of one's experience. The fulfillment of any life often awaits such completion beyond its own death, and is beholden to others who survive for its accomplishment.

This empirical presence, however, is not to be made a substitute for whatever in the nature of the ongoing stream of lived experience may occur beyond the ken of our awareness. The two may be consonant with each other, though never interpenetrating. They are two levels or dimensions of the life-spirit participating simultaneously in different structures of emerging fields of events.

One may see from these remarks that I am struggling to avoid, on the one hand, simply projecting a coherence consonant with our humanly limited structure, and, on the other hand, abandoning all critical control of reflection concerning the event of death. What has become insistent for me is the concern to take seriously the persisting dissonance within experience, which seemingly defies our efforts to establish rationality and coherence in living, by recognizing this dissonance as an accompaniment of, and a persistent— even irresolvable—surd within, our rational experience. Despite all our talk about a critical realism in recent periods of Western history, we, as Western people and as scholars, have lived from a bankrupt legacy of Idealism which somehow sees the ultimate issue as being resolved in a way that accords with our own rationality and its cherished dreams. This was too easy a reversal of the demonic account of natural man put forth in supernaturalist theories. The critique of supernatural theories must partake as well of a critique of Idealism and of the tepid forms of realism which somehow seek to salvage the investment of rationality affirmed in Idealism as an eternal treasury of good. Acknowledging, even stressing, the note of dissonance as a qualitative corrective of our rationality achieved through idealization, seems to me to offer some leverage for exerting a realistic stance that is not wholly tragic. It is, on the other hand, sufficiently sensitive to the tragic sense of life so that it takes account both of the surds of insensitivity and that which is expressive of a good not our own, a good that is beneficent and blessed.

Conclusion

What it comes down to, then, is that one is led to have concern and respect for what simple folk have mythically affirmed, though one will take this to be but a marginal apprehension beyond our own structure of experience. And one will be impelled toward a distrust of any definitive attempt to employ our own structure of rationality too readily for apprehending, or systematically formulating, what the full truth of experience might be, either as it pertains to our lived experience, or to death; and as it pertains to what may or may not concern what lies beyond death, as each of us may encounter it. There will then be more impulse to wonder and to wait, to live expectantly with openness to what can release or transform this limited structure of creatural existence in ways that emulate a new Creation.

1.   *God's Grace and Man's Hope* (New York: Harpers, 1949), pp. 163-164.

2.   Cf. Vol. I, pp. 243ff.

3.   Charles Hartshorne, *The Divine Relativity* (New Haven: Yale University Press, 1948). Cf. also, Williams, D.D., *God's Grace and Man's Hope* (New York: Harpers, 1949). Ch. II: *The Spirit and Forms of Love* (New York: Harper and Row, 1968). Chs. VIII-X: "Suffering and Being in Empirical Theology," in *The Future of Empirical Theology*, ed. by B.E. Meland (Chicago: University of Chicago Press, 1969), pp. 175-194; Meland, B.E., *The Reawakening of Christian Faith* (New York: Macmillan, 1949, Books For Libraries, 1972). Ch. III: *Faith and Culture* (New York: Oxford University Press, 1953; Paperback, Southern University Press, 1972), Chs. X-XII.

4.   William James, *Varieties of Religious Experience*. (New York, 1902).

5.   *God's Grace and Man's Hope*, p. 163. Cf., also, William E. Hocking, *Thoughts on Death and Life* (New York: Harpers, 1937), pp. 12-26.

6.   Cf. "Time, Death, and Eternal Life," *Journal of Religion*, XXXII, 2 (Apr. 1952), 97-107. Also in *The Logic of Perfection*. (LaSalle, Ill.: Open Court, 1962), Ch. X.

Bernard Eugene Meland: A Primary Bibliography 21

For some time now students and colleagues of Bernard Meland have worked toward a bibliographical tribute to his contribution to process thought. The bibliography presented here is thus a group effort. We particularly wish to thank Clark Williamson of Christian Theological Seminary, Indianapolis, Indiana, and Larry Greenfield of the Chicago Divinity School for their assistance in soliciting and collecting information on the secondary resources for this bibliography. We are also indebted to the editors of *Quest* for granting permission to use much of the primary bibliography on Meland published in volume 8 (August, 1964). Janis Rafferty, assistant bibliographical editor, and Dean Fowler deserve much of the credit for the final preparation and organization of these materials.

On the assumption that this bibliography is to provide an index to further resources in process studies, Professor Meland has agreed to include several unpublished papers which have some historical significance in the development of his thought, particularly in illuminating the transitional stages of his empirical inquiry. We are thankful for his assistance in that regard and in checking the final manuscript for inclusiveness and accuracy. In presenting this bibliography, we wish to honor Bernard Meland as a leader of the Chicago School of process theology, recognizing that he has embodied in his scholarship precisely what he most respected about that school when he wrote: "The genius of the early Chicago School in theology was its capacity to make critical scholarship in religious study vivid and exciting" (*The Realities of Faith,* p. 249).

Professor Meland may be addressed at 5842 Stony Island Avenue, Chicago, Illinois 60637.

Barry Woodbridge, Compiler

Primary Bibliography

1928
The Development of Christocentric Theology in America. D.B. Thesis, University of Chicago, 1928.

1929
A Critical Analysis of the Appeal to Christ in Present-day Religious Interpretations, Ph.D. Dissertation, University of Chicago, 1929.

1930
"Present-day Evaluation of Christian Ethics," *Journal of Religion* 10 (1930), 378-93.

A Recent Reconstruction in German Theology" (review of Karl Born-
hausen's *Schopfung: Wandel und Wesen der Religion*), *Journal of
Religion* 10 (1930), 294-97.

"Why Are Young Ministers' Minds Troubled?" *Homiletic Review* 100
(1930), 196-99.

"Why Religion?" *Methodist Quarterly Review* 79 (1930), 359-62.

1931

The Christian in Business and Civil Life (edited with H. Y. McClusky).
Board of Publications, Presbyterian Church, U.S.A., 1931.

"The Modern Liturgical Movement in Germany," *Journal of Religion* 11
(1931), 517-34.

"Must Young Ministers' Minds be Disillusioned?" *Homiletic Review* 101
(1931), 275-78.

"Toward a New Appreciation of Jesus," *Open Court* 45 (1931), 596-610.

"Toward a Valid View of God," *Harvard Theological Review* 24 (1931),
549-57.

"The Worship Mood," *Religious Education* 26 (1931), 661-65.

1932

"The Present Worth of Jesus," *International Journal of Ethics* 42 (1932),
324-30.

"A Revolt against Modernism" (review of Emil Brunner's *The Word and
the World*), *Journal of Religion* 12 (1932), 412f.

"Rudolf Otto and the New Church Worship in Germany," *Homiletic
Review* 103 (1932), 261-66.

"Trends Toward a United Christendom" (review of Friedrich Heiler's
Im Ringen um die Kirche), *Journal of Religion* 12 (1932), 286-88.

1933

"Friedrich Heiler and the High Church Movement in Germany," *Journal
of Religion* 12 (1933), 139-49.

"Is God Many or One?" *Christian Century* 100 (1933), 725f.

"Kinsmen of the Wild: Religious Moods in Modern American Poetry,"
Sewanee Review 41 (1933), 443-53.

"Modern Trends in Catholicism," *Unity* 112 (1933), 138-40.

"A Psychological Critique of Theism" (review of James H. Leuba's *God
or Man?*), *Christian Register* (December 21, 1933), 830.

"The Religion of Henry Nelson Wieman," *Christian Register* (October
19, 1933), 677-79.

"Religious Awakenings in Modern Catholicism," *Open Court* 47 (1933),
242-52.

"The Significance of Paul Tillich," *Christian Register* (December 7, 1933),
797.

1934

"The Appreciative Approach in Religion," *Journal of Religion* 14
(1934), 194-204.

"The Development of Cursing," *Open Court* 48 (1934), 232-40.

Modern Man's Worship: A Search for Reality in Religion. New York and
London: Harper and Brothers, 1934.

Reviewed by Albert E. Avey, *Philosophical Review* 45 (1936),
221f; Burdette Backus, *New Humanist* (1935); W. A. Harper,
Social Science (1937); Charles Macfarland, *Messenger* (1937); A.
C. McGiffert, Jr., *Chicago Theological Seminary Register* 25
(1935), 22f; William R. McNutt, *Crozer Quarterly* 12 (1935), 102;
Herbert W. Schneider, *Journal of Philosophy* 32 (1935), 109f; Wil-
ber P. Thirkield, *Christian Advocate* (1935); Henry P. Van Dusen,
Journal of Religion 15 (1935), 330-33; Henry Nelson Wieman,
Christian Century 52 (1935), 18f; R. Will, *Revue d'Histoire et de
Philosophie religieuses* 15 (1935), 289-91; *Anglican Theological
Review* 17 (1935), 64; *Colgate-Rochester Divinity School Bulletin*
7 (1935), 239-41; *The Living Church* 90 (1934), 717.

"Religion: Devotion or Solace?" *Christian Century* 51 (1934), 1274f.

"The Religious Situation" (review of Paul Tillich's *The Religious Situation*), *The Christian Register* (1934), 146.

"The Social Ideal of Our Age," *World Unity* 14 (1934), 225-31.

"Visual Trends in Religious Education," *Education* 55 (1934), 97-104.

1935

"Contemporary Philosophies of Religion in America," *Proceedings of the
Missouri Academy of Sciences* 1 (1934-35), 145-48.

"Mystical Naturalism and Religious Humanism," *The New Humanist* 8
(1935), 72-74.

"Religion Has Not Lost Its Hold," *Religious Education* 30 (1935), 26-30.

"The Significance of Mystical Experience" (review of Roger Bastide's
The Mystical Life), *Journal of Religion* 15 (1935), 328-33.

1936

American Philosophies of Religion (with Henry Nelson Wieman). Chicago and New York: Willet, Clark and Company, 1936; New York:
Harper and Brothers, 1948.

Reviewed by J. S. Bixler, *Christendom* 6 (1936), 719-21; Howard
B. Jefferson, *Journal of Religion* 16 (1936), 486-88; Charles S.
Macfarland, *Messenger* (1936); A. C. McGiffert, Jr., *Chicago Theological Seminary Register* 26 (1936), 22f; Randolph C. Miller,
Churchman 150 (1937); Harris Franklin Rall, *Christian Century*
52 (1936), 706f; C. L. Street, *Anglican Theological Review* 19
(1937), 58-61; A. Stewart Woodbine, *Crozer Quarterly* 13 (1936),
304; William Kelley Wright, *Review of Religion* 1 (1936), 87-91;
A. N. Wyckoff, *Saturday Review of Literature* (1936); Victor Yar-
ros, *Religious Education* 31 (1936), 313; *American Ecclesiastical
Review* 96 (1936), 430.

"First Principles as Guides to University Education," *School and Society*
44 (1946), 648-50.

"The Mystical Adventure" (review of Henri Bergson's *The Two Sources
of Morality and Religion*), *Christendom* 1 (1936), 195-98.

"Seeing God in Human Life," *Christian Century* 53 (1936), 490-92.

1937

"Attachment to Life," Xeroxed Paper, 1937.

"The Faith of a Mystical Naturalist," *Review of Religion* 1 (1937), 270-78.

"In Defense of Intuition" (review of Burnett Hillman Streeter's *The God Who Speaks*), *Christian Century* 54 (1937), 1107f.

"Man's Religious Outreach," Xeroxed Paper, 1937.

"The Mystic Returns," *Journal of Religion* 17 (1937), 147-60.

"The Quest for God through a New Vision," *The Quest for God through Understanding*, ed. Philip Henry Lotz. St. Louis: Bethany Press, 1937, 90-97.

"The Quest for God through Dreams," *The Quest for God through Understanding*, ed. Philip Henry Lotz. St. Louis: Bethany Press, 1937, 98-104.

"Primary Religion," Xeroxed Paper, 1937.

Review of D. H. Hislop's *Heritage in Public Worship*, *Journal of Religion* 17 (1937), 82-84.

"The Study of Religion in a Liberal Arts College," *Journal of Bible and Religion* 5 (1937), 62-69.

"Toward a Common Christian Faith," *Christendom* 1 (1937), 388-99.

1938

"Praise and Relinquishment," Xeroxed Paper, 1938.

"Reality in Process," Xeroxed Paper, 1938.

"Religion Rooted in Nature," Xeroxed Paper, 1938.

"Religious Awareness and Knowledge," *Review of Religion* 3 (1938), 17-36.

"Theism Philosophically Affirmed" (review of G. Dawes Hicks's *The Philosophical Bases of Theism* and Thomas H. Hughes's *The Philosophical Basis of Mysticism*), *Christendom* 3 (1938), 454-58.

"When Religion Uproots Life," Xeroxed Paper, 1938.

Write Your Own Ten Commandments. Chicago and New York: Willet, Clark and Company, 1938; New York: Harper and Brothers, 1948.

> Reviewed by Harold B. Ingalls, *Journal of Bible and Religion* 7 (1939), 135f; James Daniel Martin, *Christian Century* 61 (1939), 18; A. C. McGiffert, Jr., *Chicago Theological Seminary Register* 29 (1939), 35; R. C. Miller, *Churchman* 152 (1938), 18; G. B. Webster, *Crozer Quarterly* 16 (1939), 236; Henry Nelson Wieman, *Journal of Religion* 19 (1939), 394f.

1939

The Church and Adult Education. New York: American Association for Adult Education, 1939.

> Reviewed by W. C. Bower, *Journal of Religion* 30 (1940), 211; F. Ernest Johnson, *Library Quarterly* 10 (1940), 614; L. N. Lemmon, *Church Times* (1940); C. L. S., *Anglican Theological Review* 22 (1940), 237; Paul H. Vieth, *Yale Divinity News* (1940); Basil A. Yeaxlee, *Bulletin of the World Association For Adult Education* 20 (1940), 26-28; *International Journal of Religious Education* (1939).

"The Controlling Concept of Our Time," Xeroxed Paper, 1939.

"The Criterion of the Religious Life," *Journal of Religion* 19 (1939), 33-43.

"Mysticism in Modern Terms," Xeroxed Paper, 1939.

"The Nature of Man," Xeroxed Paper, 1939.
"The New Age of Christendom" (review of Jacques Maritain's *True Humanism*), *Christendom* 14 (1939), 611-15.
"The Present Issue in Christianity" (review of *Revelation*, ed. John Baillie and Hugh Martin), *Christian Century* 56 (1939), 156f.

1940

"Growth Toward Order," *Personalist* 21 (1940), 257-66.
"Spinoza and Modern Thought" (review of David Bidney's *The Psychology and Ethics of Spinoza*), *Christendom* 5 (1940), 291f.
"The Spiritual Outreach of the Liberal Arts College," *Religious Education* 35 (1940), 219-23.
"Tradition and New Frontiers," *Christendom* 5 (1940), 323-31.

1941

"At Home in the Universe," *Contemporary Religious Thought: An Anthology*, ed. Thomas S. Kepler. Nashville: Abingdon-Cokesbury Press, 1941, 284-89.
"Beyond Free Minds," *Christian Education* 24 (1941), 281-85.
"Comfort of the Stars," *Christian Century* 58 (1941), 559.
"Prayer," *Christian Century* 58 (1941), 616.
"Some Philosophic Aspects of Poetic Perception," *Personalist* 21 (1941), 384-92.
"The Tragic Sense of Life," *Religion in Life* 10 (1941), 212-22.
"Why Modern Cultures Are Uprooting Religion," *Christendom* 6 (1941), 194-204.

1942

"Anthology of Modern Belief" (review of Thomas S. Kepler's *Contemporary Religious Thought*), *Christendom* 7 (1942), 262-64.
"For Self-Realization—Religious Education," *Adult Education Bulletin* 6 (1942), 178f.
"Fragments of Faith," *The Baton of Phi Beta Fraternity* 21 (1942), 37f.
"God, The Unlimited Companion" (review of Charles Hartshorne's *Man's Vision of God*), *Christian Century* 59 (1942), 1289f.
"The New Language in Religion," *Religion in the Making* 2 (1942), 275-89.
"Two Paths to the Good Life," *Personalist* 23 (1942), 53-61.

1943

"Humanize the University," *Journal of Higher Education* 14 (1943), 70-74.
"The Religious Availability of a Philosopher's God," *Christendom* 8 (1943), 495-502.
"Response to David D. Henry's Critique of 'Humanize the University'," *Journal of Higher Education* 14 (1943), 394f.
"The Retreat to Tradition," *Personalist* 24 (1943), 40-45.
"Theodore Carswell Hume: His Thought and Work," *Social Action* 9 (1943).
"Theological Perspective," *Religion in Life* 13 (1943), 100-06.
"Three Poems" ("Child by the Sea," "Sea Winds," and "Relinquishment"), *The Baton of Phi Beta Fraternity* 22 (1943).

1944

"Confessions of a Frustrated Theologian," Mimeographed Paper, 1944.
"The Culture of the Human Spirit," *Journal of Bible and Religion* 12 (1944), 217-26.
Review of Roger Hazelton's *The Root and Flower of Prayer*, *Journal of Religion* 24 (1944), 285f.
"Some Unresolved Issues in Theology," *Journal of Religion* 24 (1944), 233-39.

1945

"The Ascetic Temper of Modern Humanism," *Personalist* 26 (1945), 153-65.
"A Christian Apologia" (review of *The Christian Answer*, ed. Henry P. Van Dusen, *Christian Century* 62 (1945), 1255f.
"The Creation of a World Culture," *Current Religious Thought* 5 (1945), 1-4.
"An Idealist's Preface to Theology" (review of Karl Schmidt's *From Science to God*), *Christendom* 10 (1945), 237-40.
"Why Science Needs Theism" (review of William Ernest Hocking's *Science and the Idea of God*), *Christendom* 10 (1945), 520-23.

1946

"Art, Religion, and the Cultural Mood," Mimeographed Paper, 1946.
"Education for a Spiritual Culture," *Journal of Religion* 26 (1946), 87-100.
"Inner Harvests," *Chicago Theological Seminary Register* 36 (1946), 12-16.
"Suffering and Significance," *Religious Education* 41 (1946), 37-45.
"Towers of the Mind—Autobiographical Reflections," Xeroxed Paper, 1946.

1947

"The Genius of Protestantism," *Journal of Religion* 27 (1947), 273-92.
"Is God Process or Person?" (reply to Charles Clayton Morrison's review of Henry Nelson Wieman's *The Source of Human Good*), *Christian Century* 64 (1947), 134.
"Philosophy of Religion and the War Years," *Journal of Bible and Religion* 15 (1947), 86-89.
"The Range of Our Dedications," *Divinity School News* 14 (1947), 1-4.
Seeds of Redemption. New York: Macmillan, 1947.
Reviewed by Edwin E. Aubrey, *Christian Century* 64 (1947), 1046; Roy W. Battenhouse, *Christendom* 13 (1948), 104f; Peter A. Bertocci, *Journal of Bible and Religion* 16 (1948), 120f; J. S. Bixler, *Journal of Religion* 28 (1948), 142; F. W. Dillistone, *Anglican Theological Review* 30 (1948), 188f; Roger Hazelton, *Review of Religion* 13 (1948), 202-05; Elizabeth P. Lam, *Crozier Quarterly* 26 (1949), 85f; Stiles Lessly, *Advance* (1947); Eugene MacHamus, *San Francisco Chronicle* (August 17, 1947), 17; R. C. Miller, *Churchman* 16 (1947), 116; John M. Moore, *Journal of Religious Thought* 6 (1949), 81f; *Book Chat* (1947); *Churchman* (1947); *Cresset* (1948); *Garrett Tower* (1947); *Guidepost* (1947); *Miami Herald* (July 27, 1947); *News* (Springfield, Mass.) (Jan. 14, 1948); *New York Times* (June 14, 1947); *Religious Book Club Bulletin* (1947).

Bibliography

1948

America's Spiritual Culture. New York: Harper and Brothers, 1948.
    Reviewed by William B. Blakemore, Jr., *Chicago Theological Seminary Register* 39 (1949), 36f; Arlo Ayres Brown, *Religion in Life* 18 (1948), 137f; Kenneth J. Foreman, *Theology Today* 6 (1949), 400-02; R. E. Gilmore, *Christian Century* 66 (1949), 679f; F. Ernest Johnson, *Christendom* 13 (1948), 543f; C. L. Willard, *Churchman* 163 (1949); *U. S. Quarterly Booklist* (1949).
Review of Gerald Heard's *The Eternal Gospel*, *Chicago Theological Seminary Register* 38 (1948), 42f.
"The Thought of Emil Brunner—An Evaluation," *Journal of Bible and Religion* 16 (1948), 165-68.

1949

"The Legacy of a Liberal: A Biographical Study of Raymond Cummings Brooks," *Journal of Religion* 29 (1949), 204-19.
"Presuppositions in Religious Education—An Appraisal," *Journal of Religion* 30 (1949), 214-21.
The Reawakening of Christian Faith. New York: Macmillan, 1949; paperback, New York: Books for Libraries, 1972.
    Reviewed by M. L. Eglinton, *Churchman* 163 (1949), 15; Nels Ferre, *Journal of Religion* 30 (1950), 136; Kenneth J. Foreman, *Theology Today* 6 (1949), 400-02; R. E. Gilmore, *Christian Century* 66 (1949), 679f; Waights G. Henry, Jr., *Religion in Life* 18 (1949), 626f; Daniel Day Williams, *Chicago Theological Seminary Register* 40 (1950), 27.
Review of *College Reading and Religion* (Edward W. Hazen Foundation), *Chicago Theological Seminary Register* 39 (1949), 37f.
"A Time of Reckoning" (editorial), *Journal of Religion* 29 (1949), 1-4.

1950

"A Good Not Our Own," *Current Religious Thought* 10 (1950), 3-6.
"Integrity in Higher Education," *Religious Education* 45 (1950), 7-15.
"Intelligibility in Christian Faith," Xeroxed Paper, 1950.
"Kantian Influence on Christian Thought," Mimeographed Paper, 1950.
"Theological Educators in a University Community," *Divinity School News* 17 (1950), 1-7.

1951

"Faith Regenerates the Mind" (review of Roger Hazelton's *Renewing the Mind*), *Christian Century* 68 (1951), 18.
"On Power and Goodness," *Divinity School News* 18 (1951), 1-6.
"The Perception of Goodness," *Journal of Religion* 32 (1952), 47-55.
"Radical Empiricism," Mimeographed Paper, 1951.
"Religion in Higher Education—A Symposium" (comments on Wiley's article, "Native Growth or Import"), *Journal of Higher Education* 23 (1952), 369-71.

1952

"The Pathology of Forms and Symbols," Xeroxed Paper, 1952; revised, 1974.
"Prolegomena to Inquiry into the Reality of God," Xeroxed Paper, 1952; revised, 1974.

321

1953

"Faith and Critical Thought," *Personalist* 34 (1953), 140-50.

Faith and Culture. New York: Oxford University Press, 1953; London: George Allen and Unwin, 1955; paperback, Carbondale: Southern Illinois University Press, 1970.

> Reviewed by O. Fielding Clark, *Theology* 59 (1956), 478f; E. G. Homrighausen, *Theology Today* 12 (1955), 391f; Richard J. Kroner, *Religion in Life* 23 (1954), 478f; Gerald E. Maggart, *Chicago Theological Seminary Register* 44 (1954), 64; C. C. Morrison, *Pulpit* 25 (1954), 31; Niels C. Nielsen, Jr., *Christian Century* 71 (1954), 673f; W. Norman Pittenger, *Anglican Theological Review* 36 (1954), 304f; E. T. Ramsdell, *Journal of Religion* 25 (1955), 100.

Higher Education and the Human Spirit. Chicago: University of Chicago Press, 1953; paperback, Chicago: Seminary Cooperative Bookstore, 1965.

> Reviewed by Brand Blanshard, *Saturday Review* 37 (1954), 33; K. I. Brown, *Christian Century* 71 (1954), 143; E. B. Jefferson, *Journal of Religion* 35 (1955), 52; Thomas D. Langan, *Modern Schoolman* (1955); Henry McCracken, *Journal of Higher Education* 25 (1954), 225f; Howard Parsons, *Teachers College Record* 55 (1954), 278f; W. Gordon Ross, *Journal of Bible and Religion* 22 (1954), 128, 130; T. S. K. Scott-Craig, *Christian Scholar* 37 (1954), 154f; Proctor Thompson, *School Review* 12 (1954), 432. *San Francisco Chronicle* (November 1, 1953), 23; *U. S. Quarterly Book Review* 10 (1954), 83.

"Interpreting the Christian Faith within a Philosophical Framework," *Journal of Religion* 33 (1953), 87-102.

1954

"An Age in Between," *Divinity School News* 21 (1954), 1-7.

"Renascent Protestantism," *Christian Century* 71 (1954), 458-60.

Review of Nicholas Berdyaev's *The Realm of Spirit and the Realm of Caesar,* International Journal of Religious Education 30 (1954), 33.

Review of Emile Cailliet's *The Christian Approach to Culture,* International Journal of Religious Education 30 (1954), 37f.

1955

"American Contributions to Theological Science," *Twentieth Century Encyclopedia of Religious Knowledge.* Grand Rapids, Michigan: Baker Book House, 1955, Vol. 2., 1102-04.

"The Chicago School of Theology," *Twentieth Century Encyclopedia of Religious Knowledge.* Grand Rapids, Michigan: Baker Book House, 1955, Vol. 1, 232f.

"Currents of Dissolution as Prefiguring Creative Change: Marx, Kierkegaard, and Freud," Xeroxed Paper, 1955.

Review of E. G. Lee's *Christianity and the New Situation, The Pastor* 18 (1955), 44, 46.

"The Roots of Religious Naturalism," Mimeographed Paper, 1955.

"This Upsurge of Faith," *Christian Century* 72 (1955), 562f.

Bibliography

1956

"The Student-Faculty Spring Conference," *Divinity School News* 23 (1956), 11-14.

1957

"New Dimensions of Liberal Faith," *Christian Century* 74 (1957), 961-63.
"A Profile of the Theological Field," *Divinity School News* 24 (1957), 9-19.

1958

"A Prayer," *Serampore College Magazine* 13 (1958), 15.
"Religious Zeal: A Threat to Intellectual Life?" *Christian Scholar* 40 (1958), 41-48.
"Some Glimpses of India's Faith and Culture," Mimeographed Paper, 1958.
"Together with Differences," *Divinity School News* 25 (1958), 1-6.

1959

"The Christian Encounter with the Faiths of Man," *The Resurgent Religions of Asia and the Christian Mission*. Chicago: The Center for the Study of the Christian World Mission, 1959.
"Huxley at Chicago," *Christian Century* 76 (1959), 1429f.
"The Liberal Evangel—As History Illuminates It," Mimeographed Paper, 1959.

1960

"From Darwin to Whitehead: A Study in the Shift in Ethos and Perspective Underlying Religious Thought," *Journal of Religion* 40 (1960), 229-45.
"Jesus Christ and the Problem of Power," *Encounter* 21 (1960), 59-72.
"Some Observations Concerning Theological Method," Mimeographed Paper, 1960.
"Who Regardeth the Day," *Divinity School News* 27 (1960), 1-6.

1961

"The Changing Role of Reason and Revelation in Western Thought," Mimeographed Paper, 1961.
"The Christian Faith and Empirical Method," A Mimeographed Critique of Papers presented by University Educators at Conference of Minnesota Association on Higher Education, 1961.
"Theology and the Historian of Religion," *Journal of Religion* 16 (1961), 263-76.

1962

"Analogy and Myth in Post-Liberal Theology," *Perkins School of Theology Journal* 15 (1962), 19-27.
"A Long Look at the Divinity School and Its Present Crisis," *Criterion* 1 (1962), 21-30.
"The Persisting Liberal Witness," *Christian Century* 79 (1962), 1157-59.
The Realities of Faith: The Revolution in Cultural Forms. New York: Oxford University Press, 1962; paperback, Chicago: Seminary Cooperative Bookstore, 1970.
    Reviewed by William Beardslee, *Religion in Life* 30 (1963), 307; V. A. Demant, *Journal of Theological Studies* 15 (1964), 217f; E. Dale Dunlap, *Journal of Bible and Religion* 31 (1963), 344, 346; Bernhard Erling, *Lutheran Quarterly* 15 (1963), 182-84; Philip

Hefner, *Dialog* 3 (1964), 231-33; John G. Kuethe, *Union Seminary Quarterly Review* 19 (1963), 81-83; John Lawrence, *Ecumenical Review* 16 (1964), 340f; W. Norman Pittenger, *Anglican Theological Review* 45 (1963), 324-26; Paul Schlueter, *Christian Century* 80 (1963), 805; *Lutheran World* 10 (1963), 342.

1963

"Modern Protestantism: Aimless or Resurgent?" *Christian Century* 80 (1963), 1494-97.

Review of Kenneth Cauthen's *The Impact of American Religious Liberalism, Church History* 32 (1963), 492f.

"The Root and Form of Wieman's Thought," *The Empirical Theology of Henry Nelson Wieman*, ed. Robert W. Bretall. New York: Macmillan, 1963, 44-68.

1964

"A Post-Retreat Comment to Professor Haroutunian," *Criterion* 3 (1964), 11f.

"How is Culture a Source for Theology?" *Criterion* 3 (1964), 10-21.

"New Perspectives on Nature and Grace," *The Scope of Grace*, ed. Philip Hefner. Philadelphia: Fortress Press, 1964, 143-61.

"The Self and Its Communal Ground," *Religious Education* 59 (1964), 363-69.

"A Voice of Candor," *Religion in Life* 33 (1964), 19-27.

1965

"Alternatives to Absolutes," *Religion in Life* 34 (1965), 343-51.

"Critique of Haroutunian's Paper on Theology and the American Experience," *Dialog* 4 (1965), 180-87.

"The Development of Christian Natural Theology," Xeroxed Paper, 1965.

"In Response to Dr. Faruqi, 'History of Religion: Its Nature and Significance for Christian Education and the Muslim-Christian Dialogue'," *Numen* 12 (1965), 87-95.

"My Position in Relation to Natural Theology," Xeroxed Paper, 1965.

"Rudolf Otto," *Handbook of Christian Theologians*, ed. Martin E. Marty and Dean G. Peerman. Cleveland: World Publishing Company, 1965, 165-91.

1966

"Narrow is the Way Beyond Absurdity and Anxiety," *Criterion* 5 (1966), 3-9.

"A New Morality, But to What End?" *Religion in Life* 35 (1966), 191-99.

The Secularization of Modern Cultures. New York: Oxford University Press, 1966.

Reviewed by Foster A. Durwood, *Christian Century* (June 7, 1967); Dorothy Emmet, *Religious Studies* 3 (1967), 420f; D. Greenwood, *Church Quarterly Review* (October, 1967); Raymond Hammer, *Theology* (London) (September, 1967); John Hewitt, *Activist*, (Oberlin, Ohio) (March, 1968), 25f; Robert O. Kevin, *Washington Post* (Nov. 25, 1967); Richard K. Miller, *Christian* (St. Louis) (May 14, 1967), 626; Creighton W. Peden, *Interpretation* (July, 1967); William Pinson, *Southwestern Journal of The-*

ology (April, 1968); W. Norman Pittenger, *Religion in Life* (Summer, 1967); Joseph I. Richardson, *Pacific Affairs* (Vancouver, B. C., Canada) (December, 1968), 3, 300; Lyle E. Schaller, *Church Management* (February, 1967); Richard Schaull, *Theology Today* (July, 1967), 251f; Franklin Sherman, *Literatur-Umschau* (November 4, 1967), 528; P. Tilhon, S. J., *Nouvelle Revue Theologique* March, 1968), 320f; Vasubandhu, *India Weekly* (August 10, 1967), 6; *Indian and Foreign Review* (New Delhi) (June 15, 1967); *Secularizacion* (Bozentin) 1 (1970).

1967

"Creativity in William James," Xeroxed Paper, 1967.

"For the Modern Liberal: Is Theology Possible? Can Science Replace It?" *Zygon* 2 (1967), 166-86.

"Liberalism, Theological," *Encyclopaedia Britannica,* 1967.

"Mytho-Poetic Dimension of Faith Within Modern Culture," *Criterion* 6 (1967), 5-7.

1968

"Credo," *Criterion* 7 (1968), 29-32.

"The Structure of Christian Faith," *Religion in Life* 37 (1968), 551-62.

1969

"Can Empirical Theology Learn Something from Phenomenology?" *The Future of Empirical Theology,* ed. B. Meland. Chicago: University of Chicago Press, 1969, 283-306.

"The Empirical Tradition in Theology at Chicago," *The Future of Empirical Theology,* ed. B. Meland. Chicago: University of Chicago Press, 1969.

The Future of Empirical Theology (ed.). Chicago: University of Chicago Press, 1969.

> Reviewed by William H. Austin, *Journal of the American Academy of Religion* (June, 1971); Walter E. Creery, *Theology Today* (July 1970), 244f; Lee W. Gibbs, *Journal for the Scientific Study of Religion* 10 (June, 1971); Harold E. Hatt, *Religion in Life* (Spring, 1971); J. W. Heisig, *Library Journal* 94 (Sept., 1969), 2927; Leroy T. Howe, *Perkins Journal* (Spring, 1970); Randolph C. Miller, *Religious Education* (March-April, 1970); Edward W. H. Vick, *Andrews University Seminary Studies* 10 (1972), 146f, and 12 (1974); Edward Wing, *Christian Century* 86 (December 24, 1969); *Book Review Digest* (May, 1970); *Catholic World Library* (February, 1970); *Choice Books for College Libraries* (November, 1970); *Publisher's Weekly* (September 22, 1969); *Religious Book Guide* (April, 1970); *Sisters Today* (November, 1970); *Theology Digest* (Summer, 1971).

"Some Autobiographical Reflections Bearing on Works Preceding *Faith and Culture,*" Xeroxed Paper, 1969.

1970

"Beyond Theology and What Else?—Reflections on the 100th Anniversary of Edward Scribner Ames," Xeroxed Paper, 1970.

"New Realism in Religious Inquiry," *Encounter* 31 (1970), 311-24.

"The Quest for Intelligence in Ministry at Chicago: Some Historical Reflections," Xeroxed Paper, 1970.

"Response to Citation as Alumnus of the Year," *Alumni* (November, 1970).

1971

"Analogy and Myth in Postliberal Theology," *Process Philosophy and Christian Thought*, ed. Delwin Brown, Ralph E. James, Jr., and Gene Reeves. Indianapolis: Bobbs-Merrill Co., Inc., 1971, 116-27.

"Breaking of Forms in the Interest of Importance," *Criterion* 10 (1971), 4-11.

"Evolution and the Imagery of Religious Thought: From Darwin to Whitehead," *Process Philosophy and Christian Thought*, ed. Delwin Brown, Ralph E. James, Jr., and Gene Reeves. Indianapolis: Bobbs-Merrill Co., Inc., 1971, 411-30.

"Faith and Formative Imagery of Our Time," *Process Theology*, ed. Ewert H. Cousins. New York: Newman Press, 1971, 37-45.

"The New Creation," *Process Theology*, ed. Ewert H. Cousins. New York: Newman Press, 1971, 191-202.

1972

"The Christian Legacy and Our Cultural Identity" (Working Paper), American Academy of Religion (1972), 22-42.

"History and Nature," *Religious Reconstruction for the Environment*, Proceedings Report from a Post-Stockholm Workshop at Storrs, Connecticut. Faith-Man-Nature Group. November 30-December 2, 1972.

"John Milton, Puritan or Liberal," *Encounter* 33 (1972), 129-40.

1973

"Language and Reality in the Christian Faith," *Encounter* 34 (1973), 173-90.

"Shailer Mathews," *Dictionary of American Biography*, Supplement Three 1941-45, ed. Edward T. James. New York: Charles Scribner's Sons, 1973, 514-16.

"The Unifying Moment" (review of Craig R. Eisendrath's *The Unifying Moment: The Psychological Philosophy of William James and Alfred North Whitehead*), *Process Studies* 3 (1973), 285-90.

1974

"Grace, A Dimension of Nature?" *The Journal of Religion* 54 (1974), 119-37.

"Rudolf Otto," *The New Encyclopaedia Britannica*, 1974.

1975

"The Mystery of Existing and Not Existing," *Union Seminary Quarterly Review* 30 (1975), 165-75.

"Response to Paper by Professor Beardslee, 'Narrative Form in the New Testament'," forthcoming in *Encounter*.

Review of R. C. Miller's *The American Spirit in Theology, Religious Education* 70 (1975), 82-90.

"Daniel Day Williams [1910-1973] A Tribute," *Criterion*, 14, 21-22, Spring 1975.

Bibliography

1976

Fallible Forms and Symbols: Discourses on Method for a Theology of Culture. Philadelphia: Fortress Press, 1976.

Addenda

Prolegomena to Inquiry into the Reality of God," *American Journal of Theology and Philosophy*, vol. 1, #3, pp. 71-82, 1980.

Reminscences and Reflections Concerning Wilhelm Pauck's Years in Chicago, *Criterion*, 21, pp. 3-7, Spring 1982.

"Reflections on the Early Chicago School of Modernism," *American Journal of Theology and Philosophy, vol. 5 #1*, pp. 3-12, 1984.

Special Issue of *American Journal of Theology and Philosophy,* vol. 5 #2-3, 1984 papers and discussions of Bernard Meland's thought with responses by Meland to papers by Loomer, Frankenberry, Suchocki, Miller, and Inbody.

Myth as a Mode of Awareness and Intelligibility, *American Journal of Theology and Philosophy, vol. 8 #3*, pp. 109-19, 1987.

Sources and Acknowledgements

Introduction. "The Mytho-poetic dimension of faith within modern culture," *Criterion*, (Winter 1967) 6, pp. 5-7. Used by permission.

1. "How Is Culture a Source for Theology?" *Criterion*, (Summer 1964) 3, pp. 10-21. Used by permission.

2. "The Breaking of Forms in the Interest of Importance," *Criterion* (Winter 1971) 10, pp. 4-11. Used by permission.

3. "Tradition and the New Frontiers," *Christendom* 5, 1940, pp. 323-31.

4. "Why Modern Cultures Are Uprooting Religion," *Christendom* 6, 1941, pp. 194-204.

5. "The Perception of Goodness," *Journal of Religion*, 32, 1952, pp. 47-55.

6. "The Structure of Christian Faith," *Religion in Life* 37, 1968, pp. 551-62.

7. "Faith and Critical Thought," *Personalist* 2 34, 1953, pp. 140-50.

8. "The Critical Stance in Thought," *Personalist* 46, 1965, pp. 233-44.

9. "Religious Awareness and Knowledge," *Review of Religion* 3, 1938, pp. 17-36.

10. "Interpreting the Christian Faith within a Philosophical Framework," *Journal of Religion* 33, 1953, pp. 87-102.

11. "The New Language in Religion," *Religion in the Making* 2, 1942, pp. 275-89.

12. "Analogy and Myth in Post-Liberal Theology," *Perkins School of Theology Journal* 15, 1962, pp. 19-27.

13. "Faith, Myth and Culture," Chapter 5, *Faith and Culture*, Oxford University Press, 1953, pp. 80-98.

14. "Myth as a Mode of Awareness and Intelligibility," *American Journal of Theology and Philosophy*, vol. 8, #3, 1977, pp. 109-19. Used by permission.

15. "Prolegomena to Inquiry into the Reality of God," *American Journal of Theology and Philosophy, vol. 1* #3, 1980, pp. 71-82. Used by permission.

16. "The Sense of Wonder," Chapter 15, *Modern Man's Worship*, Harper & Brothers, 1934.

17. "The Appreciative Consciousness," Chapter 5, *Higher Education and the Human Spirit*, University of Chicago Press, 1953.

18. "Religious Sensitivity and Discernment," Chapter 9, *Higher Education and the Human Spirit*, University of Chicago Press, 1953.

19. "The Significance of Religious Sensibility," Chapter 5, *The Secularization of Modern Cultures*, Oxford University Press, 1966.

20. "The Mystery of Existing and Not Existing," *Union Seminary Quarterly Review*, 30, 1975, pp. 165-75. Used by permission.

21. Bibliography, *Process Studies*, vol. 5 #4, 1975. Used by permission. Updated by the editor.

DATE DUE

HIGHSMITH   # 45220